KT-545-790

Marti&
Tel: 0.

International Women
Stage Directors

International Women Stage Directors

Edited by
Anne Fliotsos
and Wendy Vierow

Foreword by
Roberta Levitow

University of Illinois Press

Urbana, Chicago, and Springfield

Library of Congress Cataloging-in-Publication Data
International women stage directors / edited by Anne Fliotsos
and Wendy Vierow; foreword by Roberta Levitow.
    pages   cm
Includes bibliographical references and index.
ISBN 978-0-252-03781-8 (cloth : alk. paper)
1. Women theatrical producers and directors.
I. Fliotsos, Anne L., 1964– editor of compilation.
II. Vierow, Wendy, editor of compilation.
PN1590.W64159   2013
792'.082   dc23   2013009259

Contents

Foreword

Roberta Levitow

In the 1970s, when I began directing plays in the United States, I was called a pioneer. Nina Vance catalyzed the regional theatre movement by founding Houston's Alley Theatre in the late 1940s, and Zelda Fichlander founded Washington's Arena Stage in 1950. But the doors that World War II had opened for women abruptly swung shut again in its aftermath. In the 1960s, the feminist movement inspired my generation to stake our claims for women's voices in the theatre. We filled roles as playwrights and directors throughout the regional network and within the cultural capital of New York City. Today, U.S. women theatre artists participate richly in American cultural life, though far from equitably. We have established ongoing women's support organizations, and individual women artists have made fundamental contributions to the advancement of the art form.

In the aftermath of September 11, 2001, I shifted my focus from U.S.-based work to international work. My travels took me to Hong Kong, Bucharest, Cairo, Nairobi, Dar es Salaam, and Kampala. My interests became global. And I became curious about the role of women theatre artists in other countries. In European countries, not surprisingly, it seemed that women held advanced roles within the theatre just as they did in society at large. But in too many other countries, women who struggled for gender equity in the public sphere also lacked voices in the cultural scene. This imbalance made me wonder about larger questions regarding women as conveyors of our human story.

Historically and worldwide, storytelling has largely been considered the province of women. In their intimate circles, women as friends and lovers, mothers and grandmothers wove tales about dreams, loss, and longing, fulfilled and frustrated. Women used those stories to teach life lessons and to transmit cultural identity. Adept at the mechanics of story structure and suspense, storytellers are spontaneous actors and writers, compelling the attention of their audiences through humor, tension, conflict, reversal, and release—all the criteria of dramatic narrative. Practiced as storytellers, women are natural dramatists. So why, then, when the stories leave our lips to become texts for performance enacted in front of audiences, are so few women telling the tales?

When storytelling moved out of domestic intimacy and into community gathering places, women could not lead the process. For centuries, limitations on the role of women outside the home have meant that public performance in public contexts would exclude female participation, even as performers.

Happily, modern times have brought new appreciation for women's contributions within the public sphere. As women have been welcomed into productive social roles, they have rediscovered their talent for the dramatic arts. Throughout the world, as this marvelous collection demonstrates, women have achieved expertise in the crafts of theatre and performance arts. And they are not only performers and authors. They are accomplished at the discipline long considered the most demanding and ill matched for a woman's capacities—they lead the process; they steer the ship; they guide the team. They are directors. From Argentina to Tanzania, working within a range of social, economic, political, and cultural contexts, women have taken leadership roles in creating art. Just as the rise of women writers has enriched communities with the untold stories of women's experiences, the rise of women directors is enriching societies with confident women engaged as community leaders and as agents for creative social transformation.

Since 2001, when I began looking outside U.S. borders, I have been fortunate to encounter some of these inspiring women artists who have energized, preserved, protected, and rebuilt their communities through their art making.

A 2006 Fulbright Specialist grant brought me to Kampala, Uganda. Makerere University's famous Department of Music, Dance & Drama (MDD) was built and protected throughout the brutal regimes of Milton Obote and Idi Amin by the talent and courage of Rose Mbowa, a mentor to generations of Ugandan theatre artists until her too-early death in 1999. Having created the leading performing arts training program in the East African region, Rose Mbowa (with fellow professor Jessica Kaahwa) helped initiate the "Theatre for Development" movement, which utilized specific African traditional performance techniques toward social activist goals—a form that quickly spread across the continent.

Today I work as Senior Program Associate, International with the Sundance Institute Theatre Program's East Africa initiative. In Rwanda, I've met three remarkable theatre women, each of whom returned from lives in exile to rebuild Rwandan performance culture following the devastating 1994 genocide of the Tutsis. Director and choreographer Hope Azeda, a graduate of Makerere's MDD, left Uganda to found Mashirika Creative and Performing Arts Group in Kigali, where she has directed the yearly genocide commemoration in a 20,000-seat sports stadium. She travels the world to share her work as an artist/teacher focused on theatre for young people. Producer and performer Carole Karemera returned from Belgium to create the ISHYO Cultural Center. She transformed a former community center into a gathering place for Kigali's emerging artistic community, where she produced the yearly Centre x Centre International Festival in association with Brown University and Rwanda's Interdisciplinary Genocide Studies Center. Poet, performer, producer, and director Odile Gakire Katese's exquisite dance-music-theatre pieces explore recovery from loss and the search for reconciliation with the dead. With the University Centre for Arts and Drama at the National University of Rwanda in Butare, she has produced annual international performance festivals and the "Women's Initiative/Ngoma Nshya," which has transformed the lives of local women who now comprise an internationally touring women's drumming corps of more than

127 drummers—a practice formerly reserved for men. The accomplishments of these three women are welcomed in a country where women hold one-third of the cabinet positions and represent over 50 percent of the parliament.

In 2003, while on a Fulbright Specialist grant teaching at Chinese University of Hong Kong, I had the joyful opportunity to meet Stella Ma, the artistic director of the Cha Duk Chang Children's Cantonese Opera Association. Stella produces, writes, and directs original productions of Cantonese Opera for young people. The child artists, some as young as age five, work with adult performers, all of whom perform in the traditional style. New stories incorporate fresh, contemporary sensibilities in design and content. These productions not only draw large and enthusiastic audiences, they also preserve ancient Cantonese Opera and re-imagine it as a living art form. In doing so, Stella protects and invigorates Cantonese language and culture, just as Hong Kong has been returned to the protectorship of mainland China and its dominant Mandarin culture.

In 2004 I co-founded Theatre Without Borders, a volunteer, virtual, global network of individual theatre artists at www.theatrewithoutborders.com. We were motivated by the urgent need for U.S.-based artists to establish open, apolitical, artist-to-artist, people-to-people conversations across national boundaries. In 2005 Theatre Without Borders co-initiated the Acting Together Project with Brandeis University's Peacebuilding and the Arts Program to explore and document the intersection between theatre and conflict transformation: www.actingtogether.org. Not surprisingly, women theatre and performance artists figure prominently in this work.

Dijana Milosevic, artistic director of DAH Teatar in Belgrade, Serbia, recounts that her theatre company was born on the very day that Serbian forces initiated the war in the former Yugoslavia. DAH performed in the streets of the capital city with paramilitary activists in the audience. While never agitprop, DAH Teatar's work was always pro-peace. Their performances created a "safe space" where members of opposing sides would stand or sit together in appreciation of DAH's mysterious theatrical language. Dijana reflects that the artists were never harmed, perhaps because they were protected by a "discipline" that was "stronger than the situation." Throughout the war and in its aftermath, DAH Teatar provided one of the few safe places where the Serbian population could engage the painful contradictions of their national identity and culture.

The stories of these women theatre artists and those that follow are larger than the confines of their theatre buildings or performance spaces. Women around the world are again telling our human story, investing it with life lessons and deeper meanings. Women are reclaiming their place as stewards of culture and society, bravely engaging with war and violence within the home and within community, and showing the power of art to heal, to reveal truth, and to restore the balance of a healthy society. Women as leaders. Women as visionaries. Women as rebuilders. Women as protectors. Women artists as pioneers, staking their claim on the future.

Acknowledgments

There are many people who helped this book toward its creation, refinement, and publication. First and foremost, we thank the contributors for their dedication to the book. In many ways this was a labor of love, because without existing resources on women directors the research work was difficult, and in some cases language and/ or geographical barriers were added obstacles to overcome. We also thank those who passed along the call for contributors as we searched the globe for appropriate scholars in the field. Many individuals helped us as we planned and edited the volume as well, including Tom Greenfield, Valentine Moghadam, Sharon Bowker, Ann Shanahan, and Ann Marie Gardinier Halstead. We thank them for their advice, and we also thank our translators: Eric Felix, Mass Giorgini, Emilia Ismael, and Sandra Venegas. We are grateful to Purdue's Center for Research on Diversity and Inclusion for a seed grant, which provided funds for chapter translations. Finally, editors Joan Catapano and Daniel Nasset and their staff at the University of Illinois Press have given their constant support and time, answering difficult questions in this, our first international project together. A special thanks goes to our husbands, Eric Felix and Chris Whitaker, for their support. Wendy Vierow would also like to thank Anne Fliotsos for doing more than her fair share of editing and for managing the project.

International Women
Stage Directors

 Introduction

Anne Fliotsos

Although directors are the undisputed leaders of theatrical production, and women have been a part of that leadership, there is very little research and publication devoted to women as stage directors. After writing *American Women Stage Directors of the Twentieth Century*, we wondered how the stories and careers of American directors compared with those of other women directors around the globe. We were fascinated also to know how political and social contexts in various parts of the world have shaped the directing careers of those women. The result of our quest is *International Women Stage Directors*, a reference book targeted to students, researchers, and theatre practitioners as well as general readers.

The twenty-four countries in this book represent a variety of continents, economies, religions, political systems, and cultures. We do not claim to include a scientific sample representative of the entire globe and were often restricted by finding contributing authors who met our qualifications: scholars and practitioners with publications in performance, directing, and/or women in theatre. Some of our contributors are working directors and run their own theatre companies. It was important to us that the authors came from a point of authenticity rather than simply researching a foreign country; therefore, each of these authors has lived and/or worked in the country he or she has addressed.

The book is arranged alphabetically by country for ease of access, and chapters follow a parallel structure, allowing the reader to gain a sense of context before reading about individual directors and their contributions. Sections include

Women's Rights: Historical Context,
Early Women Directors,

Working Climate in the Twenty-First Century, and
Profiles of Contemporary Directors.

When available, production photographs or headshots of the directors are included, though with so many women represented, it was not feasible to include a wide spectrum of photographs. In terms of coverage, authors were forced to make difficult decisions to determine which directors to include. In some countries, such as the United States, there are hundreds of women directing professionally. Clearly, there was some subjectivity when selecting "representative" directors; considerations included geographical area, aesthetic or methodological style, impact on the profession, awards, and national/international fame, among others. In short, authors selected directors who could not be ignored for their contributions. In a few cases our contributors have included endnotes about other directors of significance.

Several other difficulties challenged our contributors, particularly since they represent a wide diversity of cultures and histories, yet they had to use the standard format we provided. In some cases they argued that women's rights—our first section in each chapter—had little or nothing to do with women stage directors, many of whom were not feminists, nor were they directing feminist productions. We recognize that not all women identify as feminists, and many do not wish to be labeled as "women directors," yet the historical context of women's rights is of special significance when examining the careers of women in any profession. We also noticed that in many countries very few, if any, women directors were working professionally before the women's movement. As would be expected, the numbers and opportunities increase with further gains in women's rights. We have cut most theoretical and critical discussion of feminism to keep these chapters as concrete as possible, though further reading is advised.

Another difficulty arose in addressing complex political and cultural histories in such a concise way. Clearly, we can only give an indication of the major factors shaping a country and its theatre; readers are encouraged to consult additional sources about the historical, cultural, and political aspects of each of these countries. Our goal here is to provide a brief framework to contextualize the contributions of these notable stage directors.

Our focus on stage direction has also meant deleting details about the various "hats" that directors wear, for most of them are also gifted artistic directors, writers, performers, choreographers, and/or designers. Our contributors were asked to separate these overlapping areas, which are often considered holistically. Where possible we have added dates and places for the productions referenced, though this information was not always available. We also tried to include production reviews. However, in many cases women directing in small venues receive no press coverage; all the more reason to record their work in this volume.

Finally, the issue of translation of titles and proper names has challenged us. We are adhering to the guidelines of the University of Illinois Press by translating proper names and titles into English first, and then including a transliteration in parentheses.

However, we have argued for some leeway for names known worldwide by their original titles, such as Théâtre du Soleil.

No doubt the curious reader will wonder what such a large group of international women directors had in common. There are several issues that women have faced simply because of their gender: gender bias in hiring, differences in communication styles (and misinterpretation), career management during child-rearing years, and glass ceilings for jobs with larger salaries are all fairly common. Ursula Neuerburg-Denzer, our contributor from Germany, writes, "The issues around child rearing, like time management, are the real obstacles women in theatre encounter in the workplace. It is over this topic that German professional women rally most easily with one another—without having to call themselves 'feminists.'" Laura Ginters, our contributor from Australia, adds, "There is also an insidious line of reasoning that states a lack of opportunities is the women directors' own fault—that they are 'responsible' for their plight because they do not network and pitch like men. . . . [H]owever, this derives from a gendered assumption that men pitch the 'right' way" (Freeman). These issues, among others, are addressed at more length in the introduction to *American Women Stage Directors of the Twentieth Century*. We commend this reading to you as you begin your study of women directors. Another excellent source of information particular to women in theatre in New York is "Report on the Status of Women: A Limited Engagement?" by Susan Jonas and Suzanne Bennett for the New York State Council on the Arts. Books that may be of interest for English-language readers include Elaine Aston and Sue-Ellen Case's edited volume, *Staging International Feminisms*, which provides a critical feminist frame for international performance; Helen Manfull's *In Other Words: Women Directors Speak*, which examines British directors, as well as Manfull's *Taking Stage: Women Directors on Directing*, which addresses directors' preparation, process, production, and passion; Rebecca Daniels's *Women Stage Directors Speak: Exploring the Influence of Gender on Their Work*, which provides a gender study of women directors in the United States; and Ellen Donkin and Susan Clement's edited volume, *Upstaging Big Daddy: Directing Theatre as if Gender and Race Matter*, which analyzes feminist directors and their application of feminist theory to performance of the canon. Those interested in women directing Shakespeare may consult Elizabeth Schafer's *Ms-Directing Shakespeare: Women Direct Shakespeare* and Nancy Taylor's *Women Direct Shakespeare in America: Productions from the 1990s*.

As this book demonstrates, women continue to grow in numbers as directors, and their work is being recognized and celebrated. We hope this introduction may whet your appetite for the further study of women directing around the globe—or perhaps even induce women readers to join their ranks.

Sources

Aston, Elaine, and Sue-Ellen Case, eds. *Staging International Feminisms*. New York: Palgrave Macmillan, 2007.

Daniels, Rebecca. *Women Stage Directors Speak: Exploring the Influence of Gender on Their Work.* Jefferson, N.C.: McFarland, 1996.

Donkin, Ellen, and Susan Clement. *Upstaging Big Daddy: Directing Theatre as if Gender and Race Matter.* Ann Arbor: University of Michigan Press, 1993.

Fliotsos, Anne, and Wendy Vierow. *American Women Stage Directors of the Twentieth Century.* Urbana: University of Illinois Press, 2008.

Freeman, Lucy. "The Underrepresentation of Victorian Women Directors on the Main Stage." Victorian Women Network Meeting, "3 Three Minute Pitch." *Australian Women Directors Alliance.* September 16, 2010. Available at http://australianwomendirectorsalliance.blogspot.com (accessed January 15, 2011).

Jonas, Susan, and Suzanne Bennett. "Report on the Status of Women: A Limited Engagement?" Executive Summary. New York: New York State Council on the Arts Theatre Program, 2002.

Manfull, Helen. *In Other Words: Women Directors Speak.* Portland, Maine: Smith & Kraus, 1997.

Manfull, Helen, et al. *Taking Stage: Women Directors on Directing.* London: Methuen, 1999.

Schafer, Elizabeth. *Ms-Directing Shakespeare: Women Direct Shakespeare.* New York: St. Martin's, 2000.

Taylor, Nancy. *Women Direct Shakespeare in America: Productions from the 1990s.* Madison: Fairleigh Dickinson, 2005.

 Argentina

May Summer Farnsworth
and Brenda Werth

Women gained visibility as stage directors in Argentina during the 1980s and 1990s, in the aftermath of a repressive military dictatorship. Prior to that time, women's participation in the theatre was mostly limited to acting, though a few pioneering women worked as stage directors as early as the 1920s. In the twenty-first century, Argentine women directors work in diverse theatrical arenas, from small experimental theatres to main-stage, big-budget productions. The national economic crisis of 2001 had widespread destabilizing effects on Argentina's social, political, and cultural life. As a result, many contemporary Argentine artists, including some women directors, struggle to find adequate funding and suitable facilities for their projects.

Women's Rights: Historical Context

The women's rights movement in Argentina began to take shape in the first decades of the twentieth century at a time when women lacked voting rights, divorce was illegal, and women were considered minors in the civil code. Married women could neither hold property nor work without their husbands' permission. Unmarried women remained under the legal authority of their fathers, even after reaching adulthood. Mothers, regardless of marital status, were denied full legal custody of their children (Lavrin 194–96, 228). Between 1900 and 1910, a series of feminist organizations emerged that challenged the nation's paternalistic attitude toward women. Groups such as the Women's Socialist Center (Centro Socialista Femenino), the Anarchist Women's

Center (Centro Femenino Anarquista), the National League of Freethinking Women (Liga Nacional de Mujeres Librepensadores), and the National Women's Council (El Consejo Nacional de Mujeres) worked to promote the inclusion of women in the cultural and political life of Argentina. In addition, early feminist activists, including anarchist journalist María Abella Ramírez; Argentina's first woman physician, Dr. Cecilia Grierson; and socialist political campaigner Dr. Alicia Moreau, maintained close ties to feminist activists in Europe and North America. Buenos Aires became the site of the 1910 International Feminist Congress (Congreso Feminista Internacional) through the collective efforts of national feminists and their international allies. Among the subjects of greatest interest were the legalization of divorce, women's suffrage, female education, and the treatment of women in the national civil code.

In 1919 one bold woman activist, Dr. Julieta Lanteri Renshaw, created the Feminist Party (Partido Feminista) and ran for public office. (Although women could not vote, no prohibition existed against women running for public office.) Lanteri campaigned in public parks, on street corners, and at movie theatres but ultimately lost the election (Dreier 225–26). In the years following, the Feminist Union (La Unión Feminista) and the Women's Pro-Suffrage Committee (El Comité Pro-Sufragio de la Mujer), headed by Moreau, staged "mock elections" for women wishing to publicly protest their lack of suffrage (Lavrin 270, Moreau de Justo 164). These organizations worked in tandem with Lanteri's Feminist Party, using public forums to raise awareness about women's political and social marginalization. The 1926 Law of Women's Civil Rights represented the first legislative victory for feminists. This law gave women citizens full adult status, allowed married women to manage their own incomes, and freed wives from their husbands' debts. It also officially recognized the unwed mother's authority over her children (Lavrin 210).

In the 1930s women entered the labor force in greater numbers and, by the early 1940s, one quarter of the country's workforce was female; meanwhile, however, the government moved increasingly to the right and became ever more hostile toward the women's movement (Carlson 185–86). In 1943 a military regime took power and began censoring theatre, tango lyrics, the arts, and the press through its campaign of "moral purity" (184). Censorship in the arts continued after the 1946 democratic election of populist leader Juan Perón, a cabinet member in the former military regime (Mogliani 78–79). In 1947 Argentina finally granted women the right to vote, after Perón and his wife Eva (Evita) Duarte took over the campaign for women's suffrage. Also during Perón's presidency, divorce was legalized and women gained more visibility in politics, public life, and the workforce. Despite these events, Evita and Juan Perón considered woman's role in society to be, above all, that of nurturer and mother to a new generation of Peronist citizens (Zink 17–18). Evita died in 1952, and a right-wing coup ousted Juan Perón in 1955. Perón returned to power in 1973—after a long period of political upheaval—with his third wife, Isabel, serving as vice president. Isabel Perón became the country's first woman president when Perón died in 1974. However, just two years later, a military junta under General Jorge Videla seized power in a coup (Taylor 53–54).

The junta terrorized civilians between 1976 and 1983 in what became known as the "Dirty War." Military forces abducted, imprisoned, tortured, and frequently assassinated individuals suspected of government opposition, though most of the persons they detained were not actually involved in subversive activity (Taylor 130). Female prisoners, who made up about one-third of the detainees, were routinely subjected to rape and other forms of brutal sexual violence. Babies born in prison were often forcibly taken from their mothers and given to military families (84). According to human rights organizations, between ten thousand and thirty thousand civilians were killed or "disappeared" during this time (Project of the Disappeared). Surprisingly, the most visible and vocal opponents of this repressive and violent regime were a group of previously nonpolitical women. The Association of Mothers of the Plaza de Mayo (La Asociación de las Madres de la Plaza de Mayo) started with a group of fourteen mothers who met while searching for the whereabouts of their missing children. As early as 1977, these women began staging weekly protests in front of the presidential palace, La Casa Rosada, in the Plaza de Mayo. Over time, their membership grew and their protests continued despite the government's attempts to silence and intimidate them by threatening, attacking, and "disappearing" individuals in the group (186–87). In a series of protests and marches, the Association of Mothers displayed photos of their missing children and demanded their safe return, bringing international attention to the human rights abuses of the "Dirty War." In the years following the return to democracy, the Association of Mothers has continued to stage weekly protests in the Plaza de Mayo and to hold perpetrators accountable for human rights abuses (189).

In the twenty-first century Argentine women participate significantly in politics, the professional workforce, and public life. Balanced election slates ensure that one-third of the seats in both houses of Congress are held by women. In 2007 Cristina Fernández de Kirchner became the second female president of Argentina and the first woman to win a presidential election. Goals of feminist organizations include decriminalizing abortion, eradicating violence against women, and closing the gender wage gap.

Early Women Directors

In the 1920s and 1930s women playwrights occasionally acted as stage directors. Feminist dramatist Lola Pita Martínez, for example, directed two plays in 1924 for a nonprofessional theatre company, run by women, called the Argentine Women's Theatre Club (Compañía de Comedias del Club Argentino de Mujeres): *The Mother* (*La Madre*), by Santiago Rusiñol, and *Arms and the Man*, by George Bernard Shaw (Seibel, *History of the Argentine Theatre: From Its Rituals Until 1930* 644). As another example, Alfonsina Storni directed a children's theatre troupe in the 1930s (Nalé Roxlo 126). Nevertheless, the women who exerted the most influence in the theatre industry

Angelina Pagano

Angelina Pagano (1888–1962) was one of the most influential leading ladies of the early 1900s. She was born in Buenos Aires but moved to Europe as a young child, where she began a successful acting career at age fourteen. By the time she returned to Argentina in 1912, she had already performed in Italy, Austria, Germany, and the United States (Sosa de Newton 469). Pagano headed two successful theatre companies in Buenos Aires in the 1920s, the Angelina Pagano company and the Pagano-Ducasse company, which promoted the works of women playwrights. In fact, many of the nation's earliest feminist debuts were actually Angelina Pagano productions, including *Marcela*, by Lola Pita Martínez, in 1922; *Salvation* (*La salvación*), by Alcira Olivé, in 1923; and *Songs and Tears* (*Cantares y lágrimas*), by Alcira Obligado, in 1924. Pagano herself starred in all of the above-mentioned plays, personally embodying the newly emerging Argentine feminist heroine. In Buenos Aires, Pagano also created the School for Children's Theatre (La Escuela de Teatro Infantil) in 1914, and in 1928 she directed another youth troupe called the Labarden Children's Theatre (Teatro Infantil Labarden) (469). Finally, in 1929, Pagano joined the Company of United Artists (Companía de Artistas Unidos) in Buenos Aires and was named scene director, becoming the first woman to act as scene director in a professional company (Seibel, *History of the Argentine Theatre: From Its Rituals until 1930* 714).

of this period were undoubtedly the lead actresses. The popularity of divas like Camila Quiroga, María Gámez, Angelina Pagano, Blanca Podestá, Iris Marga, and Mecha Ortiz earned them prominent positions in the theatre industry. It was not uncommon for women celebrities to manage their own theatre companies, despite the fact that women were underrepresented in other areas of the Argentine labor force. In the 1940s María Herminia Avellaneda and Eugenia de Oro made names for themselves as radio theatre directors, and celebrated actor Gloria Ferrandíz headed her own theatre company and began directing for the stage (Sosa de Newton 46, 458; Seibel, *The History of Argentine Theatre, 1930–1956: Crisis and Changes II* 588).

Alejandra Boero (1918–2006) paved the way for women directors currently working in Argentina. Actor, director, and teacher, Boero was a key figure in promoting independent theatre in Argentina and provided a role model for women working in theatre from the 1940s onward. Her theatre training began at La Máscara Theatre in Buenos Aires. She co-founded the company Nuevo Teatro with Pedro Asquini, and she founded a number of theatres in Buenos Aires, among them La Lorange, El Planeta, and Andamio 90 (Geirola 23).

Working Climate in the Twenty-First Century

The end of the military dictatorship in 1983 ushered in the recovery of artistic freedom and an outpouring of creative expression. Theatre flourished in this newfound climate, and women directors began to have more opportunities available to them in a variety of theatrical venues, including the commercial theatres on Corrientes Avenue, the National Cervantes Theatre (Teatro Nacional Cervantes), the city-subsidized Buenos Aires Theatre Complex (Complejo Teatral de Buenos Aires), and low-budget, more experimental spaces, commonly referred to in Argentina as "under" or "off" venues. Under the direction of Kive Staiff at the San Martín Theatre, Laura Yusem, Vivi Tellas, Ana Alvarado, and Cristina Banegas, among others, found support as directors.

In the wake of Argentina's debilitating economic crisis of 2001, artists have found it increasingly difficult to support themselves exclusively with their creative work. Women directors, like their male counterparts, often teach acting and directing classes in order to stay afloat financially. Many contemporary artists in Argentina, including directors, depend on international funding to carry out their projects. All of the women directors featured in this chapter have received international support and have toured extensively with their work.

Profiles of Contemporary Directors

Laura Yusem

Laura Yusem has employed a range of styles and techniques in the direction of more than forty productions staged in independent, commercial, and national theatre venues since 1970. Though Yusem is first and foremost a director, she also writes and acts, and her earliest training was in dance and literature (Yusem). She was five years old when she started dance classes and twelve when she began to study with Ana Itelman, a pioneer of contemporary dance in Argentina. Itelman taught her choreography and played an instrumental role in steering her toward theatrical direction. Yusem began studying literature at the University of Buenos Aires but left after three years to pursue theatre. In addition to writing and directing theatre, Yusem currently holds acting and directing workshops out of the Actors' Patio (Patio de Actores) in Buenos Aires, which she founded jointly with director Clara Pizarro.

The first play Yusem directed, *A Slightly Fat Gray Bird with a Short Beak* (*Un pájaro gris medio gordo, de pico corto*), premiered at the Teatro del Centro in Buenos Aires in 1970. Based on a short story written by her friend and collaborator Hebe Uhart, this first production received very little critical attention. Yusem spent the next ten years learning and polishing her technique, except during the period between 1974 and 1978 when Yusem was forced into internal exile because of state repression surrounding the dictatorship (Yusem).

In 1980 Yusem directed the play *White Wedding*, written by the Polish author Tadeusz Rozewicz and staged at the Teatro Planeta in Buenos Aires. This production was a great success and marks a turning point in Yusem's career because of the visibility she received as a director. Yusem relates that *White Wedding*, which won a Molière Prize for best direction, caught the attention of Staiff and the distinguished Argentine playwrights Griselda Gambaro and Eduardo Pavlovsky, who saw the play and subsequently asked Yusem to direct their work (Yusem).

In 1982 Yusem directed *Bad Blood* (*La malasangre*), written by Gambaro and staged at the Teatro Olimpia in Buenos Aires. Yusem has continued to collaborate with Gambaro consistently, and though Yusem cites a wide range of European artistic influences, including Pina Bausch, Samuel Beckett, Anton Chekhov, and Tadeusz Kantor, she maintains that Gambaro remains her true dramaturgical voice. Yusem finds Gambaro's *Bad Blood* particularly fulfilling to direct because it features strong female characters in lead roles (Yusem). The main character in the play, Dolores, defies her father and attempts to escape an oppressive patriarchal system, actions that at the time of the premiere were read metaphorically as resistance to the military dictatorship. One of Yusem's most political stagings, *Bad Blood* generated a particularly heated response; in one of the first performances, Yusem relates that a group of national revisionists upset with the portrayal of a polemical nineteenth-century leader (Juan Manuel de Rosas) stormed the stage with guns, though tensions were ultimately defused and nobody was hurt (Puga 168).

Continuing in a political vein, Yusem collaborated with the playwright Roberto Cossa to direct *The Crazy Uncle* (*El tío loco*) for the groundbreaking theatre movement Teatro Abierto (Open Theatre) in 1982. Teatro Abierto brought together theatre practitioners and human rights activists in a collective act of resistance against the dictatorship, which was still in power when the movement was founded in 1981 (Graham-Jones 89–122). Yusem relates that she inherited her interest in political engagement through theatre from her parents, and specifically from her mother, who was particularly politically minded (Yusem).

In the middle of the 1980s Yusem asked Gambaro to write a version of *Antigone* as homage to Argentina's Mothers of Plaza de Mayo, and Gambaro wrote *Furious Antigone* (*Antígona furiosa*), based on Sophocles's tragedy. Premiered at the Goethe Institute in Buenos Aires in 1986, Antigone was played by the classically trained dancer Bettina Muraña. Yusem and Muraña rehearsed for two full years before the play's premiere. The goal of the director was to envision an Antigone through a fusion of theatre and dance. Stage designer Graciela Galán, also a longtime collaborator of Yusem's, created a pyramid-like structure consisting of crisscrossing bars that framed Antigone's movement throughout the play. In his review of the play, critic Osvaldo Quiroga observed that each movement in space was also a movement in the spectator's mind (10). The scene in which Antigone performs the burial rites for her brother Polynices held particular resonance at the time of the premiere in the early post-dictatorship period, when the whereabouts of many of the country's thirty thousand disappeared were still unknown.

Susana Torres Molina

Susana Torres Molina first became involved in theatre as an actor in the play *Liberty and Other Toxins* (*Libertad y otras intoxicaciones*), written by Mario Trejo and staged at the Torcuato di Tella Institute, one of the most significant venues of avant-garde experimentation in Latin America in the sixties. From 1971 to 1975 she studied with actor and director Beatriz Matar, and toward the end of this training she wrote the dramatic text *Strange Game* (*Extraño juguete*), which she then premiered as her first authored play in 1977 under the direction of Lito Cruz at the Payró Theatre in Buenos Aires. From 1974 to 1975 she studied stage design with Alberto Ure, and from 1978 to 1981, while exiled in Madrid during the military dictatorship, she participated in a workshop on performance with Lindsay Kemp and in a dramatic seminar with Roberto Villanueva. Since returning to Buenos Aires, Torres Molina has studied directing with David Amitin, Eugenio Barba, and Augusto Fernándes (Torres Molina).

In 1981 Torres Molina began directing her own plays, the first of which was *And On to the Next One* (*Y a otra cosa mariposa*),[1] a text she had written in Madrid and staged at the Teatro Planeta upon her return to Buenos Aires. The play exposes gender and machismo as social constructions through five scenes depicting key moments in the lives of the four main male characters. Torres Molina wanted a woman to direct the play, but in the early 1980s there were not many women directors working in Argentina, so she decided to direct the play herself. In staging *And On to the Next One*, Molina insisted that all of the male characters be played by female actors. The play opens with the gradual illumination of the stage while the women actors undress and put on men's clothing. An interest in deconstructing gender roles permeates

Susana Torres Molina

much of Torres Molina's work; she explains that plays such as *And On to the Next One* in 1981, *Amantíssima* in 1988, *Mystic Union* (*Unio mystica*) in 1991, and *Siren's Song* (*Canto de sirenas*) in 1995 reflect a phase in which she worked predominantly with women actors, though later plays, such as the 2005 production of *She* (*Ella*), feature all-male casts (André 95).

Torres Molina prefers to direct her own plays, and she values a methodology that is versatile and adaptable. Instead of structuring the rehearsal process a priori, she focuses on drawing out the unique energies and potentials of each actor over the course of rehearsals. She believes an essential objective of the director should be to create moments of improvisation and then to integrate the creative output generated in these moments into the work. Aesthetically, her work is predominantly minimalist and is defined through its functionality. For example, in the award-winning play *She*, written and directed by Torres Molina and premiered at the Teatro Payró in Buenos Aires, the stage space is converted into the austere interior of a sauna in which the two male characters are engaged in an emotionally charged conversation, wearing nothing but towels around their waists (Torres Molina).

Premiered at the Camarín de las Musas Theatre (Teatro Camarín de las Musas) in Bueno Aires in 2010, Torres Molina's *That Strange Form of Passion* (*Esa extraña forma de pasión*) examines the violence of the dictatorship period through the perspectives of six characters divided into three separate but related stories juxtaposed onstage. It is one of her most satisfying projects as director, as Torres Molina unsettles audiences by exposing the complexity of resistance, complicity, and responsibility through nuanced and sometimes contradictory points of view (Rosso). Whether contesting stereotypes relating to gender or to the country's memory politics, Torres Molina demonstrates an ongoing commitment to engaging contemporary social issues through her work as playwright and director (Torres Molina).

Ana Alvarado

Originally trained in visual arts, the director Ana Alvarado has pioneered cutting-edge work in object theatre, puppetry, and interactive multimedia. In addition to maintaining an active agenda directing plays, Alvarado has taught courses on theatre direction at the National University Institute of Art (Instituto Universitario Nacional de Arte) in Buenos Aires and a course on playwriting for the stage at the National San Martín University (Universidad Nacional de San Martín) in the province of Buenos Aires.

Her entrance into the theatre world began at the San Martín Theatre, where she trained with the prestigious Puppeteer Group (Grupo de Titiriteros de Teatro San Martín de la Ciudad de Buenos Aires). In 1989, together with Daniel Veronese and Emilio García Wehbi, Alvarado co-founded the experimental object theatre group The Peripherals of Objects (El Periférico de Objetos). Alvarado co-created and directed critically acclaimed works by the group, including Heiner Müller's *Hamletmachine* in 1995, *Zooedipus* in 1998, and *Monteverdi War Method* (*Monteverdi Método Bélico*) in 2000, staged nationally and presented internationally at venues such as the Kunsten Festival des Artes, the Festival D'Avignon, Theatre der Welt, and B.A.M.[2] Spanning fifteen years, the works of the Periférico de Objetos explore the relationship between humans and objects onstage and, in dialogue with Freud's notion of the uncanny, seek to make visible onstage that which remains culturally invisible (Dubatti 25).

In 1990 Alvarado received a grant to study puppetry at the International Institute of the Marionette in Charleville-Mézières, France, where she came in contact with different object theatre and puppetry traditions from Asia and Europe. Alvarado references a wide spectrum of artistic influences, including Argentine puppeteer Ariel Bufano; stage directors Laura Yusem, Tadeusz Kantor, and Romeo Castellucci; Dadaist Marcel Duchamp; and playwright Samuel Beckett. The first work Alvarado wrote and directed was a children's play involving puppets, called *The Travels of Manuela* (*La travesía de Manuela*), staged at the San Martín Theatre (El Teatro San Martín) in 1994.

Since then, Alvarado has continued to incorporate objects into many of her stagings. Premiered at the People's Theatre (Teatro del Pueblo) in Buenos Aires, the play *Balsam* (*Bálsamo*), written by Maite Aranzábal and directed by Alvarado in 2007, depicts a forgotten museum in Patagonia, wherein mannequins exhibited in display cases representing historical figures from the nineteenth century come to life. In 2008 Alvarado premiered *Visible* in Buenos Aires as part of the Tecnoescena Theatre Festival. Written by Ana Laura Suárez Cassino and created in collaboration with La Fase (The Phase)—a group composed of students of visual and theatre arts—*Visible* juxtaposes characters against an enormous computer screen onstage and investigates the ways everyday use of communicative technologies—e-mail, SMS, cell phones, computers—affect their identities and interaction with others. In addition to featuring objects prominently, both *Balsam* and *Visible* highlight Alvarado's interest in multimedia (Alvarado).

Alvarado also has directed plays that do not rely as heavily on formal experimentation through objects and technology. In the direction of *La Chira (el lugar donde conocí el miedo)* (*La Chira*[3] [*The Place Where I Met Fear*]), a play about exile and dictatorship based on poetic writings by Ana Longoni, Rodrigo Quijano, and Lilian Celiberti and produced in Buenos Aires at Teatro del Abasto in 2004, Alvarado collaborated very closely with Longoni in adapting the text to theatre. Alvarado's direction of Ricardo Monti's *A South American Passion Play* (*Una pasión sudamericana*) at the National Cervantes Theatre in 2005 likewise demanded rigorous engagement with the written text. In her staging of Dea Loher's *The Final Fire* (*El último fuego*) at Espacio Callejón in Buenos Aires in 2010, critics identified a shift in Alvarado's work away from experimentation and toward a focus on working with actors (Hopkins).

Vivi Tellas

Since the 1990s Vivi Tellas has pioneered imaginative projects exploring the boundaries between fiction and reality in theatre, the role of the autobiographical in theatrical creation, and the engagement of performance and urban space. Tellas first studied fine arts before specializing in theatre direction at the Municipal School of Dramatic Art (Escuela Municipal de Arte Dramático) in Buenos Aires. Her entry on the performing arts scene dates to the 1980s, when she began playing in a music band called Bay Biscuits, and then founded a theatre event called *Teatro malo* (*Bad Theatre*).

Tellas has held a number of important, institutional posts in which she has developed and implemented creative initiatives in the arts. She established and directed the Center for Theatrical Experimentation (Centro de Experimentación Teatral), housed at the Ricardo Rojas Cultural Center (Centro Cultural Ricardo Rojas) at the University of Buenos Aires from 1990 to 2002, and she was director of the Sarmiento Theatre from 2001 to 2009, a venue known for its experimental stagings. Throughout her career Tellas has also taught and served as advisor for artistic projects in and outside of Argentina. In 2009 she was a visiting professor at New York University, where she taught a seminar on creative writing and participated in the Teatro Vivo Festival; and in 2007, under the auspices of the British Council, she served as advisor to students working on live portraits in a series called *The Other People* (*La otra gente*) (Tellas, website).

While director of the Center for Theatrical Experimentation, Tellas proposed a project called *Project Museums* (*Proyecto Museos*). From 1994 to 2001 the project sought to investigate the relationship between museums, history, and the politics of exposition in urban space (Tellas and Pauls). Tellas assigned museums—excluding art museums—to theatre directors in Buenos Aires and asked directors to create stagings inspired by their visits to one of fifteen museums, ranging from the mainstream Museum of National History to the obscure Medicinal Herb Museum. Motivating the project was the desire to perceive the city differently and reflect on the translatability of the museum to the space of theatre (Tellas and Pauls). Works produced as part of this project include Mariana Oberzstern's *Dens en Dente* in 1997, an exploration of the Dentistry Museum; Federico León's *Miguel Ángel Boezzio Museum* (*Museo Miguel Ángel Boezzio*) in 1998, based on the Aeronautical Museum; and Emilio García Wehbi's *Vile Bodies* (*Cuerpos Viles*) in 1999, an interpretation of the Morgue Museum.

Project Biodrama (*Proyecto Biodrama*), Tellas's second major artistic project, encompassed fourteen plays staged from 2002 to 2009 at the Sarmiento Theatre. For this project Tellas invited playwrights and directors to create works that narrated the real stories of living Argentines. The project helped Tellas further develop her interest in theatre as a vehicle of documentation, whether of history, as in *Proyecto Museos*, or biography, as in *Proyecto Biodrama*. Forming part of the project are works such as Daniel Veronese's *The Unfolding Form* (*La forma que se depliega*) in 2003, which dealt with a family's pain after the loss of a child; Mariana Oberzstern's *The Surrounding Air* (*El aire alrededor*) in 2003, a portrait of a woman living in the Argentine Pampa; Stefan Kaegi's *Sit!* (*¡Sentate!*) in 2003, a piece about the relationship between pets and their owners; and José María Muscari's *Fetish* (*Fetiche*) in 2007, a work inspired by the life of a female Argentine body builder.

The desire to explore "theatricality outside of the theatre" informs Tellas's most recent project, *Project Archives* (*Proyecto Archivos*), which began in 2003 and builds on the premise that people are archives with "a reserve of experiences, knowledge, texts, images" (Tellas, website).[4] To carry out the works in this project, such as *My Mom and My Aunt* (*Mi mamá y mi tía*) in 2003, *Three Moustached Philosophers* (*Tres filósofos con bigotes*) in 2004, *Cozarinzky and His Doctor* (*Cozarinsky y su médico*) in 2005, and *Disc Jockey* in 2008, Tellas provided a space for nonactors—including her relatives, philosophers, disc jockeys, and the like—to narrate stories that reflect the inherent theatricality integral to the everyday rituals of their lives.

The intimacy of *Project Archives* contrasts notably with the large-scale direction project of Federico García Lorca's *The House of Bernarda Alba* (*La casa de Bernarda Alba*), which Tellas undertook in 2002 in conjunction with the Argentine artist Guillermo Kuitca. Staged at the San Martín Theatre, the critically acclaimed production was praised for breaking free from the mythology surrounding the famed work and revitalizing the play (Pacheco).

Over the past century women directors in Argentina have played key roles in shaping the country's vibrant theatre scene. Contemporary women directors such as Yusem, Torres Molina, Alvarado, Tellas, and many others not mentioned here continue to nourish this legacy through their unique directorial interventions in the aesthetics and politics of Argentine theatre and performance.

Notes

1. Translation by Graham-Jones in *Exorcising History*.

2. Alvarado co-created *Zooedipus* with Veronese and García Wehbi. According to some sources, it is a loose adaptation of Sophocles's *Oedipus*, though on the Periférico website, it claims not to be an adaptation of any one author's work. *Monteverdi War Method* is based on Claudio Monteverdi's *Madrigals*.

3. La Chira is the name of a town in Perú, a reference to Longoni's childhood in exile.

4. Translation by Sarah Townsend.

Sources

Alvarado, Ana. Interview with Brenda Werth. August 2, 2010.

André, María Claudia. "Conversations on Life and Theatre with Susana Torres Molina"

["Conversaciones sobre vida y teatro con Susana Torres Molina"]. *Latin American Theatre Review* 35.2 (2002): 89–95.

Carlson, Marifran. *¡Feminismo! The Woman's Movement in Argentina from Its Beginnings to Eva Perón*. Chicago: Academy Chicago, 1988.

Dreier, Katherine Sophie. *Five Months in the Argentine from a Woman's Point of View*. New York: Frederic Fairchild Sherman, 1920.

Dubatti, Jorge. "The Dramaturgy of the First Daniel Veronese 1990–1993." Introduction to *Body of Proof I* ["La dramaturgia del primer Daniel Veronese 1990–1993." Introduction to *Cuerpo de prueba I*], by Daniel Veronese, edited by Jorge Dubatti. Buenos Aires: Atuel, 2005.

First International Feminine Congress in the Argentine Republic [*Primer Congreso Femenino Internacional de la República Argentina*]. Buenos Aires: Ceppi, 1911.

Geirola, Gustavo. *The Art and Work of Theatre Directors in Latin America* [*Arte y oficio del director teatral en América Latina*]. Buenos Aires: Nueva Generación, 2007.

Graham-Jones, Jean. *Exorcising History*. Cranbury, N.J.: Associated University Presses, 2000.

Hopkins, Cecilia. "I Had to Do It in Order to Reflect." *Page 12* ["Necesité hacerlo para reflexionar." *Página 12*], September 16, 2009.

Lavrin, Asunción. *Women, Feminism, and Social Change in Argentina, Chile, and Uruguay (1890–1940)*. Lincoln: University of Nebraska Press, 1995.

Mogliani, Laura. "Continuity of the Microsystem of the First Modernity (1949–1960)." In *The History of Argentine Theatre in Buenos Aires* ["Continuidad del microsistema teatral de la primera modernidad (1949–1960)." In *Historia del Teatro Argentino en Buenos Aires*], edited by Osvaldo Pellettieri. Vol. 4, 77–90. Buenos Aires: Galerna, 2003.

Moreau de Justo, Alicia. *Women in Democracy* [*La mujer en la democracia*]. Buenos Aires: Ateneo, 1945.

Nalé Roxlo, Conrado. *The Intelligence and Character of Alfonsina Storni* [*Genio y figura de Alfonsina Storni*]. Buenos Aires: Editorial Universitaria de Buenos Aires, 1964.

Pacheco, Carlos. "A Different Bernarda Alba." *The Nation* ["Una Bernarda Alba diferente." *La Nación*], July 21, 2002.

Project of the Disappeared [*Proyecto Desaparecidos*]. Available at http://desaparecidos.org (accessed December 3, 2012).

Puga, Ana Elena. *Memory, Allegory, and Testimony in South American Theater: Upstaging Dictatorship*. New York: Routledge, 2008.

Quiroga, Osvaldo. "Interview with Laura Yusem." *The Nation* ["Entrevista con Laura Yusem." *La Nación*], September 25, 1986, 10.

Rosso, Laura. "Impassioned." *Page 12* ["Apasionados." *Página 12*], March 5, 2010.

Seibel, Beatriz. *The History of the Argentine Theatre: From Its Rituals until 1930* [*Historia del teatro argentino: Desde los rituales hasta 1930*]. Buenos Aires: Corregidor, 2002.

———. *The History of Argentine Theatre, 1930–1956: Crisis and Changes II* [*Historia del teatro argentino, 1930–1956: Crisis y cambios II*]. Buenos Aires: Corregidor, 2010.

Sosa de Newton, Lily. *Biographical Dictionary of Argentine Women* [*Diccionario biográfico de mujeres argentinas*]. Buenos Aires: Plus Ultra, 1985.

Taylor, Diana. *Disappearing Acts: Spectacles of Gender and Nationalism in Argentina's "Dirty War."* Durham, N.C.: Duke University Press, 1997.

Tellas, Vivi. Personal website at http://www.archivotellas.com.ar (accessed December 3, 2010).

Tellas, Vivi, and Alan Pauls. *Museos Project* [*Proyecto Museos*]. Buenos Aires: Libros del Rojas, n.d.

Torres Molina, Susana. "Re: Directors" ["Re: Directoras"]. E-mail message to Brenda Werth. August 13, 2010.

Yusem, Laura. Interview with Brenda Werth. August 4, 2010.

Zayas de Lima, Perla. *Dictionary of Directors and Stage Designers in Argentine Theatre* [*Diccionario de directores y escenógrafos del teatro argentino*]. Buenos Aires: Galerna, 1990.

Zink, Mirta. "Mothers for the Nation: 'The Peronist World' and the Interpelation of Women." In *Women, Maternity, and Peronism* ["Madres para la patria: 'Mundo Peronista' y la interpelación de las mujeres." In *Mujeres, maternidad y peronismo*], edited by María Herminia Di Liscia et al., 11–37. Santa Rosa, Argentina: Fondo Editorial Pampeano, 2000.

# Australia

Laura Ginters

Women performed in theatre in Australia from its earliest days as a penal colony in the late eighteenth century, and by the 1840s several were running their own companies and producing plays. Despite their early and continuing participation as actors, managers, directors, and playwrights, women remain underrepresented in Australian theatre. This is especially the case for women directors, and even more so in mainstream theatre.

Women's Rights: Historical Context

Feminism in Australia has largely followed the model of other western nations: a first wave of feminism in the late nineteenth century was mainly concerned with suffrage, and the vote was seen as symbolic of the self-determination that women sought in all areas of their lives. In 1893 Australia's neighbor, New Zealand, was the first country in the world to grant women the vote, and the state of South Australia followed in 1895. The federation of the individual states into the Commonwealth of Australia in 1901 marked the beginning of a democratic and egalitarian modern nation, and in 1902 federal voting rights were given to Australian women, though Indigenous women and men did not receive the vote until 1962.[1]

A second wave of feminism developed from the 1960s, focusing on legal and economic equality, as well reproductive and sexual freedom, and it saw many significant reforms. For example, the ban on married women in the public service was lifted in 1966, and the principle of "equal pay for work of equal value" was accepted by the Commonwealth Conciliation and Arbitration Commission in 1969. This paved the way for other changes: by 1984 the federal Sex Discrimination Act had made it illegal to discriminate on the basis of sex, marital status, or pregnancy, and this was supported by state-based antidiscrimination or equal opportunity legislation. Since 1999 the federal Equal Opportunity for Women in the Workplace Act has required organizations with more than one hundred people to establish a workplace program to remove the barriers that prevent women from entering and advancing in their organizations.

A third wave in the 1990s might best be characterized by its plurality. As well as some sense of revolt against Second Wavers, issues of class, ethnicity, and sexuality also became part of the debate and nuanced what feminism might encompass. Postfeminism, antifeminism, postmodern feminism, power feminism—even DIY feminism—have all been used to describe the feminist thought and activity of this period.

At the beginning of the twenty-first century women made up more than 50 percent of the population and more than half of university graduates. By 2011 women occupied a number of senior positions in Australia, including the top two governmental positions with Prime Minister Julia Gillard and Governor General Quentin Bryce. Fewer than 30 percent of the Federal Parliament's members were women, however. Well represented in the public service, with 57 percent of the jobs and 36 percent of senior executive positions, the situation was much less balanced in the private sector, where women held only 12 percent of senior executive positions and 9 percent of board directorships (Department of Foreign Affairs). Even in the face of generally accepted, legislatively supported principles of equal rights, and the peculiarly Australian belief in a "fair go," there remain structural and cultural impediments that prevent women from equal access to, and participation in, all areas of public life; the theatre remains a pertinent example of this.

Early Women Directors

In 1840 Anne Clarke became the first woman to run an Australian theatre, the Royal Victoria Theatre, in Hobart. Her disciplined rehearsals, well-run theatre, and programs set new performance standards (Winter 650). She was the first of a number of nineteenth-century female actor-managers, including May Holt, Marian Willis, and Maggie Moore, the former wife of the famous entrepreneur and theatrical manager, J. C. Williamson. Kate Howarde, a well-known and popular actor, director, dramatist, and entrepreneur, founded the Kate Howarde Company in 1886 at age seventeen and toured widely in Australia, New Zealand, and South Africa. She enjoyed a forty-year career that included becoming the first Australian woman to direct a feature film—producing, directing, and starring in a film version of her hugely successful bush comedy *Possum Paddock* in 1920.

The advent of the talkies dealt commercial theatre a severe blow from the late 1920s, and while J. C. Williamson's company continued to present popular fare in the cities' big theatres, the "serious" theatre took place in small theatres in the nation's capital cities. These were amateur theatres insofar as performers were mostly unpaid. They championed modern and innovative drama from around the world, believed in the social and cultural benefits of a lively theatre culture, advocated for developing local Australian playwrights and actors, and in some cases also ran training schools. These companies were, very often, established and run by entrepreneurial women directors who made a major contribution from the 1920s to 1950s. By the early 1940s, for example, *all* of Sydney's serious theatres were run by women who had established them and also directed for them: the Metropolitan Players by May Hollinworth, Bryant's Playhouse by Beryl Bryant, the Independent Theatre by Doris Fitton, and the Minerva Theatre by Kathleen Robinson.

The work of these small theatres set the scene for the shift to subsidized, professional theatre, which began in the 1950s and was consolidated in 1968 by the creation of the federal government's arts funding body, the Australia Council for the Arts. A few companies managed to turn professional, but for many it marked the end of their influence and viability. As professional theatre grew, the number of women directing theatres—or even just plays—seemed largely to evaporate.

The New Wave of Australian theatre and drama from the early 1970s embraced a masculine, larrikin culture, centered around the Nimrod Theatre in Sydney and the Australian Performing Group (APG) in Melbourne.[2] The APG was political, radical, and committed to collective decision making and theatre making. Nevertheless, the women in the group did not find themselves writing or directing plays, and in 1972 a breakaway group devised the groundbreaking *Betty Can Jump*, which examined women's historical and contemporary place in Australia. It had a sellout six-week season and led to the formation of the Women's Theatre Group (WTG), also in Melbourne, in 1974. The WTG was committed to radical politics, collective work processes with all female production teams, and social change using theatre (Tait, "Act of Forming Anew" 24). The radicalism of their projects increased and was pioneering but ultimately unsustainable: unlike the APG, WTG was unfunded, and it folded in 1977 (Tait, e-mail).

The 1980s saw the emergence of a number of other explicitly feminist companies such as the Home Cooking Theatre in Melbourne and Vitalstatistix in Adelaide. While many of these feminist companies were relatively short-lived, three decades later Vitalstatistix continued to work primarily with women playwrights and directors. There were also specific programs instituted by government and theatre companies to encourage and increase the participation of women artists in theatre, but it was not until 1993 that a woman was first appointed to run a state theatre company.

By 2001, however, a former artistic director of the Sydney Theatre Company (STC) was attributing the dire state of theatre to, among other things, the "political correctness" that he claimed was driving the STC's employment of women directors (Wherrett 4)—despite the fact that fewer than half of the directors employed there at that time were women. Fensham and Varney have pointed out that the number of women employed as directors in mainstream theatres nationally rose from just under 19 percent in 1990 to peak at around 30 percent early in the years from 2000 to 2010; since that time there has been a sharp decline (55).

Working Climate in the Twenty-First Century

The commercial theatre sector is mostly limited to large-scale musicals that have been successful in the United Kingdom and United States. Such productions also often import their own directors, and there are few opportunities for local women directors. At the other end of the music theatre spectrum, Opera Australia and several smaller state opera companies have occasionally employed a few women directors, including Gale Edwards, Lindy Hume, and Elke Neidhardt. In late 2011, Lindy Hume was appointed artistic director of Opera Queensland.

The professional theatre is almost exclusively composed of theatre companies whose operations are subsidized by government funding bodies. While the level of subsidy has decreased dramatically in real terms for many companies since the 1970s—amounting to less than 10 percent at the STC, for example—public accountability and their role as public institutions impose a broad mission that goes beyond the provision of profit-making entertainment. This mission includes artist, art form and audience development, maintenance of the classic repertoire, and also, arguably, a commitment to broader principles of social inclusion, including representation of gender and cultural diversity. These companies continue overwhelmingly to be run by white, middle-class men, and this can be a source of ongoing tension and exclusion for women directors.

Directors are not covered by a professional union in Australia, though the Australian Women Directors Alliance (AWDA) provides a forum for support and advocacy.[3] Examining the production statistics for several major, mainstream theatre companies reveals how necessary this is. Sydney's highly regarded, and second largest, subsidized theatre is Belvoir Street Theatre, and from 1999 to 2009 it produced sixty-one works. Four women directed a total of just eight of these productions, amounting to 13 percent. Eighteen men enjoyed the other fifty-three directing opportunities (Boland 14). Similarly, of the fifty productions staged by the Melbourne Theatre Company (MTC) up to late 2009, only ten were directed by women (Bailey 13).

Between 2008 and 2010 women assumed the role of artistic director at four significant subsidized theatre companies in New South Wales, Victoria, and Western Australia. A woman artistic director has not always guaranteed more opportunities for women directors, but it is noteworthy that the Western Australian companies, Perth Theatre Company and Black Swan, were the only ones among eleven major companies nationwide to employ more female than male directors in 2009 (Lyall-Watson). Further, Marion Potts, who was appointed artistic director at Malthouse Theatre in Victoria in 2010, signaled her intention to establish two internships for women directors at Malthouse in what she described as her "brazen commitment to affirmative action" (Neill 4).

There is also a flourishing "independent" scene of professional actors and directors, especially in Sydney and Melbourne, producing high-quality theatre in small venues on a profit-sharing basis. In practice these practitioners are scarcely better off than their amateur forebears in terms of being able to make a living from their work. Women directors are better represented here than in the mainstream, and a small number, including Kate Gaul and Lee Lewis, have made the leap to freelance work with subsidized companies.[4]

In late 2010 AWDA held a national forum for more than one hundred professional women theatre directors and theatre makers to discuss issues related to the visibility and recognition of, and opportunities for, women theatre directors. Their report concluded that "[o]ur gender is not a problem in our art making, rather the professional challenges we face are related to professional development, employment opportunities and accountability to equal opportunity legislation in funded organisations" (AWDA).

While women are underrepresented in mainstream theatre, they continue to play significant roles as creators, facilitators, and directors in the education wings of subsidized companies, in youth and community theatre, in circus and physical theatre, and in contemporary performance.

Profiles of Contemporary Directors

Robyn Nevin

Trained as an actor—she entered the first class of Sydney's National Institute of Dramatic Art (NIDA) in 1959 at age 16—Robyn Nevin moved into directing in 1981 with a one-act play, Mil Perrin's *Is This Where We Came In?*, starring Mel Gibson, for the recently formed STC. She continued a highly successful career as an actor, director, and producer, and became one of the very few prominent mainstream women directors in the country. Associate directorships at the STC from 1984 to 1987 and the MTC from 1994 to 1996 were followed by the artistic directorship of the Queensland Theatre Company (QTC) from 1996 to 1999 and the nation's largest company, the STC, from 1999 to 2007. Nevin was the first woman, and the first actor, to lead the STC, and while at the helm she also performed in nine plays and directed a further twelve.

Nevin made a deliberate choice not to seek an international career but instead sought to "paint [her] own landscape" (Nevin). Her commitment to developing an Australian voice—in terms of both texts and actors—is well known. She has, for example, often directed and acted in the plays of David Williamson, Australia's best-known and most popular playwright.

She has also delivered directorial successes with productions of contemporary adaptations of Ibsen's plays, which she commissioned from Australian playwrights for the STC. These adaptations maintained the settings of the originals but reinvigorated British translations, which often sound stiff to Australian ears. Nevin's production of Henrik Ibsen's *A Doll's House* in 2002, adapted by Bea Christian, was critically and publicly acclaimed, and two years later she directed Ibsen's *Hedda Gabler*, with Cate Blanchett in the title role, in an adaptation by Blanchett's husband Andrew Upton.

Like *A Doll's House* the production was sumptuously designed and highly realistic. No museum theatre piece, Nevin's production was "reverential but not embalmed, elegant but not stuffy, engrossing, psychologically piercing and just beautifully performed" (Rose 27). *Hedda Gabler* was hugely successful and toured to the Brooklyn Academy of Music (BAM) in New York City.

Both *A Doll's House* and *Hedda Gabler* were also examples of one of Nevin's key attributes as a director—her ability to enable great performances: Miranda Otto was nominated for a Helpmann Award and won a Mo Award for best actress in the role of Nora; Blanchett was awarded both honors for her portrayal of Hedda.[5] Blanchett rates this attribute highly in Nevin, commenting that "[h]er rehearsal rooms—like the best I've been in—are open, fluid and focused on what each actor needs [in order] to realise the best they can offer" (Hallett, "Robyn Nevin" 6).

Nevin had herself played Hedda some years before, and her work as an actor has undoubtedly enriched her directorial approach. Her move into directing was in fact partly inspired by a disenchantment with directors whose "concepts got in the way [for me] as an actor" (Hallett and Morgan 33). Nevin affirms, "I don't come to a production with a concept and overlay that on a play. I try to tell the play as it was written and let the audience make of it what it will" (33). Blanchett describes Nevin as having "a very clear internal metronome: the text, the text, the text" (Hallett, "Robyn Nevin" 6).

Nevin's legacy stretches beyond the outstanding and often award-winning performances she has delivered and the carefully detailed productions she has directed over a career of more than half a century. Her deep commitment to nurture and support the artists with whom she works is also manifest in the many positive changes she introduced as artistic director at the QTC and the STC. While her direct support for women directors seemed to wane after the early years of her artistic directorship of the STC, Nevin may also be credited with launching the theatre directing careers of a number of prominent actors, among them Cate Blanchett and Judy Davis.

Jenny Kemp

At age seventeen, Jenny Kemp spent a year training as an actor at NIDA in 1967 and went on to work as a performer and as a visual artist. She is the daughter of abstract painter Roger Kemp, whose work was influential on her. Finding a way to look at nonrepresentational art developed in her a sense of spatial dynamics and energy in relationship to the frame that has translated directly to her meticulously choreographed and spatially organized stage work. Kemp joined the Stasis group at Melbourne's Pram Factory theatre in 1977, eventually writing and directing her own work, because, she said, "I can't find plays to satisfy me. I need to build my own" (Tait, *Converging Realities* 86).

One of the few Australian theatre artists who could rightly be called an auteur, Kemp is a visionary writer-director who makes innovative, psychoanalytically informed works that operate in the space between the everyday and the fantastic. She imaginatively uses light, soundscapes, and multimedia to create her worlds. Uninterested in naturalism and the linear narratives of traditional mainstream drama in her own work, her focus instead is on creating a dialogue with the disjunction between interior and exterior worlds. She has developed very specific approaches to her writing and rehearsal processes: directing becomes the completion of the writing act.

The White Hotel in 1983 and *Good Night Sweet Dreams* in 1986 reflected Kemp's preoccupation with the subconscious and the world of dreams. Her next four works—*Call of the Wild, Remember, Black Sequin Dress*, and *Still Angela*—made between 1989 and 2002, developed these themes, and each mise-en-scène was influenced by the paintings of surrealist Paul Delvaux. Like Delvaux, Kemp foregrounds the female in this series of works, which marks moments of transition in women's lives. A new triptych cycle, examining characters "on the edge," also focused on the female psyche. *Kitten—A Bi-Polar Soap Opera* in 2008 was followed in 2010 by *Madeleine—A Schizophrenic Tragedy*.[6] Both leaned more on narrative and character than earlier works, but within a performative frame that "no less than her previous works . . . compels us to enter an unfamiliar state of consciousness" (Gallasch 46).

Alongside her own projects—best described as contemporary performance—Kemp also successfully directs plays for mainstream companies, including the STC, the MTC, Malthouse, HotHouse, and the South Australian Theatre Company. She confirms that "text is crucial, but in its relationship to the visual," which leads to her pre-direction preparation: "[I] must create a visual setting that leads me to understand the world [the play] sits in" (Gill and Burchall 5).

Kemp has been artistic director of Melbourne's Black Sequin Productions since 1989 and has won a number of awards for her directing work in theatre and in dance, including the Kenneth Myer Medallion for outstanding and distinguished services to the performing arts. She has worked to train the next generation of practitioners, both by teaching directing at the Victorian College of the Arts from 1990 and with her generative writing workshops, which have been in great demand nationally since the 1990s.

Gale Edwards

Gale Edwards is the only Australian woman director who has achieved a sustained national as well as international career, and her career has been full of "firsts." Her trajectory is all the more remarkable given its unconventional beginning. She is a graduate of the Flinders University Drama Centre in Adelaide, where she obtained a bachelor of arts in 1974; Adelaide University, where she was awarded a bachelor of education in 1976; London's Mime Centre in 1979; and NIDA's directors' course in 1981. She worked initially, however, for some years as a high school drama teacher, and following her training as a director, she joined NIDA as a staff director. In an interview, she explains, "If I was ever to be a director of merit in this country, I knew I had to unlock those productions I'd seen in Europe, and no one was going to give me [as a woman] a chance to direct Shakespeare, Chekhov and Ibsen" (Evans 48).

A subsequent appointment to the State Theatre Company of South Australia (ST-CSA) as associate director in 1987 saw her strategy pay off, and she directed *Much Ado About Nothing* and *The Winter's Tale* in her first year—the first time a woman had directed Shakespeare on the main stage of a major theatre company in Australia. *The Winter's Tale* concluded unconventionally, with Leontes falling to his knees to beg Hermione's forgiveness. Edwards went on to apply a feminist twist to her 1995 production of *The Taming of the Shrew*, the first main stage production to be directed by a woman, or an Australian, at the Royal Shakespeare Company (RSC) in Stratford, England. She double-cast the roles of the couples, Petruchio/Kate and Sly/Mrs. Sly, reframing the play as Sly's dream *cum* nightmare, and he awoke in distress at the end of the play, aghast at what "he," as Petruchio, had done to subjugate Kate. Her production was controversial, but it was a box office success. It launched her career with the RSC, for which she also directed Friedrich Schiller's *Don Carlos* in 1999, as well as John Webster's plays *The White Devil* in 1996 (restaged in 2000 for the STC, and touring to BAM) and *The Duchess of Malfi* in 2000.

Edwards also developed a strong reputation in musical theatre. After assisting British director Trevor Nunn on the Australian production of *Les Misérables* in Sydney in 1987 and directing the European premiere in Vienna, she directed the Australian premiere of Andrew Lloyd Webber's *Aspects of Love* in 1992 in Sydney. She was the first woman director that Lloyd Webber employed, and the two then worked together on the book for *Whistle Down the Wind*, which Edwards directed for the Sydmonton Festival in the United Kingdom in 1995 and later in the West End in 1998. She also directed a new West End production of his *Jesus Christ Superstar* in 1996; she won an International Emmy for the film of the production. Edwards co-created (with Nick Enright and Ben Gannon) and directed the first production of the landmark Australian musical *The Boy from Oz* in Sydney in 1998, and she won the first Helpmann Award for her direction. This became the first Australian musical to make it to Broadway, but Edwards was "devastated" (Perkins 16) when the American producers replaced the Australian creative team with locals, including a male director. She has also worked internationally in opera since 1992.

Edwards describes her goal as "try[ing] to lead a group of actors to become great story-tellers and to have everyone on stage harnessed to the same story. That process, for me as a director, which is rigorous, disciplined, fun, hard-hitting and analytical, is exactly the same in any production" (Lambert 81). This focus on clear storytelling is key and applies equally to the texts she interprets as it does to the works she creates. Enright attributed *The Boy from Oz*'s success to Edwards's "relentless pursuit of clarity and meaning" (Hallett, "That's Our Boy" 11).

Edwards is accomplished at directing on a big landscape, filling large stages with large casts and confident, bold, and energetic productions, but her approach also benefits smaller-scale plays. Actors praise her communication abilities, commenting on the way in which she gives them the skills and confidence to "enlarge" their performance.

A desire to work in her own culture flagged a return to Australia in the early years of the new century, and Edwards turned down an offer to direct Shakespeare's *Julius Caesar* at the RSC to do so. However, she found herself again taking up projects overseas due to the small number of employment opportunities locally. Her expertise and versatility have continued to lead to new directing opportunities, such as her first feature film, *A Heartbeat Away*, in 2011.

As of 2010, Edwards had won twenty awards for best director or production, in addition to several other prestigious awards for her contribution to the performing arts.

Marion Potts

Marion Potts graduated with a bachelor of arts with honors in French in 1988 and a master of philosophy in performance studies in 1995 from the University of Sydney. A member of the student dramatic society, she was already directing striking shows as an undergraduate, and she went on to complete the directors' course at NIDA in 1991. Her training in French and semiotics have informed her work, beginning with adaptations and independent productions of French classics early in her career. She later created, with Andrew Upton, vigorous, colloquial, and contemporary translations/adaptations of Edmond Rostand's *Cyrano de Bergerac* in 1999 and Molière's *Don Juan* in 2001, both of which she also directed for the STC.

The 1997 STC production of Peter Whelan's *The Herbal Bed*, her first main stage production, was praised as "superb" (Waites 12) and toured interstate. It began a series of well-regarded productions she directed while at the STC from 1995 to 1999, and for other major companies: her direction of Albee's *The Goat or Who is Sylvia?* in 2006 at STCSA earned her a Helpmann Award, winning over more established, international directors Ariane Mnouchkine and Declan Donellan.

Her work on poetic adaptations has been a recurrent feature, most recently in her staging of Jane Montgomery Griffiths's *Sappho . . . In Nine Fragments* in 2010 at Malthouse Theatre. A self-proclaimed career highlight was her playful and erotically charged adaptation of Shakespeare's *Venus and Adonis* in 2008 (Neill 4), the first project she undertook as artistic director of Bell Shakespeare Company's (BSC) development arm, Mind's Eye, both based in Sydney. Other notable productions she directed for BSC as its associate artistic director from 2007 to 2010 included BSC's first ever production of *Othello* in 2007, with an Indigenous actor in the title role, and an all-female *Taming of the Shrew* in 2009. *Shrew* is often regarded as problematic for modern audiences due to its misogyny, and casting all women was, Potts reports, "the only way I could find of doing the play without my own reservations about its politics getting in the way" ("Women" 19).

Contemporary cultural or social concerns are often revealed by her interpretations and she feels strongly that "Australian artists are instrumental in expressing the concerns that we have as a culture and community. And this carries a degree of responsibility" (de Jager). This applies as equally to an *Othello* featuring an Aboriginal man and thus inevitably touching on contemporary race relations, as it does to a production of Molière's *Don Juan*, which raised serious ethical questions about the Australian government's treatment of asylum seekers (Kiernander 112), or Ben Jonson's *Volpone* in 2002 at the STC, which subtly evoked parallels between the early seventeenth-century character and modern-day corporate moguls.

Potts has a strong track record in both developing and directing new and contemporary work.[7] Text remains at the core of her work as a theatre maker, and Potts makes the point that "the danger with attacks on text-based theatre is the text is seen to be at fault, rather than the directors who direct in a way that is unpalatable and boring" (Dunne 4). While text is the departure point, she is committed to an art form which unfolds in space and has another, nonlinguistic level of meaning beyond the text. Critical responses to her work are remarkably consistent and pay tribute to the rigor she brings to her productions as an astute, intelligent, and thoughtful director. Often stylized and highly choreographed, her work is understated and spare, even austere, and brings a sense of stillness to the stage.

In 2011 Potts became the first woman to run a major theatre company in Melbourne. She opened her first season at Malthouse that year with her own adaptation of John Forde's *'Tis Pity She's a Whore*. A play she had long wanted to direct, it is, she says, "extremely confronting" and "presents an aggressive, male-dominated world that still causes ongoing tension today" (Usher 16). Its final line, "'Tis pity she's a whore," places the blame for the mayhem of the play—actually initiated by the male "hero"—squarely on the youngest female of the cast, and it has not lost its power to shock, provoking audible gasps from the audience. Potts clearly relishes the opportunity granted by her position: "That's one of the things about pioneering these jobs. You have to take the opportunity to try and affect the culture" (Neill 4).

Affecting the culture in positive ways is certainly the legacy of these outstanding practitioners, and it bodes well for a shared theatrical future for artists—and audiences—that reflects more evenly the composition and aspirations, as well as the creative ambitions and vision, of the society in which they make their work.

Notes

1. Australia's Indigenous peoples prefer "Indigenous" to be capitalized.
2. Larrikinism is a longstanding tradition and part of Australian popular (and especially

male) culture. It implies an attitude of strong irreverence, and a disregard for authority and propriety, often combined with self-deprecating or understated humor.

3. AWDA is a nonprofit coalition of professional women directors and theatre makers.

4. Lewis was then appointed artistic director of Sydney's Griffin Theatre in 2012.

5. The Helpmann Awards are Australia's most prestigious performing arts industry awards and Mo Awards are broader entertainment industry awards. Both awards are annual and national.

6. With the exception of *Black Sequin Dress,* which was commissioned for the Adelaide International Festival of the Arts, Kemp's works all premiered at various theatres in Melbourne.

7. Potts was artistic director of World Interplay 2001, a young playwrights' festival, and the Australian National Playwrights' Conference 2003.

Sources

Australian Women Directors' Alliance (AWDA). "Creating Change" Forum. *Australian Women Directors' Alliance,* December 1, 2010. Available at http://australianwomendirectorsalliance.blogspot.com.au (accessed January 15, 2011).

Bailey, John. "A Dramatic Imbalance." *Sunday Age,* October 18, 2009, 13.

Boland, Micaela. "Women Act Up over Directionless Careers." *Australian,* December 4, 2009, 14.

de Jager, Christa. "Big Ideas." *Artlook* 227 (April 2003): n.p.

Department of Foreign Affairs and Trade. "About Australia: Women—Towards Equality." *Australian Government,* n.d. Available at http://www.dfat.gov.au (accessed January 15, 2011).

Dunne, Stephen. "New Directions." *Sydney Morning Herald,* November 23, 1996, 4.

Evans, Bob. "Edwards' Theatrical Balancing Act." *Sydney Morning Herald,* October 17, 1987, 48.

Fensham, Rachel, and Denise Varney. *The Dolls' Revolution: Australian Theatre and Cultural Imagination.* Melbourne: Australian Scholarly Publishing, 2005.

Gallasch, Keith. "Madeleine." *RealTime* 99 (October–December 2010): 46.

Gill, Raymond, and Greg Burchall. "Accentuating the Visual." *The Age,* April 29, 1997, 5.

Hallett, Bryce. "Robyn Nevin: She Who Must Be Obeyed." *Sydney Morning Herald,* February 25, 2006, 6.

———. "That's Our Boy: 200 Today and Still Going Strong." *Sydney Morning Herald,* August 26, 1998, 11.

Hallett, Bryce, and Joyce Morgan. "Nevin Rings Up Curtain on Next QTC Season." *Australian,* September 27, 1996, 33.

Kiernander, Adrian. "Abjected Arcadias: Images of Classical Greece and Rome in Barrie Kosky's *Oedipus, The Lost Echo* and *Women of Troy.*" *Australasian Drama Studies* 56 (April 2010): 109–16.

Lambert, Catherine. "Gale's Home on the Stage." *Sunday Herald Sun,* April 25, 1999, 81.

Lyall-Watson, Katherine. "Gender Equity in Theatre." *Brisbane City Council,* September 7, 2009. Available at http://www.ourbrisbane.com/blogs (accessed January 15, 2011).

Neill, Rosemary. "Danger Woman." *Weekend Australian*, January 15–16, 2011, 4.

Nevin, Robyn. "2004 Australia Day Address." *Australia Day Council of New South Wales*, n.d. Available at http://australiaday.com.au (accessed July 12, 2011).

Parsons, Phillip, with Victoria Chance, eds. *Companion to Theatre in Australia*. Sydney: Currency Press / Cambridge: Cambridge University Press, 1995.

Perkins, Corrie. "Return to Oz." *Australian*, July 22, 2006, 16.

Rose, Colin. "Smitten by Blanchett's Siren Call." *Sun Herald*, August 1, 2004, 27.

Tait, Peta. "The Act of Forming Anew: The Melbourne Women's Theatre Group." *Australasian Drama Studies* 21 (October 1992): 24–32.

———. *Converging Realities: Feminism in Australian Theatre*. Sydney: Currency Press / Melbourne: Artmoves, 1994.

———. E-mail message. July 18, 2011.

Usher, Robin. "Potts Plots Own Path." *The Age*, November 9, 2010, 16.

Waites, James. "Oh Susanna, What a Beauty." *Sydney Morning Herald*, January 17, 1997, 12.

Wherrett, Richard. "Terrible Deception, Monumental Con, Giant Fraud." *Sydney Morning Herald*, January 20, 2001, 4.

Winter, Gillian. "Women in Theatre." In *Companion to Theatre in Australia*, edited by Philip Parsons, with Victoria Chance, 650–51. Sydney: Currency Press / Cambridge: Cambridge University Press, 1995.

"Women Take Centre Stage." *Canberra Times*, November 8, 2008, 19.

 Brazil

Alessandra Vannucci

translated by Massimiliano Giorgini

Women directors conquered Brazilian theatre starting in the 1980s, dealing with both cultural and logistical obstacles, such as the clearing of time for artistic activity from the day's domestic work and earning a living wage. The rigid social morality, the reason for most women's withdrawal from the arts during the twentieth century, persisted even after the end of the military dictatorship in 1985, yet in the twenty-first century the same driving force seems to heighten the creativity, charisma, and diversity that are characteristic of the women who stand out in the field of theatre direction. One common factor that seems to be an advantage for women directors is either foreign nationality or training abroad, either in Europe during the 1970s or in the United States for those who emerged later. In addition, the public recognition of early women directors was influenced by the fact that many were wives and daughters of recognized male artists, in contrast to the modern situation, in which success arises from several different and highly individual paths. While the beginning of the twenty-first century is characterized by a strong policy of equal opportunity in all public and private spaces, the theatre seems to continue to present a traditional resistance to equal opportunity, much more so than in the other arts.

Women's Rights: Historical Context

In the evolutionary framework of women's emancipation, Brazil offers some provocative surprises. Census data indicates that in 1872 women represented almost half of the working population, falling to less than 20 percent during the 1920s, and then maintaining this incidence of inclusion in the national workforce until the 1970s.[1] To understand these data, one must take into account the state of slavery, which was considered "full employment" for women, and the predominance of agricultural work for the majority of the workforce until abolition in 1888. The massive industrial development at the turn of the twentieth century employed an almost exclusively male workforce for some fifty years. In the 1970s the unskilled female workforce began to fill the service sector, doing domestic chores outside of their own homes, thus giving women few opportunities to complete their studies and succeed in their own careers. Especially for those with low incomes, partially or completely illiterate, extra work undertaken in the public sector ensures the minimum conditions for family survival.

Gender discrimination can be traced through the changing laws of Brazil. The Civil Code of 1916 considered women "relatively incapable" and therefore, when married, legally subject to conjugal guardianship. Unmarried or widowed women were effectively obliged to be dependent on their families, rather than to find independent employment for self-sustenance. Any nondomestic employment was barely tolerated, unless it was for activities considered "feminine" inasmuch as they were compatible with daytime domestic, maternal, and filial chores. Gender discrimination has been prohibited by law in Brazil since the 1930s, but the same law restricts nighttime female employment as a form of social "protection," a noose that the feminist movement only loosened in 1969. The rhetoric of "family values" continued to be applied during the military dictatorship, from 1964–1985, as a strategy of restraint that made any employment of women at night—as is the case with the dramatic arts—seem incompatible with good morals. These working practices in theatre—unlike in the fine arts, whose practice has always been allowed in the upper classes—tend to be associated with the introduction of foreign customs or with foreign artists and sometimes with prostitution.

With regard to women's education, illiteracy prevailed among all classes in the mid-nineteenth century. A woman was considered "educated enough when she could properly read her prayers and knew how to follow the recipe for marmalade" (Expilly 269). Books were not recommended for women because it was believed that excessive intellectual activity for an "undeveloped brain" could cause respiratory difficulties and "congestion of the optic nerve."[2] With the exception of foreigners, the social life of wealthy women was limited to morning Mass and to appearances at the opera, seated in private boxes reserved for them and their "mulatto" women servants. Brazilian women who wished to engage in artistic activities endured the obligatory accompaniment of their husbands. Biographical dictionaries reveal many women artists who for one reason or another had to set aside their professional dreams by interrupting their careers, remaining unpublished, or continuing as amateurs.

Things did not go any better during the regime of Getulio Vargas, from 1930 to 1945, when with universal suffrage, established by the Constitution of 1934, the idea of separate education also came into vogue, a sign that actually opposed the acquisition of equal rights. Career paths for women included ones that required a gentle disposition, patience, and attention to detail, such as the fields of medicine that focused on nursing, dentistry, and pediatrics, in addition to teaching and the fine arts. Such use of the concept of vocation is one of the most durable devices for inequality, forcing the gender with less bargaining power to choose lesser-valued professions.

Brazilian feminism, which arose during the military dictatorship in the 1970s, originally focused on social demands while serving as a means to defy the regime. It identified itself more with political militancy rather than gender issues. Unlike European women involved in the resistance against fascism—which included women who laid down their arms, put on their aprons, and got back in the kitchen once the war was over—the militant women in Brazil took advantage of the greater access to active politics following the resumption of democracy. Increasing representation in the highest offices of the State in the twenty-first century[3] has also generated a much broader concern about granting women full rights, including the right to produce and enjoy art and culture—a privilege from which the vast majority of Brazilian women has been excluded, thanks to class disparity.

Early Women Directors

In the *Brazilian Women Dictionary* (*Dicionário de mulheres brasileiras*) of 850 biographies of women from 1500 to 1975, only four are categorized as theatre directors. This group consists of four pioneering women who were born or trained in Europe and were the daughters or wives of artists. Their directing techniques do not deviate substantially from their male counterparts. However, it is important to understand the shift in theatre from traditional to modern techniques during the course of their careers in the twentieth century.

The modernization of the national dramatic art was largely affected by innovations in two cities, Rio de Janeiro and São Paulo, where a mass-market art industry attracted the necessary human resources. What cosmopolitan intellectuals required—the importation of European masters—finally was provided at the end of war, with increasing immigration to South America. Between 1941 and 1955 young directors from Poland, France, Belgium, and Italy landed in Brazil; collaborators followed them, all men, except the occasional costume designer or make-up artist. It was their task to train a new generation of actors, as well as to shape a whole system of production centered on the pivotal axis of direction, which would replace the "old" national theatre that centered around actors. The "directors' generation" strengthened the idea of women as muses; leading actresses with a high profile on stage were directed or led by their powerful husbands behind the scenes.

The first of the four pioneering women directors began working before the period of modernization in Brazilian theatre. Born and educated in Italy, Italia Fausta (1879–1951) began her career as an amateur actor in São Paulo, autonomous in her choices and sometimes daring in both repertoire and acting. Despite that, as a director Fausta enacted a traditional concept of staging, focusing on the distribution of actors across the stage and being faithful to the text. Her script, annotated with indications of entrances and exits and without any interpretative comment, did not differ much from that of most stage directors, except for the license she exercised in the cuts to the text of Shakespeare to adjust to the limited abilities of amateurs (Bevilacqua 348–52). At age sixty she directed a version of *Romeo and Juliet* in 1938 in Rio de Janeiro at the invitation of a diplomat who financed a university group, the Student Theatre of Brazil (Teatro do Estudante do Brasil, TEB). After renouncing the direction of Edmond Rostand's *The Romantics* (*Les romanesques*) at TEB a year later, Fausta returned to performing in the late 1940s.

In 1940 three other women took the helm of the TEB: Mary Jacintha (1906–2004), a writer honored just two years before by the Brazilian Academy of Letters, with assistants Dulcina de Moraes (1908–1996) and Esther Leão (1892–1971). Jacintha took charge as artistic director and left the rehearsals to Leão. Portuguese by birth and educated in her home country, Leão took over the preparation of the Rostand text left half-finished by Fausta. After that, she rehearsed almost all "modern" groups in the 1940s, meaning almost all of the new actors who became major players in the Rio–São Paulo axis passed through her hands. However, her practical work on stage was diminished beside the public recognition of her artistic director, Jacintha, who remembered her as "a rather extravagant woman, for the work she did." Jacintha wrote that Leão "deserves our respect . . . for her legacy as a rehearsal director (*ensaiadora*) of the Brazilian theatre" (33). The case of the other assistant, Moraes, was different. Born into a family of artists and heavily booked even as an adolescent by major touring companies, she founded her own company with her husband Odilon Azevedo in 1934. She made ties to the new generation of actors and began directing, becoming an award-winning innovator for the elegance and technical mastery displayed in her productions of contemporary texts, thereby winning over the elite of the cosmopolitan audience, who despised the "old manner" of the national theatre. Later, she taught drama for thirty years and returned to the stage as an actor in 1981 for a farewell soirée that evoked her early successes, directed by yet another woman actor-director from a family of artists, Bibi Ferreira.

Born in 1922, Ferreira entered the arts scene when less than a month old in the arms of her comedian father, Procópio. She founded her own company at age twenty and signed several female contemporaries, including French actress Henriette Morineau as a director. In 1946 she moved to London to study directing at the Royal Academy; in this manner she prepared for her debut as her father's director a year later in Rio de Janeiro with *Divorce* by Clemence Dane. She established herself by directing comedies and revues in Brazil and Portugal, and later, during the 1960s and 1970s, theatre programs for television. Her reputation did not prevent her from venturing into costume extravaganzas such as *Gay Fantasy* in 1981, the first revue performed entirely by transvestites, which ran for over a year in Rio de Janeiro. Ferreira and Moraes were educated, enterprising women who took advantage of unique opportunities offered by friends and family. As such, they do not reflect the true conditions of access to the theatrical world for a woman of the era, which were very limited outside the possibility of being an actor.

Another notable exception is the French actor-director Henriette Morineau (1908–1990). Trained at the Paris Conservatoire and with an early acting career, she immigrated to Rio during World War II and in 1941 joined the company of Luis Jouvet for a tour of Latin America. When the director left, she established herself as a director, founding her own company, the United Artists (Os Artistas Unidos), with a vast bilingual repertoire. Known as "Madame Morineau," she enjoyed a long career both as an actor and as an "actor's director"—a practical, maternal guide who studied roles with the actors and illustrated roles to them by example.[4] Her rehearsal technique went against the tide of male directors who were led by "concept," which was imposing itself as the agent of reform in Brazil.

Working Climate in the Twenty-First Century

Statistics from the late twentieth century reveal the situation for women directors who continued to work into the next century. On the website for the *Itaú Cultural Encyclopedia* (*Enciclopedia Itaú Cultural*), of the total of 448 theatre artists registered as active in Brazil in the twentieth century, there were only twenty-three women directors—just over 5 percent.[5] Of the thirty or so professionals who made their debut in the 1980s, some are still active and successful nationally and internationally, with careers both in theatre and cinema. Of the most important permanent companies on the Rio–São Paulo axis, very few are led by a woman; some are led by a couple, as is the case with Amok Teatro in Rio de Janeiro, directed by Ana Teixeira and Stephan Brodt—both educated in France, where Brodt was part of the Théâtre du Soleil. Other respected actor-directors who have worked between Rio and São Paulo include Neyde Veneziano, Cybelé Forjaz, Ana Kfoury, Tiche Vianna, Karen Accioly, Celina Sodré, Maria Thaís, Georgette Fadel, Christina Streva, and Christiane Jatahi.

In order to complete the contemporary panorama of women directors, it is necessary also to include the choreographers, who make up the majority of their sector and are dedicated to exploring a creative area that tends to identify itself as "dance theatre." In addition, multimedia artists work on the borders between music, the visual arts, and performance and should be counted as directors, such as the composer Jocy de Oliveira. For forty years, both in Brazil and abroad, she has combined projected images with instruments and the voices of actors, including text, to create site-specific urban performances. Nevertheless, in comparison with other fields in which women now fully assert themselves—including television and cinema, where women directors clearly stand out in terms of quality, success, and even numbers—the minimal presence of women stage directors and the slow pace at which they have appeared is still surprising. Few women directors stand out on the Brazilian scene for their charisma, perseverance, experimentalism, and leadership, whether that be in terms of conceptual authority or in the hands-on, technical aspects of the craft. What they share is the exceptional effort they are forced to put forth in dealing with the double workday of both domestic and artistic tasks, especially given that directing demands total attention, availability at all hours, and frequent travel. Modern Brazilian society demands an equitable division of family tasks, but this notion is more easily achieved in careers compatible with motherhood. Therefore, when they don't give up, women stage directors in Brazil withdraw from the profession for a time to raise children, or opt to decline maternity altogether.[6]

Profiles of Contemporary Directors

Bia Lessa

The most notable person in the theatre of the 1980s, alongside Gerald Thomas, was a woman. Born in 1958 in São Paulo, Beatriz Ferreira Lessa debuted as a very young performer in a children's show and in an adaptation of Brecht for street theatre. In order to fully devote herself to the stage, she dropped out of school. In 1981 she completed her theatre training in São Paulo, acting under the guidance of a rigorous director of the realist school, Antunes Filho. She made her directorial debut in 1983 in Rio de Janeiro, almost by chance, with a children's adaptation of a novel by Graciliano Ramos, *The Land of the Naked Children* (*A terra dos meninos pelados*). Her first step toward theatre research was working with a group of amateur actors on "trascriAzioni" (transcription/creations/actions) of literary works in scenic sequences, characterized by fragmented and allusive language. As playwright and director, Lessa presented her work in the concept of "experiments" in Rio de Janeiro, in Theatre SESC-Tijuca: *Experiment Number 1—A Brazilian Tragedy* (*Ensaio n°1—A tragédia brasiliera*) in 1984; *Experiment Number 2—The Painter* (*Ensaio n°2—O pintor*) the following year; and *Experiment Number 3—A Musical of Gestures* (*Ensaio n°3—Um musical de gestos*) in 1986, a composition of fragments by Jorge Luis Borges, Júlio Cortázar, and Lygia Bojunga. A very sparse dialogue was sustained by continuous soundtrack by Caique Botkay. The result was an open and postdramatic show, with strong influences from the theatre of Polish director Tadeusz Kantor, requiring an unusual stretch of the imagination of the viewer. This production earned Lessa the Molière Award for best director in 1986, the first awarded to a woman.

After 1986 the score took the upper hand over the word in Lessa's work, thus beginning the series of "exercises" such as *Exercício n°1*, a composition of obsessively repeated actions from the universe of *The Demons* by Dostoyevsky. The production included scenic environments of great impact that used the aerial space as a zone of potential interference and creation, and which formed a solid link with set designer Fernando Mello e Costa. In the same series she created her first work with professional actors: *Experiment Number 4—The Possessed* (*Ensaio n°4—Os possessos*) in Rio de Janeiro in 1987.

In 1989 Lessa experimented with the opening of the stage space to natural elements such as the flowers, leaves, sand, and stones in *Orlando*, based on Virginia Woolf's novel and two years later with water and aquatic plants in *Portuguese Letters* (*Cartas*

Portuguesas), based on the letters of Mariana Alcoforado. She directed her first opera in 1990, Puccini's *Suor Angelica*, with an unconventional and ironic style. Lessa continued directing many other operas, including the heralded *Il Trovatore* by Verdi in 2010, which inaugurated the reopening of the Municipal Theatre (Teatro Municipal) of Rio de Janeiro after a complete restoration. These contemporary stagings show the dominion of the director over increasingly impressive performing spaces, designed by Gringo Cardia. A certain impatience with the narcissism of the theatrical system and the conventional reductionism of scenic art drove Lessa to seek out realistic staging for her adaptation of Thomas Mann's *The Holy Sinner* (*O eleito*) in 1996. Lessa's long journey in Ceará, a state in northeastern Brazil, in which sacred and profane elements come together in a rich liturgical mass culture, produced material for the movie *Believe Me* (*Crede-mi*), made in 1997 with Dany Roland. Lessa's return to the theatre is almost a negation: in 2002 the stage became home to filmed reality for Ibsen's *A Doll's House*, in which an actor only appeared live for a monologue in the final scene.

Verdi's *Il Trovatore,* directed by Bia Lessa, Municipal Theatre of Rio de Janeiro, 2010. Photographer: Carlos Fernando Teixeira de Macedo.

Verdi's *Il Trovatore,* directed by Bia Lessa, Municipal Theatre of Rio de Janeiro, 2010. Photographer: Carlos Fernando Teixeira de Macedo.

Since 2000, Lessa increasingly evades the world of drama. By directing operas or concerts and events such as parades, fashion shows, and museum exhibitions, Lessa acts as a multimedia artist, redesigning the space as an interactive concept, an approach she has been pursuing since her first exhibition in 1999,[7] requiring the participation of the spectator as a determining factor in modern Brazilian museology. Innovative projects such as the Brazilian Pavilion at EXPO 2000 in Hanover, Germany, or Baroque Gallery (*Modulo Barocco*) at the São Paulo Biannual that same year stimulate in the visitor a complete experience, not just a visual one. The fact that this concept is valued is highlighted by Lessa's creation of the first "conceptual" museums, such as the *Museum of the Portuguese Language* (*Museu da Língua Portuguesa*) in São Paulo and the *Brazilian Oral History Museum* (*Museu Oral Brasileiro*) in Paraty, works that have made the director a mandatory reference for contemporary museum design. Recently, she created the acclaimed exhibition Humanidade 2012 for the United Nations Conference, Rio+20. Despite the apparent institutionalization of her work, Lessa still sees it primarily as a means of experimentation based on the idea of interaction and risk—a manifestation of the concept of experiments (*ensaio*). She explains, "because they are permanent, museums are a challenge that was not foreseen, in the sense that for me to stage exhibitions or theatre is almost the same thing: there with hammer and nails, here with human material" (Lessa).

Both the experimental vocation and the sequential method of "trascriAzioni" continue to inform Lessa's direction. She states:

> The author creates the problem and the director organizes the formal equation so that the problem can be solved; the actors or the materials are part of this equation. The function of the director is then to create the space and create a scenic language to make them obvious and effective for the specific content. Before there were categories, genres, codes, while today a director must create, for each job, a language and a code that the public can decode so that the work successfully communicates. The viewer, then, is the one who sees and creates, or rather creates what he sees, builds within himself what he imagines he is seeing, which is in truth a different show for each individual spectator. (Lessa)

Christiane Jatahi

Born in 1968 and raised in Rio de Janeiro, Christiane Jatahi made her debut as an actor, directed by influential directors such as Miguel Falabella and Aderbal Freire Filho. Particularly attracted by contemporary Spanish drama, she refined her talent in Barcelona in 1992 with Spanish playwright José S. Sinisterra. On her return to Rio de Janeiro, she founded Grupo Tal, for which she wrote and directed in the same year three children's shows under the title of *Trilogy of Initiation* (*Trilogia da Iniciação*). Starting in 2000 she directed Rio de Janeiro's Vertex Company (Cia.Vertice), whose name alludes to a triangle whose vertex is the audience; this was a research path that developed into her creation and direction of the trilogy *A Chair Is Solitude, Two Is Dialogue, and Three Is Society* (*Uma cadeira para a solidão, duas para o diálogo, três para a sociedade*), and her radical exploration of naturalism with plays: *Connected* (*Conjugado*) in 2004, *The Fault That Moves Us* (*A falta que nos move*) in 2005, and *Clean Cut* (*Corte seco*) in 2010. Creating situations of extreme proximity between stage and auditorium in which the boundaries between interpretation and reaction, fiction and reality were confused, Jatahi made her actors interact and mingle with the audience in an intimate and abstract way—making the performance meta-theatrical. In *Clean Cut* the montage of short scenes was created by the director live, with the lighting and audio boards in full view, as if the audience were viewing the scene from the inside of a film-editing booth. Her attempt was to provoke new scenic possibilities by addressing casualty. The support of video technology—pointed toward the outside of the theatre through the security cameras—questioned unique points of view and encouraged the audience to renew its own. Jatahi kept the production "open" so that the audience would recognize itself as "part of the show in the present" and mobilize its imagination to complete the open-ended stories while actors perceived themselves as both being "in character" and at the same time, themselves (Jatahi). The purpose of the director was that the meeting of actor and audience be kept alive and transformational, as in real life.

From here the transition to film seemed obvious, a medium in which *The Fault That Moves Us* debuted in 2011, and earned unprecedented success for a national experimental production. The film was close to absolute naturalism, with the actors playing themselves for a thirteen-hour tracking shot (1:30 edited) in which they received instructions from the director over a cell phone, were called by name, were interrupted, argued, and took drink breaks, all in real-time. The intrusion of the cinema in the theatre and of the theatre in the cinema is justified by the search for a "vision from within." According to Jatahi,

> I open things on stage not to show my abilities but to capture the possibilities for interaction in that moment. To strip naked and experience the unveiling: perhaps one can build something here and now. When the actor who plays a part is called by his real name, a series of instinctive reactions takes over, and lives, one that does not reason. The function of direction is to build in a state of absolute difference, to risk. To assemble a mosaic of these fragments in the scene. The theatre itself is a slice of reality. The director chooses, cuts. Dance with handcuffs, as Nietzsche wrote. Create from the limit: the less needs to become more. (Jatahi)

Denise Stoklos

From outside of the Rio–São Paulo axis, exceptional artists like Denise Stoklos have managed to prevail over economic difficulties and to artistically distance themselves from the metropolitan mainstream. Stoklos, who is from the state of Paranà, had a versatile and autodidactic education as a mime and performer, further enriched in London and New York, where she has lived since the mid-1980s. This background nourishes the expressive work of the "essential" theatre that the artist writes, directs, and performs, dealing with issues that are "universal, urgent, human, therefore political" with a minimum of technical effects and maximum theatricality ("Denise Stoklos"). Without costumes or scenes, the "essential performer" as Stoklos describes herself, only has her body, voice, and mind to tell a story. As the director describes on her website, she is "always militant; her quest is a search for a possibility of improvement, reflection, action and transformation; her intention is for the audience to come out stronger from its theatrical encounter with the essential performer's struggle for freedom" ("Denise Stoklos"). The distance creates an experimental genre, the one-woman show, which she successfully created, directed, and performed with *Elis Regina*, created in California in 1980, and *Mary Stuart*, created in New York in 1987 at La Mama Experimental Theatre Club.

Back in Brazil, Stoklos began to produce her own repertoire with authorial shows like *House* (*Casa*) in 1990, which was subsequently performed in several languages; *A Fax from Denise Stoklos to Christopher Columbus* (*Um fax de Denise Stoklos para Cristóvão Colombo*) in 1992; and *DisMedea* (*Des-Medéia*) in 1994. In others she reclaims the voices of committed authors, such as the anarchist Henri Thoreau, Gertrude Stein, and the protester, Bartleby, from Herman Melville's story *Bartleby the Scrivener*.

The author of several books about her method, Stoklos exercises a mastery of a very personal scenic grammar, based on her own skills and a refined style of montage that includes an organic score of continuous rhythmic variants. Her methodology allows her to retain absolute autonomy in her path of theatricality, expansive and untamed. She explains,

> Theatricality is when one is completely run through by affects, as Spinoza says. I feel alive this way, when I can tell stories about something that moves me, dramatize what has happened. You stage it so that it can be observed, in order to reflect upon it and do things better. It is such an unquestionably free horizon that it reminds us of all that can still possibly save us in this world of war and intolerance. I see the theatre as a resistance movement, one of affirmation: never negative, always of affirmation. (Pardo 78)

Awarded in Edinburgh in 1994 and, the following year, in Brazil with the medal of the Ordem do Rio Branco, Stoklos is among the Brazilian artists of greatest international significance.

Leo Sykes

Born in London but educated in primary school in Italy, Leo Sykes was an assistant of Eugenio Barba's from 1991 to 1996 in Barba's Odin Teatret in Denmark. She studied Barba's directorial method for her doctoral dissertation in performing arts, granted from the University of Warwick in 1996. Sykes lives in Brasilia and travels the world with the circus-theatre company Udi Grudi, which she has directed since 1998. The group, made up of three clown-musicians, had no director before her arrival. The first Brazilian show Sykes directed in 1998, *The Barrel* (*O cano*), developed the already extravagant language typical of Udi Grudi in an experimental environment, with particular attention to the comedic timing of sound production. This and her direction of the Udi Grudi productions of *The Egg* (*O ovo*) in 2003 and *In ConSerto* in 2008 all go on extensive international tours, allowing her to devote herself to the parallel production of videos and documentaries such as *In Transit* for the Odin Teatret in 1996, *Tale of Two Heads* (*Racconto delle due teste*) for the Teatret Om in 1998, and *The House of Master Andre* (*A casa do mestre André*) for Udi Grudi in 2006. Teatret Om is a group of women actors in Denmark with whom Sykes has maintained a regular contribution as director since 1995, producing shows that tour throughout Europe, such as *Ciota, Matoc e Gulliver* in 1995, and *79 Fjord* in 2009. Her work develops on two fronts: that of gender and the linguistic, since she works with women performers in Denmark and with male clowns in Brazil.

Sykes says she is interested in "feminine direction" rather than in women directors, explaining:

> Eugenio [Barba] to me is a feminine director; he lets the material guide him, his work is all based on the spontaneous responses of the actors reacting to his proposals. It's a game. . . . How can a director communicate and grow, given that her work is

invisible, or should be so in the final product? We use our internal organs in order to work: but who sees my heart, who sees my stomach? All of this is just mine, it is invisible but I have to make the public feel it; if the scene moves me, I hope it can also excite the viewer. . . . For me, the actor may use whichever process she wants, [but] I'm interested in the audience. In this sense, the director is the audience, in other words, he represents it: she is the first spectator, and stays there to see what the audience will see. The external look has to do with quality. The director in this sense protects the viewer, is his eyes, but also protects the actors from the audience. She is a bridge between two worlds. From the stage we try to encourage a meeting, to reclaim the humanity of the people present, to remember that we are spiritual human beings, and that we can cry, laugh, open ourselves up to the game. (Sykes)

Independent of gender, the few yet brilliant Brazilian women directors negotiate every inch of their personal professional success both on the entertainment market and in the family.

Notes

1. According to the 2010 census, the inclusion of women in the workforce, while considerable, is lower than it is for men in terms of the hierarchy of employment positions and earnings, on average 30 percent lower than for men of the same age and educational level.

2. Organization of Secondary Education for Females (Organização do Ensino Secundário para o Sexo Feminino), 1884 (Costa 266). More recently, the incidence of illiteracy for adult women has decreased from 27 percent in 1990 to 11 percent in 2010, thanks to equal access to compulsory education, though women are still far from achieving equal rights.

3. President Dilma Roussef intends to distribute 50 percent of public posts to women, according to her 2011 mandate.

4. It is curious that Morineau chose to reveal her French nationality with her stage name. Other foreigners camouflaged their names while the nationalist phase was in full swing.

5. As of August 2011 the site had not yet catalogued any twenty-first-century names, among which would include at least three other foreign women directors resident in Brazil: German Nehle Franke, British-Italian Leo Sykes, and Italian Alessandra Vannucci.

6. Lessa states, "One time I quit and ended up becoming a horse breeder. I got married, I made babies, and I spent years doing laundry, ironing and cooking" (Nagib 260).

7. *Brazilian Like Me* (*Brasileiro que nem eu*), to the FAAP (Fundação Armando Alvares Penteado) in São Paulo.

Sources

Bevilacqua, Ana. "Corporal Space in *Romeo and Juliet* by Italia Fausta." *Annals of the 1st Congress of Research and Post-Graduate Performing Arts* ["Espaços do corpo no Romeu e Julieta de Itália Fausta." *Anais do I° congresso de pesquisa e pós-graduação em Artes Cênicas*]. São Paulo: USP, 1999.

Costa, Albertina, and Cristina Bruschini. *A Question of Gender* [*Uma questão de gênero*]. São Paulo: Fundação Carlos Chagas, 1992.

"Denise Stoklos." Available at http://denisestoklos.uol.com.br (accessed December 10, 2011).

Expilly, Charles. *Women and Customs of Brazil* [*Mulheres e costumes do Brasil*]. São Paulo: Companhia Editora Nacional, 1977.

Itaú Cultural Encyclopedia [*Enciclopédia Itaú Cultural*]. Available at www.itaucultural.org.br (accessed December 10, 2011).

Jacintha, Maria. "Presence of Esther Leão" ["Presença de Esther Leão"]. *Dionysos* 23 (1978): 33.

Jatahi, Christiane. Interview with the author. May 2011.

Lessa, Bia. Interview with the author. May 2011.

Nagib, Lucia. *The Resumption of the Film: Testimony of 90 Filmmakers in 90 Years* [*O cinema da retomada: Depoimentos de 90 cineastas dos anos 90*]. São Paulo: Editora, 2002.

Pardo, Ana Lúcia, organizer. *The Theatricality of Human* [*A teatralidade do humano*]. São Paulo: SESC, 2011.

Schumaher, Schuma, and Érico Vital Brazil, eds. *Brazilian Women Dictionary* [*Dicionário de mulheres brasileiras*]. São Paulo: Jorge Zahar, 2000.

Sykes, Leo. Interview with the author. February 2011.

Bulgaria
Vessela S. Warner

Bulgarian women made assertive steps in theatre directing after 1944, when the communist state granted free professional training in the performing arts, built and subsidized some thirty-five theatres, and provided equal-gender employment opportunities. Comprising a small number in the heavily politicized occupation of directing during the totalitarian period, women often persevered through professional and moral compromises. Since the collapse of Eastern European communism in 1990, Bulgarian women stage directors have fearlessly faced the challenges of an open-market economy and free competition. Although in the beginning of the twenty-first century they still represented a minority in the business, their achievements have gained high national and international recognition.

Women's Rights: Historical Context

The women's rights movement in Bulgaria was intertwined with and impeded by the country's thwarted early modern history. In the time of the European Renaissance and Enlightenment, Bulgaria existed as a colonized country with a patriarchal society within the feudal Ottoman Empire (1393–1878). After its national liberation, it remained generally conservative to modern gender perceptions. The void of liberal traditions and distinct capitalist structures during the first half of the twentieth century was quickly filled by the masculine drive of various lower-class, nationalist, and leftist forces which eventually established a Soviet-like proletarian dictatorship at the end of World War II.

Women's emancipation in Bulgaria was integrated in the objectives of the socialist revolution the Bulgarian Communist Party carried out in coalition with other antifascist organizations in 1944. For the first time in Bulgarian history, policies of class and gender equality were included in the new socialist constitution, and their legislative power granted suffrage and employment rights to women. Principally progressive and irrevocable, these policies also secured women's support of the communist government as well as their much-needed participation in a primitive economy that heavily relied on physical labor and mass numbers. On the premise that women's emancipation was achieved with the victory of the socialist revolution, the new government dissolved all previous feminist organizations. The formalistic and politically complacent Bulgarian Women's Committee was mostly concerned with women's international solidarity (Nikolchina). The Bulgarian totalitarian government disallowed the existence of grassroots organizations and public forums that addressed any internal political issues.

Between 1944 and 1989, Bulgarian women silently suffered the injustices of a sociopolitical system that disregarded basic human freedoms and nourished political and gender favoritism. State-granted education and emancipation through employment proved to be an illusionary victory for Bulgarian women, who were compelled to support their families financially while overcoming the burdens of primitive living conditions. Furthering their education was often compromised by the need to care for young children and aging parents. In the 1960s, Bulgaria's national deficit increased and the market sustained a shortage of basic commodities. Downplaying a much larger sociopolitical crisis, the Communist Party recognized the disintegration of the Bulgarian family and addressed women's difficulties in balancing advancement at work and mounting duties at home. The measures taken—considered by many to be a return to gender division and traditional family hierarchy—were generally futile due to ideology-governed policies. The place of women in the new political and cultural environment of totalitarian communism was precarious: they were generally protected and encouraged to compete in every social arena, yet they were exposed to acts of gender bias and sexism on a daily basis.[1]

In the postcommunist years, the totalitarian practices mutated into economic chaos, inadequate legislature, and pervasive criminal violence, which altogether exacerbated women's lives. The lingering transition from state ownership to privatization of industry pushed some women to "risky but prosperous entrepreneurial activity" in the private sector, mainly in retail and service, while "others, after years of guaranteed jobs, [were] facing unemployment" (Kostova 215). After 1990 many nongovernmental organizations embraced the women's rights cause, but they engaged mostly in cultural and educational projects. The passing of the antidiscrimination bill in 2003 was a major political victory, but the problems that specifically identified women as a dynamic yet vulnerable social group were not sufficiently addressed.

Early Women Directors

The women pioneers in stage directing were not specifically trained in directing but relied on their acting education and experience to lead their casts. From this small group, Zlatina Nedeva (1878–1941) could likely take the credit for being the first Bulgarian woman director. Nedeva studied theatre arts in Zagreb, then part of Austria-Hungary, and in 1904 became an actor in the first troupe of the Bulgarian National Theatre (now Naroden Teatar Ivan Vazov). Between 1921 and 1924 she founded and led the Chamber Theatre (Kameren Teatar), and in 1934–35 she briefly served as artistic director of two provincial theatres. The women immediately following in Nedeva's steps were either trained actresses or graduates of established directing programs in Moscow. They plowed new territories for the art they loved: Vesselina Stefanova and Stefka Prokhaskova headed small theatre companies, and Mara Penkova and Liliana Todorova started auxiliary theatre projects like Theatre for the Village and Children's Theatre Academy, respectively. Director Mara Penkova Sr. was among the creators of the professional puppet theatre, while Rebeca Arsenieva directed programs for Bulgarian radio and television.

In 1948 the State Theatre School (Durzhavno Teatralno Uchilishte) received the status of national academy and started providing graduate education in all areas of the performing arts. Until the 1990s, this conservatory-type institution, late known as NATFIZ (National Academy of Theatre and Film Arts), offered the only professional and highly competitive program in stage directing in the country. The first domestically trained women directors had equal opportunities to further their educations and strengthen their competitive power by studying under famed Soviet directors after graduation.[2] Some of the most established practitioners who started their careers in the 1950s included Tsvetana Stoyanova, Gertruda Lukanova, Elka Mikhailova, Nikolina Tomanova, Nadezhda Seikova, Yulia Ognyanova, Dimitrina Gyurova, Margarita Venkova, and Vesselina Ganeva. The increased number of women directors in this period reflected the Communist Party's determination to maintain gender equality in every professional area, theatre included. But theatre was not like any other occupation in communist Bulgaria; considered a major ideological weapon for invasive political propaganda, it was heftily financed and strictly controlled by the government. As a result of these austere political conditions, Bulgarian theatre turned into a bureaucratic institution where nepotism, careerism, and ideological obedience flourished.[3]

From the 1950s through the 1970s, most women directors occupied administrative and educational positions in the arts. Women professors in acting and directing were often staging productions as guest artists in various theatres at home and abroad. Their work was never in serious competition with that of men directors, who were employed by the largest theatres and entrusted with the politically engaged repertoire. Women stage directors could much more easily find employment in the provinces than in the totalitarian "bastions" of ideological culture in the Bulgarian capital of Sofia. An example of political and gender preferences is the fact that until 1990 only a couple of women were invited as guest directors in the Bulgarian National Theatre.[4] Generally, stage directors had little to no input in the selection of the repertoire, which was determined by complacent theatre management under the censorship of the Central Committee of the Communist Party. The productions directed by women during the totalitarian period included early and modern classical drama as well as contemporary Bulgarian and Soviet plays.

The lack of creative freedom and fair competition explain why women pursued less prestigious but also less risky academic careers in the theatre. The failing socioeconomic infrastructure further contributed to their desire to secure a politically safe occupation and stable conditions for raising a family. Women directors, like many women intellectuals, continued to feel vulnerable when in a position of artistic or administrative authority. They needed stronger political backing in order to survive in men's professional territory.

Bulgarian theatre received a short respite from the political demands of realism in the productions of four young directors at the Burgas State Theatre between 1957 and 1960. Sheltered by a valiant management and encouraged by the emerging of experimental theatres in the Soviet Union after the death of communist dictator Joseph Stalin in 1953, these talented artists began to explore various nonrealistic styles (Buchvarov 2). The only woman among these nonconformists was Yulia Ognyanova, who was born in 1923. Ognyanova was privileged for being an active participant in the communist insurgency before the socialist revolution and sent to earn a master's in theatre history and criticism from the State Institute for Theatre Arts (GITIZ) in Moscow, after which she was hired as a dramaturge at Burgas Theatre. Soon she began to direct her own shows, which embraced the principles of theatricality and Epic Theatre. In 1958, still in Burgas, she directed *Mother Courage and Her Children*, which was the first production of Brecht's play in communist Bulgaria. In a heated public discussion, the work of the four avant-garde directors was slammed by dogmatic critics and incompetent party officials, to whom Ognyanova responded courageously by defending artists' freedom of expression. She accused Bulgarian theatre of leaning toward false romanticism and deadly "socialist realism," protesting that, of the communist Eastern European countries, only in Bulgaria and Albania had the name Bertolt Brecht remained taboo.[5]

After the Burgas troupe was dissolved in an act of political punishment, Ognyanova worked mostly as a freelancer, showing preference to epic-style adaptations and satirical fables in works by Vladimir Mayakovski, Nikolai Erdman, Peter Weiss, and Josef Kafka. She directed activist theatre companies in Italy and France, and educated unorthodox actors and directors in the puppet theatre program at NATFIZ from 1981 to 1990.

The aesthetic dogmatization and political control of theatre in the 1960s and the 1970s negatively affected the number of productions by women directors. With the political thaw in the early 1980s, a new generation of women directors, including Elena

Baeva, Bina Haralampieva, Snezhina Tankovska, and Elena Tsikova, started to break away from the conventions of socialist realism by directing aesthetically diverse or previously censored foreign drama.

Working Climate in the Twenty-First Century

With the collapse of the communist state in 1989, Bulgarian theatre went into a deep financial crisis and painful adjustment to capitalist economy. Until 2010, the forty-one theatre companies in the country relied primarily on state funding and less on box office receipts and private sponsorship. The new economical conditions forced theatres to shrink their troupes and incorporate freelance contracts. Directors have been especially interested in working at different venues in order to survive financially. The Union of the Bulgarian Artists, the only professional union for all employed in the theatre, has protected the equity in compensation and working conditions, but without differentiating between the needs of men and women.

The 2010 reform aimed to propel the Bulgarian theatre into the free market. It merged established theatre troupes in order to cut down administrative costs and introduced funding criteria based on ticket sales. In return, companies have tried to be creative in their selection of repertoire, efficient in the use of existing resources, and wise in balancing avant-garde and commercial productions. In an environment of major political and cultural transformations, women stage directors have preferred small-cast chamber plays with heavy intellectual content. As the following section will illustrate, their productions have leaned toward creative adaptations and experimental theatre.

Profiles of Contemporary Directors

Margarita Mladenova

One of the most successful Bulgarian directors, Margarita Mladenova is also an internationally known theatre instructor and the talented manager of the oldest independent theatre in communist Bulgaria. Born in 1947, Mladenova completed her education in directing at NATFIZ in 1972. In 1988, together with fellow director Ivan Dobchev, she founded the experimental Theatre Workshop Sfumato (Teatralna Rabotilnitsa Sfumato). Since its inception, Sfumato has been the most vibrant, intellectually engaging, and internationally acclaimed Bulgarian troupe. The company's name reveals the directors' desire to return theatre to its sacredness by unraveling invisible psychological, archetypal, and philosophical meanings of the text through effective visual language.

Mladenova's penchant for the spiritual and ethical in theatre was inspired by the creative inquests of Jerzy Grotowski, Anatoly Vasiliev, and Peter Brook (Vandov and Decheva 86). The director tested her "sfumato" approach with the poetic realism of

Anton Chekhov, Ivan Turgenev, and Lyudmila Petrushevska. Her refined work on classical and contemporary Russian texts produced polyphonic structures of complex characterizations and visual asceticism. Actor-director Atanas Atanasov writes about Mladenova's and Dobchev's Sfumato debut, the production of Chekhov's *The Seagull* in 1989: "[I still carry] the painful curiosity to explain how this [theatre] worked and why it worked in such a way. . . . This was a theatre without being THE theatre. This was Chekhov but not THAT Chekhov" (54).[6] The postmodern meta-text of Mladenova's 1991 production *P.S.*—a compilation of Chekhov's texts that envisioned the characters of *The Seagull* after Treplyev's death—astonished and perplexed the critics. In an article for *Theatre* magazine, Svetlana Bajchinska declared: "[The] show cannot be 'read,' i.e. interpreted. The only thing left is to feel it" (Vandova and Vandov 62).

Some of Mladenova's most original productions were part of Sfumato's signature seasons' programs, in which the theatre co-founders each directed works by the same author. In her own adaptations, Mladenova surprised the audiences with an inexhaustible variety of stylistic choices. She explored folkloric and mythological territories in the 1993 *Sin Named Zlatil* (*Grekhat Zlatil*), based on Yordan Yovkov's *Boryana*, and the 1998 *Mortal Antigone* (*Antigona Smurtnata*) based on Sophocles's play. Mladenova drew upon Epic Theatre techniques and elements of Grotowski's "poor theatre" in creating the metaphysical space of the nation in Yordan Radichkov's *Crazy Grass* (*Luda Treva*) in 1994.

As a director-auteur, Mladenova has been unafraid to adapt a variety of texts for the stage, including poetry, documentary material, collected folklore, and classical novels. In her 2004 production of Dostoyevsky's *The Brothers Karamazov*, titled *The Valley of the Deadly Shadow: Alyosha* (*Dolinata na Smurtnata Syanka: Alyosha*), she depicted a cast of godless, agonizing souls contrasted with and attracted to the sacred figure of Alyosha Karamazov, the protagonist. Dostoyevsky's text was presented as a collage of monologues: a scenic poem about the battle between sacred and satanic. In collaboration with Dobchev, Mladenova also created two powerful examples of anthropological theatre: *Apocrypha* (*Apokrif*) in 1997 and the internationally acclaimed *The Black Fleece* (*Chernoto Runo*) in 2000. Conceived after an extensive research of archaic texts, songs, old dialects, and firsthand observations of the nomadic Karakachan tribe, *The Black Fleece* articulates the anxiety between ancient consciousness and modern rationalism. French critics described the production as "a legend in perfect aesthetics," a "primitive mystery . . . [that] moves with its archaic beauty," and compared it to Peter Brook's African-history-inspired *The Iks* from 1975 (Vandova and Vandov 163–64).

In 2007 Mladenova offered two powerful interpretations of August Strindberg's drama: *Julie, Jean, and Christine*, based on *Miss Julie*, and *The Dance of Death*. Set in a chromic kitchen, where metal pots boil on open fire and wastewater drains onto the floor, the fall of Miss Julie resembled a clinical examination of man's physical self-destruction. Critic Nikolai Yordanov described Mladenova's visual language as a "blend of ecstasy and symbolism in a hyperrealistic environment" (Vandova and Vandov 228–29). In *The Dance of Death* the characters' abstracted relations unfold behind a mysterious black scrim and with choreographed physical gestures that revitalized the languages of expressionism and the absurd. Mladenova explains her leading concept: "[*The Dance of Death* proves how] the civilization's big plan for Man fails in man himself, how Nietzschean Superman is denigrated to a beast. From this point, the tragicomic absurd and Beckett's *Endgame* are only a step away" (Mladenova). Mladenova's variations on Strindberg were performed at La Pavris in Tarbes, France, and the Theatre de la Bastille in Paris. Captivated by the production's visual expressiveness, French theatre critic Stéphane Boularaud commented that in the most intense moments of the show one seems to "forget that it is being performed in Bulgarian" (Vandova and Vandov 238).

In her productions, Mladenova uses classical texts to pose difficult philosophical questions and offer contemporary perspectives. Often her rehearsals are preceded by open ateliers: workshops which bring together intellectuals of various backgrounds to discuss the challenges of the literary source. By delving deeply into the phonetic rhythms and complex meanings of a given text, the director creates striking images of metaphysical presence. In her aesthetically diverse productions, Mladenova "rejects the boundaries between living, dreaming, and yearning, and between hidden and apparent realities" (Vandov and Decheva 87).

Mladenova is a recipient of the highest Bulgarian awards in directing and, together with her Sfumato associate, is frequently invited to lead workshops in France. Sfumato's productions have toured more than twenty countries. Whether working in the ideological restrains of communism or in the market-oriented culture of post-communism, Mladenova has always sustained high artistic standards and the belief that "morality always accompanies true talent" (Vandov and Decheva 94). As part of her selfless efforts toward purer theatre forms, Mladenova has, with Sfumato, given opportunities to young, untraditional directors—many of them women—to showcase their work during the theatre's summer seasons.

Vazkresia Viharova

The earliest and most drastic opposition to psychological realism in Bulgarian theatre belongs to another woman director, Vazkresia Viharova. Born in 1957, Viharova studied Stanislavsky's methods of directing and acting in NATFIZ and graduated in 1983, then became interested in developing an alternative actor's training as well as testing it in experimental productions. Her early study of physical theatre familiarized her with the methods of Yevgeny Vakhtangov, Vsevolod Meyerhold, and Michael Chekhov, but it was only after she specialized in Noh theatre, psychodrama, Waldorf education, and Feldenkrais Method, that Viharova started to apply a multidisciplinary approach to theatre practices.[7] She began experimenting with actors' resources that are set in archetypal impulses and uncontrolled energies, as explored by Grotowski or sculpted in the unsteady "architecture" of human body much like Oskar Schlemmer's work on constructivist costume and non-anthropomorphic performance.

Viharova created and directed two riveting avant-garde productions at Theatre Tear and Laughter (Sulza i Smjah): *Dingdong* (*Dzun*) in 1988, based on Evgeni Haritonov's play, and *Living* (*Bit*) in 1990, based on Ivan Hadjiiski's book, *Optimistic Theory of Our People* (*Optimistichna Teorija za Nashia Narod*). These innovative works gave her the confidence to create an alternative theatre program at the New Bulgarian University (NBU) in 1990. Since then she has been directing casts of students and professional actors at the NBU's Theatre of the Slug (Teatarut na Golia Ohliuv).

Dingdong is a bold experiment in the deconstruction of text into syllables and musical phrases, through which the actors create new relationships and meanings. For this show, as well as for most of her later work, Viharova worked closely with architect Zarko Uzunov in creating props and costumes that challenged actors' physical reactions. Uzunov's costumes included sticks fixed at different angles, which restrained the actors' bodies and changed their rhythm, energy, and emotional expressions. The "stickman technique" was also implemented in the NBU's co-production with Theatre 199 of Maurice Maeterlinck's *The Blind* in 1992.

Viharova's *Living* was based on a nondramatic text: Ivan Hadjiiski's academic study of Bulgarian national psychology. The performance deconstructed/reconstructed traditional dances and the bagpipe music that accompanies them. Between 1990 and 1994, Viharova created a sequel of four more productions of *Living*, in which she also included and trained NBU students. Until 1996, the director's professional and school projects were shown at more than fifty festivals in Europe and Australia, including

Dingdong, directed by Vazkresia Viharova at Theatre Tear and Laughter, Sofia, 1988.

Living, based on Ivan Hadjiiski's book, *Optimistic Theory of Our People,* directed by Vazkresia Viharova, Theatre Tear and Laughter, Sofia, 1990.

the 1993 and 1994 Edinburgh Fringe Festival. The international critics called *Living* a
Balkan *butoh*[8] and referred to the actors onstage as "Chinese princesses of the Balkans"
(Viharova E-mail). The intercultural comparisons came to depict a theatrical vision
that was original and cohesive in its ethnic-universal hybridity. Viharova describes her
aesthetic principles as "intuition on the wings of understanding," quoting the Swiss
painter Paul Klee. She summarizes the nature of her experiments:

> Although these attempts could be considered a formal deconstructionist flirt with
> performance, they were actually a result of investigating the pre-text of a given text:
> that something which precedes the word in a sentence, character, or situation. The
> word [was treated] as a sign of a psycholinguistic gesture of the mind with the actor's
> body being its only interpreter and energy carrier. . . . [My first experiments] were
> accompanied by psychoanalytical approach to the text that aimed at adjusting it to
> the performers and to the propensity of human psychophysics to seek expressions
> through rhythm and melody while in a situation of affect. Very often the text was
> reduced to a phonetic and melodic structure, which stimulated the actor's body
> during rehearsal and produced defensive mechanisms during performance. (E-mail)

Viharova's psychomechanical theatre "simultaneously creates and rectifies itself," but
despite its formalistic nature, it evokes strong emotional responses (Viharova E-mail).

With her following productions, the director continued to work with the deconstruction of classical and contemporary texts, pushing the boundaries of psychodrama

and surrealism. The audiences were often infuriated to find in her shows nondramatic etudes rather than stories and self-reflective "happenings" instead of dramatic action. Viharova was the first Bulgarian director to introduce multimedia in Jean Cocteau's *Les Parents Terrible* at Razgrad Theatre in 1991. She continued to explore this multiplying and deconstructing device in *The Crazy Woman of the House!* (*Ludata na Doma*), based on texts by Jean Cocteau, in a co-production by Razgrad Theatre and NBU in 1994, and in Peter Turrini's *Alpenglühen* (*Alpijsko Siyanie*) at the National Palace of Culture in 1997. Her nonrealistic theatre naturally complemented the parody in Michael Green's *The Cherry Sisters* at the Theatre of Satire in 2003 but challenged the aesthetic conventions of Lorca's *The House of Bernarda Alba* in 2005 and Shaw's *Heartbreak House* in 2009, both of which played at the Bulgarian National Theatre.

Viharova pioneered the alternative theatre in Bulgaria by designing, probing, and teaching an advanced system of nonpsychological performance. Comparing her attempts at anthropological theatre to those of Jerzy Grotowski and Eugenio Barba, or her treatment of text-body-space to other examples of postmodern performance, will not fully explain—nor diminish—her artistic originality. Viharova's former female students, who have made a significant mark in the contemporary Bulgarian theatre as directors, include Elena Panayotova, Dessislava Shpatova, Deliana Manova, and Anelia Christova.

Lilia Abadjieva

Born in 1966, Lilia Abadjieva began her professional career in 1998 after she graduated from NATFIZ with a degree in theatre directing. She learned from the experience of post-communist directors, especially the stylistically compressed, theme-oriented theatre of Vazkresia Viharova. Since 1998 Abadjieva has exhibited "cruel" expression and intellectual irony in her deconstructions of classical works by Shakespeare, Gogol, Strindberg, Dostoyevsky, Chekhov, and Goethe. Her work has been shown at the Bulgarian National Theatre; Moscow Art Theatre; Luna Theatre in Moscow; Lobero Theatre in Santa Barbara, California; and Freie Kammerspiele in Magdeburg, Germany, where she received prestigious theatre awards. Abadjieva was a distinguished artist-in-residence at the University of Köln, Germany, and in 2010 became one of the two permanent directors at the Bulgarian National Theatre. She is the only contemporary Bulgarian director whose work has been recognized in the United States. After the successful performance of her postmodern *Romeo and Juliet*, a Bulgarian National Theatre production at the University of California, Santa Barbara in 2006, Abadjieva was invited to work at Westmont College, California. With a cast of students, teachers, and alumni, she mounted the stage fusion *Othello / Measure for Measure*, which was presented at Lit Moon World Shakespeare Festival in Santa Barbara in 2008. The production won Abadjieva the Indy Award for directing by the *Los Angeles Times* and *Santa Barbara Independent* theatre critics.

Abadjieva's style thrives on the deconstruction of classical texts and an emphasis on cultural travesty. Her stage adaptations extract only main dramatic situations and reveal characters as "absurd and contemptible, quivering in their choice making" (Vandov and Decheva 233). Approaching the texts from a new and original angle, Abadjieva condenses classical plays to a few images or leitmotifs, which she then presents in a fast, MTV-inspired montage of selected scenes. Charles Donelan from *Santa Barbara Independent* compares her style in *Othello / Measure for Measure* to the "aesthetic of punk rock." He writes, "Rather than exhibiting anything so clichéd as disdain for the audience or contempt for the material, Abadjieva's direction resembles the Ramones in its purity and dedication to the three essential chords of a song, or, in this case, a situation" (Donelan). Language and text are only a starting point for the semantically rich vision of the avant-garde director. Abadjieva's theatre overtly manifests the director's "distaste for the stereotyped and reductionist expression of feelings in human communication" (Vandov and Decheva 230).

Abadjieva's 2009 "mix" from three Shakespearean texts—*Measure for Measure*, *Othello*, and *Macbeth*—was produced by the Little City Theatre off the Channel (Maluk Grandski Teatar zad Kanala) in Sofia. The distilled conflicts from the plays were united by the themes of passion and dissatisfaction. Typical of all her takes on the Bard, the all-male cast interchanged roles and swung from one play into another, conveying a boldly fresh sense of overwhelming desire and discontent. In this clever intercultural performance, Abadjieva introduced theatrical signs of various epochs and aesthetic codes: Elizabethan costumes, rhetorical gestures of the romantic stage, as well as classical and popular songs. In the words of critic Violeta Decheva, the parody of the classic "reveals the semantic emptiness of the codified theatre gestures in order to visualize the grotesque quivers of the flesh" (4).

The re-envisioning of classical works does not only exhibit Abadjieva's postmodern distrust in language and tradition: beyond the parody and grotesque physicality, there emerges a new poetic expression of the metaphysical human condition. The clear emotional and semantic structures "draw you in, as if borders between audience and acting are overstepped and there is no 'there' but only 'here' and 'now.' . . . [The] blend of light, music and movement never calls into question the locality of the scenes: [that] psychological dimension where love, gnawing doubt, fear, delusion, and mad rage dwell" (Daskalova).

The original, innovative, and internationally recognized work of Mladenova, Viharova, and Abadjieva is a strong declaration of the prominent position of women stage directors in contemporary theatre. In the beginning of the twenty-first century Bulgarian theatre has witnessed a rise in the quantity and quality of productions by women directors. Artists like Diana Dobreva, Dessislava Shpatova, Ida Daniel, Vassilena Radeva,

Elena Panayotova, and others, continue to challenge the aesthetic canons and existing cultural perceptions.

Notes

1. For an example of the continuing cultural attitudes towards Bulgarian women, see Bilefsky.

2. The most promising or just politically loyal directors were sent by the government to work with prominent Soviet artists.

3. For an overview of the propaganda role of theatre during Bulgarian communism, see Liljana Stancheva, *Theatre and Totalitarianism*, and Vasil Stefanov et al., *100 Years National Theatre*. In his memoir *Behind the Curtain of the National Theatre: An Experience*, Diko Fuchedjiev unveils the political machinations in the first Bulgarian theatre, which he headed between 1976 and 1990.

4. Between 1944 and 1990 only one woman director was on staff at the Bulgarian National Theatre, and she was part of the "reserve" group of artists who did not produce regularly. The practice of overstaffed institutions was typical of the bureaucratic communist management (Stefanov 246, 285).

5. The style of "socialist realism" was formulated in Stalinist Russia in the early 1930s and became a compulsory model for the arts in most of the communist countries. This doctrine prescribed a "realistic" (understood as optimistic and often romanticized) representation of the working-class life and its struggle under the guidance of the Communist Party.

6. All the translations from Bulgarian belong to the author.

7. The Waldorf education method, based on Rudolf Steiner's anthroposophy, involves integral learning that stimulates the physical, artistic, and conceptual abilities of man. The Feldenkrais system of education was designed to bring awareness of the human body in order to improve the functioning of its nervous and muscular systems.

8. *Butoh* is an avant-garde Japanese dance first performed in 1959. Its grotesque elements combine traditional Japanese performance with improvisation, Expressionist dance, and theatre.

Sources

Atanasov, Atanas. "Margarita Mladenova—The Unconventional Convention" ["Margarita Mladenova—Bezuslovnata uslovnost"]. *Homo Ludens* 6–7 (2003): 52–68.

Bilefsky, Dan. "Women's Influence Grows in Bulgarian Public Life." *New York Times*, February 7, 2010. Available at http://www.nytimes.com (accessed January 4, 2011).

Buchvarov, Kiril. "Burgas State Theatre 'Adriana Budevska' 1957–1960." *Theatre* ["Burgaski naroden teatar 'Adriana Budevska' 1957–1960." *Teatar*] 1–2 (1994): 2–7.

Daskalova, Radina. Review of *Othello*, by William Shakespeare. *PlaystoSee.com, 2009*. Available at http://playstosee.com (accessed December 20, 2010).

Decheva, Violeta. "Poor Soul, the Center of My Sinful Earth." Review of *Measure for Measure*, by William Shakespeare. *Culture* ["Dusha neshtastna, iadko na platta." *Kultura*], October 30, 2009, 4.

Donelan, Charles. "Shakespeare Fest Kicks Off at Center Stage." *Santa Barbara Independent*, October 23, 2008.

Fuchedjiev, Diko. *Behind the Curtain of the National Theatre: An Experience* [*Zad Zavesata na Narodnija Teatar: Prezhivjano*]. Sofia: Izdatelstvo Christo Botev, 1998.

Kostova, Dobrinka. "Women in Bulgaria. Changes in Employment and Political Involvement." In *Women and Democracy: Latin America and Central and Eastern Europe*, edited by Jane S. Jaquette and Sharon L. Wolchik, 203–22. Baltimore: Johns Hopkins University Press, 1998.

Mladenova, Margarita. *The Dance of Death* by August Strindberg. *Sfumato.info.* Available at http://sfumato.info (accessed June 8, 2011).

Nikolchina, Miglena. "Gender Studies and the University: The Bulgarian Case." Author's typescript. Published in *Gender Studies: Trends/Tensions in Greece and Other European Countries*, edited by Th.-S. Pavlidou, 117–28. Thessaloniki: Ziti, 2006.

Rusev, Ivan. "That Wonderful and Captivating Cinderella." *Theatre* ["Tazi chudna magnetichna Pepeliashka." *Teatar*] 1–2 (2003): 20–22.

Stancheva, Liljana. *Theatre and Totalitarianism* [*Teatar i Totalitarizum*]. Sofia: Academic Publishing House Prof. Marin Drinov [Akademichno izdatelstvo Prof. Marin Drinov]. Sofia: Idea, 2000.

Stefanov, Vasil, Kristina Tosheva, Violeta Decheva, and Romeo Popiliev. *100 Years National Theatre* [*100 Godini Naroden Teatar*]. Sofia: Damyan Yakov, 2004.

Tosheva, Kristina, Vasil Stefanov, Svetlana Bajchinska, and Svetla Beneva, eds. *Encyclopedia of the Bulgarian Theatre* [*Entsiklopedia na Bulgarskia Teatar*]. Sofia: Trud, 2008.

Vandov, Nikola, and Violeta Decheva. *The Directors of the 1990s: Interviews* [*Rezhisiorite na 90-te: Razgovori*]. Sofia: Izdatelstvo Valentin Trayanov, 2003.

Vandova, Maria, and Nikola Vandov, comp. *Theatre Workshop Sfumato 1989–2009* [*Teatralna Rabotilnitsa Sfumato 1989–2009*]. Sofia: Izdanie na Teatralna Rabotilnitsa Sfumato, 2009.

Viharova, Vazkresia. E-mail message to the author. November 14, 2010.

———. Interview with Daniela Strelkova-Djankova. *Theatre* [*Teatar*] 9–10 (1995): 29–30.

 Canada

Gordon McCall

As the second-largest landmass country in the world and defined as the largest country in the Western Hemisphere, Canada is a nation made up of ten provinces and three territories with a population of thirty-four million citizens. Spread across its vast expanse, Canada's bilingual regional and independent theatre scene serves as a connective tissue of the nation's social, cultural, and political identity.

In addition to the formation of an ever-increasing number of English and French language theatre companies beginning in the 1970s, the national theatre scene experienced significant growth in the number of important women directors, such as Brigitte Haentjens, Jackie Maxwell, Jillian Keiley, Diane Roberts, and Sarah Stanley. It is directors like these, inspired by a new age of gender equality and led by their passionate artistic imaginations and theatrical visions, who have brought a new sense of urgency and vibrancy to Canada's national theatre scene.

Women's Rights: Historical Context

As far back as the late nineteenth century, Canadian women fought for their rights, often against great odds but always with courage, tenacity, and imagination. The right to vote, the right to equal pay for equal work, and the right to freedom from violence are just some of the seminal issues that have engaged the hearts and minds of women nationwide.

The first political engagement on the road to equality for Canadian women, the battle for the right to vote, was ignited by a visionary who wouldn't take no for an answer, Dr. Emily Howard Stowe (1831–1903). Seeking the same provincial and federal electoral rights as men, Stowe fought for women's rights until her death. In 1916 Alberta, Manitoba, and Saskatchewan became the first provinces to pass legislation allowing women to vote. By 1919 Canadian women had won the right to vote in federal elections. However, it was not until 1940, with Quebec implementing its provincial right to vote for women, that suffrage was finally established in its entirety on both a federal and provincial level.

The struggle for equality continued on other fronts. Even though women had been granted the right to vote in federal elections and to hold seats in the House of Commons, it was not until 1929 with the famous Persons Case that women were considered "persons" and awarded equal rights. This case came about when five Alberta women campaigned to have a woman named to the Senate the previous year but were denied because "women were not included among the 'persons' eligible for Senate appointments under Section 24 of the British North America Act (1867)" (Parks Canada).

Suffrage and equality in the eyes of the law were not the only issues requiring dedicated and courageous action by and on behalf of women. Women struggled to have laws and legislation enacted that would protect them from physical and emotional violence. The 1970s saw the opening of Canada's first rape crisis centers as well as shelters and transitional housing for abused women. On another front, Canadian women continue to be engaged in attempting to gain equality in the workplace. As of 1978, pay equity has been a part of the Canadian Human Rights Act. However, women continue to find a gender pay gap, due in part to "discriminatory attitudes toward women and the jobs they have traditionally held, attitudes that have become ingrained in the economic system" (CHRC).

Early Women Directors

In the spirit of women seeking a better quality of life, one woman stands at the forefront of the development of Canadian theatre and its everlasting contribution to the lives of Canadians.[1] That woman is Dora Mavor Moore (1888–1979), often called the founder of professional theatre in Canada.

Moore was born in Glasgow, Scotland, but immigrated to Canada at the age of four. As a teenager she attended the University of Toronto, where her father served as a professor of political economy. Perhaps it was in her role as Rosalind in a University of Toronto production of *As You Like It* that the seeds were sown for Moore's later connection to Canada's Stratford Festival. Following her graduation Moore studied at the Margaret Eaton School of Literature and Expression in Toronto. From there she earned a scholarship to the Royal Academy of Dramatic Art (RADA) in London and in 1912 became the academy's first Canadian graduate (Leonard). Her journey to RADA was part of a growing tradition of Canadian actors leaving the Great White North to apprentice in the birthplace of Shakespeare.[2]

Upon her return from overseas after World War I, Moore began producing and directing theatre for amateur groups, and in 1938 she took the bold step of forming her first amateur theatre company, the Village Players, based in Toronto. For many years the company toured productions of Shakespeare to high schools. However, following World War II Moore's attention turned to professional theatre and her dream of founding a fully professional company. The Village Players came to an end and the New Play Society (NPS) was born. Author Paul Leonard chronicles that Moore directed NPS's first production in 1946, when "Millington Synge's *Playboy of The Western World* . . . was performed at the 435-seat theatre of the Royal Ontario Museum in downtown Toronto. . . . These [play] series continued until 1950, offering Torontonians the 'balanced season' that would become a staple of the regional theatre movement a decade later in Canada: contemporary British and American hits, classics, and original Canadian plays" (n.p.).

Another of Moore's lasting contributions to Canadian theatre was her role in recruiting Sir Tyrone Guthrie from England to become the first artistic director of the Stratford Festival, in Stratford, Ontario (Sperdakos). For her service to her country, Moore was awarded a Centennial Medal on the country's hundredth birthday in 1967. She subsequently was made an officer of the Order of Canada in 1970. Since 1980 one of the greatest tributes to her is the annual presentation of the Dora Mavor Moore Awards, produced by the Toronto Theatre Alliance.

Working Climate in the Twenty-First Century

Inspired by the contributions of Moore and other pioneering women and aided by a renewed sense of purpose generated by the second wave of feminism in the 1960s, the stalwart efforts of dedicated, talented, and visionary directors, academics, and political activists of the 1970s and 1980s provided true foundational blocks upon which aspiring women directors could build.

In their 2006 research article, "Women in Theatre: Here, There, Everywhere, and Nowhere," Rebecca Burton and Reina Green point out that while there is no doubt the number of women directors employed in Canadian professional theatre has increased from approximately 10 percent in the early 1980s to 30–35 percent at the turn of the twenty-first century, gender inequity remains in place with male directors and artistic directors still dominating the scene. They reference Rina Fraticelli's 1982 report, "The Status of Women in Canadian Theatre," which addressed playwrights, directors, and artistic directors. Fraticelli found that "women accounted for a paltry 11 percent of the country's artistic directors, a mere 13 percent of its directors, and only 10 percent of its produced playwrights" despite comprising "the vast majority of theatre school graduates as well as the vast majority of amateur (unpaid), volunteer and community theatre workers" (Burton and Green 58; Fraticelli, "Any Black" 9). The Fraticelli report had no immediate effect on mainstream theatre practices of the 1980s, but it became a galvanizing force for women in theatre, giving rise to additional studies as well as new theatre companies, organizations, festivals, and conferences (Burton and Green 60).

In the summer of 2005, a group called Equity in Canadian Theatre: The Women's Initiative collected statistics through nationwide surveys that reflected "an incremental improvement has been made since the release of Fraticelli's report, with an equivalent increase of 10 percent per decade in the numbers of women represented, but this advancement is not sufficient to constitute genuine equality in the theatre sector" (Burton and Green 60–61).

Profiles of Contemporary Directors

Brigitte Haentjens

Born in 1951 and raised in Versailles, France, Brigitte Haentjens, the artistic director of the French Theatre (Théâtre français) of the National Arts Centre (NAC) of Canada, came to her adopted country in 1977. Before coming to Canada Haentjens completed her university studies in France, then enrolled in the famous Theatre School of Jaques Lecoq (Ecole de théâtre Jaques Lecoq) in Paris. Looking back at that turning point in her life, Haentjens says that she realized she would have to leave her country of origin "in order that theatre could become my whole life" (Haentjens).

Haentjens made her way to the bilingual city of Ottawa, Ontario, but did not find the opportunity she was seeking. Instead, it was the small northern Ontario mining town of Sudbury that gave her the start of her career. Sudbury had a large Franco-Ontarian population, a small French language theatre, and an opening for a new artistic director. As artistic director at Theatre of the New Ontario (Théâtre du Nouvel-Ontario) from 1982 to 1990, Haentjens excelled at developing original plays from local writers. It was just such a writer, playwright Jean Marc Dalpe, and his play *The Dog (Le Chien)* that propelled Haentjens into the national spotlight. Her 1988 direction of the play had immediate impact and was invited to the Limoges Festival in France and Festival TransAmerica (Festival Transameriques) in Montreal.

By 1991 Haentjens's reputation was continuing to grow, and she moved to Montreal to be at the center of French-language theatre in Canada. In her new artistic leadership position as head of the New Theatrical Company (Nouvelle Compagnie Théâtrale), she directed a memorable production of Albert Camus's *Caligula* in 1993. The following year she founded her own company, Sybellines, the name inspired by the Sybelline Prophecies. At Sybellines, Haentjens's direction of classics such as Sophocles's *Electra* and *Antigone* highlighted her unique theatrical vision. As one author describes, "Through her subjective interpretation of texts, often influenced by psychoanalysis, she particularly explores the hidden weaknesses of the feminine identity, the games between power and sex, and the zone where myths and the unconscious collide" ("Canadian Directors").

Of her 2009 production of Georg Büchner's *Woyzeck*, produced by Sybillines at l'Usine C in Montreal, the critics were unanimous in their praise. Natasha Gauthier of the *Ottawa Citizen* newspaper wrote of the mise-en-scène:

Haentjens stages the action as a series of jagged tableaux, as hallucinatory and unsettling as the original text. The language is current, the setting 1960s-ish, the men in mechanic's coveralls or high-waisted trousers, the girls in short skirts, but Büchner's stuttering, cubist dialogue is so extemporaneous that the modern update hardly registers. The set consists chiefly of a long, suspended inclined platform, dimly lit in red, like a bloody gash across the stage, a harbinger of the violence to come. Haentjens demands extraordinarily physical, exaggerated performances from her actors.

Gesture and tableaux, metaphor physicalized into striking scenic imagery, and a bold contemporary sensibility with language and movement are hallmarks of Haentjens's productions. She aims to provoke the audience's sensibilities, to jar them into an unforgettable viewing experience. In June 2011 *Just Like Her* (*Tout Comme Elle*) received its premiere at the Luminato Festival, Toronto to rave reviews. Conceived and directed by Haentjens and co-authored by poet Louise Dupre with translation by Erin Moure, it explored the complexity of mother-daughter relationships with a cast of fifty women. Critic Jon Kaplan wrote, "Award-winning director Brigitte Haentjens . . . turns the production into an evening of movement, a cappella song and gesture, adding suggestive emotional levels that expand on the spoken word."

In honor of her sustained excellence in directing, Haentjens was awarded the $100,000 Elinor and Louis Siminovitch Prize in Theatre in 2007.

Jackie Maxwell

Artistic director of the Shaw Festival in Niagara-on-the-Lake, Ontario, since 2002, Jackie Maxwell is a directorial force to be reckoned with. The first woman to helm this acclaimed festival, for years prior to accepting this directing engagement she dedicated herself to the development and production of new plays. She has also long been a champion of the cause of women theatre artists, particularly directors. Now that she holds one of the most powerful positions in Canadian theatre, she continues to take bold steps to emphasize the importance of women in today's theatre.

Born in 1956 in Belfast, Northern Ireland, Maxwell credits her mother with sparking her first interest in theatre. In an interview with the *Toronto Star* she stated, "Mom was an English and drama teacher, which is where I got my love of theatre, and my father was a bookie which is where some people would say I learned how to be an artistic director" (Ouzounian). Leaving Ireland for England, Maxwell graduated in 1977 with a bachelor of arts in drama, with honors, from the University of Manchester. Following graduation, she performed in small roles on television and was an usher in theatres. After meeting her future husband, Canadian actor Ben Campbell, she moved to Canada in 1978.

Maxwell began her directing career in the late 1970s when John Wood, artistic director of the National Arts Centre (NAC) in Ottawa, offered her the job as assistant director to himself as well as luminary and legendary Canadian directors John Hirsch and Jean

Gascon. Soon thereafter she directed her first show at the NAC, Thomas Middletown and William Rowley's *The Changeling* (Ouzounian).

In the early 1980s came a fateful meeting with Sharon Pollock, preeminent Canadian playwright, who showed Maxwell how to work with writers and run playwriting workshops. Once people came to know how good Maxwell was at developing new plays, her reputation as an outstanding dramaturge began to grow. Bob White, artistic director of Toronto's Factory Theatre from 1977 to 1987, asked Maxwell to take over for him while he was on sabbatical one year. She did so and became associate director of the theatre in 1983, then artistic director from 1987 to 1995. While there, she dedicated herself to the development and production of new plays, including "some of Canada's most respected and vital playwrights such as George Walker, Michel Marc Bouchard, Sharon Pollock, Ann-Marie MacDonald and Michel Garneau" ("Jackie"). After her work at the Factory Theatre, Maxwell freelanced and was head of new play development at the Charlottetown Festival in Prince Edward Island from 1997 to 2000.

Since 2002 Maxwell has been the artistic director of the Shaw Festival, one of Canada's most venerated theatrical companies. As its artistic leader, she has taken bold steps to emphasize the importance of women in contemporary theatre. In addition to hiring women directors on a regular basis, she has expanded the mandate of the festival to include not only plays by George Bernard Shaw and his contemporaries, but also contemporary plays that focus on social and political issues that concerned Shaw.

As a director, Maxwell is sensitive to the voices and nuances of character with a strong lyrical sensibility that lends her best productions an engaging and entertaining layering of voice and music. In addition, she is able to bring old plays to life for contemporary audiences. For her 2007 acclaimed Shaw Festival production of Shaw's *Saint Joan*, presented at the Chicago Shakespeare Theatre in 2008, the *Chicago Tribune* noted, "That sensation of prescience and the gaining of a larger historical context for events of the moment—which Jackie Maxwell's superbly spoken and also profoundly moving production greatly engenders—is the best rationale going for attending revivals of 85-year-old plays" (Jones).

However, where Maxwell truly excels is with contemporary plays. Her 2006 staging at the Shaw Festival of Argentine-American playwright Lillian Groag's *The Magic Fire*, about an immigrant Italian and Jewish family living in politically volatile Buenos Aires in 1952 under the Peron regime, was luminous in its revelations of the complexity, volatility, and inherent musicality of this family dynamic. Reviewer Steven Berketo wrote, "Director Jackie Maxwell firmly establishes an array of moods that allows the effervescent comedy and formidable drama to swing back and forth like a pendulum. Her efforts fully compliment the playwright's original writing style."

Among her awards for her achievement in theatre are the 2005 Gascon-Thomas Award, bestowed by the National Theatre School of Canada, and the 2008 Herbert Whittaker/Drama Bench Award, given by the Canadian Theatre Critics Association. In addition, she received an honorary doctorate from Windsor University in 2007.

Looking to the future, Maxwell states, "We must now, more than ever, continue to move forward—embracing new writers, revealing new worlds, exploring new approaches to our classic plays" ("Artistic").

Jillian Keiley

Jillian Keiley, artistic director of English Theatre, National Arts Centre of Canada, and founder/artistic director of Artistic Fraud theatre company in St. John's, Newfoundland, is a leader among theatrical innovators in Canada. Along with artistic associate and playwright Robert Chafe, Keiley has created a defining element of her directing and creative process called Kaleidography, which has won her national and international acclaim.

Born in 1970 and raised in Newfoundland, Keiley's seminal artistic years included six seasons as an assistant director for Memorial University Newfoundland (MUN) Drama Summer Shakespeare under Dr. Gordon Jones. In 1994 she earned a BFA from Toronto's York University, specializing in directing. As a university student, the work of directors Peter Brook, Robert Lepage, and director-designer Gordon Craig became formative influences in Keiley's creative growth, but it was during her investigations into the inner workings of commedia dell'arte that she found the inspiration for what would become the heartbeat of Kaleidography: timing (Devine 33). Keiley explains, "In 1994 I was having trouble making a commedia scene work and my teacher (Anatol Schlosser) explained that the commedia actors had perfect timing because they were families. So then I thought I could impose a family by pre-arranging the timing" (Keiley). She further explains how Kaleidography makes time central to creating "synchronized movement harmonics": "[E]very second is contained and measured using music notation. Using our system of music notation and grid placement, we are able to create visually complex scenes through relatively simple choreography. . . . This works both in movement and aural aspects of performance; an actor has his monologue anticipated and reverberated by a twenty-person chorus through an underscored whispered fugue, with key phrases perfectly falling on the whispered echoes of the full group" ("Kaleidography").

Many productions that have further developed the Kaleidography system have followed that original burst of creativity. In *Chekhov Variations*, adapted from Chekov by Chafe and directed by Keiley for Artistic Fraud in 2002, four characters from *The Seagull* and other Chekhovian classics interpreted their roles accompanied by musicians. The exact rhythm and pitch of how each actor said the lines in rehearsal composed the music of the piece. The Artistic Fraud website clarifies, "Each character was assigned a player from our string quartet to represent their voice. The viola personified Irina; the cello, Konstantin; the violin, Nina; and the bass, Trigorin" ("Chekov Variations"). In performance the actors never spoke. They acted silently while the musicians became their voices.

Keiley first directed Chafe's *Fear of Flight* with students at Sir Wilfred Grenfell College in 2005 as part of a teaching residency for Artistic Fraud. A collection of characters, monologues, and choral work integrated with music and movement follows the anxious moments of fourteen passengers on a flight across Canada. *Fear of Flight* was subsequently produced professionally in various parts of Canada, garnering a variety of reviews. In the 2010 *Canadian Theatre Review*, Barry Freeman and Robin C. Whittaker wrote of the production at the Factory Theatre: "Here, shifting in seats, flipping the pages of a newspaper, closing laptops and unfolding menu cards are components of the piece's music, timed precisely to punctuate, or sometimes to act in counterpoint to, the monologues . . . [However,] transitions between the monologues are often unprovoked, and about forty minutes into the eighty-minute piece the predictable spotlight / monologue / switch pattern begins to grate."

Writing about Keiley's mixed critical reception, stage director Michael Devine comments, "[In] a stream of kinetic and engaging productions, Keiley's work remains, at times, unconvincing in its ability to plumb darker emotions and reach the deepest depths of psychological complexity or emotion. It needs to be said, however, that this could only be considered a deficiency within the conventional mindset of North American psychological realism" (35). According to Devine, her strength is in her theatricality: "Large casts, swirling images, and the use of music and direct address engage audiences" (35). Keiley has been described as a "visionary, innovative artist whose experiments with form and content have magical results for audiences and performers alike" ("Recipients").

Robert Chafe's *Fear of Flight*, directed by Jillian Keiley, Artistic Fraud of Newfoundland. Photographer: John Lauener.

Keiley's major awards include the Canada Council's John Hirsch Prize in 1998 and the $100,000 Siminovitch Prize in Theatre for excellence in directing in 2004. She also had the honor of representing Canada at the Cultural Olympiad of the Vancouver 2010 Winter Olympics with *Fear of Flight*.

Diane Roberts

African Canadian director Diane Roberts is an excellent example of a Canadian theatre artist who has dedicated herself to animating social and political issues through her art of theatre directing focused primarily on Aboriginal artists and artists of color. Her goal, along with the theatre company she leads, urban ink, is "to champion Aboriginal and minoritized artists to take control of not only their voice and visions, but the process and integrity in which their work is brought to an audience" ("About UI").

Born in England and immigrating to Montreal when she was three years old, Roberts fell under the spell of theatre at a young age when she witnessed an Ice Capades production of *Peter Pan* (Roberts). Years later another revelatory moment occurred when she directed an all-white cast in a university production of *for colored girls who have considered suicide/when the rainbow is enuf*, by Ntozake Shange. By concentrating on the references embedded in the text and demanding of her actors that no one be allowed to "white wash" any of the words or cadences, Roberts felt she achieved an authentic representation of the play (Roberts). Always a dedicated learner, she earned a bachelor of fine arts in 1988 and master of fine arts in 1998, both from Toronto's York University.

During her career, Roberts has directed for a wide variety of theatre companies from regional theatres to feminist theatres, to African Canadian theatres, to Indigenous Peoples theatres. Before arriving at urban ink, she founded Obsidian Theatre and backforward collective, and was co–artistic director, with Alisa Palmer, of Toronto's Nightwood Theatre from 1994 to 1996, where she "spearheaded the Groundswell Festival of New Works by Women" ("Artistic Direction").

Her 2002 direction of the Black Theatre Workshop production at the Montreal, arts interculturels (MAI) of Andrew Moodie's play *A Common Man's Guide to Loving Women* firmly established her status as an effective director of a well-made play. The *Montreal Gazette* proclaimed in its review: "Amazing team effort in a drama that goes from comedy to rape-crisis drama" (Radz) and montreal.com concurred: "Under the inventive and crackling direction of Diane Roberts all the elements were there, and it made for a memorable night" (Brouillet).

However, it is in the world of devised theatre created through interdisciplinary theatrical collaboration, and far from traditional play forms, where Roberts excels. A prime example is her ongoing theatrical initiative, *The Arrivals Project: A Personal Legacy Workshop Series*, "bringing together First Nations and Minoritized Artists in a meaningful creative interplay between artistic voice, ceremony, and Ancestral recovery" ("Artistic Directon"). She has designed a process to create new performance works drawing on

Valerie Sing Turner's *Confessions of the Other Woman,* directed by Diane Roberts and Gerry Trentham, Performance Works, Vancouver, 2012. Photographer: Tim Matheson.

ancestry and has worked all over the world inspiring artists to delve into their roots as a source of theatrical inspiration. In 2012, in residence at Chapter Arts in Cardiff, Wales, Roberts worked on an international exchange between dance artists from Nigeria and interdisciplinary artists from across Canada called *Atlantic.*

Of her directing process she states: "I prepare through research and exploration of the script or performance work. Then I go in and create an atmosphere where collaboration can thrive. I step into the abyss with my collaborators and see the work with new eyes. Together we discover the nuance in performance" (Roberts).

Sarah Stanley

Born in Montreal in 1963 and raised in Westmount, Quebec, Sarah Stanley is a proponent of new works of theatre and self-identifies as a queer theatre director. Associate artistic director of English Theatre, National Arts Centre of Canada, she earned a bachelor of arts from Queens University in Kingston in 1987 and graduated from Vancouver Film

School in 2001. It was while in Kingston that she founded her first theatre company, The Baby Grand, in 1985. In 1992 she helped to form a Montreal theatre collective, along with other young women directors, called Women Making Scenes, which focused on alternative and controversial works. The next year her career took off when she staged a production of *Romeo and Juliet* under the Bathurst Street Bridge in Toronto. According to Stanley, that production was very significant. She states, "It gave birth to a company that I'm still involved in—Die in Debt Theatre. The piece was something we did in collaboration with Kensington Youth Theatre. It caused a huge media sensation, which was fantastic. It was not necessarily where we were headed but given that I was able to bring together scenes of homeless youth into a story such as *Romeo and Juliet* and set it in an environment where theatre-goers would find off their beaten track was the big achievement. . . . The following year we did a new version of *Oedipus* under the Gardner Expressway and that won a Dora [Award]" (Stanley "Sarah").

As co–artistic director of Die In Debt Theatre with Troy Hansen, Stanley created site-specific theatre productions. Subsequently, she expanded her repertoire to programming and directing new plays as artistic director of Toronto's Buddies in Bad Times Theatre, co–artistic director of Self-Conscious Theatre (with Michael Rubenfeld), associate director of the Factory Theatre, dramaturge-in-residence of Montreal's Playwright's Workshop, and as the first festival associate and symposium coordinator for the traveling Magnetic North Theatre Festival. In addition she was co-director of the directing program at the National Theatre School of Canada and worked as an instructor at Concordia University, both in Montreal. Her body of work has brought her numerous accolades, including a nomination for the 2007 Siminovitch Award for directing.

Stanley directs a wide variety of theatrical genres and styles. In 2007 she directed Peter Quilter's hilarious play, *Glorious*, based on the true story of the flamboyant but tone-deaf singer Florence Foster Jenkins, for Montreal's Centaur Theatre. Praise for her direction was generous, with the *Montreal Gazette* proclaiming, "Stanley's controlled, subtle direction registers perfect pitch in handling the play's comic mayhem and its satirical rhythms without losing sight of the characters' humanity" (Donnelly).

Turning from comedy to drama in 2008, Stanley directed a co-production between Montreal's Tessri Duniya Theatre and Vancouver's Neworld Theatre at Vancouver's Havana Stage with the Canadian premiere of *My Name Is Rachel Corrie,* based on the writings of Rachel Corrie and adapted to the stage by Alan Rickman and Katherine Viner.[3] Other productions of this controversial play had been canceled by or withdrawn by theatres in New York and Toronto for political reasons. The play is based on the events regarding the violent death of twenty-three-year-old American activist Rachel Corrie, a member of the International Solidarity Movement who was protesting the destruction of Palestinian homes and was crushed to death by an Israeli Defense Forces bulldozer in the Gaza strip (Wasserman). Unafraid to enter tempestuous political waters, Stanley's direction received praise for a script that was admittedly unbalanced in its portrayal of the politics of the real-world situation.

In 2010 Stanley once again exemplified her active social conscience and belief in new plays that speak of local issues but that resonate with universal meaning. She directed a premiere of Berni Stapleton's *The Oracle of Gros Morne* at the Gros Morne Theatre Festival, Theatre Newfoundland Labrador, in Gros Morne Provincial Park. Stanley summed up the experience, stating, "[T]his apocalyptic play grabs a portion of Newfoundland's psyche by the throat and wrestles it through music, comedy and pathos into a gorgeous moment of realization regarding the role we all play in the ongoing environmental despair we are all facing" (Stanley "Info").

Sarah Stanley is a director who remains very much in touch with her times, continuing to affect social change with her theatrical vision. As she so eloquently states: "Theatre that doesn't engage in some profound way with both the mysteries and agonies of human existence holds little interest for me. The theatre is a place of options and the very best theatre offers a great sense of possibility in the face of difficulty" (Stanley "Oracle").

Directors Haentjens, Maxwell, Keiley, Roberts, and Stanley represent five unique and highly respected approaches to the art form of live theatre directing. All have achieved significant success and continue to contribute to the status of women directors in Canadian theatre and to the overall betterment of the theatre art form. They represent a microcosm of the vibrant, talented, and growing number of women directors throughout the country who are continuing the journey begun by Dora Mavor Moore so many years ago.

Notes

1. Another pioneer was Joy Coghill, who became co-producer at Vancouver's Everyman Theatre in the early 1950s and also co-founded Holiday Theatre, Canada's first professional children's theatre. From 1953 through 1965 she directed all of the forty-nine productions the theatre produced. She also served as artistic director of the Vancouver Playhouse and headed the English section of the National Theatre School of Canada in the early 1970s.

2. Britain's Royal Academy of Dramatic Art has stood as a beacon of actor training for aspiring Canadian thespians, who have historically turned to England or France for cultural cues.

3. *My Name Is Rachel Corrie* was directed by Sarah Garton Stanley with collaborating director Marcus Youssef.

Sources

"About UI." *urban ink productions,* 2012. Available at http://urbanink.ca (accessed February 28, 2012).

"Artistic Direction." *urban ink productions,* 2012. Available at http://urbanink.ca (accessed February 28, 2012).

Berketo, Steven. "Effervescent Comedy and Formidable Drama Collide."*torontostage.com*, 2006. Available at http://www.torontostage.com (accessed February 28, 2012).

Brouilett, Neil. "Far from Common." Review of *A Common Man's Guide to Loving Women*, by Andrew Moodie. *monteral.com*. Available at http://montreal.com (accessed February 28, 2012).

Burton, Rebecca, and Reina Green. "Women in Theatre: Here, There, Everywhere, and Nowhere." *Theatre Research in Canada / Recherches théâtrales au Canada* 27.1 (2006): 56–80.

"Canadian Directors." *ArtsAlive.ca,* n.d. Available at http://www.artsalive.ca (accessed February 28, 2012).

Canadian Human Rights Commission (CHRC). "Equal Pay for Work of Equal Value: Employer's Guide." *Canadian Human Rights Commission*, October 6, 2010. Available at http://www.chrc-ccdp.gc.ca (accessed February 28, 2012).

"Chekov Variations." *Artistic Fraud*, n.d. Available at http://www.artisticfraud.com (accessed February 28, 2012).

Devine, Michael. "Keileydography: The Symphonic Theatre of Jillian Keiley." *Canadian Theatre Review* 128 (September 2006): 31–36.

Donnelly, Pat. "Glorious Is Certainly That!" Review of *Glorious*, by Peter Quilter. *Montreal Gazette*, February 5, 2007.

Fraticelli, Rina. "'Any Black Crippled Woman Can!' or A Feminist's Notes from Outside the Sheltered Workshop." *Room of One's Own* 8.2 (1983): 7–18.

———. "The Status of Women in the Canadian Theatre." An unpublished report prepared for the Status of Women Canada. June 1982.

Freeman, Barry, and Robin C. Whittaker. "Fear of Flight, Fear of Fright: Artistic Fraud of Newfoundland and Eight 'Trans-Canadian' Playwrights Touch Down at Factory Theatre." Review of *Fear of Flight,* by Robert Chafe. *Canadian Theatre Review* 142 (Spring 2010): 88–90.

Gauthier, Natasha. "Haentjens' Woyzeck a Disturbing, Original Interpretation." *Ottawa Citizen*, February 10, 2010. Available at http://www.canada.com (accessed February 10, 2012).

Haentjens, Brigitte. Acceptance speech. *Siminovitch Prize,* 2007. Available at http://www.siminovitchprize.com (accessed February 28, 2012).

"Jackie Maxwell." *Shaw Festival,* n.d. Available at http://www.shawfest.com (accessed February 28, 2012).

Jones, Chris. "Now Is the Moment for This Wonderful 'Saint Joan' at CST." Review of *St. Joan* by George Bernard Shaw. *Chicago Tribune*, January 11, 2008.

"Kaleidography Workshop." *Rumble Productions,* 1999. Available at http://www.rumble.org (accessed February 28, 2012).

Kaplan, Jon. "Tout Comme Elle (Just Like Her): 50 Outstanding Actors Define the Nuanced Mother-Daughter Relationship." *NOW Daily Stage*, June 17, 2011.

Keiley, Jillian. "Re: Almost There." E-mail message to author. March 1, 2012.

Leonard, Paul. "Dora Mavor Moore." *Dictionary of Literary Biography*. Thomson Gale, 2005–2006: n.p. Available at http://www.bookrags.com (accessed February 22, 1012).

Maxwell, Jackie. "Artistic Directors Message." *Shaw Festival,* 2012.

Ouzounian, Richard. "Ouzounian: Jackie Maxwell Is Shaw Festival's Champion." *thestar* *.com*, May 28, 2010 (accessed February 28, 2012).

Parks Canada. "Person's Case." *Parks Canada,* n.d. Available at http://www.parkscanada .gc.ca (accessed November 2011).

Radz, Matt. "When Loving Women Goes Too Far." Review of *A Common Man's Guide To Loving Women* by Andrew Moodie. *Montreal Gazette*, November 30, 2002.

"Recipients of the Elinore & Lou Siminovitch Prize in Theatre." *Siminovitch Prize.* Available at http://www.siminovitchprize.com (accessed February 9, 2013).

Roberts, Diane. "Last-minute stuff." E-mail message to author. February 28, 2012.

Sperkados, Paula. *Dora Mavor Moore: Pioneer of the Canadian Theatre.* Toronto: ECW, 1995.

Stanley, Sarah. "Sarah Stanley's Directorial Decree." *TorontoStage.com,* 2004. Available at http://www.torontostage.com (accessed February 28, 2012).

———. "Info needed for book chapter." E-mail message to author. February 29, 2012.

———. "The Oracle of Gros Morne." E-mail message to author. March 1, 2012.

Wasserman, Jerry. Review of *My Name Is Rachel Corrie* by Rachel Corrie, edited by Alan Richman and Katherine Viner. *Vancouver Plays* 43 (January 2008). Available at http:// www.vancouverplays.com (accessed February 28, 2012).

 China

Jiangyue Li

Contemporary Chinese theatre has become increasingly dynamic because of the growing role of women directors. Women stage directors in China are contributing to the intercultural global context by integrating modern, postmodern, and traditional forms of theatre while exploring gender politics. Although women directors emerged in the late 1500s, it was not until the 1900s that they made significant inroads in Chinese theatre, particularly with modernist and feminist productions.

Women's Rights: Historical Context

Opportunities for women in China surpass those of women who live in many other countries (LaFleur 166). Most women work outside their homes and have equal employment rights with men. These working women receive respect from both outside and within their families, and many of them become medical doctors, artists, scientists, and governors. However, the *New York Times* reports that although there are many opportunities for Chinese women, there is still gender discrimination with "unfair hiring practice, dismissal on grounds of pregnancy or maternity leave, or sexual harassment" (Tatlow). Throughout the two thousand years of Imperial China (221 BCE–1911 CE), women had limited rights due to patriarchal conventions, and women were discriminated against since birth. Marriages were arranged, women did not have inheritance rights, and women could not work outside the home, making them economically dependent on their fathers and husbands. In addition, women had to obey patriarchal principles developed by Confucius, termed the "three obediences" and "four virtues," which required women to serve their spouses and their husbands' relatives, give birth to male heirs, and remain chaste even if their husbands died. Otherwise, they would be discarded by their families and even physically punished or killed by angry mobs. According to these traditional principles, it was difficult for women to divorce, and they suffered unequal treatment. Likewise, numerous Chinese women in ancient times were physically and psychologically abused by feudal habits, such as foot binding and domestic violence. Women entered a dark age during the late Qing Dynasty (1644–1911) founded by the Manchu who used and distorted traditions to oppress, manipulate, and control the large population. The Qing government forcefully promoted Confucianism, especially those aspects regarding women's chasteness, although some oppressive regulations were not applied to high-class women. Nonetheless, there were early well-educated Chinese native feminists who fought against patriarchal principles via their work as dramatists, writers, publishers, poets, and private teachers while confined to the inner chambers of the household. Most of these early women fighters were geishas, courtesans, noble women, officials, gentlewomen, and Taoists or Buddhist nuns, who were intellectuals but could not get married because of specific religious rules.

The status of Chinese women was dramatically changed during the early years of the republic, founded in the 1911 revolution, when women's rights were considered an important priority. During the 1920s, the first wave of Chinese feminists encouraged women to defend their rights and identify themselves as participants of the new era, coinciding with the introduction of Ibsen's *A Doll's House* in China (He 49). Women were encouraged to get higher education and to pursue their professional ambitions. Additionally, marriage laws were enacted to protect women from being forced into abusive arranged marriages (LaFleur 166). Since the 1900s, many Chinese women writers have demonstrated feminism in their dramas and literature. These literate, upper-class women left their secluded inner chambers and took on significant social roles in public (Yan 3).[1]

Later, in the 1950s, women's liberation was highlighted by the People's Republic of China (PRC), especially in rural China. The second wave of Chinese feminists, inspired by Marxism, were generally working class and leaders of the new government. As materialist feminists, they emphasized "the dominance of economic factors" and thus made efforts to promote and improve women's rights about property and employment (Fortier 152). A fundamental change in the gender income gap occurred in 1950 with the implementation of the Land Reform Act, which allowed women equally to enjoy ownership of land, property, and work opportunities.

During the Great Leap Forward (1958–1960) and the Cultural Revolution (1966–1976), women as warriors, leaders, model workers, and farmers were continually presented on stage. The idea of Chinese women's legendary equality with men was first interpreted and promoted by Mao Zedong's thoughts during the Cultural Revolution in China (Xiaomei Chen 4). Encouraged to fight for their rights in an effort to develop modernity in China, women became significant performers and audiences in theatre. Zedong's second wife, Jiang Qing, an ambitious stage producer and actor, strongly promoted a genre of modern Chinese drama called model operas, the synthesis of Peking Opera, musical theatre, spoken drama, and ballet. Using women as major characters, model operas such as *Red Detachment of Women* (*Hong Se Niang Zi Jun*) and *The White Haired Girl* (*Bai Mao Nv*) and the Peking opera *Sha Family Stream* (*Sha Jia Bang*) received warm receptions from the working class and peasantry as well as some scholarly critics. The iconic images of women on stage, with an overemphasis on their professions, displayed disenchantment about women's rights and gradually became stereotypes of women's physical power during the Cultural Revolution.

The third wave of Chinese feminists in the 1980s were usually scholars and elites who had finished their further education in China or abroad and worked at academic institutes, professional theatres, or departments of government. They introduced a number of feminist theories to China and articulated their own thoughts through criticism, writings, and public speeches.

Thanks to the efforts of these three waves of Chinese feminists throughout the twentieth century, women's rights in China improved enormously. However, women are still facing challenges from the remnants of patriarchal traditions and global social issues such as domestic violence, prostitution, and access to medical care.

Early Women Directors

The women pioneers in directing who appeared in the late 1500s learned the fundamentals of directing through their work as actors. The first well-known Chinese woman stage director was Ma Xianglan (1548–1604), a geisha who lived in the late Ming Dynasty (1368–1644). She was celebrated as one of the "eight beauties of South China"[2] who worked at yachts on the Qinhuai River in Nanjing, a booming city full of music and drama. Ma Xianglan had her own troupe and worked as a director, producer, stage manager, dramaturge, actor, and musician (Hua 151–52). She coached her group of young geishas to play the northern version of a traditional opera entitled *The West Chamber* (*Xi Xiang Ji*) and other plays in the theatrical forms of northern China's Zaju variety play as well as the south's Kun or Kunqu opera. Ma Xianglan was also a famous woman writer who published fictional works and verses. Because of her celebrated achievements in performing, directing, and painting, the public was very interested in her private life, including her love life. As a shining star on stage and in literary circles, she was affiliated with a group of many well-known dramatists, including Liang Chenyu and Wang Xideng, who strongly supported and inspired her theatrical activities. In addition, her highly technical artistic style, invigorating personality, and fascinating personal life influenced many dramatists who wrote about her in plays or created plays in which she could appear (Hua 151–77).

Despite Ma Xianglan's early success, women's inferior status and lack of rights limited opportunities for Chinese women directors in the premodern period. Moreover, in 1772, women were banned from performing on stage, leaving few employment opportunities for Chinese women in theatre. It was not until the turn of the twentieth century that Western feminist theories and modern dramaturgical techniques influenced Chinese theatre. By the 1930s professional modern theatres and amateur theatre companies flourished in the city of Shanghai. Those modern theatres not only offered stardom to women but also disseminated feminist and revolutionary thoughts, encouraging many women to work in theatre.

In the early twentieth century, Sun Weishi (1921–1968) was the most influential woman director who started her career as an actor. She was the daughter of a revolutionary martyr and then was adopted by the first premier of the People's Republic of China, Zhou Enlai. In 1939 Sun Weishi accompanied Zhou Enlai to Moscow, where she studied Russian. She remained in Russia to pursue her acting and directing studies and in 1945 returned to China to work at the Fine Arts Department of Huabei University in Zhangjiakou as a theatre artist (Lee, Stefanowska, and Wiles 497).[3] Her first directing success, a musical entitled *False Alarm* (*Yi Chang Xu Jing*), was produced in the same year in Yan'an. During the 1950s, as the director of the China Youth Art Theatre in Beijing, Sun Weishi's productions included Russian classics, such as Nikolai Gogol's *The Government Inspector* in 1952 and Anton Chekov's *Uncle Vanya* in 1954, and original modern Chinese dramas that combined Russian dramatic techniques with traditional Chinese opera to create a new socialist realist form, including Lao She's *Xi Wang Chang'an* in 1956 and Ding Ling's *Happy Events on Sanggan River* in 1959. She translated a textbook, *Stanislavsky Directs*, by Russian director Nikolai M. Gorchakov, who described Stanislavsky's directing process for eight plays. By 1956 Sun Weishi had published translations of Carlo Goldoni's Italian comedies, *The Mistress of the Inn* and *Servant of Two Masters*. After becoming the founder and general director of the Central Experimental Theatre in Beijing in 1956, she directed productions there including Ostrovsky's *The Storm* (*Da Lei Yu*), her own adaptation of *Uncle Tom's Cabin* in 1961, and Vsevolod Kochetov's *Brothers Yershov* (*Ye Er Shao Fu Xiong Di*) in 1964 (B. Tian 352). In directing these works, she was influenced by Stanislavsky's realistic stage techniques as well as those of Bertolt Brecht, with an attempt at breaking the fourth wall. *The Rising Sun* (*Chu Sheng De Tai Yang*), Sun Weishi's first popular success in playwriting, was also her last staged production. The play, which premiered in 1964 in Beijing, received strong, positive reception from the public. However, Sun Weishi did not live to see her last play published and died in prison in 1968 during the Cultural Revolution (Lee, Stefanowska, and Wiles 497–500). In the late 1970s *The Rising Sun* was restaged in Beijing after her husband Jin was released from jail in 1975, and it was published to commemorate Sun Weishi's influence on modern Chinese theatre and the development of spoken drama.

Chen Yong (1929–2004) was another important figure in the history of Chinese theatre. As a woman director who started her theatrical career as an actor in 1946 and then went to Russia for further education, she became a Russian theatre expert. Despite her Russian influences, she directed the largest number of Brecht's plays in China as of 2010 (Liu, *Top Ten* 96). In 1959, when she finished her directing studies in Moscow, Chen Yong directed her first production at Beijing People's Art Theatre, *Aesop* (*Yi Suo*), by Brazilian dramatist Guilherme Figueiredo. It was well received by both audiences and critics, as indicated in reviews in *People's Daily*, China's most important newspaper. Historian Nuo Niansheng called this production a "reproduction of the open-air performance in ancient Greece" (Liu, *Top Ten* 85). After the Cultural Revolution, Chen Yong directed more than fifty plays. Unfortunately, she died on stage in 2004 when directing her last masterpiece in Beijing, Yao Baoxuan's *Autumn Begins*. Chen Yong's output was predominantly influenced by Confucianism as well as Western staging techniques. Like the majority of Chinese intellectuals, she had profound humane feelings, and her works were created with compassion. In addition, she was knowledgeable about Russian and German directing approaches and scenic architecture. She expanded the Russian genre of classical dramas into Chinese modern stagings in addition to promoting Brecht's plays and theories.

Working Climate in the Twenty-First Century

In Chinese history, the term "contemporary" refers to the period from 1978 up to the present. During these times and the end of radical Maoism, the Chinese government shifted its focus from promoting political struggles among different classes toward economic development by opening the country to the rest of the world (Gladston 195). Furthermore, with the end of the cruel censorship of the Cultural Revolution, the contemporary work climate in theatre offered more opportunities for directors and artists to present their creations. According to a 2012 interview with famous stage and film director Liu Liexiong, since the 1980s, Chinese directors can decide what to show on stage, and scripts need only to be reviewed by producers instead of governors (Liu Interview).

The late 1970s were a period of revival for professional companies after ten years of repression during the Cultural Revolution (Mackerras 203). Several distinguished directors of both genders became major leaders of Beijing People's Art Company, the most important Chinese theatre company, which supported and promoted a number of women actors and stage directors. These directors studied abroad and brought back new and influential staging techniques and theories, infusing contemporary Chinese theatre with a global influence. Moreover, some small companies founded by individual artists instead of the government thrived during these times. These small companies and studios created more diversity and choices for both dramatists and audiences, as well as more viewpoints. The Chinese theatre mainly flourished in such major cities as Beijing and Shanghai as well as some provincial capitals like Guangzhou, Wuhan, Changsha, and Xi'an.

Most of China's famous directors graduated from the Central Academy of Drama in Beijing, founded in 1950, which focused on spoken drama. Xu Xiaozhong, a radical avant-garde stage director who studied Stanislavsky in the Soviet Union, served as the dean of the Department of Directing from 1984 to 2000 and mentored multiple women directors who graduated from the academy. The premiere of his 1988 experimental production of Zidu Chen, Yang Jian, and Zhu Xiaoping's *The Sangshuping Chronicles* (*Sang Shu Ping Ji Shi*) was a milestone of Chinese avant-garde theatre in symbolist manners and impacted many women stage directors in terms of their radical explorations. In China's universities and educational institutions, feminist thought became popular and spread through the mass media to the public. Several women scholars, such as Dai Jinghua and Li Yinhe, received abundant academic attention from many parts of world for their insights on Chinese feminist theatre and cinema.

In the late twentieth century, especially since the 1980s—a golden age for women in Chinese theatre—influential women playwrights of Chinese spoken drama became partners of Chinese women directors.[4] These feminist directors echoed feminist conventions of women's writing and were more radical than the playwrights because of their power to control what was on stage. A woman director named Lin Yinyu noted in her autobiography: "I have my own voice on the stage and I can speak out about what I am concerned with in my productions. That's the best condition for me. I became fascinated by the theatre since I was aware of my power" (147–48). Because of this power, some women writers and actors became stage directors. In addition, women directors often collaborated with women playwrights because they could understand their writings intimately and conceptualize the work onstage.

Although women in theatre made strides during the 1980s, dramatists had to face serious competition with the rising popularity of cinema and television, which caused theatre to lose audiences and theatrical performances (Fu 167). There were also struggles within the theatre world itself. Traditional opera suffered challenges from the spoken drama, which was more popular among the younger generation. However, since the 1990s, a radical tendency toward deconstruction affected the texts of spoken drama causing several dramatists to initiate experimental movements. Accordingly, in the world of traditional drama, not only the Peking Opera but also regional operas such as Kun Opera, Yueju Opera, Sichuan Opera, and Huangmei Opera were resurrected or revived because theatrical innovators were exploring them. With these innovations, the contemporary Chinese theatre is moving in a dynamic way to encourage women theatre artists, including avant-garde artists. These artists integrate modern and traditional forms while exploring feminism and the politics of embodiment. According to Liu Liexiong's book, *The Top Ten Stage Directors in China*, remarkable women including Chen Yong (profiled earlier), Chen Xinyi, and Cao Qijing are three of the most successful masters of stage directing, while Tian Qinxin represents a younger generation of feminist directors who integrates multiple forms of theatre and cinema (223–35).[5] Though no statistics exist on the number of women directing as compared with men, director Liu Liexiong estimates that the ratio is likely one woman to every five men. However, those women directors are successful in earning top dollars along with men in large venues. Some of them also work in smaller experimental settings (Liu Interview).

Profiles of Contemporary Directors

Chen Xinyi

Born in 1938 in the city of Xi'an, Chen Xinyi is the daughter of a military governor of the Chinese Nationalist Party and was adopted by his new wife because Chen Xinyi's mother went to Beijing to pursue acting studies. As a little girl she left home after her father went to Taiwan in 1949 because she had trouble getting along with her stepmother's relatives. She began to learn Qinqiang Opera acting in Xibei Provincial Academy in order to live independently. Although she worked diligently, she recognized that she was not good at performing opera. She then became a typist and assisted playwright Ma Jianling, learning from her while she also studied Chinese literature, Shakespeare, and Stanislavsky on her own. In 1957 she passed the selection exam and became an acting student in the Spoken Drama Company of Shanxi Province. Unfortunately, her former supervisor, teacher, and friend, Ma Jianling, died in the Cultural Revolution, and she had to study independently like other actors, for theatre companies and schools were forced to shut down during the ten years' chaos from 1966 to 1976.

In 1978 Chen Xinyi was accepted into the Central Academy of Drama, the finest academic institute of Chinese spoken drama. She started her professional directing career in her forties; the stress of her early personal life profoundly influenced her work. In 1980 her first directing credit was her own play, *The Return of Mr. Li Zhongren*, produced by the Shanxi People's Theatre Company. The production, a biographical epic play about a military commander, was influenced by her early memory of her father and his colleagues (Chen, Ma, and Mao 4–5). During those years of her early professional life, she strived to survive and negotiate with agencies and producers to provide funding for her productions. Because of her tight schedule, she did not spend much time with family and eventually divorced, raising her daughter alone. In 1980 Chen Xinyi left Xi'an for Beijing and Shanghai, since her company did not support her staging of *Othello*. However, her production of *Othello* became a huge success at Shanghai's Shakespeare Festival in 1986.

Chen Xinyi has been a productive director. From the 1980s to 2012, she directed more than one hundred productions. She is widely recognized for her achievements in integrating Chinese traditional opera and multiple modern forms. In 1982 in Xi'an, she directed *Life of a Woman* (*Nv Ren De Yi Sheng*), her own adaptation of a Japanese play. The play, which she wrote for her acting students, was a touching story about an Asian "Cinderella" who becomes a successful businesswoman. Performed more than seventy times in the first season, the play was popular, Chen Xinyi says, because it manifested a woman's toughness, and it remains inspiring for women (Chen Xinyi, "Spirit").

In 1999 Chen Xinyi received the highest national prizes in Beijing for her directing and playwriting of the Huangmei Opera, *Huizhou Women*, her original production with the assistance of Qijing Cao, another accomplished woman director. Its popularity lasted for ten years, and the company toured across the country. In 2002 Chen Xinyi again staged *Huizhou Women*, which told the story of a housewife who waited for her absent husband for several decades, only to find he did not recognize her upon his return. The production dominated Chang'an Grand Theatre in Beijing—often described as "Chinese Broadway"—for the whole season. The play had already won commercial triumph in Taiwan, Anhui, Shanghai, and Tianjing before its Beijing premiere. Critic Gong Hede at the Drama Institute of China Academy of Art considered its poetic dialogue and prosaic structure to be greatly innovative (Y. Wang 24–26). Chen Xinyi used theatrical techniques, including metaphor, symbolism, foreshadowing, meta-theatre (a play within a play), song, dance, and plot twists to stage the tragic story. Fu Jin, a well-known theater critic, remarked that the highest achievement of its performance was choreography (Y. Wang 27).

In 2010 Chen Xinyi put Cao Yu's *Wilderness* (*Yuan Ye*) on the Beijing stage to celebrate the centennial of the Chinese playwright. Influenced by expressionism, the play was about the revenge of a farmer who had lost his land and lover. It included scenes of the farmer's hallucinations as well as haunting ghosts to display the inner voice of the role. She reinterpreted this modern Chinese classic to explore humanistic concerns and philosophical meanings instead of focusing on Marxist ideas, as in some previous productions. Critic Zhu Guang at the *Xinmin Evening News* noted three reasons for the production's popularity: every character is controversial; the play is full of poetry; and the cast is well known (Zhu A-24). Chen Xinyi's life experience and perception has affected her theatrical creation. The heroes she created, especially women of courage, express her own pursuit of love and beauty on stage.

Chen Xinyi is not afraid to push her actors in order to achieve an optimal performance. Portraying a slave's mother, actor Zhou Xiaoquain recalled an effective but "cruel" technique from one rehearsal: "She said I didn't act like a slave's mother and asked me to take off my earrings. Still, she was not satisfied. Then she told me to shoulder a three-step prop and walk the rehearsal room for many rounds. Finally, she even told an actor to whip me. I dogged and burst out growling 'I quit.' But she shouted back 'read your lines now.'" The result was "mesmerizing," and Zhou performed with renewed energy ("Drama Queen").

Cao Qijing

Born in 1941 in Beijing, Cao Qijing became a professor of theatre at the Central Academy of Drama and has worked as a stage director since 1964, directing more than sixty plays from 1964 to 2012. As a visiting scholar at Yale University and Columbia University in the United States, she is familiar with Western theatre. Her stage productions include spoken drama and opera in the Western tradition, as well as Kunqu Opera, Beijing Opera, and other local dialect operas. Her productions are deeply influenced by cultural memory and include specific traditional Chinese features. Cao Qijing gives rich or layered portrayals of women in her plays, which range from Puccini's opera *Turandot* to the realist spoken drama *Mother* by Zhao Ruitai. For instance, *The Mortgaged Wife*, which she directed in 2002 at the Ningbo Art Theatre in Ningbo, was adapted by the illustrious playwright Luo Huaizhen from Rou Shi's novel, *Slave Mother*. It told the story of a destitute woman who was mortgaged by her husband to have a baby for a wealthy gentleman and his wife. When the woman returned home, she found her elder son had died, and her husband was sick and addicted to alcohol and gambling. Cao Qijing states:

> This play is not grand, but a very delicate, fascinating presentation. It penetrates a genuine emotion and earnest intenseness to the audience, rather than its visible impact. . . . The form, Yong drama, flourished in China of the sixties in the twentieth century, which was mainly popular in rural areas but gradually vanished due to its obsolete way of performance. Therefore, we do not only maintain major characteristics of the genre but also add gorgeous dances to the play to make it more graphic. In addition, the famous text enhances its literary taste. (Zhou 14)

To suit the desires of audiences in Ningbo and Shanghai, the director intentionally compressed lyrics that were usually significantly longer in traditional Yong drama and absorbed the naturalistic performing skills of television drama. Moreover, Cao Qijing's extensive use of body language sped up the rhythm of the folk opera. *The Mortgaged Wife* received a warm reception at the Shanghai International Art Festival in 2002 and sold out, attracting the most media attention in the theatre festival. Experts applauded the production as "a small drama" with a "great transformation" because it was converted from a small township theatre to a large urban theatre (Zhou 14). In addition to its reception in mainland China, the play also earned encores in Hong Kong, Taiwan, and other areas.

Cao Qijing continues to inject renewed vitality to the ancient Chinese traditional operas, dramas, and musicals by amalgamating various forms and enriching their performing techniques.

Tian Qinxin

Tian Qinxin is a pivotal avant-garde director. Born in 1968 in Beijing, she became the youngest and the only woman director in Beijing's National Theatre of China in 1997. Tian Qinxin visited England and Japan to study stage directing when she attended the Central Academy of Drama from 1991 to 1995. Before becoming a director in 1997, she was a Peking Opera performer specializing in martial arts roles. During her acting career, she audited a course of the famous feminist Dai Jinhua at the Beijing Film Academy. At the academy, she was acquainted with the theatre producer Li Dong, who commented that Qinxin studied very hard and that her class notes were even better than those of the official students there (K. Wang).

In 1997 Tian Qinxin directed professionally for the first time in Beijing's National Theatre of China, while also serving as dramaturge for her play *Broken Wrist* (*Duan Wan*), written to commemorate her lost first love. She utilized smooth body movements of modern dancers, portraying a queen who had to face the ministers' rebellion after the emperor's death. The queen cut off her hand at the wrist and put it into the buried coffin, then killed her enemies to calm down the riots. Tian Qinxin exploited cross-gender casting by using a man to play the queen; she realized that the queen had to take on a male role after her husband's death, highlighting the inherent gender politics. Although the play had grand historical themes, Tian Qinxin was more inclined to represent the characters' inner voices and mental conflicts. Due to a lack of promotion the production was not popular, yet it affected audiences with its unique performance style, attracting the attention of academic critics. The critic Ma Rongrong remarked in *Life Week* magazine, "Such plays as *Broken Wrist* included themes of pursuit of love, morality and justice" (Ma Rongong).

In Beijing's National Theatre of China in 1999, Tian Qinxin made a name for herself by directing the well-known masterpiece, *The Field of Life and Death*, her adaptation of Chinese feminist novelist Hsiao Hung's work. This symbolist work was inspired by her adviser Xu Xiaozhong's experimental theatre explorations, and the play portrayed a group of women suffering during the war with Japan in the 1930s. It began with a symbolic scene of a woman's childbirth, while the men ignored the woman's groaning. Tian Qinxin states on the official website of the National Theatre of China, "We are tenacious, because we suffered. . . . Day after day, like the play, we had come across the apathy, ignorance, joy, longing and a long way of struggle" (National). The play was considered an extraordinary success. Critic Man Yan at Beijing Evening News noticed that the director made adjustments and trade-offs of the original text, and used techniques of film, splicing modern painting on stage, which had the capacity to create a forceful effect (Tian Qinxin, *I Put on a Show* 226–27).

Tian Qinxin usually works on Chinese traditional subjects or themes in theatre. Moreover, she also deals with contemporary social issues in her productions by combining Western tradition and Asian aesthetics. She explains, "The Modern Chinese spoken drama was a successor to the Western theatre world and thus had to curry favor with foreigners in the past. However, dramatists need to choose and enrich themes from the inside of China's five thousand years' vast civilization" (Tian Qinxin Interview). In addition, she has emphasized physical expression and poetic language through her direction. Her productions usually have complex structures of time and space, and impress audiences with strong visuals and sound. For instance, her 2012 Beijing production of *Red Roses and White Roses*—her adaptation of Zhang Ailing's novel—contains a rock concert, while the 2012 Beijing production of *24 Hours Store*—her adaptation of Yang Qin's movie—has a pop music chorus. She often presents traditional Chinese dramas or stories, tales, and legends in Western forms, such as spoken drama. However, she is also familiar with traditional operas and popular comedies and has had commercial triumphs by adapting movies and operas into spoken drama.

In addition to her work as a director, Tian Qinxin is also a playwright. In 2001 she directed her own play, *Hurricane* (*Kuang Biao*), produced by the China Central Experimental Theatre in Beijing. In this biographical play about the distinguished playwright Tian Han, Tian Qixin combined refinement and passion, a trademark of her personal style. She encouraged young actors to present their own artistic feelings and cultural memories while performing techniques of diverse schools. The meta-theatre in *Hurricane* revealed aspects related to cultural memory and imagination of modern China in the late nineteenth and early twentieth centuries. Drawing from a variety of source material, meta-theatre has become a significant characteristic of many of her works.

With her distinctive interpretations, the general style of Tian Qinxin's works are tragic and show compassion. When talking about her latest comedy, in 2011, she wrote in her Weibo—the Chinese local Twitter—"This comedy is not only good for a laugh. Indeed, there is sadness in this comedy" (Tian Qinxin's Weibo). To remedy the scarcity of original plays, she strongly promoted a playwriting project to send new playwrights to study in England and also lectured in public to encourage young writers to provide more high-quality original texts. Tian Qinxin is an avant-garde feminist and has become one of the most promising directors in China.

Chinese women directors of the twentieth century were heavily influenced by the theatrical theories of Stanislavsky and Brecht, but in the twenty-first century women directors have expanded their sources of influence, often mingling traditional Chinese forms with experimental ideas. They have promoted feminism and modernism, and they have sought to inspire their audience to work on national issues, including education and quality of life. Stage directing has become an effective way for Chinese women to advertise their political views and pursue their art.

Notes

1. Feminist author Qiu Jin, who usually appeared in theatre auditoriums disguised as a man, abandoned her arranged marriage and studied in Japan. She returned to China as a feminist activist in 1905 and helped to lead the political movement for the women's literary and social revolution as well as for the democracy and the well-being of the nation.

2. See *Gender and the City Before Modernity*, online edition, edited by Lin Foxhall and Gabriele Neher (Chichester, U.K. / Malden, Mass.: Wiley, 2012). "Eight Beauties" was first seen in Yu Huai's book *Slate Anthology*, including Gu Hengbo, Dong Xiaowan, Bian Yujing, Li Xiangjun, Kou Baimen, and Ma Xianglan (Ma Shouzhen). The descendants added Liu Rushi and Chen Yuanyuan to the list called "eight (brilliant) beauties."

3. The university was renamed as the Renmin University when the People's Republic of China was founded in 1949.

4. Important feminist playwrights in both mainland China and Taiwan include Bai Fengxi, Tian Fen, Shen Hongguang, Bei Ying, Xu Yan, and He Ji Ping.

5. Additional well-known women directors include Lei Guohua, Lin Yinyu, Xu Jinglei, Lou Naiming, and He Ji Ping.

Sources

Chen, Xiaomei. *Acting the Right Part: Political Theater and Popular Drama in Contemporary China*. Honolulu: University of Hawaii Press, 2002.

Chen, Xinyi. "The Spirit of the Theatre." *Speeches at the Shanghai Library* ["Xi ju de shi dai jing shen yu ren wen guan huai." *Shang tu jiang zuo zhuan kan*]. Presentation. December 1, 2004.

Chen, Xinyi, Bomin Ma, and Shian Mao. *Live Archives: Xinyi's Director's Notes*. Shanghai: Social Science Press [*Sheng ming dang an: Chen Xinyi dao yan shou ji*. Shanghai: She hui ke xue yuan chu ban she], 2006.

"The Drama Queen." *china.org.cn,* n.d. Available at http://www.china.org.cn (accessed September 1, 2012).

Fortier, Mark. *Theory/Theatre: An Introduction*. London: Routledge, Taylor & Francis, 2004.

Fu, Jin. *Chinese Theater: Happiness and Sorrows on the Stage*. Beijing: China Intercontinental, 2010.

Gladston, Paul. "Problematizing the New Cultural Separatism: Critical Reflections on Contemporaneity and the Theorizing of Contemporary Chinese Art." *Modern China Studies* 1.1 (2012): 195–270.

He, Chengzhou. "Women and the Search for Modernity: Rethinking Modern Chinese Drama." *Modern Language Quarterly* 69.1 (2008): 45–60.

Hua, Wei. "Ma Xianglan and the Late Ming Theatre World" ["Ma Xianglan yu ming dai hou qi de qu tan"]. *Chinese Opera Series* 37 (June 2008): 151–77.

LaFleur, Robert André. *China: A Global Studies Handbook*. Santa Barbara, Calif.: ABC-CLIO, 2003.

Lee, Lily Xiao Hong, A. D. Stefanowska, and Sue Wiles. *Biographical Dictionary of Chinese Women: The Twentieth Century, 1912–2000*. Vol. 14. Armonk, N.Y.: Sharpe, 2003.

Lin, Yinyu. *Director's Notes*. Beijing: China Drama Press [*Dao Yan Dang An*. Beijing: Zhong guo xi ju chu ban she], 1999.

Liu, Liexiong. *The Top Ten Stage Directors in China*. Beijing: Renmin University of China Press [*Zhongguo shi da xi ju dao yan da shi*. Beijing: Zhongguo ren min da xue chu ban she], 2005.

———. Interview. June 28, 2012.

Ma, Rongrong. "Tian Qinxin: Love and Justice in Theater" [Tian Qinxin: xi ju chang li de qing yu yi]. *Life Weekly* [Beijing], January 11, 2010.

Mackerras, Colin. *Chinese Drama: A Historical Survey*. 1st ed. Beijing, China: New World, 1990.

National Theatre Company of China. *National Theatre Company of China* [*Guo Jia Hua Ju Yuan*]. Available at http://www.ntcc.com.cn (accessed August 1, 2012).

Tatlow, Didi Kirsten. "For China's Women: More Opportunities, More Pitfalls." *New York Times*, November 25, 2010.

Tian, Benxiang, *The History of Chinese Spoken Drama* [*Zhongguo hua ju bai nian tu shi*]. Taiyuan Shi: Shanxi jiao yu chu ban she, 2006.

Tian, Qinxin. *I Put on a Show Because I Am Sad*. Beijing: Writers Publishing House [*Wo zuo xi, yin wei wo bei shang*. Beijing: Zuo jia zhu ban she], 2003.

———. Interview with Chen Shudi. *culture.ifeng.com*, December 21, 2011. Available at http://culture.ifeng.com (accessed September 6, 2012).

———. Tian Qinxin's Weibo (accessed June 22, 2011).

Wang, Kai. "Tian Qinxin in the Rehearsal Space" ["Tian Qinxin zai xi ju chang"]. *Life Weekly* [Beijing], September 5, 2011.

Wang, Yunming. "Huizhou Woman's Innovative Thinking" ["Huizhou nv ren chuang xin de si suo"]. *Chinese Drama* 10 (1999): 24–33.

Yan, Haiping. *Chinese Women Writers and the Feminist Imagination, 1905–1948*. London, New York: Routledge, 2006.

Zhou, Yuan. "Truly Concerned about Women's Fate: Director Cao Qijing's Interpretation of *The Mortgaged Wife*" ["Zhen qie guan zhu nv xing ming yun"]. *Xi'an Evening News*, October 14, 2003: 14.

Zhu, Guang. "Chen Talk about *Wilderness*" ["Chen Xinyi tan yuan ye"]. *Xinmin Evening News* [Shanghai]. Wenxin Press, May 10, 2012.

Cuba

Ileana Azor

translated by Sandra Venegas and Emilia Ismael[1]

Women Cuban theatre directors presented their first scenic works at the turn of the 1940s. Without a doubt, the long road traveled from then has been more than successful. These women, most of them actors in their origins, have combined personal poetics with the most artistic influences from Europe, the United States, and Latin America.

Women's Rights: Historical Context

Since the mid-nineteenth century, Cuban women have been part of the feminist movement. According to historian Julio César González Pagés, there are four periods of the women's movement, from the beginning of their struggles in 1880 until they won the right to vote in 1934. In the first period from 1880 to 1912, the focus was on social feminism. It was during this period, in 1902, that the Republic of Cuba was officially established.[2] The first suffragists appeared in the second period, which spanned from 1912 until 1917, and their main purpose was to obtain the right to vote. The third period, which lasted from 1918 until 1933, saw the acceleration of liberal feminism and the spreading of feminist institutions, such as different kinds of feminist parties. In addition, suffrage became a more comprehensive issue with regard to the rights inherent to any woman, no matter her social origin, educational level, or race. The fourth period started in 1934 and ended in the same decade, when the government provisionally approved the law that gave women the right to vote as a result of the Revolution of 1933, in which dictator Gerardo Machado y Morales was overthrown. The feminist movement joined the left political wing, which was in charge of the government that decade and responsible for the many social changes of the period. By 1940 the new constitution guaranteed the right to vote to both men and women, increasing the number of voters but at the same time generating a lack of unity among the various women's movements.[3]

A more detailed examination of these periods reveals the names and organizations at work. Two women were the most visible exponents of women's movements in the early years. Beginning in 1841 Gertrudis Gómez de Avellaneada y Arteaga (1814–1873), a poet and novelist often compared to American author Harriet Beecher Stowe, focused her narrative work on abolitionist themes as well as interracial and interclass love. Ana Betancourt Agramonte (1832–1901), wife of the revolutionary leader Ignacio Agramonte, was active in the fight for Cuba's independence. She always included the importance of considering women's rights as part of the liberating movement in her fight.

During the first two decades of the twentieth century, feminists founded magazines, newspapers, and political parties.[4] In 1917 a law allowing women to have parental custody regardless of their marital status was approved, followed by the Divorce Law, which allowed women to divorce their husbands. Also, in 1917 the Female Club (Club Femenino) was founded. The outstanding women intellectuals who composed this institution had been part of the struggle for the right to vote and other social accomplishments, such as night schools for working class women. In the female prison in Guanabacoa, they centered their efforts on rehabilitating the inmates through education. The incarcerated women could take classes to improve their literacy, and they could learn clothing design, thus creating better living conditions for themselves through their work. In 1923 the National Federation of Female Associations of Cuba (Federación Nacional de Asociaciones Femeninas de Cuba) convened the First National Women's Conference (Primer Congreso Nacional de Mujeres) in Havana. The second conference took place in 1925 and summoned outstanding researchers and essayists as well as social leader Enrique Loynaz del Castillo. That same year, the National Organization of Female Associations (Organización Nacional de Asociaciones Femeninas), consisting of eleven different affiliates, conducted campaigns to increase women's access to education.

Female associations like the Civic Front of Martiana Women (Frente Cívico de Mujeres Martianas) and United Opposing Women (Mujeres Oposicionistas Unidas) played an important role in the struggle to overthrow the tyranny of dictator Fulgencio Batista in the 1950s, resulting in the triumph of the Revolution of 1959. The new government created a state policy that presumed equality of gender. However, prejudices and cultural stereotypes were deeply rooted in the society, causing rejection of feminist ideals—wrongly associated with capitalism—by some revolutionary leaders and other social figures.

Since the 1970s important women who have worked primarily as writers and university professors, such as Camila Henríquez Ureña, Ofelia Domínguez Navarro, Mirta Aguirre,

Vicentina Antuña, and Luisa Campuzano, debated openly through their publications and actions, which favored women's rights. During the 1990s it was possible to see a more open approach to the ideas of feminism, which was accomplished through the spread of gender and women's studies, research, conferences, and books. Although perpetual topics such as abortion rights and salary equality remained basic principles of discussion, feminists had to address their collective aspirations as well (López Cabrales 23).

Early Women Directors

The first women directors began working on the stages of Havana in the 1940s. The American actor, director, and professor, Lorna de Sosa (1913–2009), studied theatre, music, and literature at the University of Cincinnati, where she founded the Cincinnati Theater Guild. During the fifteen years she stayed in Cuba from 1940 to 1955, she taught at the Academy of Dramatic Arts of the Free School of Havana (Academia de Artes Dramáticas de la Escuela Libre de la Habana), also known as ADADEL. Her directing credits at ADADEL in the 1940s favored British and American plays such as *Becky Sharp*, based on William M. Thackeray's novel *Vanity Fair*; Noel Coward's *Hay Fever;* Eugene O'Neill's *Desire under the Elms;* and Somerset Maugham's *Theater.*

Spanish-born Isabel Fernández de Amado Blanco (1910–1999) and Cuban-born Celia (Cuqui) Ponce de León (1916–2009) became a creative pair in the Cuban theatre in the mid-twentieth century. They wrote two comedies together and directed several productions for the Theatre Council (Patronato del Teatro) in Havana. In 1947 both women received the Talía Award from the Theatre Council as recognition for their brilliant work directing Rafael Suárez Solís's *The Mad Man of the Year* (*El loco del año*).

Fernández, who graduated in 1932 from the University of Madrid (Universidad de Madrid) with a degree in philosophy and literature, came to Havana with her husband in 1936 and worked as a journalist and essayist (Cuadriello 69). Ponce de León graduated with a degree in art history in 1979 from the University of Havana (Universidad de la Habana). Besides being one of the founders of CMQ—the only Cuban television broadcasting station active in the 1950s—Ponce de León had a long professional career as a theatre director. She founded a theatre company called Rita Montaner in Havana in 1962 and directed there during the 1960s.

The Hungarian artist Clara Ronay started her directing career in 1949, working with experimental pieces at the Free Stage Group (Grupo Escénico Libre) in Havana. The group's puppetry troupe collaborated with Ronay who, in collaboration with the Cuban director and actor Vicente Revuelta Planas, wrote and directed *The Magic Chalk* (*La tiza mágica*) the same year. Then, in 1950, the two of them directed another project—but this time for television: *Creole Puppets* (*Títeres Criollos*), a show that was created by Revuelta and Ronay for adults. For the rest of the decade, Ronay continued producing and directing for television. In 1960 she also started working with Revuelta's Studio Theatre (Teatro Estudio) in Havana. Her first production was *Death of a Salesman* by

Arthur Miller in 1960, followed the next year by *Gloria*, written by Cuban playwright Ingrid González. Years later Ronay moved to Spain to continue working on television productions.

Another important Spanish-born woman who worked as a director and actor in Cuban theatre was Adela Escartin (1913–2010). She studied in 1947 at the Royal Conservatory of Music and Declamation (Real Conservatorio de Música y Declamación) in Madrid. A year later she moved to New York, where she studied direction with Erwin Piscator and Lee Strasberg. Beginning in the 1950s, she helped mentor several generations of performers in Cuba. In 1958 Escartin directed her own theatre venue, Prado 260 Theatre (Sala Teatro Prado 260), in Havana. One of the works she directed there, Ramón Ferreira's *A Color for This Fear* (*Un color para este miedo*), was a production she took to Mexico in 1958 for the Pan-American Theatre Festival. Between 1963 and 1970 Escartin worked as a professor of acting and directing at the School of Theatre Instructors (Escuela de Instructores de Arte) in Havana, where she directed Ibsen's *A Doll's House*. Other credits during that period include Arnold Wesker's *The Kitchen*; Verdi's opera, *La Traviata*; Franz Lehar's operetta, *The Happy Widow*; Sophocles's *Antigone*; Leroy Jones's *Dutchman*; and Georg Büchner's *Woyzeck*. Escartin moved to Spain, where she continued to teach after two decades of work in Cuba.

In the area of a more commercial theatre, it is possible to find the work of talented women actor-directors such as Enriqueta Sierra, Pilar Bermúdez, Mary Munné, and Socorro González (González Freire 156).

Working Climate in the Twenty-First Century

Women directors have received public recognition very slowly, although their recognition started increasing during the 1980s. Most of these artists did not receive formal education to become directors, except for some training classes in various theatre schools. The Superior Institute of Art created a specialized theatre training program in 1990; however, this did not mean that all its graduates would dedicate their lives to the directing profession (Azor, "Cuban Actor" 223). One can certainly find performers who decided to direct their own groups and productions; they also teach, and their work in academia has furthered the education of new artists, who in many cases became new members of their own companies. Although women directors have received more public recognition, illustrated through awards and invitations to be part of international festivals, the proportion between men and women is far from well balanced.

Cuba's Secretary of Culture has organized the theatre system through the National Committee for the Stage Arts (Consejo Nacional de las Artes Escénicas) since the late 1980s. Although its efforts do not supply enough funding and theatre spaces for all the companies, the committee still provides possibilities for many of them to develop their creativity, and the government funding does not have gender restrictions. Many women directors lead their own companies.

Pioneers Raquel Revuelta and Berta Martínez

Although Raquel Revuelta and Berta Martínez did not have formal university educations, they were part of several workshops and professional productions in Cuba and abroad, and both received honorary degrees (Doctor Honoris Causa) from the Superior Institute of Art (Instituto Superior de Arte) in Havana in 1985 and 2000 respectively. Revuelta and Martínez also became important pioneers as women directors in Cuba.

Revuelta (1925–2004) started her career as a performer in Cuban radio in 1936, where she stayed for eleven years. In 1941 she joined a theatre group called the Eugenia Zuffoli Company in Havana as an actor, and in 1956 she starred in Maxwell Anderson's *Joan of Lorraine* in Hubert de Blanck Theatre (Sala Hubert de Blanck) in Havana (Leal 128). She received numerous awards for this production, and three years later she starred in a movie for the first time. Revuelta became one of the most important promoters of contemporary theatre in Cuba.

Revuelta was the artistic director of the highly regarded Studio Theatre—founded by her brother, Vicente Revuelta in Havana—for more than thirty-six years. The first production she directed with the studio in 1980 was Federico García Lorca's *Ms. Rosita, the Single One* (*Doña Rosita la soltera*). Other productions she directed with this company in the following two decades included Arthur Schnitzler's *La Ronde*; *Baroque Concert* (*Concierto Barroco*), inspired by Alejo Carpentier's novel of the same name; and Molière's *Tartuffe*. She received several awards during her long artistic and political trajectory, among them the National Theatre Award (Premio Nacional de Teatro) in 1999 and the Orders Félix Varela and Juan Marinello.

Revuelta's acting training comes from teachers such as Enriqueta Sierra and her brother Vicente Revuelta, who had very different styles. Sierra closely followed the theatre tradition "del buen decir" (good speaking),[5] but her brother was known for his peculiar eclectic style inspired by Stanislavski, Brecht, Grotowski, and Brook. As a result of this background, Raquel Revuelta focused on acting as the key to success for her directing work. She was not considered an experimental director but rather an actor who decided to work as a director. However, she has been recognized as the builder of a trajectory that broke the boundaries of the Spanish traditions of the nineteenth century and for being a promoter of a directing style that focused on the coherence of internal work in the construction of a character.

Like Revuelta, Berta Martínez—known for a career spanning more than five decades—started as an actor and then moved to directing, at first in the style of Vicente Revuelta, her teacher. Martinez's choices for productions were always dictated by the high quality of the texts whose complexity created big challenges for the construction of characters (Azor, "Return" 15).

The complexity of the design in her repertoire—which consisted of groups of performers substituting for the actual scenic pieces and sound elements—came together in an integrating aesthetic purpose, which dialogues with Spanish culture as the origin of the Cuban theatre. Famed actor-director Nuria Espert and several international critiques praised Martinez's approach to Lorca and Tirso de Molina and extolled her as a director who revises classics to interrogate the present (Azor, "Return" 15).

Martínez likes to explore different theatrical styles: from Alejo Carpentier's *The Witch's Apprentice* (*La aprendiz de bruja*), a serious drama about the Conquest of

America, to merrier, musical fare, such as the Spanish zarzuelas *The Festival of the Dove* (*La verbena de la paloma*) and *Uncle Francisco and the Leandras* (*El Tío Francisco and las Leandras*). She almost always twists the nicer side of a play with the purpose of achieving a deeper approach to the themes, focusing on those that have a bigger impact on the audience (Azor, "Return" 16). Her work is a tribute to the "cómicos de la legua" (comics of the league),[6] the century-old Cuban lyric tradition, as well as contemporary cultural Spanish influences. The legacy left by Martínez certainly explains her various prizes, such as the National Theatre Award, as well as her tremendous success with European and Latin American audiences.

Profiles of Contemporary Directors

Flora Lauten

Like Revuelta and Martínez before her, Flora Lauten did not obtain a formal university education but received an honorary degree (Doctor Honoris Causa) in theatre from the Superior Institute of Art in 2001 based on her body of work. By the end of the 1950s, Lauten became a disciple of Vicente Revuelta in the academy of his Studio Theatre. After several experimental works, including a Grotowski-based project using a ritual text by José Martí, she decided to submerge herself in a theatrical and sociological research project in El Escambray, a mountainous zone of heavy class conflict located in the center of Cuba. With a group of actors, sociologists, university professors, and psychologists, she started to explore the political, economic, and social conflicts of the area. This research and artistic project initiated the most important community-based theatre in Cuba, the Escambray Theatre (Teatro Escambray), founded in 1968 in El Escambray. The problems of the peasantry were the main focus for this theatre, which included plays, performances, and community debates as collective theatre creations. As such, this theatrical work developed in parallel to theatrical activity in Colombia, Brazil, and other Latin American countries. Artists presented their theatre performances, improvisations, and their collective writings on important social issues through the Escambray Theatre.

Because she needed to find better schools for her young children, Lauten decided to leave El Escambray in 1973, but she established herself in a nearby town, Mataguá. Here, with the municipal government's help, she founded the La Yaya Theatre (Teatro La Yaya). The main goal of this new theatre group was to depict the people's most urgent conflicts. Author Rine Leal explains that Lauten used "*acts or games (actos o juegos)*, short pieces—that she wrote based on her sociologic research—in which the problems were presented in a direct way" in order to stimulate change through confrontation (Leal 163). These short pieces included themes such as the incorporation of women into the workforce, thus breaking centuries of tradition steeped in different social and economic dynamics.

While a professor at the Superior Institute of Art, Lauten founded the Buendía Theatre Company (Teatro Buendía) in 1985, the company where she still works. It started in the basement of an Orthodox church in Havana, with actors who were the first graduates under Lauten's professorship. From the beginning she started applying the methodology for collective creation that she had learned while working with Colombian and Danish teachers in the 1970s and 1980s. Improvisation, dance, actor's dramaturgy, gesture, live music, and masks became her main tools to create productions that eventually toured five continents.

Examples of some of Lauten's directorial credits with Buendía Theatre include *The Pearls in Your Mouth* (*Las perlas de tu boca*) in 1989, *Candida Erendira and Her Heartless Grandmother* (*La Cándida Eréndira y su abuela desalmada*) in 1992, *Another Tempest* (*Otra tempestad*) in 1997, *Life in Pink* (*La vida en rosa*) in 1999, *Bacchanals* (*Bacantes*) in 2001, *Charenton* in 2005, *Woyzeck's Ballad* (*La balada de Woyzeck*) in 2008, and *The Old Lady's Visit* (*La visita de la vieja dama*) in 2009. These theatre pieces were all formed by a collaborative theatre company, which was guided by Lauten and Raquel Carrió, a dramaturge who has worked with Lauten since the beginning of the Buendía Theatre Company. Each one of the productions starts with an iconic classic play which is retold through the creation of a parallel text that explores themes such as power, seduction, spiritual and material scarcity, dysfunctional families, risks, memory, exile, migration, or myths.

One example of Lauten's working process is *Another Tempest*, in which the wish to follow the Shakespearean text is contrasted by aspects that are key to Cuban culture. In an article for *American Theatre,* Caridad Svich explains,

> In response to Shakespeare's *The Tempest,* Lauten and her longtime dramaturge Raquel Carrió envisioned not merely a post-colonial critique of Shakespeare's text, but also a collision of Prospero, Caliban and the other inhabitants of Shakespeare's mythic "islands" with the Orishas of Yoruban culture. In this syncretic collision, which incorporated texts from Carpentier, Paz, Marti and others, audiences were made witness to questions of cultural and societal displacement—questions that arose from the labyrinth of Shakespeare's text that contest easily read signs of behavior, class, sexuality, gender and race. (Svich)

In 1998 the Teatro Buendía company received the Ollantay Award from the Latin American Center of Theatre, Creation and Research (Centro Latinoamericano de Creación e Investigación Teatral [CELCIT]), as recognition for the quality of its productions and its contribution to Latin American and Caribbean theatre. In 2005 Lauten received the National Theatre Award, and she continues accumulating professional success beyond the borders of her country.

Miriam Lezcano

Miriam Lezcano graduated as an actor from National School of Art (Escuela Nacional de Arte) in Havana in 1968, though her career has always focused on directing. Lezcano also earned a master of arts in directing in the Soviet Union at the Moscow Art Theatre in 1979 as well as a bachelor of arts in history at the University of Havana in 1981. When she returned from Moscow in the early 1980s she directed several Russian and Cuban plays in a company called Bertolt Brecht. In 1987 she and her husband, the prominent playwright Alberto Pedro Torriente, founded My Theatre (Teatro Mío) in Havana, giving the Cuban theatre the most polemic plays of the next two decades. *Weekend at Bahia* (*Weekend en Bahía*) in 1987, *Animal Fat* (*Manteca*) in 1993, *Havana Delirium* (*Delirio Habanero*) in 1994, *Our Sea* (*Mar nuestro*) in 1997, and *Waiting for Odiseo* (*Esperando a Odiseo*) in 2001, all written by Pedro Torriente, are some of the productions that shook audiences in Cuba and overseas because of their treatment of the most conflictive themes on the island. For example, in *Weekend at Bahia*, two former lovers are reunited after one of them is exiled, and in *Havana Delirium*, an imaginary, impossible meeting takes place between the two Cuban musical icons, one of whom was exiled and one of whom passed away shortly thereafter. Also, in *Animal Fat*, a family debates Cuba's principal economic and ideological problems. Audiences follow My Theatre productions because they can participate in a social forum about urgent issues.

Lezcano and her company have received awards such as Atlantis of Cadiz (Atlántida de Cádiz) from Spain; The Golden Mask (La Máscara de Oro) from Rostock, Germany; Próspero Morales from Colombia; and several others from the Cuban critics who recognize her as an undeniable pioneer of a symbolic and critical political direction during the last few decades.

Inspired in the most polemic and typical style of the early years of Soviet culture, such as Mijail Bulgakov's plays and novels from the 1930s, Lezcano emphasizes a critical vision of political and social authoritarianism but not with a direct language. Instead, her stage creations seduce audiences with mysterious images coming from dreams, combined with a hilarious tone. Her own aesthetic identity is a mixture between magical realism and satire.

Fátima Patterson

Fátima Patterson does not have a formal university education and works from the eastern part of the island. She founded her group Macubá Studio Theatre (Estudio Teatral Macubá) in 1992 in Santiago de Cuba. In her company, in which she works as an actor, director, and playwright, she emphasizes themes that make reference to the Caribbean woman through dance, music, and oral narration.

Ringing for Mafifa (Repique por Mafifa) was a hit and won three awards in 1992. Co-written by Patterson and Marcial Lorenzo Escudero, the play is a monologue performed by Patterson herself. It is based on the life of musician Gladys Linares Acuña—known as Mafifa—who had twenty-five years' experience performing in the Conga de los Hoyos, a musical carnival group—*comparsa*—in Santiago de Cuba. Although she had been described by society as being a lesbian and sometimes a prostitute, Mafifa received honors when she died in 1984. The play begins with Mafifa's death; without fully realizing that she has died, she goes over her own life in a sort of assessment. Critic Adonis Sánchez Cervera describes that Mafifa "makes associations with life from death itself, which is not assumed or she doesn't realize it yet, until the end of the play, reaching a high level of lyricism. Two other planes are also present: the living and the dead, and both converge in the music, just as palpable as it is in the soliloquies that her character holds with the musicians, who can't see her" (Sánchez Cervera). At the end, a battle breaks out between Mafifa and a percussionist representing Iku, the Death, but finally they leave the scene with the rhythm of the conga.

In 2000 Patterson's production of *The Small Square* (*La plazuela*)—which was her own adaptation of Carlo Goldoni's play by the same title—demonstrated a strong influence from the Relations Theatre (Teatro Relaciones) and the Carnival of Santiago. Both of these popular traditions from the city of Santiago de Cuba have a powerful theatricality. Relations Theatre, for instance, retells Afro-Cuban mythological narrations, while the Carnival is the most popular celebration of the city. Physical and verbal performances at the Carnival include musicians, singers, and dancers, and these aspects are all incorporated in *The Small Square*.

Patterson is not only an actor, she is also a dancer and a singer. The style of this director incorporates the aesthetics of contemporary theatre and ritual aspects of music and dance from Cuban culture. Some ritual traditions such as the Yoruban ceremonies of Santeria and oral tradition from Palo Monte[7] survive through the Macuba Studio theatre productions directed by Patterson. One article noted, "Memory, dream interpretation, and Antillean poetry are also some of the main components of her aesthetics as director" (López Jimenez). Her work has been widely presented throughout the American continent and Europe.

Nelda Castillo

Nelda Castillo graduated as an actor from the Superior Institute of Art in 1984 and directed her first productions, which she also wrote, with material adapted from authors such as Jorge Luis Borges and Laura Devetach. Her works with the Buendía Theatre Company include *Rag Doll in the Sand* (*Monigote en la arena*) in 1987, *An Elephant Takes Up Too Much Room* (*Un elefante ocupa mucho espacio*) in 1989, and *The Circular Ruins* (*Las ruinas circulares*) in 1991.

In 1996 she founded The Enchanted Deer (El Ciervo Encantado) with a group of her former students who had just graduated from the Superior Institute of Art. They were preoccupied with clarifying the forces that articulated Cuban history through the years, so they embraced the idea of investigation that would give them back the image—the genesis and evolution—of the island through personal discoveries. This group has tried to unveil the dark zones in the Cuban soul in the company's own language and theatrical point of view, which is characterized by a strong interest in the training of the actors. This allows the metamorphoses of the actor in a "channel body" through which ancestors and unknown beings, which are part of the genetic map of the performer, are able to express the collective unconscious of the entire nation.

The productions of The Enchanted Deer are known for their exploration of the visual and sonic elements, as well as for their use of literary, historical, plastic, musical, and dance sources toward an original, artistic language that differs from traditional expression. For example, *The Enchanted Deer*—the production that gave its name to the group—tries to uncover a mirror in which both the actors and the audience can see the nation. Three characters—an indigenous, a native (*criollo*), and an Afro-Cuban—are looking for a deer, a spirit in which they believe they could find their patriotic desires realized. The music drags them into that search while they recite verses from Virgilio Piñera, a prominent Cuban writer from the twentieth century, and fragments from a battle diary from the war of independence against Spain in the nineteenth century.

The company's research around important Cuban authors such as Esteban Borrero, Virgilio Piñera, Fernando Ortiz, Severo Sarduy, Reinaldo Arenas, and Guillermo Cabrera Infante is very relevant, for the last three were exiled and practically unknown to Cubans. Thus, the experimental calling of The Enchanted Deer is focused on exploring the margins of the Cuban cultural identity and recovering the richness and complexity that distinguishes it. Among its most significant productions, which were directed by Castillo, are *Visions of Cubanosofía* (*Visiones de cubanosofía*) in 2005 and *Galiano Varieties* (*Variedades Galiano*) in 2010.

In *Visions of Cubanosofía* Castillo includes subjects such as faith, power, slavery, prostitution, frustration, prepotency, dementia, hallucinations, shame, creation, resistance, solitude, abandonment, and absence. All of these are visions of the Cuban being, who observes from his or her greatness the sparks of a historical, psychic, and social development of the island, always under construction, always under resistance. The Cuban critic and researcher Roberto Gacio expressed, "The action develops in complicity with the audience, as if it was a hidden secret that turns into an open one. We [the audience] have to decipher codes and vital keys, since some scenes are presented almost as a cryptic, accompanied by others that are more comprehensible. All this happens through a very fragmented structure that encloses different frames, each one of them with a different purpose that is essential to the storytelling" (Gacio).

As a director, Castillo has presented her work in theatre festivals in Argentina, Australia, Belgium, Brazil, Canada, Colombia, England, France, Germany, Holland, Korea, Mexico, Russia, Scotland, Singapore, South Africa, and Spain, among other countries. She has received numerous awards from several artistic Cuban institutions.

In addition to women who live and work as directors in Cuba, several women have been exiled or have obtained jobs directing in other countries. For example, the veteran actor and professor Teresa Maria Rojas founded the Teatro Prometeo (Prometheus Theatre) in 1975 at Miami Dade College in Florida and led the company until 2006; Lilian Vega (Lauten's daughter) also works in Miami, where they both have developed reputations as directors.

Twentieth and early twenty-first century Cuban women directors have achieved noteworthy significance with their work, and this has paved the way for those who want to begin the same journey.

Notes

1. With additional editorial assistance by Sandra Venegas and Emilia Ismael.

2. Tomas Estrada Palma, the first president of Cuba, was very interested in improving the level of education in the country.

3. The new constitution also addressed labor laws, which included maternity leave.

4. In 1912 several parties were formed: the Feminist Popular Party (el Partido Popular Feminista), the Cuban Voters Party (el Partido de Sufragistas Cubanas), and the Feminist National Party (el Partido Nacional Feminista).

5. "Del buen decir" (good speaking) refers to the Spanish theatre tradition that privileged the versed text and to a specific acting style that became very popular in Cuba during the first half of the twentieth century.

6. "Cómicos de la legua" (Comics of the League) refers to the artists from the Spanish Golden Age, who would travel as small companies from town to town.

7. The Palo Monte is an African Cuban religion from Bantu people who came as slaves in the sixteenth century to Santiago de Cuba from Cameroon, Mozambique, and Angola. Palo Monte had an oral tradition that the Cuban descendents combined with different magical elements to transmit their legends about gods (Nkisi, Orishas, Christian saints) and mythological elements in nature. Santeria is another African Cuban religion that came with Lucumi slaves from the Yoruba culture. The Cuban descendents created a syncretism with saints from Christian religions and other magical beliefs. Santeria celebrates many rites related with prophecies and corporeal spirits, and incarnations by dances and singing performances. The orishas or gods of Santeria are very venerated by Cuban people today.

Sources

Actualidad Escénica Cubana. El Centro Nacional de Investigaciones de las Artes Escénicas (CNIEA), n.d. Available at http://cniae.cult.cu (accessed January 5, 2011).

Armada, Alfonso. "Adela Escartín, maestra de actores." *ABC*, August 11, 2010. Available at http://www.abc.es (accessed December 16, 2010).

Azor, Ileana. "The Cuban Actor, a Model Kit." *Mask* ["El actor cubano, modelo para armar." *Máscara*] 26–30 (January–April 1999): 217–23.

———. "The Return of the Zarzuela." *Latin American Stage* ["El retorno de la Zarzuela." *La Escena Latinoamericana*] 5 (December 1990): 15–21.

Castro Rodríguez, Manuel. "Luchas y conquistas de la mujer cubana durante el período 1901–1940." *insurrectasypunto,* February 24, 2009. Available at http://www.insurrectasypunto.org (accessed January 6, 2013).

Cuadriello, Jorge Domingo. *The Spanish in Cuban Literature of the Twentieth Century* [*Los españoles en las letras cubanas durante el siglo XX*]. Sevilla: Renacimiento, 2002.

CUBAESCENA. "Consejo Nacional de las Artes Escénicas." *CUBAESCENA,* 2004. Available at http://www.cubaescena.cult.cu (accessed January 5, 2011).

Cuban Theater Digital Archive. University of Miami Libraries, 2002. Available at http://cubantheater.org (accessed February 12, 2013).

Gacio, Roberto. "The Enchanted Deer Shows Its Visions" ["El ciervo encantado muestra sus visiones"]. *Entretelones* 16 (June 2005): n.p.

González Freire, Natividad. *Cuban Theatre (1927–1961)* [*Teatro Cubano (1927–1961)*]. La Habana: Ministerio de Relaciones Exteriores, 1961.

González Pagés, Julio César. "Feminism, Suffrage and Machismo in Cuba: Three Concepts and Two Women" ["Feminismo, sufragismo y machismo en Cuba: Tres conceptos y dos Mujeres"]. *masculinidades en cuba,* March 19, 2009, n.p. Available at http://www.masculinidadescuba.blogspot.com (accessed December 7, 2010).

Leal, Rine. *Brief History of Cuban Theatre* [*Breve historia del teatro cubano*]. Havana: Letras Cubanas, 1980.

Lobato Morchón, Ricardo. *The Theatre of the Absurd in Cuba* [*El teatro del absurdo en Cuba (1948–1968)*]. Madrid: Verbum, 2002.

López Cabrales, María del Mar. *Warm Sands out to Sea: Interview with Contemporary Women Cuban Writers.* Santiago de Chile: A Room of One's Own Editorial [*Arenas cálidas en alta mar: Entrevista a escritoras contemporáneas en Cuba*]. Santiago de Chile: Editorial Cuarto Propio, 2007.

López Jiménez, María Elena. "The Peculiarity of Santiago Theatre, a Fatima Patterson Way" ["Lo peculiar del teatro santiaguero, a lo Fátima Patterson"]. *CUBAESCENA,* November 17, 2010. Available at http://www.cubaescena.cult.cu (accessed February 23, 2011).

Sánchez Cervera, Adonis. "I Have Been a Real Woman." *The Bearded Alligator* ["Yo he sido una mujer de verdad." *El Caimán Barbudo*], April 4, 2010, n.p. Available at http://www.caimanbarbudo.cu (accessed May 19, 2011).

Svich, Caridad. "A Flower in Havana: Flora Lauten and Cuba's Teatro Buendía Make Their U.S. Debut." *American Theatre* (May 2010): n.p.

 Czech Republic

Miřenka Čechová[1]

The oldest record of women's participation in cultural events in the Czech region comes from the twelfth century, when Czech language was added to Latin plays or performed by conjurers during "profane" festivities. Although the oldest Czech-language drama dates from the fourteenth century, the first plays and performances in modern Czech emerged in the final third of the eighteenth century, when the Czech National Revival raised cultural awareness and helped to solidify the national identity. As a result, the Czech language was restored as the official language of the Czech people, and this led to the founding of the first official theatres in Prague that performed in Czech.

Women first gained recognition in the theatre as actors. Beginning with the founding in 1881 of the National Theatre (Národní Divadlo) in Prague, women performers provided a model of morality and nationalism. Historical evidence reveals that women who worked in the theatre as producers, managers, translators, and actors were forced by circumstances to assume the role of directors as well.[2]

Women's Rights: Historical Context

In the second half of the eighteenth century, women maintained traditional roles as caregivers and housekeepers. They were not allowed to attend secondary school, colleges, or universities and had access only to a private home education and a compulsory primary education, as established in the Kingdom of Bohemia in 1774. Women were also not allowed to actively participate in political or cultural movements or to pursue any type of profession. Among the first women who fought for and gained emancipation from the patriarchal hierarchy was Božena Němcová (c. 1820–1862), one of the most influential Czech authors and an important collector of traditional Czech folklore. She was an inspiration and role model for future generations of Czech women.

Women slowly realized the importance of gaining independence from men and began to seek education and professional careers. Karolína Světlá founded the Czech Women's Production Association in 1871, through which women could acquire a practical education in subjects ranging from business to foreign languages to sewing. Another educational landmark for women was the opening of the Municipal High School for Girls in 1863, where women could get a secondary education, and the American Club of Czech Ladies in 1865, which contained a library and organized lectures by prominent individuals on the subjects of culture, science, and politics. In 1890 the Minerva gymnasium, the first college preparatory high school for girls, was founded, facilitating women's access to universities. Women actors and writers were also acknowledged and accepted in the second half of the nineteenth century, including authors such as Němcová, Světlá, Eliška Krásnohorská, Sofie Podlipská, and Marie Riegrová-Palacká, who were also the first Czech feminists.

The early twentieth century saw improvements in women's rights and a new presence of women in politics. In 1912 Božena Viková-Kunětická, who began her career as an actor, playwright, and writer, was the first woman in Czech history to achieve a political position, becoming the first female member of parliament and in 1920 a senator. In her novels, she propagated women's emancipation and feminist ideas. At the end of World War I, the Czechoslovak Republic was established and included equal political, social, and cultural rights for both women and men. Charlotta G. Masaryková, the American wife of the first Czechoslovakian president, T. G. Masaryk, was a strong proponent of the emancipation of women, who gained both full suffrage and the right to higher education in 1920. Little by little, women were able to establish themselves.

The Munich Agreement of 1938 destroyed democratic Czechoslovakia and permitted Nazi Germans to occupy large borderline areas. Consequently, Czech inhabitants were driven out and civil liberties were taken away. Married women in public service were involuntarily retired in order to relinquish their positions to people displaced from the borderline areas. The Czech region was changed into the Protectorate of Bohemia and Moravia. This act of violence became a prologue to World War II. Young Czech women, men, and Jews were drafted for forced labor and deported to concentration and extermination camps in Germany. During the occupation, thousands of Czech inhabitants were killed.

The Communist coup d'etat in 1948 and the subsequent totalitarian régime, which lasted until 1989, completely interrupted the progress of women's rights. Women with no children were required to undertake physical work. Mothers were financially obligated to begin working soon after childbirth. The communist ideal of "woman" encouraged nationalism, physical labor, and socialism.[3] As early as 1948 the communist regime established labor camps for political opponents and those labeled inconvenient individuals, who were subject to unjust trials, executions, and imprisonments. One of the accused intellectuals was Milada Horáková, an attorney and women's rights activist, who, as a member of the National Women's Council, was engaged in women's emancipation in the legislature. She was imprisoned by the Gestapo during World War II. In 1950 she acted as her own lawyer in a public trial, scripted in advance by the authorities. She was condemned to hanging, provoking many negative international reactions. There are numerous theatrical productions of the trial of Milada Horáková that invoke a strong spectator response.

The communist state was overthrown in the nonviolent Velvet Revolution of 1989 that led to the creation of a Czech democracy. In the new Czech Republic, separated from the Slovak Republic in 1993, numerous women's rights organizations and feminist associations were founded.

Early Women Directors

Many new progressive theatres emerged in the creative atmosphere between the two world wars, providing women directors their first true chance to succeed. These small studio theatres created innovative performance pieces, combined dramatic theatre with music and dance numbers, reflected political and cultural life, and fostered close relationships between the artists and the audience. Another important influence in the formation of women directors in the 1920s and 1930s was through modern dance, performed in Prague's avant-garde theatres. The most important dancers from this period were creators of their own movement performances, mime scenes, and dance pieces.

Early women theatre producers and managers had occasional directing credits. Probably the first true Czech woman director was a performer in Vladimir Gamza's studio theatres: Emílie Hráská (1900–1978) (Kazda, Král, and Pavlovský). Hráská took various acting classes and afterward graduated in dramatic arts from the Prague Conservatory (Pražská Konzervatoř). She followed Gamza to Czech Studio (České Studio), Sečestal Studio (Sečestal Studio), and Art Studio (Umělecké Studio), where in 1927 she directed George Bernard Shaw's *Candide* and Henning Berger's *Flood* (Potopa). Despite artistic successes, these avant-garde studios were usually forced to close after one season, mainly because of financial problems. Beginning in the 1920s, Hráská performed and directed in some of Prague's theatres, including the Liberated Theatre (Osvobozené Divadlo), the Intimate Theatre (Intimní Divadlo), and also in regional theatres.

Another woman working as a director in the 1930s was Míla Mellanová (1899–1964). After taking private acting classes she learned the director's craft with the well-known Czech director Jan Bor, and afterward she began her directing career in Prague at the Uranie Theatre and Švandovo Theatre. In 1935 Mellanová founded Prague Children's Theatre (Pražské Dětské Divadlo), which became the first professional theatre for children

Avant-garde Women Choreographers Pave the Way
for Independent Women Directors

After World War I the immense expansion of cultural life in the new Czechoslovakia, which was founded in 1918, led to the emergence of inventive avant-garde dancers and choreographers. The artists had a profound impact on the formation of independent women directors. These women were engaged in Prague's avant-garde scene, which included the Liberated Theatre (Osvobozené Divadlo), the Dada Theatre (Divadlo Dada), and the Modern Studio (Moderní Studio) as creators of their own dance, movement, or pantomime pieces. They were also important founders and leaders of dance schools and their own companies.

Their legacy originated from experience with the Swiss musician Emile Jacques Dalcroz's school of rhythmic gymnastics in Hellerau, Austria, and from the influence of the Hungarian dance teacher Rudolf von Laban. Czech choreographers closely cooperated with the most significant avant-garde directors, including Jindřich Honzl, Emil František Burian, and Jiří Frejka in the theatres the Modern Studio, Dada Studio, Liberated Theatre, and D34 Theatre.

As a director of movement performances, Jarmila Kröschlová, one of the founders of the Modern Studio, created scenic choreographies and pantomimes. She called her choreographic style "a theater of movement" because it was close to mime and physical theatre. In 1923 she founded her own theatre company, Jarmila Kröschlová's Company (Skupina Jarmily Kröschlové), which was introduced to Parisian audiences at an expo where her company received a bronze medal for its work. In the 1930s she directed children's theatre performances. Beginning in 1931 she led her own dance school in the Phoenix Palace (Palác Fenix) in Prague, and from 1949 to 1958 she taught at the Academy of Performing Arts (DAMU). She also wrote theoretical books on movement for actors and dance techniques. The inspiring choreographer Jožka Šaršeová was a member of Kröschlová's company.

Another important representative of scenic dance is Míra Holzachová, who opened her new avant-garde theatre, Unitarie, in Prague in 1933 with the premiere of *The Clown Chocolate* (*Klaun Čokoláda*), for which she created the choreography and libretto. Before World War II Holzachová escaped to the United States, where, under the name Mira Slavonica, she produced antiwar dance projects such as *Dance of Liberation* (*Tanec Osvobozeni*) in 1942; taught dance at the Free School in Riverdale, New York; and performed dance productions with her students on television. After 1946 she continued teaching and choreographing in Czechoslovakia.

Other important avant-garde dancer-choreographers who paved the way for women stage directors include Míra Holzachová, Milča Mayerová, Nina Jirsíková, and Jarmila Jeřábková. These accomplished women were independent creators and artistic leaders who gained respect in the environment of Prague's avant-garde theatres and among the general public. Thanks to their contributions, they became models for aspiring women theatre directors.

in Czech. She was the artistic director there until 1945. Later, she directed at other theatres for children and youth in Prague and taught acting classes there at the Department of Puppet Theatre in the Academy of Performing Arts (DAMU).

Among the avant-garde actors who turned to directing in Prague was Lola Skrbková (1902–1978). She studied acting, graduated from Prague Conservatory in 1924, and during the second half of the twentieth century started performing in the Liberated Theatre. Later she contributed to the founding of Emil Frantisek (E. F.) Burian's politically left D34 Theatre, where she was engaged as a director, music conductor, and experimenter with voiceband—Burian's term for people reciting texts as if they were a musical band (Bartoš). After World War II, Skrbková continued to direct and teach as part of the Theatre Faculty at Janáček's Academy of Performing Arts (JAMU) in Brno and in regional theatres.

Another important artist who was active following World War II was Zuzana Kočová (1922–1988), the wife of the multitalented writer, musician, and theatre practitioner E. F. Burian. Kočová founded her own touring Caravan Theatre (Maringotka), where she directed and acted.

Crucial to the equality of women directors after World War II was the founding of two important theatre departments in the main universities of DAMU and JAMU. Both universities formed theatre faculties where directing and dramaturgy were offered independently. Women graduates from these programs were far fewer than the number of male directors, and the hiring of women as directors in established theatres was almost inconceivable. In the 1960s and 1970s it was still rare to find working women directors in Czech theatre. Women were more typically engaged as radio broadcast directors or as television directors. Later, they worked in regional theatres or small studio theatres.

One of the most distinguished women directors was Eva Tálská, who was born in 1944. At age twenty-four she became the second woman ever to graduate from JAMU. While still a student, Tálská co-founded the Goose on a String Theatre (Divadlo Husa na Provázku) in 1967 in Brno, where she began her professional directing career. This was one of the most important artistic and political theatres in the country. Tálská became one of its leading personalities and house directors. Her innovative directing style had a strong influence on this theatre until 1989. Afterward, she founded her own theatre school, Studio A House (Studio Dům), an experimental laboratory for young people to learn essential theatre education. Most of her pupils later became well-known actors, directors, theatre theorists, or scenographers. Tálská's directing aesthetic is strongly stylized and often focused on the poetic line of the story. Her work is influenced by traditional folklore, poetry, musical structure, puppets, and circus—such as her creation and direction of *The Circus or Else a Death and a Horse with Me* (*Cirkus aneb se mnou smrt a kůň*) at the Goose on a String Theatre in 1999. The seventy-minute production included a nonverbal circus atmosphere and required rehearsals with professional circus people. Her performances were repeatedly nominated for the prestigious Alfred Radok Awards, presented for achievement in Czech theatre.

One of the first women graduates at the Theatre Department of DAMU who became a professional director was Helena Glancová, who, as a Jewish child, was imprisoned at the concentration camp Terezín, located in what is now the Czech Republic. She first directed at a regional theatre in Pardubice from 1962 to 1965 where she directed productions such as Jaroslav Dietl's *The Accident* (*Nehoda*) in 1963 and Friedrich Dürrenmatt's *The Physicists* (*Fyzikové*) in 1964. Following that she worked in the intellectually exceptional Beyond the Gate Theatre (Divadlo Za Branou) in Prague, where she directed such productions as Shakespeare's *Love's Labour's Lost* in 1970.

Another of the first DAMU women graduates was Lída Engelová, who is profiled below. Tálská and Engelová, both strong individuals, became pioneers for the introduction of women directors into established theatres.

Women also won recognition in puppet theatres, studio theatres, and children's theatre. In the 1960s Markéta Schartová started her career as a director in professional studio theatres and puppet theatres, later becoming an artistic director. In 1993 she directed Julius Zeyer's *Radúz and Mahulena* on the main stage of the National Theatre in Prague, one of only two women who have had the chance to direct on its main stage. A respected teacher in the Puppet Department at DAMU, Schartová became Dean of Theatre Faculty there. She has received an impressive total of ten awards in directing and best performance from various festivals throughout the Czech Republic.

Working Climate in the Twenty-First Century

Since 1989 women in professional theatres have continued to struggle to assert themselves in directing. The Velvet Revolution brought democracy and opened the door into foreign countries. As a result, Czech theatres started to produce plays from Western playwrights whose works were formerly forbidden. The number of women who aspired to be directors increased, though no statistics are available to chronicle this growth. Also, women who graduated in directing earlier could now start their careers in professional theatres. For example, Jaroslava Šiktancová, who was expelled from DAMU for placing her signature on a political document opposing the communist régime, was able to direct again after 1989.

Despite the achievements of certain women directors, since the beginning of the twenty-first century there is still little chance to see women directing on the main state-owned theatre stages. In the complex of Prague's National Theatre buildings—which include the National Theatre, the Estates Theatre (Stavovské Divadlo), the New Stage (Nová Scéna), and the Kolowrat Theatre (Divadlo Kolowrat)—only eight women have had the opportunity to direct. In 1993 the first woman directed a production on its main stage that had only five performances. One year later, the second (and last, as of

2011) woman directed on the main stage. Three women directed at the Estates Theatre, while three women directed at Kolowrat, a small attic theatre. No women at Prague's National Theatre had the opportunity to direct there on an ongoing basis.[4]

Since 2000 the number of women working in the professional field has increased dramatically thanks to the graduates of DAMU and JAMU. Young women directors from the Department of Alternative and Puppet Theatre in DAMU founded their own independent theatre groups that attract new, young audiences and have established themselves as a progressive contrast to official theatre scenes.[5] These groups, all in Prague, include Theatre Na Blízko, which experiments with sign language; Theatre Letí, which introduces contemporary foreign plays in translation; Spitfire Company, which experiments with physical and visual theatre; and numerous others.

The rate of men and women graduates of directing at DAMU became more balanced around 2010, with the number of women graduates in the field actually being slightly more than half. Despite this, however, in terms of general theatre awards, there is still a conspicuous absence of women award recipients. By 2010 there was only one woman, Hana Burešová, whose four plays were awarded the Alfred Radok Award for best production of the year.[6]

Profiles of Contemporary Directors

Lída Engelová

Born in Prague in 1944, Lída Engelová's career started as an actor and screenwriter. In 1967 she was one of the first women directors who graduated in the field of directing from DAMU. During her years of study and from 1968 until 1973 she served as an assistant director to many significant directors in Prague's National Theatre. At this time, she began to work with Jan Grossman, a Czech director and theorist, in Prague's Theatre on the Balustrade (Divadlo na Zábradlí). Engelová discusses her experience, stating, "In my time it was unusual to see women stage directors. There was always an obstacle to trusting women concerned with this 'male' profession. Until now there has been a problem for many people inside and outside of the theater for women to be the head, to be an authority for men."

Two important events in the early 1970s helped propel Engelová's directing career forward. She began an internship in 1970 with British director Peter Brook, for which she observed, discussed, and took notes on his rehearsals of *A Midsummer Night's Dream* at the Royal Shakespeare Company in London and in Stratford. Engelová adopted Brook's idea that for the creation of a theatre piece, it is enough to have a space, an actor, and good subject matter. Her book, *Brook's A Midsummer Night's Dream* (*Brookův Sen noci svatojanské*), published in 1971, explored her experience with this project. In addition, in 1973 she directed her first big theatre production in Pilsen at J. K. Tyl

Theatre (Divadlo Josefa Kajetána Tyla), where she remained for fifteen years. As the first woman ever engaged as a director there, Engelová went on to direct about forty-five performances, ranging from Jean Anouilh's *Medea* to Oldřich Daněk's *Moravian Field Battle* (Bitva na Moravském poli).

Together with Zdena Kratochvílová, a member of the renowned Ladislav Fialka's Mime Company, Engelová established Prague's Pocket Theatre (Kapesní Divadlo) in 1975, which produced more than thirteen hundred mime performances for children and adults and played in fifteen countries. A television documentary film, *How to Make a Clown (Jak se dělá klaun)*, was about their Pocket Theatre.

Engelová was employed or hired as a director in many Czech theatres and abroad. Of note, she directed Manuel Puig's *Vabang* in Prague's National Theatre and Franz Kafka's *Trial* in Saint Petersburg and London. Many of her productions were adapted for television. As a broadcasting director, she directed more than sixty plays.

Engelová's directing methods are built upon detailed work with an actor and with the text. Rather than relying on elaborate technical effects, her work points to purity and simplicity of expression on the stage. She likes to change and combine different genres and working methods. Her directing repertoire consists of dramas, comedies, burlesques, physical theatre performances, broadcast productions, and operas. Engelová describes the purpose of her work, saying, "All work has to point to the interest of rehearsing that allows us to open ourselves as human and to touch our uttermost possibilities. The audience should later be able to see the result of our work as a thrilling spectacle that will touch their souls. And inside of that the humor is not missing."

Zoja Mikotová

Zoja Mikotová, who was born in the former Czechoslovakia in 1951, started her career in the visual arts, which provided her with unique insights into the world. She continued as an actor and, later, as the author of short pieces for mime theatre. Her interest in the visual arts is recognizable in her directing. She graduated in directing at JAMU in 1980, only the fourth woman to graduate from the program. She discusses obstacles at the start of her career, stating, "When I was starting my professional career there was no tradition of female directors in Czechoslovakia. There were only isolated instances. They were telling me that I can succeed rather as a dramaturge, that I have too tiny a figure and that I don't speak loud enough to be a director."

As a student, Mikotová created her first successful directing works, which led to offers for directing in professional theatres. At the start of the 1980s, she was a director in the professional puppet theatre The Joy (Radost) in Brno for ten years. Mikotová was hired as a director and a choreographer in multiple theatres in the Czech Republic and abroad, where she created many performances for adults as well as children.

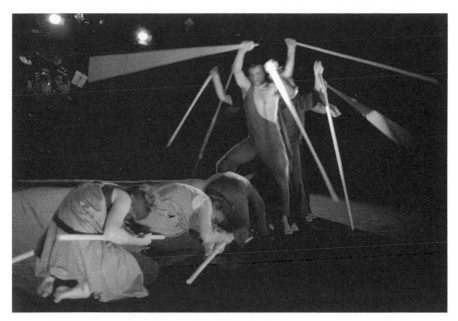

Genesis, translated from the Bible into sign language by Zoja Mikotová with Václav Gottwald, written and directed by Mikotová. First performed at DIFA JAMU, Brno, 1997. Photographer: Pavel Nevsvadba.

Above all, she is well known for her work with deaf actors, with whom she created numerous performances that were presented at various international theatre festivals in Europe, and in countries spanning from China to the United States. In 1992 she founded the Atelier of Deaf Educational Drama at JAMU. This studio became an artistic laboratory that explored new possibilities of expression for deaf actors in the field of education and theatre, especially physical theatre. The many distinctions that her studio received are a testimony to the ability of art to break down the barriers between people.

Visual art, physical theatre, mime, and puppets are essential to the means of expression that Mikotová plays with in her directing style. The two elements that are most important to her are the work with actors and storytelling—through movement, image, and the inner dialogue between actors and the audience rather than through words. When she creates performances for children, she focuses on cultivating their imaginations and avoiding literal interpretation. The most worthwhile thing for her is the moment of shared experience between the actors and the children in the audience—the experience of the story that will remain in their subconscious.

Through her pedagogical and artistic activities Mikotová has received numerous awards, and in 2000 she became professor of dramatic arts at JAMU. In 2010 she directed a piece with a deaf actor performing as a professional singer sang. That year she also worked as an author and director on a performance of Carlo Goldoni's *Pinocchio* in the Slovácké Theatre in Uherské Hradiště. In her directing she never recedes from sensitiveness, inwardness, or an emotional approach to the themes and collaborators.

Viktorie Čermáková

Born in Prague in 1966, Viktorie Čermáková started her career as an actor in a non-professional theatre group, A Studio, that was associated with the Theatre on the Fringe (Divadlo na Okraji). It was one of the experimental theatres in Prague at the time of Normalization—a period from 1969 to 1989—when the communist régime asserted its values on society. Later, Čermáková pursued an education as a photographer. In A Studio she received a well-rounded theatre education, learning the craft of directing by experimenting at the group. Everyone in this theatre worked together on the script, discussed the literature, cleaned the theatre, listened to and discussed music, and tried to find his or her place and a free expression of opinion in the world of Czechoslovakia during Normalization. Čermáková experienced her first directing with this theatre group in 1980 and went on to become one of the group's artistic directors. After that, she worked as a professional actor in various Prague theatres.

Karel Steigerwald's *Marina's Thirtieth Love (Třicátá Marinina láska)*, adapted from Vladimir Sorokin's novel, directed by Viktorie Čermáková, Factory Studio of The New Stage Theatre, Prague, 2011. Photographer: Jiří N. Jelínek.

She also directed independent alternative projects in experimental theatre venues. From 2002 to 2005 she studied directing at DAMU. In 2006 she co-founded the Theatre Studio A Factory (Divadelní Studio Továrna), which focuses on new works and contemporary Czech drama that deals with sociocultural questions. Her latest projects were realized at official theatre stages, such as the New Stage at the National Theatre in Prague and the National Theatre in Brno. Čermáková discusses her beliefs about directing, exclaiming, "My directing credo is non-violence and I find that it is, in many cases, nearly impossible. I realize that people have to deserve freedom here in the rehearsals as well as in life. The ones who were not born in freedom are not able to deal with freedom in art and because of this they are not able to realize themselves in cooperation with others."

Inspired by contemporary dance and physical theatre, Čermáková's directing style has a strong sense of rhythm and dynamics. She works most often with strong and distinct personalities, powerful common themes, and whole-group involvement. These elements were evident in her direction of Karel Steigerwald's *Horáková x Gottwald* in the theatre La Fabrika in Prague in 2006.

Although Čermáková is a well-prepared director, she depends on cooperation and authorial contributions from all actors and collaborators. She notes, "All the time I am fighting against the uninformed, traditional opinion that says the director has to be a self-confident dictator that punishes and mandates." She discusses her weaknesses, stating, "My main obstacle is my hypersensitivity and a lack of operational skill which causes me painful work primarily with my male collaborators."

In 2007 Čermáková was nominated for an Alfréd Radok Award as talent of the year. In the years ahead, she will surely utilize her talent to create many more engaging works of theatre.

Natálie Deáková

Natálie Deáková belongs on the list of the most significant women directors mainly because as a twenty-three-year-old graduate in directing from DAMU in 2003, she received the position of artistic director at the important regional theatre the Drama Theatre (Činoherní Studio) in Ústí nad Labem. She is one of very few women to assume a leadership role in an established theatre. She discusses her choice to go into theatre, stating, "My theater career began unawares by a driving need to do theater. I was fascinated by the metamorphosis of an actor into his/her character and was captivated by the fact that the theater stage is a magic space where everything is possible. My decision was entirely intuitive and until now I wonder how I have conformed to it whole my life."

Since she began her work at the Drama Theatre, Deáková has attracted a young, ambitious generation of actors who are influenced by the pop and media epoch and by

Natálie Deáková and Johana Součkova's *Alice in Wonderland*, based on a book by Lewis Carroll, directed by Deáková, Činoherní Studio, Ústí nad Labem, 2011. Photographer: Klára Žitňanská.

Coolness Drama, or in-yer-face-theatre, which emerged in the 1990s in Great Britain. Her goal is to speak to young audiences, to bring a new generation into the theatre and, at a time when personal relationships are lost, to give them the feeling of life. That is also why she produces and directs new plays and experiments with forms. She says she is "playing," but at the same time she deals with serious, rough themes.

Deáková combines the approaches of dramatic theatre with alternative theatre and the visual side of performance with lighting design. Her theatre direction is usually contemporary and topically shocking. This may work in tandem with the choice of play—for example, her decision to direct Mark Ravenhill's *Some Explicit Polaroids* (*Polaroidy*) for her degree at the Academy. Critical for her is to give actors the feeling of inner freedom no matter how strict a form they must follow. The audiences should be able to touch the beauty that is a reflection of something godlike within them.

Deáková discusses her role as a woman director, stating, "I don't like to limit myself by the moniker of 'female director.' Except for a certain amount of decisiveness (and some testosterone too) I don't consider this work strange when it is done by women. . . . In the theater, the female element that brings a certain sensitivity and receptivity is always a contribution. I only wonder why we are so few[,] contrary, for example, to female documentary film makers."

In 2011 Deáková left her position at the Drama Theatre and started to work as a freelance director. With her exceptional experience and many years before her, Deáková hopes to introduce a new generation to the world of theatre.

These profiled women directors represent strong artistic individuals who were able, by exceptional quality and artistic vision, to accomplish significant positions in the Czech theatre. This is exemplified by their courage to experiment and by the desire and strength required to maintain independence.

Notes

1. With special thanks to Dr. Ladislava Petišková, Jana Soprová, and Nancy Jo Snider.

2. Saša Kokošková was the first woman to acquire a license to produce theatre events. She managed a touring theatre company and performed with her company in public houses such as Deutsch's Pub in Prague around 1894. Her efforts were supported and followed by other theatre women who managed and produced theatre, notably Eliška Zollnerová (1822–1911), Marie Zieglerová (1881–1966), and Eliška Pešková (1833–1895).

3. Many theatre artists were silenced by the communistic regime, but others decided to fight against it. An important event was the founding of Vlasta Chramostová's The Apartment's Theatre (Bytové Divadlo), where the actor Chramostová organized and performed illegal protest performances during the 1980s that influenced other dissident artists.

4. The following women were directing a production at established theatres under the National Theatre in Prague as of 2010:

The main stage of the National Theatre: Hana Burešová, Markéta Schartová

The Estate Theatre: Hana Burešová, Oxana Meleskina Smilková, Zoja Mikotová, Lucie Bělohradská

Theatre Kolowrat: Lída Engelová (two productions), Irena Žantovská (two productions), Lucie Bělohradská

Summer stage at the Bouda: Viktorie Čermáková

5. For example, DAMU graduate Natálie Deaková achieved the position of the artistic leader and house director in the established Drama Studio (Činoherní Studio) in Ústí nad Labem in 2005.

6. Hana Burešová, born in 1959, graduated from DAMU in 1983 and worked in regional theatre. She started her career in Prague at the Theatre Labyrint in 1992 when she was hired to direct a new production of C. D. Grabbe's *Don Juan and Faust*, which won the Alfred Radok Award for the best performance of the year. Three years later, with another director, she won a competition held by the city to establish a permanent theatre in Old Town in Prague, where they founded Theatre in Dlouhá Street (Divadlo V Dlouhé). This theatre promptly gained recognition primarily for original dramaturgy, which combined classical plays, new dramatizations, and small theatre forms. Burešová became its artistic director in 1996. As of 2012 she is the only woman in the Czech Republic to receive the Alfred Radok Award and the second woman to direct on the main stage of the National Theatre in Prague.

Her directing is characterized by a variety of styles and genres that nevertheless remains faithful to the aesthetic intention of the author.

Sources

Bartoš, Petr. "Lola Skrbková." *Czech-Slovak Film Database* [Česko-Slovenská Filmová Database]. n.d. Available at http://www.csfd.cz (accessed February 22, 2012).

Čermáková, Viktorie. E-mail message to Miřenka Čechová. December 6, 2010.

Deáková, Natálie. E-mail message to Miřenka Čechová. December 25, 2010.

Engelová, Lída. E-mail message to Miřenka Čechová. December 13, 2010.

Kazda, Jaromír, Karel Král, and Petr Pavlovský. "Studio Theatres." *Theatre Revue* ["Studiová divadla." *Divadelní Revue*]. Arts and Theatre Institute [Divadelní Ústav], 2001.

Mikotová, Zoja. E-mail message to Miřenka Čechová. December 12, 2010.

 Egypt

Dalia Basiouny[1]

The first Egyptian woman to direct for the stage was Fatma Roushdy in 1930. Though her seven plays as a director were successful, the work of this actor-turned-director did not encourage many women to follow in her footsteps. The directorial efforts of women in the theatre were sporadic throughout most of the twentieth century, and, with a few exceptions, they did not reflect a clear vision or commitment to the craft until the rise of contemporary Egyptian women directors in the last decade of the century. In the 1990s a few women artists started carving names for themselves in the independent theatre world in Egypt. A handful of women directors established their own theatre companies with clear missions and visions and started competing with male directors for the limited funding and performance spaces available in Cairo. Outside the Egyptian capital, women directors are still a rare phenomenon in the regional theatres.

The journey from Roushdy's first attempt at directing Tolstoy's *Anna Karenina* in 1930 to director Laila Soliman's productions revealing the atrocities of the Military Council against the rebels of the Egyptian Revolution in 2011 distills the journey of Egyptian women theatre artists searching for their voice and mission in the public sphere, and honing that voice and their artistic skills to create their unique aesthetics.

Women's Rights: Historical Context

The Egyptian feminist movement started in the late nineteenth century and gained much strength and momentum at the beginning of the twentieth century. It was closely connected to the nationalist struggle for independence and shaping the country's future. In her article "Egyptian Feminism in a Nationalist Century," Margo Badran sums up that connection: "The first half of the century was marked by a fierce anti-colonial struggle; the second half in constructing a new, more independent nation. During the course of the century, women have given shape to a newer, modern identity—a new way of thinking, a new mode of analysis and a new guide for everyday and collective political activism. Women articulated feminism within the discourses of both Islamic modernism and secular nationalism" (Badran).[2]

The revolution of 1919 is often seen as the true beginning of women's open involvement in the public arena: marching against the colonial British occupation, organizing the first public protests demanding the country's independence, and dying to defend their right to live in a free country. The period between 1919 and 1922 was an important period of transformation from the invisible social feminism to a highly public and organized collective feminism. The second decade of the twentieth century witnessed public women's activities on a number of fronts. The first group of female students officially enrolled in degree programs at Cairo University in 1927. Women producers and directors participated in the birthing of the new industry of Egyptian filmmaking. On another front, women owned and published women's magazines. Retired stage actor Rosa Al Youssef established a magazine carrying her name in 1925 that is still in print, and Roushdy established a magazine in 1928, which was short lived. Women also wrote for the theatre for the first time. May Zeyada wrote two plays that were not performed, while actor Dawlat Abyad wrote two one-act plays tackling women's problems.

Badran notes that with the 1952 revolution, women's independent public militancy was about to come to an end. The new state granted women the vote in 1956, thirty-two years after feminists had made their first demands for suffrage. That same year the government forced the closure of the Egyptian Feminist Union, as it did all independent organizations. It was allowed to reconstitute itself as a social service organization under a new name, the Huda Sha'rawi Association.

The last decades of the twentieth century and the beginning of the twenty-first century bore the fruit of women's activism throughout the century, represented in major advancements in family laws to protect women and their children, and new divorce laws that guarantee women's rights. As of 2012, the number of women exceeds men in higher education, and there is a large number of women in the workforce, from manual and office work to high executive positions and ministerial offices. Yet there are some serious backlashes to the status of women in society due to the irrational religious waves. Even though the breadwinner in one out of every four Egyptian households is a woman, there are extremist religious calls for women to leave the work force and return to the home. Many women performers choose to veil and leave the profession, while others adopt the veil and continue to act in "veil suitable" roles.

The 2011 revolution was another landmark in Egyptian women's political participation and public engagement. Women took to the streets with men, marching, protesting, and joining in the occupation of Cairo's Tahrir Square and other squares throughout the country. Women of every background and affiliation demonstrated to topple the regime and demanded the ousting of the president. Many women found their political voice for the first time during this revolution, which created a safe space for expression and dissent, allowing for more artistic expression and creativity than the country had ever witnessed before. However, after the president stepped down, very few women took on leadership roles. The parliamentary elections that followed at the end of 2011 and beginning of 2012 showed very weak representation of women in the post revolution People's Assembly, with only six women elected out of more than four hundred representatives. On the other hand, the aggression from the Military Council did not spare women demonstrators who continued to protest to free Egypt from the military rule. They subjected women protestors to virginity checks, beating and stripping them, subjecting them to tear gas bombs, and targeting them with rubber bullets and live ammunition. This coincided with a rise in the irrational interpretation of religion and a growing extremist faction, which has gained more power in society and parliamentary and political presence. The extremists in turn have targeted women and their freedoms, threatening a reversal to their societal advancements.

Forces of modernity are in a constant battle with the traditionalists and the fundamentalists. The twenty-first-century moral codes are at odds with the nineteenth-century values, especially with regard to women and their role in society. The pioneers of directing fought similar battles earlier in the twentieth century, as the country was finding its independence and questioning its national identity.

Early Women Directors

Before Roushdy made history as the first woman director in Egypt, she was a famous actor of the 1920s. She left Youssef Wahby's company and established a new company with her husband, Aziz Eid, in Cairo in 1927. Eid directed most of the performances of Fatma Roushdy's Company—the first theatre company bearing a name of a woman in Egypt and the Arab world.

In 1930–31 Roushy directed three plays herself: Tolstoy's *Anna Karenina*, Victor Hugo's *Mason de Leon*, and Mahmoud Kamel's *Fatma*. Her directorial work extended overseas; she directed two plays in Morocco in 1937–38 and two plays in Tunisia in the 1940s. Roushdy also tried her hand at film—directing, producing, and performing in *Marriage* in 1932.

There is mention of other women performers who had to direct plays as part of their jobs in the Popular Theatre Companies established by the government in 1947. Amina Rezk, the famous tragedian, directed two or three one-act plays in 1950, while actor Zozo Nabeel managed the Popular Theatre Company and possibly directed some plays for them. Their efforts are not well documented, and there are no records of the names and exact dates of these performances. It is worth noting that the early directors—women as well as men—were all working actors who also produced or managed theatre companies, as there was no established program to study directing at the time.

After the 1952 military coup that overthrew the king, many changes happened in Egyptian society, which adopted a socialist agenda, offering free education, encouraging the arts, and sending some artists to study abroad. However, the first few generations of theatre artists and academics sent to study abroad had no women among them. The first notable woman director in the second half of the twentieth century was Laila Abou Seif, who earned a bachelor of arts at American University in Cairo (AUC), a master of arts from the University of Chicago, and a doctorate from the University of Illinois. She taught in the United States before returning to Egypt in the early 1970s to teach in the Higher Institute of Theatre in Cairo. She directed some student productions at the Theatre Institute, in the Academy of Arts, as well as plays that were performed in government theatres in Cairo. Abou Seif established a theatre company and directed two films produced for the Egyptian Television. She directed thirteen plays in Egypt before immigrating to the United States in the late 1970s. Her journey from directing Tom Stoppard's *New Hamlet* in 1973 to Brecht's *Mother Courage* in 1981 included a number of stops with Egyptian contemporary plays, in addition to a few translated texts by international writers.

Menha El Batrawy, the renowned theatre critic, tried her hand at directing a few times. Her first attempt was with the theatre group of the leftist party Al Tagqmou' in downtown Cairo where she directed *The House* (*Al Beet*) in 1977. She followed that with *The Ghoul* (*Ommena El Ghoula*) in 1983 for the Touring Theatre, which is based in Cairo and tours different cities in Egypt. Almost two decades later El Batrawy directed and acted in Sameh Mahran's *The Umbrella* (*Al Mazalla*), which was performed only once in El Netaq Downtown Festival in Cairo in 2000. El Batrawy also directed a number of children's plays through the French Cultural Center in Cairo, both in Arabic and French.

The two major challenges for twentieth-century women directors in Egypt were the constraints of patriarchal society and financing their theatre work. The unstable situation of the theatre in general, because of the economic instability connected to the Great Depression of the 1930s and its repercussions, led to dismantling many theatre companies, affecting the early works of pioneering women directors. The difficulty of securing consistent funding for the arts continued to afflict theatre, affecting the continuity of women directors' work. In addition, the roles expected of women in society and the working conditions of theatre—daily rehearsals, late hours, working in a male-dominated world, lack of rehearsal space—posed and continue to pose a challenge for many women who are interested in directing for the stage.

Working Climate in the Twenty-First Century

Most of the productions by women directors are fringe productions, usually performed by independent theatre companies during festivals, or in short runs funded by foreign cultural centers or embassies; in many cases they are self-funded. There are no women directors working in the state-run companies or commercial theatre. At the

Women Directors in the Arab World: Lebanon and Syria
by Anne Fliotsos and Watfa Hamadi

In the twentieth century, the Arab world saw a new phase of feminism emerging, with issues of gender equality driving the quest for new laws and new freedom. Gradually, women gained new opportunities to study theatre, producing a first generation of women stage directors in Lebanon and Syria, mainly in the late twentieth century. As with most developing theatre artists, these budding directors have worn many hats—as performers, writers, designers, and producers; they have also worked in several mediums and across national borders. Most women directors in Lebanon and Syria work with smaller casts and within the constraints of minimal budgets in this field so long dominated by men.

In Lebanon Latife Moultaka became a pioneer, directing as early as the 1960s. Born in 1932 in Bisshareh, Lebanon, she earned bachelor of arts and bachelor of laws degrees, becoming a lawyer in 1956. She started working in the theatre in 1959, at first as a writer and performer alongside her husband, Antoine Moultaka, an actor and director. Moultaka later earned her doctorate in theatre in Beirut in 1960 and became a professor of dramatic arts at the Lebanese University's Institute of Fine Arts in Beirut in 1966. With her husband she founded the Lebanese Theatre Circle (Masrah al-Halaka) in Beirut in 1970, and together they created and directed works that they presented both in Lebanon and at international festivals ("Latife Moultaka").

A second pioneer in Lebanon is the actor and director Nidal Al Achkar, born in Dick El-Mehdi, North Metn. She is a graduate of the Royal Academy of Dramatic Arts (RADA) in London and has trained and worked with British director Joan Littlewood, who had a major effect on her life and work. Al Achkar played a significant role in Lebanese theatre in the 1960s when she founded The Beirut Theatre Workshop in 1966. This group of artists "shook and provoked Lebanese society because they dealt boldly with contemporary social, political and regional issues" (*Al Madina*). She founded an Arab Actors Theatre in the mid-1980s, based in Amman, Jordan, and consisting of artists from thirteen Arab countries. In 1994 she founded the Al Madina Theatre in Beirut, which became the Al Madina Theatre Association for Arts and Culture in 2005. With this enterprise, Al Achkar aims to "promote dialogue and to create a space of free expression for all issues facing the Lebanese and Arab societies" (*Al Madina*). Her many national and international awards include Knight of Arts and Letters, bestowed upon her by the French Government in 1997.

As theatre degree programs at Lebanese universities developed, a new generation of women directors began to emerge in Lebanon, first in the 1980s, including Lina Abiad, Jana Al-Hassan, Sawsan Bou Khaled, Kholoud Nasser, Siham Nasser, Lina Sanne, and Maya Zbib.

Born in Beirut, Zbib is an example of a new generation of directors from the twenty-first century. She earned a bachelor of arts from the Lebanese University's Institute of Fine Arts in 2003, followed by a master's in performance making from Goldsmiths, University of London, in 2007. Zbib is the co-founder and manager of Zoukak Theatre Company and Cultural Association in Beirut and also teaches at the Institute of Fine Arts ("People"). She has won a number of honors, including the opportunity to work with American director Peter Sellars in 2010–11 as part of the Rolex Mentor &

Protégé Arts Initiative. In an interview for Rolex, Zbib discussed her broader goals as a director and writer: "I hope to bring more people to the theatre in Lebanon and to create a movement where going to the theatre becomes a need. And try to give back to theatre its political and artistic aspects, those that consumerism and the corrupt political environment have sadly managed to dissolve." Zbib states that the biggest challenge in Lebanon is funding, as the government provides no support for theatre, which she feels is "regarded as a trivial profession" ("Maya Zbib").

In Syria women made inroads as performers by the 1960s and gradually began directing and producing theatre. With the creation of the Higher Institute of Dramatic Arts in Damascus in 1977, new opportunities for women emerged. Pioneering Syrian directors include Maha Saleh as well as Naila al-Atrash, who studied directing at Bulgaria's High Institute of Dramatic Arts in Sofia in the 1970s (Hamadi).

In her career of more than three decades, Atrash has worked her way up to higher-profile directing jobs, including work with the Syrian National Theatre (SNT) in Damascus. In December 2008 Atrash directed SNT's production of Sadallah Wannus's *Wretched Dreams* (*Ahlam Shakiyya*) at the esteemed Damascus Theatre Festival. Edward Ziter, a theatre professor at New York University, preempted his review of the festival by stating, "Arab theatre is highly political, addressing present events through historical analogies or fables that are open to interpretation, or by addressing social developments that are directly tied to heads of state" (617). Ziter sought out political productions and found Atrash's direction of *Wretched Dreams* to be "a smart and moving interpretation" (619). Set in 1963 after a political coup, the play focuses on two women, both oppressed by their husbands and the patriarchal culture in which they live. Ziter was impressed with Atrash's use of a simple bed, used as a metaphorical space, where the women presented "their aspirations and hopes" along with frank sexual discussions "performed with arresting seriousness" (619, 620). Explaining why political theatre is risky, Atrash states, "Theatre is about being in the same house with someone else. . . . That's the importance of theatre and that's what makes it so dangerous. It builds in the audience a collective consciousness of the same issues and ideas" (Hines). Atrash spent 2009–10 as a visiting professor at the University of North Carolina at Greensboro (UNCG), helping American students understand the political theatre of the Arab world.

According to Hamadi, other women directors working in Syria from the late twentieth and early twenty-first century include Rolla Fattal, Nora Murad, Nada Homsi, Oula Al Khatib, and Raghda Chaarani. She adds, "These new directors provided free shows, mainly dealing with feminism and social and political issues."

beginning of the second decade of the twenty-first century, there were a dozen women directors; some established a name for themselves at the end of the previous century, while others started taking their first steps.

Some of the promising young directors with one or two credits include Doaa Teyma, Yousra El Sharqawy, Heba Sami, Manar Zien, Maison Hussien, and Mram Ahmed. Though there is a surge in the numbers of women directors, they are still a minority in the field. While some of the early women actors who tried directing lacked a specific vision or a particular aesthetic, contemporary women directors have more clarity about

Interview with Dalia Basiouny

Note from the editors: This chapter's author, Dalia Basiouny, is a woman director, artistic director, playwright, and performer whose world was shaken by Egypt's Revolution in 2011. Here she reflects on her own work, highlighting her artistic responses to political events.

Describe your directorial style and aesthetics. Have they changed over the years?

The Arabic culture is highly verbal and auditory. This influenced my choices aesthetically when I started my stage work. Gradually, I moved away from focusing on the "power of the words" toward multilayered sensory and visual performances. *The Courage Just to Be,* a performance piece I presented in Cairo in 2000, required the audience members to take off their shoes and be blindfolded as they walked one at a time through a corridor of textures and smells and sounds before they were led to a room where they met the performer one to one and heard her words. My later productions rely heavily on multimedia, utilizing projections of images and film.

You have lived in both Egypt and the United States. Did the events of 9/11 influence your work?

In 2001, I moved to New York to pursue my doctorate in theatre studies at the Graduate Center of City University of New York (CUNY) and was involved in the Arab American theatre movement that galvanized in response to 9/11 and the backlash against Arabs and Muslims. I curated a number of performances, directed plays by Arab American writers, and participated in the Arab American Comedy Festival. My last U.S. production was Elmaz Abi Nader's *Country of Origin*, which was performed in Arabesque Festival at the Kennedy Center in 2009.

How has the Egyptian Revolution shaped your work as a theatre artist?

The first play I wrote, *Solitaire,* was awarded a production grant from the Arab Fund for Arts and Culture in 2010 in Amman, Jordan. I was in rehearsals for this production when the Egyptian revolution started and altered our reality. I stopped rehearsals and participated in the revolution. I started a blog about it and tried to collect some of the amazing stories of heroism I was hearing all around Tahrir Square. In February 2011, my theatre group, Sabeel, presented the first performance documenting the Egyptian revolution. We presented a ritual performance with verbatim testimonies of rebels, honoring the names of the martyrs. The first performance was in Hanager Art Center, Cairo, followed by three other performances in March 2011.

When I went back to rehearse *Solitaire* so much had changed, so the performance, as a living thing, had to change. I wrote a new section about the revolution that fit perfectly well with the theme of the Egyptian American character dealing with the aftermath of 9/11 and a growing political awareness. This multimedia performance had visuals from demonstrations in New York in addition to footage and images from demonstrations in Cairo. I felt obliged to perform it myself, as I carry the visceral memory of these unique moments that I personally experienced. The play opened in Cairo in March 2011. The response to this timely performance weaving major political events to a personal story of growth and empowerment has been overwhelming. To date we performed it in Iraq, Morocco, Zimbabwe, Germany, Abu Dhabi, and toured in the United States in 2011, 2012, and 2013.

How would you describe your role as a director?

I am feminist and I am not afraid of the label. I strongly believe in people's right to enjoy peace and justice. I think of myself as an "artivist" an artist and an activist, and my theatre work reflects both.

the trajectory of their theatre work, often working in a specific genre or with recognizable aesthetics that constitute their own mark.

Profiles of Contemporary Directors

Abeer Ali

Abeer Ali is a graduate of the School of Fine Arts in Cairo. After training for a few years as an assistant director and working as a set designer in a number of performances for the Authority of Cultural Palaces in Cairo, she established her theatre company, El Mesaharaty, which means "the waking drummer."[3] The company has produced fourteen performances since its inception in Cairo in 1989, all of them directed by Ali. Most of the plays are based on traditional stories and folk tales, which the company members adapt while Ali offers the final dramaturgical touches. The performances usually utilize storytelling modality and rely heavily on music and popular or folk songs. Ali not only adapts and directs her plays but also designs the sets and costumes and creates the visual effects of the company's performances herself. The final effect is that of folk-based performances with simple sets inspired from the environment.

The first production for El Mesaharaty was *El Shater Hasan* in 1990, written by Fouad Haddad and Metwally Abdel Latif and performed in Cairo's Manf Hall. This was followed by *Egyptian Ghosts* in 1991, a group adaptation based on Ibsen's *Ghosts* as well as stories collected from interviews. The company revisited their first folk-based performance again in 1993 and re-presented *El Shater Hasan*, a group-writing based on the original folk story, adapted by Sayeed Shoeeb.

Describing their typical way of devising a performance, theatre critic and Academy of Arts professor Nehad Selaiha writes about *No Condolences* (*Wa La ʿAzaaʾ*), a piece about rituals for death burial first performed in 2000: "Ali and her troupe drew upon several sources, including the ancient Egyptian *Book of the Dead*, collections of traditional elegies and lamentations, and studies of folk songs and literature, as well as their own personal experiences. The material was then collectively pieced together, shaped, and written in the light of an overall concept provided by Ali, who wrote the final script and also designed and directed it. Besides the many folk songs, choral lamentations, and funerary chants interwoven in the text, she also incorporated bits of relevant, contemporary poems. The result was a gently nostalgic performance text, subtly interlaced with earthy humor, despite the sad theme, and deeply engaged with contemporary Egyptian reality as viewed through the experiences of the various mourners" ("Women" 640–41).

One of the ambitious projects of El Mesaharaty was collecting stories from people around the country about pivotal moments in Egyptian history and presenting them in a number of performances fashioned after the *Arabian Nights* (*The First Night, The Second Night*, etc.). Ali received the award for best young playwright from the Egyptian National Theatre Festival in Cairo for her dramaturgy of *Viva Mama* in 2009.

Effat Yehia

Effat Yehia graduated from AUC with a major in chemistry and a minor in theatre. She established an independent theatre company named Al Qafela (The Caravan) in Cairo in 1991, for which she produced and directed more than a dozen performances about women's issues. Yehia often works on foreign translated texts that she adapts or reworks with her cast. She started with *Virginia*, based on *Who's Afraid of Virginia Woolf?* in 1992, and followed it by the group-created piece *Daily Sketches* (*Esketshaat Hayatyya*) in 1993. The following year she worked on an adaptation of Caryl Churchill's *Top Girls*, naming it *Sahrawya*. She revisited the same theme in 2010 with a play that has her credited as a playwright as well, *The Character Maker*, produced in an unusual venue, "a theatre attached to the Supreme Council for Youth and Sports" ("Character").

Yehia sees herself as an experimental director, trying different styles of work in each production. She likes the fluidity of the creative process and uses rehearsals to experiment on acting and visual styles. Unlike Abeer Ali, most of Yehia's performances do not have an authentic Egyptian feel; the staccato language and lack of flow give her performances a sense of translation. Selaiha describes Yehia's collaborative working process, writing that once she translates a text, she invites trusted theatre colleagues to share it as a group, "allowing each member to relate to it in their own way, through extensive improvisation sessions centering on its major theme. When the casting is finally decided, the actors are asked to phrase their parts in the language they would normally use in similar situations without straying from the main drift of the dialogue. . . . The end product is usually something rich and strange—at once intimately personal and neutrally universal, profoundly disconsolate and hilariously comic, even farcical" ("Don't").

Yehia's career highlight was her devised piece *Memory of Water* (*Zaherat Al Meyyah*), which she first presented at the Alexandria Library in 2004. This performance was repeated in 2007 and won Yehia the award for best young director from the National Theatre Festival in Cairo.[4] Describing the restaging of *Memory of Water* for El Ghad Theatre in 2007, Selaiha gives a sense of Yehia's aesthetic, writing that Yehia "had to rethink and slightly modify her quirky representation of the dead mother as two women . . . : one completely inert, except for the head and eyes—and pinned to, or rather crucified on an upright bed, stage-left, throughout the performance; and her ghost which wanders around freely, haunts the daughters, particularly Mary—and often goes to the window, stage-right, to gaze dreamily out at the sea. . . . For nearly 75 minutes, the former stood on a box, her whole body inert, stuck to a white wooden board, but following all that is happening with her head and eloquently communicating with her daughters, and with her ghostly double through eye language, while the latter, even when drunk, befuddled and mad, seemed to embrace everybody, the whole of human suffering, in a warm, agonized look" ("Don't").

In addition to many productions in Egypt, Yehia has directed college productions and performances abroad: *Give Me Sweets* in 1999 in the USA and *Bahyya* in 2002 in

Brazil. Her achievements continue as a director, but also as a playwright. She published a book of three original one-act plays entitled *I Have Had Enough* in 2008.

Nora Amin

Nora Amin is an active writer, dancer, director, and translator. She graduated with a master of arts in French literature from Cairo University in 1993 after undergraduate work there ("Nora"). As a student she participated in a number of amateur plays, and upon her graduation she danced in a number of performances, establishing a name for herself in the dance world. She founded the performance group La Musica in Cairo in 2000 and has produced and directed more than twenty performances. Her productions rely on foreign funding from cultural centers and international organizations.

La Musica's productions are based on translated and adapted text or improvisation and physical movement pieces that Amin writes and choreographs. The director also performs in most of her productions, often playing the main role. Some of these productions do not use any sets. She has a long list of directorial credits that starts with *The Text* (*Al Nass*) in 1999. Her 2000 performance *The Braid* (*Al Defeera*) established her name as an artist with an eye on feminist issues. This performance depicted the relationship between a mother and a daughter, and the tensions between them as the mother forces the child into conformity. Selaiha writes, "With a minimal spoken text and the imaginative uses of set, costumes, lighting, movements, and gestures, Amin presented a series of haunting images that show a mother and daughter cooped up in a tiny, derelict, dark, and windowless room, and hopelessly interlocked, as in a fatal embrace, in a love/hate relationship, with death as their only hope of release" ("Women" 642). In 2003 the British Council in Cairo commissioned Amin to create *Nine*, a devised piece about nine women. The success of this performance led to another performance in 2004, *Ten*, which was a collaboration between British and Egyptian artists. She has directed some performances overseas as well: Fat-hya El Assal's *Women Prison*, performed in the United States in 2005, and *Hecabe*, performed in Germany in 2006.

Nora's Doors (*Abwaab Nora*), her 2009 adaptation of Ibsen's *A Doll's House*, which opened at the Cairo Opera House's Gomhoryya Theatre, was controversial in the way she interpreted the original text, presenting many of her female characters as victims and making the central figure in her dance performance a male. The production earned Amin and her company an Ibsen Scholarship in 2009. Their website describes, "*Nora's Doors* reflects upon the Egyptian Noras of today. The symbolic act of slamming the door, finding an exit and finally searching for a path is the center of the theatrical search. . . . Five performers with five different motivations, aspirations and attitudes will give a performance of five different Noras. The action that triggers the performance is the slamming of the door, and the scenes will circulate around this action. The door is placed on stage, both concretely and in a philosophical and symbolic sense" ("Nora's Doors").

Laila Soliman

Born in 1981 and based in Cairo, Laila Soliman has become one of the most prolific and renowned woman directors in Egypt. Soliman studied theatre at AUC and made her debut with her senior project in 2004. She searched for a politically and socially conscious monodrama and came across Naomi Wallace's *The Retreating World*, in which a former Iraqi soldier reminisces about the First Gulf War. It was first performed at AUC's Howard Theatre in 2004, only a few months after the U.S. invasion of Iraq. The performance was well received by both audiences and critics. They had a strong emotional reaction to it, considering the exploding situation in Iraq at the time.

When asked who has influenced her work she replied, "I could say no one and everyone. Every good show has been an inspiration, and everybody I worked with has been an influence" (Soliman). Examples of influential figures include Stefan Kaegi, one of the Rimini Protokoll Collective, and Egyptian puppeteer Nagy Shaker, whom she considers her mentor.

Soliman does not have a fixed company, only collaborators who repeatedly join her projects. She frequently works with the same actors, designers, technicians, and musicians, often with Mustafa Said, an Egyptian composer and Oud player. In her independent theatre productions she plays a number of roles: director, production manager, fundraiser, public relations–publicity person, stagehand, and sometimes costume and set designer.

One highlight of Soliman's career as a director is *Spring Awakening in Egypt*, which premiered in April 2010 at Rawabet Theatre in Cairo and then toured internationally. Based on Frank Wedekind's *Spring Awakening*, Soliman highlights the parallels between the trials of a teenager in nineteenth-century European society and the contemporary youth of Egypt. She cut the adult characters and foregrounded the teenagers, conducting her own research by interviewing Egyptian teens and leading workshops with improvisation at some schools. Critic Nehad Selaiha reflected that Soliman "sensitively captured many of the subtle shades of the original text, eloquently communicating the disorienting mixture of fear, heady excitement, joy and wonder that accompanies sexual awakening, while preserving the full force of its socio-moral criticism and cautionary message . . . a haunting and profoundly moving experience, alternately funny and poignant and emotionally intelligent and honest throughout" ("Humane").

Since her first play, Soliman says she has developed as a director, especially in her attempt to combine documentary with fiction onstage, not just in the writing. Her father's paintings are a major source of inspiration aesthetically in terms of color, composition, and visuals (Soliman).

Since the start of Egypt's revolution Soliman has been keen on exposing the practices of the Military Council that overtook the leadership of the country. In 2011 she created and directed a series of documentary performances under the title *No Time for Art*, "to confront Egyptian and other audiences with the realities of living under a brutal military junta" ("No Time for Art"). First performed in the Al-Fan Midan street art festival in May 2011, the minimalist productions toured internationally in 2012. Also in 2011 Soliman premiered *Lessons in Revolting* at Cairo's Rawabet Theater. Co-created and co-directed with Belgian artist Ruud Geilens in collaboration with a group of Egyptian theatre artists, the production gave voice to individual reactions to the revolution. Soliman explained, "It is about . . . using your experience to create something, to react, and to act" (Stuhr-Rommereim). Reviewer Helen Stuhr-Rommereim wrote that the emotional impact on the audience was "undeniable," in particular the final dance sequence through the audience, with performers marching, beating their chests, and clanging metal rods. The production toured Europe "to create an alternative narrative" to the media's portrayal of Egypt (Stuhr-Rommereim).

Like most of the directors of her generation, Soliman has had to overcome many hurdles, including limited rehearsal and performance space, minimal funding, and restricted time with the actors, as most of them can work only part time on such projects. But she believes that the problems she confronts while walking in the streets of Cairo as a woman make her challenges as a woman director insignificant and minor in comparison.

Soliman does not describe her work as feminist, though others definitely do. She works on the issues she feels passionate about. "If, as a woman, I feel an urge to talk about women's issues among other issues," she says, "then feminist it may be, but I think this labeling weakens the position a woman is starting from and not the opposite" (Soliman).

Egyptian women directors in the twenty-first century deal with many challenges in order to produce stage plays. They face limited funding, lack of rehearsal and performance spaces, uncommitted actors, and logistical problems with the same courage they tap into to face the challenges of negotiating daily life in a troubled country attempting to continue its revolution.

Notes

1. Published with additional text by Anne Fliotsos.

2. Badran states that 1909 was a landmark in Egyptian feminism because of the number of firsts in education and healthcare for women.

3. El Mesaharaty is a traditional figure that roamed villages and towns during Ramadan to wake people up in order that they could eat their meal before sunrise and the beginning of next day's fast. This name choice indicated the company's focus on folk culture and reviving traditions.

4. Additional directorial credits include *Carnival of Sketches* in 1995, *Moving Sand* in 1996, *The Swing* in 2000, *Stories from Memory* in 2001, *Fatima's Diaries* in 2002, *Coffee* in 2003, *Once Upon a Time* in 2003, and *Embroidery* in 2008.

Sources

Abdel Fattah, Hadia. "The Role of Women in Developing Theatre Directing in Egypt: A Semiotic Study of [the] Egyptian Woman Director from 1990 to the Present" ["Door Al Mar'a Fi Tatweer Harakat El Ekhrag Al Masrahy Fi Masr"]. Master's thesis. Higher Institute of Criticism, Academy of Arts, 2009.

Al Madina Theatre, n.d. Available at http://www.almadinatheatre.com (accessed February 6, 2012).

Amin, Dina. "Women in Arab Theatre: Finding a Voice." *World Encyclopedia of Contemporary Theatre*. Vol. 4. Edited by Don Rubin. London: Routledge, 1999.

Badran, Margot. "Egyptian Feminism in a Nationalist Century." *Al-Ahram Weekly*, December 30, 1999–January 5, 2000.

"The Character Maker by Effat Yehia." *Notes from Over There. . . .*October 31, 2010. Available at http://www.notesfromoverthere.blogspot.com (accessed February 12, 2012).

Hamadi, Watfa. Unpublished manuscript. Translated by Eric Felix. January 13, 2011.

Hines, Michelle. "Being in the Same House: Professor Bridges Cultures with Drama." University of North Carolina at Greensboro, March 5, 2010. Available at https://ure .uncg.edu (accessed October 25, 2011).

Ismael, Sayed Ali. *The Path of the Egyptian Theatre 1900–1935: The Musical Companies, Part 1* [*Maserat Al Masrah Al Masry 1900–1935: Feraq Al Masrah Al Ghena'y*]. Cairo: General Egyptian Authority for Books, 2003.

"Latife Moultaka." *Who's Who Amongst Arab Women*, n.d. Available at http://www .whoswhoarabwomen.com (accessed October 19, 2011).

"Maya Zbib." *Rolex Mentor & Protégé Arts Initiative*, October 2010. Available at http://www .rolexmentorprotege.com (accessed October 25, 2011).

"Nora Amin." *Arab World Books*, n.d. Available at http://www.arabworldbooks.com (accessed March 1, 2012).

"Nora's Doors." *Ibsen Awards*, 2009. Available at http://www.ibsenawards.com (accessed February 12, 2012).

"No Time for Art." *notimeforart.com*, n.d. Available at http://notimeforart.com (accessed January 11, 2013).

"People; Maya Zbib." *British Council / Creative and Cultural Economy*. 2009. Available at http://creativeconomy.britishcouncil.org (accessed October 25, 2011).

"Sawsan Darwaza." *IMS / International Media Support*, n.d. Available at http://www.i-m-s .dk (accessed October 21, 2011).

Selaiha, Nehad. "Don't Call Me Mother." *Al-Ahram Weekly Online*, January 25–31, 2007. Available at http://weekly.ahram.org.eg (accessed February 12, 2011).

———. "Humane Trafficking." *Al-Ahram Weekly Online*, May 20–26, 2010. Available at http://weekly.ahram.org.eg (accessed February 12, 2011).

Selaiha, Nehad, with Sarah Enany. "Women Playwrights in Egypt." *Theatre Journal* 62 (2010): 627–43.

Soliman, Laila. E-mail interview with the author. September 2010.

Stuhr-Rommereim, Helen. "'Lessons in Revolting': The Revolution Continues." *Egypt Independent*, August 20, 2011.

Ziter, Edward. "Damascus Theatre Festival." *Theatre Journal* 61 (2009): 617–20.

 France

Kate Bredeson[1]

There is no correct way to refer to a woman who practices stage directing in France. All French nouns are gendered, and the term for director (*le metteur en scène*) is masculine. Some women stage directors go by *metteur en scène femme* or *femme metteur en scène* (basically, "director woman" or "woman director"); others call themselves *metteuse en scène* or *metteure en scène*, adding a feminine ending to the masculine term. As Marie-Josée Brakha points out, this terminology is unsettling. Using only the masculine form of the word, she argues, "[I]t allows us once again to deny women their place in history: . . . it tells you that only men practice these noble trades rightfully, that women have never become prominent in them and have never achieved anything noteworthy in these domains. And it seems bizarre to call oneself 'woman director.' . . . You don't say 'man-writer'" (Brakha 9).

There is a general sense of unease and a relative lack of information about the state of French women stage directors. Many theatre scholars and practitioners can only name one or possibly two French women who direct for the stage. Yet many women directors have succeeded in France. The story of French women theatre directors shows how women have worked with and against the grammar that confines them, made space for themselves on and off stages throughout centuries, and redefined collaboration in the artistic process.

Women's Rights: Historical Context

French history is marked by significant moments of feminist activity, as well as several sustained waves of feminism. In 1791 playwright Olympe de Gouges published the *Declaration of the Rights of Women and the Female Citizen*, a revision of the French Revolution document the *Declaration of the Rights of Man*, in which she substituted "woman" for "man" in every instance of the word's occurrence. During the 1848 revolution, feminists founded a newspaper, advocating equal rights for men and women in the new republic, and an active women's union organized during the Paris Commune in 1871. In 1903 Jeanne Schmahl founded the French Union for Women's Suffrage, and women replaced men at work in both world wars. French women gained the right to vote in April 1944. In 1949 Simone de Beauvoir published *The Second Sex*, a landmark interdisciplinary meditation on the role of women in society; in this and her other works de Beauvoir calls into question women's agency, duties, and sense of being "other" in society.

The events of May 1968—a time of massive rupture in the political and cultural sphere, marked by enormous protests, strikes, and the occupations of factories, universities, and the Odéon National Theatre—were a rallying point for the feminist movement, known as the MLF, the Movement for the Liberation of Women (Mouvement de libération des femmes). Feminists at this time rallied largely around issues of gender equity in the workplace and rights to abortion and birth control. In April 1971 the "Manifesto of the 343" was published, signed by de Beauvoir, writer Marguerite Duras, and other women who admitted to having had abortions. The law prohibiting abortion was repealed three years later, and in 1974 the French League for the Rights of Women was founded. Writers including Hélène Cixous, Monique Wittig, and Julie Kristeva published significant works that often engaged in the psychoanalytic turn associated with French feminism of this time.

Since 2000, a primary concern of French feminists has been the question of "otherness," not only about gender but also about class, race, and immigrant rights. This speaks to the changing demographics of France and the continued marginalization of large parts of the French population. In the wake of decolonization, France has seen increasing numbers of first-generation French born of immigrants from formerly colonized countries in North Africa, as well as large numbers of undocumented immigrants. Feminist organizations were founded to combat continued violence against women in immigrant-heavy areas outside of major cities. The first decade of the twenty-first century was also significant for women in politics: in 2007 Ségolène Royal became the first woman to be nominated by a major party for the presidential candidacy; she ran and lost against Nicholas Sarkozy.

Early Women Directors

Women have long made significant and vital contributions to theatre in France. They appeared as performers in medieval mystery plays and some—like Madeleine and Armande Béjart—had significant roles in early companies and commedia troupes. Women operated theatres during the French Revolution; eighteenth-century Marguerite "La Montansier" Brunet is one of the earliest known French women who directed in the modern sense.

The great stage figures of the French nineteenth and early twentieth century—Sarah Bernhardt, Gabrielle Réjane, Céleste Mogador, Alice Cocéa, and others—also functioned often as both star performers and directors of their own work, and they sometimes ran their own theatres. These women were at the forefront of the scene in what remained a male-dominated field.

Yet very few women worked exclusively as directors or playwrights. This was due to two main obstacles: the continuing perception of theatre women as being affiliated with something licentious and immoral; and the fact that men owned most of the theatres, only men were granted theatre licenses, and men continued to govern most of the decision making. Culturally, too, it was not accepted for women to be in positions of strength and authority. The very idea of a strong woman—an inherent part of being a director—was suspect.

A significant event for women in French theatre occurred in June 1897, shortly after the 1896 International Feminist Congress, when Marya Chéliga created Le Théâtre Feministe, an organization to produce work by women. Soon thereafter, women emerged as part of the avant-garde theatre movements of the early twentieth century. Nelly Roussel and Vera Starkoff were two influential women directors of the early twentieth century, known as performers and directors of militant plays. But they, like many women artists of this time, were affiliated primarily with experimental or fringe endeavors.

A leap forward for women in theatre occurred in 1959 when Ariane Mnouchkine founded the ATEP—the Theatrical Association of Parisian Students (L'Association théâtrale des étudiants parisiens)—which became the Théâtre du Soleil in 1964. Mnouchkine remains the first and often only director mentioned in discussions about women directors in contemporary France.

Between 1968 and the end of the twentieth century, women directors in France emerged with force and prominence in the theatre world. From performance artists who wrote and directed their own work, like Orlan, to playwright/directors like Catherine Anne, to master directors like Mnouchkine, Julie Brochen, and Sophia Loucachevsky, women directors occupied many stages leading up to the year 2000. Yet the scene remained dominated by men. According to scholars Sabine Cornille, Paulette Soubeyrand, and Monique Surel-Tupin, by 1995 only three women had reached the position of head of a National Dramatic Center (Centre Dramatique National) (Ivernel 41).[2] Further, they note that in 1993–94 only one out of seven stage directors was a woman (41).

Working Climate in the Twenty-First Century

Since 2000 there remain fewer professional women directors than men, though women hold significant positions in many French theatres of all sizes and continue to direct in every kind of theatre in France—from intimate experimental venues to big-budget Parisian commercial houses.

Training programs in France continue to train both women and men directors. Since 2001 the prestigious École du Théâtre National de Strasbourg (TNS) has had as many women as men in the directing program (Benhamou 4). In terms of artistic directorships, women hold several key positions, including Muriel Mayette as the general administrator of the Comédie Française, the first woman to occupy this position in more than three hundred years of the prestigious institution's existence. A 2012 study, "Where are the Women?" by the Society of Dramatic Authors and Composers (SACD), notes of the 2012–13 announced season: in France's five National Theatres, of the 104 productions, 12 are directed by women. In the National Dramatic Centres, of the 459 productions, 73 are directed by women. Overall, they report, women direct only 25 percent of France's plays. The authors of the study write of these statistics: "it is urgent to act" (SACD).

Despite women's increasing presence in the field of stage directing, there remains a significant lack of writing in French or English about women directors in France and a general attitude that the profession remains a difficult one for women. In a 2005 issue of the theatre journal *Beyond the Stage* (*Outre Scène*) devoted to directing, only two of the seventeen directors represented were women. Two years later the same publication produced an issue called "Women Directors: The Theatre, Does It Have a Gender?" The journal editors noted that there exists a tremendous hole in scholarship on the subject, reporting that "almost no recent book or journal volume has been dedicated to women in theatre" since 1995 (Benhamou 5). As another example, David Bradby's *Modern French Drama 1940–1980* discusses in detail not one woman director besides Mnouchkine.

Profiles of Contemporary Directors

Ariane Mnouchkine

Ariane Mnouchkine is not only one of France's most famous theatre directors, but she is also internationally acclaimed, studied, and debated. The Théâtre du Soleil is located in the woods of Vincennes on the eastern side of Paris, in a complex called La Cartoucherie—a walled enclave that originally housed a munitions factory and is now home to multiple theatres. Since 1959, when she was twenty, Mnouchkine has spearheaded the troupe, filling the paradoxical role of the director of a collective. She has changed French theatre, challenged the notion of the collective, and created a stunning legacy of decadently theatrical, defiant performances that are enormous in scope, scale, and ambition.

The daughter of filmmaker Alexandre Mnouchkine, Ariane Mnouchkine's exposure to her father's work, as well as his support of her later endeavors, significantly influenced her path as an artist. As a student, she studied at the Sorbonne from 1959 to 1962 and for a year at Oxford in 1957. In 1959 she asked the director of the Sorbonne classical theatre group if she could join. She recalls: "And Jean-Pierre Miquel, who directed the company, said to me: 'Yes, of course, we need girls, but with us girls don't act, don't direct, they also don't assistant direct, they don't do sound, they don't do lights, they sew. . . . ' The response was immediate! I said: 'Bye!' I went downstairs to the concierge and asked for a room, and I created the ATEP that then became the Soleil. That wasn't even negotiable, there was nothing to discuss; it seemed to me entirely ridiculous, entirely old-fashioned. I thought we'd passed that, that it was something out of the nineteenth century" (Benhamou 12).

Other early influences on Mnouchkine include her training with the actor and physical theatre specialist Jacques LeCoq, her travels to Asia in the early 1960s, and the worker and student strikes and occupations of May 1968. During this turbulent time in French culture and politics, Mnouchkine emerged as a director alongside French feminists like Hélène Cixous—with whom she would develop a career-long collaboration—and Simone Benmussa.

Mnouchkine's work is known and celebrated for many reasons, from the logistical to the aesthetic. The Soleil has long functioned as a collective, where everyone

Simone Benmussa

Since her death in 2001, Simone Benmussa has remained influential as a groundbreaking playwright and director. Born in Tunisia in 1931, Benmussa studied philosophy at the Sorbonne before joining the Compagnie Renaud-Barrault in Paris and becoming the editor-in-chief of the journal *Cahiers Renaud-Barrault*; she worked with actor-director Jean-Louis Barrault at the Odéon in Paris, and also at Gallimard Press. She was a preeminent theatre artist, editor, and feminist during the time when women emerged as theatre professionals in France. In her directing and writing, she committed herself to a career of telling and staging the lives of the marginalized.

Benmussa is best known for her adaptations and productions of the works of others, including Virginia Woolf, Nathalie Sarraute, and Edith Wharton. Her most celebrated project remains her 1977 play *The Singular Life of Albert Nobbs*, an adaptation of the story by George Moore about a woman who dresses and lives as a man in order to work as a butler in nineteenth-century Ireland. Benmussa directed multiple productions of *Nobbs*, including premieres at Paris's Petit Orsay in 1977, London's New End in 1978, and New York City's Manhattan Theatre Club in 1982. She also directed Hélène Cixous's *Portrait of Dora*—a dramatization of Freud's first case study, but with Freud and Dora's relationship voiced and staged through Dora's perspective—at the Petit Orsay, which toured to Geneva, Lyon, Vienna, and Zurich. Both *Nobbs* and *Dora* were significant not only in terms of embodying stories about living as an "other," but also in terms of Benmussa's innovations as a director who sought to create total theatre experiences. Both plays feature elaborate dreamscape stage directions and thorough production notes that precede the published scripts to help embody her total theatre vision.

Benmussa continued to write and direct until 2000 and died in Paris the following year.

earns the same salary and shares duties. On any given day at a Soleil performance, a lead performer might serve salad to a spectator during one of the intermissions, and Mnouchkine herself tears tickets. The group trains together, develops roles together, and shares research and technical work. Their process, too, defies convention. Unlike many directors, Mnouchkine does not lead the company through traditional table work. Scholar Judith Graves Miller explains, "From the beginning, Mnouchkine and the actors are in a mode of discovery and creation, rather than interpretation or repetition. The set is not built, other than the empty 14x14 square meter platform on which the actors rehearse; and scenes are not worked in any special order. Mnouchkine tells the story of what they will attempt to create" (49–50). This unusually long rehearsal process is one of improvisation, of trying and playing, and only then do choices begin to be fixed. "There will usually be two or three months of rehearsals before a consensus is reached that they feel is right. Then the designers go ahead and execute the performance costumes, the set pieces, and the final music. Casting is also done at this point" (50). When developing a new performance, the actors sometimes switch roles multiple times during the rehearsal process until they are cast in their prescribed roles for the production. Those not cast work on food preparation, in administration, or in artistic and technical realms (50).

Each production is an enormous undertaking, and the Soleil only produces a new one every few years. In between, they travel, research, improvise, develop character and company training, and attend to business. Each new work typically performs in Paris and then tours internationally. The actual performances are also quite long: up to eight hours in length, with multiple intermissions.

To go to the Soleil is a total theatre experience involving a bus ride into the Vincennes woods, a shuttle to the Cartoucherie, and a walk through the other theatres. Upon arrival at the Soleil, tickets are collected en route to their theatre lobby/restaurant/gallery. For each performance, the Soleil alters the space to suit the theme of the production. For Cixous's *The Last Caravanserai (Odysseys)* (*Le dernier caravanserail* [*Odyssées*]) in 2003, the walls were painted ochre, with maps of immigration routes from the Middle East to North Africa to Europe sketched out on them. Company members cooked and served Middle Eastern food before and after the performance, as well as during intermissions.

While every production by the Soleil is different, common elements include a defiant and sumptuous theatricality, as well as a commitment to long-term collaboration and ensemble work. The world of the Soleil is one of bold color and gesture, trademark lyrical soundscapes concocted by Jean-Jacques LeMêtre, puppetry, marionettes, and bold visible mechanisms of theatricality. En route to the seating area at the beginning of the spectacle, the performers are visible, applying makeup and costumes in a purposefully exposed dressing area.

Mnouchkine specializes in international subject matter and theatrical practice, as well as political themes and discussions. For example, works by Cixous focused on a conspiracy to flood a town of peasants in ancient China in *The Flood Drummers* (*Tambours sur la*

The audience eats a meal served by the company of the Théâtre du Soleil during a break in *The Survivors of the Mad Hope*, Paris, 2010. Photographer: Kate Bredeson.

The company of the Théâtre du Soleil's *The Survivors of the Mad Hope* at curtain call with director Mnouchkine (center). Paris, 2010. Photographer: Kate Bredeson.

digue) in 1999, quiet moments of personal reflection on memory and family in *Ephemera* (*Les Ephémères*) in 2006, and the staging of a silent film production on the eve of World War I in *The Survivors of the Mad Hope* (*Les Naufragés du fol espoir*) in 2010.

As a director, Mnouchkine has been a trailblazer in terms of her aesthetic, working methods, and global preoccupations. She won an honorary doctor of letters degree from the University of Oxford in 2008. She has been equally significant and influential to other women directors in France, a "pioneer in the domain" (Féral 11). Miller writes: "Given the exceptionally male-dominated milieu of French theater, the story of her success is all the more compelling" (2). Mnouchkine responds: "It took me a long time to realize that I belonged to . . . a race [laughs] . . . how can I say this? . . . to an oppressed community. Probably because I myself was very lucky. . . . [I]t took me a long time to accept that being a woman could be a problem" (Benhamou 8–9).

Brigitte Jaques-Wajeman

Born in Switzerland in 1946, Brigitte Jaques-Wajeman's directorial debut in 1974 was considered audacious by many of her senior colleagues and fellow artists. After collaborating with François Regnault on a new translation of *Spring Awakening*, Frank Wedekind's opus of youthful rebellion, she directed the French premiere of the integral version of this play as her first professional directing endeavor—part of the Festival d'Automne à Paris. Jaques-Wajeman's directing career has been marked by tremendous ambition, bold choices, and reverence for the classics.

Jaques-Wajeman, who initially went professionally by the name Brigitte Jaques, is one of several French women directors who were educated by influential director Antoine Vitez at the National Conservatory of Dramatic Arts (Conservatoire National Supérieur d'Art Dramatique) in Paris;[3] she studied with him from 1969 to 1974. At the conservatory, Vitez quickly became known for educating and encouraging young women artists in a style marked by "his total absence of misogyny" (Cornille, Soubeyrand, Surel-Tupin 42). Of her career, Jaques-Wajeman writes, "Vitez's art was my main influence" (Jaques-Wajeman).

Like Vitez, Jaques-Wajeman has worked in a variety of significant French theatres, founded her own company, and throughout has devoted herself to educating theatre students. In 1976 she founded La Compagnie Pandora with playwright and philosopher François Regnault. From 1980 to 1987 she was a professor at ENSATT, the National School of the Arts and Techniques of Theatre (Ecole Nationale Supérieure des Arts et Techniques de Théâtre) in Lyon, and from 1991 to 1997 she continued her collaboration with Regnault as co-director of the Théâtre de la Commune d'Aubervilliers. Throughout she has continued her professional career as a director, and in 2006 she began teaching at the Ecole Normale Supérieure in Paris.

She is best known for directing the French premiere of Tony Kushner's *Angels in America*, translated by Gérard Wajeman, in 1994 at the Festival d'Avignon, as well as for her career-long devotion to French neoclassical playwright Pierre Corneille. She has directed more than a dozen productions by or about Corneille, who is sometimes criticized for his female characters. Through deep work on his plays, and crafting new plays about him, Jaques-Wajeman has strived to make his characters contemporary, tap into their desires, and transform "the view of his female characters, notably the queens in his later plays" (Benhamou 27). She writes that her preferences for directing are for "Good plays, old or new! I love staging Corneille, Racine, and Molière, as much as Tennessee Williams and Tony Kushner" (Jaques-Wajeman). Other directing projects include the nationally and internationally toured *Elvire Jouvet 40* at the Théâtre National de Strasbourg, which she wrote and for which she won the 1989 Arletty Prize; *The Night of the Iguana* by Williams at the Comédie Française in 1991; *The Good Person of Szechuan* by Bertolt Brecht at ENSATT in 2001; and two plays by Corneille, *Suréna* and *Nicomède*, staged with one acting company at the Théâtre de la Ville in Paris in 2011.

As a director, the fact of her gender was not one she initially considered: Cornille, Soubeyrand, and Surel-Tupin write, "The question of femininity posed itself later, inside her work, as she moved forward, 'unmasked by her work'" (44). When asked if being directed by a woman creates something different for performers, she answers, "Without a doubt. . . . some were very shocked to have to deal with a woman. When you're a director, you become a bit of a father or mother figure: the relationship of the actors to the director is one of transference" (Benhamou 31). She describes her directing style as "very close to the actors, very attentive to the choreography of the body and to the music of the voices, a very bare stage, great attention to the lighting" (Jaques-Wajeman). Ultimately, the world of Jaques-Wajeman as a director is one of great texts and close collaboration.

Catherine Anne

Catherine Anne is another student of Vitez's who has gone on to a distinguished directing career. Born in 1960 in St. Etienne, she is an alumnus of the acting programs of ENSATT, which she attended from 1978 to 1981, and the National Conservatory, where she studied from 1981 to 1984. Since 1987, when she founded her own company in Paris, A Brûle-pourpoint—which roughly translates to "out of the blue," but originally meant "point blank"—Anne has directed more than twenty-five plays that she has written, including multiple dramatic works for young people. Throughout her career, she has worked extensively as an actor, writer, and director.

Like Mnouchkine, many regard Anne as a pioneer of women stage directors in France; in 2002, she became one of the first women to direct a prominent public theatre when she took over l'Est Parisien. She is also known for directing work for young audiences and by new playwrights. Anne's directorial process is one of experimentation and exploration of words and production elements; she writes that, for her, "directing is a path of discoveries and meetings. I don't know at all when the work starts what will be the final form of the production. I don't set moments in space or acting intentions until late. It's the blocking that I set very last." She elaborates: "I realized that what I love in the theatre is the rapport between the body and the words. . . . I love spaces that are very empty or clean. I love a form of discretion in the direction. I love when light is a sensible and sensual element. I love playing with silence. As a director, I strive to work with actors on the incarnation of their characters. I don't have preconceived ideas about the way the characters should be played. I propose all sorts of games and improvisations to search for that with the actors. I don't hesitate to go far away from the text and the written situations" (Anne).

Her own work as a writer and director has been devoted to breaking boundaries. Her writing has focused on transgression and on using the stage to tell women's stories. In Anne's *Agnès*, which she directed in 1994 at the Théâtre Gérard Philipe in St. Denis, she explored themes of incest between a father and daughter and staged the title character at three different key ages in her life—sometimes portraying all three onstage at once. In *The Happiness of Wind* (*Le Bonheur du vent*) in 2003 at l'Est Parisien, Anne wrote and directed a protagonist inspired by Calamity Jane, who wants to escape the condition of being a woman.

Anne has staged her work not only for traditional theatre audiences but also for nontraditional ones, including social workers and youth. By targeting nontraditional audiences and exploring taboo themes, she embodies her mission of exploring the human condition and giving voice to the voiceless. Theatre scholar Monique Surel-Tupin writes, "For her, the theatre is first of all a space of human sharing, a space where the most intimate things can be said out loud, where one can share stories, sensations, emotions, and thoughts on subjects buried deep inside of us" (72). Of her preoccupations and style, Anne says to interviewer Nathalie Trotta: "I feel like an activist, I do have a willful attitude, but not in my art. . . . What is complicated is to assert one's identity while refusing to be categorized by one's gender" (Ivernel 43).

Since leaving the Théâtre de l'Est Parisien in 2010, Anne has directed multiple productions around France, and in 2012–13 she directed a project titled *Agnès Yesterday and Today: Stage Diptique* (*Agnès hier et aujourd'hui: diptyque en scène*) that featured both her *Agnès* and Molière's *The School for Wives*. Both plays were presented in their entireties, but on one set with one acting company composed entirely of women. In this project, she spoke of her desire to play with the male/female dynamic, the construction of gender roles, power and seduction, the mixture of comedy and tragedy, as well as the mélange of the modern and the classical. Of this period in her career, Anne wrote: "I'm like someone who is coming out of . . . a very intense work in a rather closed off space. I'm adapting with a mix of joys and fears to a completely different situation. After having worked with an important company, after having programmed hundreds of artists, I am in a space of great lightness and artistic freedom" (Anne).

Irina Brook

Irina Brook is one of France's most successful and recognized theatre directors. Her work is marked by a great reverence for the classics, a dedication to international production and touring, and large-scale spectacle. Born in France in 1962, Brook grew up shuttling between France and England, always immersed in theatre. Her mother, Natasha Parry, is a performer, while her father is acclaimed stage director Peter Brook, who settled his company at the Théâtre des Bouffes du Nord in Paris in 1974. Irina Brook went to New York to study acting with Stella Adler when she was eighteen. After landing several roles in off-Broadway productions, she returned to Paris to play in Chekhov's *The Cherry Orchard*, directed by her father, and went on to a multinational career first as a performer and then as a director. Of the transition from acting to directing, she says: "This transition didn't happen in a thought-out way, but came about in a more organic fashion, without me really having a choice. The more I worked as an actress, the less that role satisfied me, and curiously, the more I got better at acting, the less interested I was in my work. Over the course of several years, I had more and more ideas about how such-and-such a play should be produced, about the directing and the design, and I realized that these ideas didn't necessarily have anything to do with my profession as an actress" (Féral 93). Since turning to directing, Brook has enjoyed widespread success, become one of the best-known directors in Europe, and traveled and worked not only in France and England, but also in Italy, Japan, Russia, Switzerland, and the United States.

In her work, Brook emphasizes a collective, joyous rehearsal process and one of collaborative experience: "For me, the reason to be in the theatre isn't just artistic. It's a life choice, a manner of living collectively, of trying—in the microcosm of theatre—to create a better world. That doesn't mean that the work and the creative research lose importance, but it's the human, and even a sort of utopian dream that guides me above all else" (Féral 96). She does not ask her actors to arrive at rehearsal with their parts memorized, nor does she favor a psychological approach to acting. She classifies some of her work as "excessive" and "theatrical, like the work I did on Brecht's *The Good Person of Szechwan*." (Féral 98). Her work is marked by physicality and spectacle.

Brook's love of creating a better world drives her theatre, as does a great passion for plays as texts. Throughout her career, Brook has often chosen to direct well-known plays, touring productions, and operas, and she often works internationally. Her production of Williams's *The Glass Menagerie* played at the Théâtre de l'Atelier in 2001 and subsequently toured to Japan. She directed *Romeo and Juliet* in 2002 and *The Good Person of Szechuan* in 2003 at the Théâtre de Chaillot in Paris. She has won consistent acclaim for her work, including winning five Molières (French theatre awards)—best director among them—in 2001 for her production of Richard Kalinoski's *Beast on the Moon* (*Une Bête sur la lune*) at the Théâtre de l'Oeuvre in Paris. Following this success, Mnouchkine invited her to the Cartoucherie, where she directed Shakespeare's *All's Well*

That Ends Well, which she then toured to the Avignon Festival. In 2003 she founded her own troupe, the Company (Compagnie) Irina Brook, one year after she was awarded the title of Knight of Arts and Letters by the French government. From 2008 to 2009 she worked a residency at Shakespeare and Company in Lenox, Massachusetts, where she directed her original adaptation of Oscar Wilde's *The Canterville Ghost*. In addition, she has directed opera in France, Italy, and Spain.

Thirty-five years after her father's groundbreaking 1970 production of *A Midsummer Night's Dream*, Irina Brook directed her own innovative adaptation and production of Shakespeare's play. According to one source, "She saw it [Peter Brook's 1970 production] over fifty times and could recite most of the play by heart" (Broadway World). In her adaptation, *Waiting for the Dream* (*En Attendant le songe*), Brook staged *Midsummer* with only six male performers and minimal props, costumes, and set pieces. In an interview, Brook declared, "I had a dream! I dreamt that with six actors (all men like in Shakespeare's day) it was possible to do a joyful, pared down *Midsummer Night's Dream*, which could be accessible to everyone. We created this *Dream* to be performed for only half a dozen special one-off performances in the roughest suburbs of Paris, in the cobbled courtyard of a medieval farm in the deepest countryside, on the grounds of a town hall, in an abandoned campsite, in the middle of a forest. . . . And in each different spot something magical occurred—thanks to the enduring magic of Shakespeare's extraordinary and timeless text" (Broadway World); it toured around the world, including to La MaMa in New York City in 2010, and was reprised in 2011 at the Théâtre de Paris.

Brook's invitation to work at the Cartoucherie as a director represents a homecoming. She remembers going to the Cartoucherie as a child to see the Théâtre du Soleil's *The Golden Age* (*L'Age d'Or*). She counts Mnouchkine as one of her mentors from an early age. Like Mnouchkine, Brook expresses a degree of ambiguity about being a woman and being a director: "As a director, I right away felt androgynous" (Féral 103). When asked what advice she would give to a woman considering going into directing, Brook writes: "I don't think that it would be any different than that which I'd give to a man. The only advice I could give concerns the way in which I started to work as a director, and the reason for why I continued: it's simply about doing things that you feel passionately about. Then everything is possible" (Féral 107).

"Everything is possible" is indeed a quality that Mnouchkine, Benmussa, Jaques-Wajeman, Anne, and Brook share. None of these artists set out to be a "woman director," and yet, while French grammar does not accommodate them, they occupy tremendous space in French theatre. On stage they craft worlds for voices popular and marginalized—from immigrants to children to women to ancient and contemporary refugees. They retell well-known stories, but with different players and configurations. Bucking the male director-centered theatre trend of most of the twentieth century, they work collaboratively and sometimes collectively. They are artistic and intellectual visionaries. In this way they are the inheritors of the May 1968 shift that posited the great utopian slogan: "underneath the paving stones, the beach" ("sous les pavés la plage"). As directors and as women, they embody alternative worlds on stage that reflect and refute the world in which they live, and point to how life in France and beyond could be.

Notes

1. Unless otherwise noted, all French-English quotations in the chapter have been translated by the author, with special thanks to Joelle Rameau.
2. Brigitte Jaques (Théâtre de la Commune d'Aubervilliers), Arlette Téphany (Théâtre de Limoges), and Agathe Alexis (Théâtre de Béthune).
3. Others include Anne Delbée, Catherine Anne, Ewa Lewinson, Bérangère Bonvoisin, Sophie Loucachevsky, and Claudia Stavisky.

Sources

Anne, Catherine. E-mail interview. Translated by Kate Bredeson. January 10, 2012.

Benhamou, Anne-Françoise, ed. *Beyond the Stage, the Review of the National Theatre of Strasbourg* 9: "[Women] Directors: Does the Theatre Have a Gender?" [*Outre Scène, la revue du Théâtre National de Strasbourg* 9: "Metteuses en scène: le théâtre a-t-il un genre?"]. Théâtre National de Strasbourg, Strasbourg, France. May 9, 2007.

Benmussa, Simone. *Benmussa Directs: "Portrait of Dora" by Hélène Cixous, and "The Singular Life of Albert Nobbs" by Simone Benmussa.* London: Calder, 1979.

Bradby, David. *Modern French Drama: 1940–1980.* Cambridge: Cambridge University Press, 1984.

Brahka, Marie-Josée. "The Work of Women in France Today." ("La Création des femmes au théâtre en France de nos jours"). Master's thesis (Maîtrise de l'U.E.R.), Sorbonne Nouvelle Paris III, 1985.

Broadway World News Desk. "Irina Brook's Production of Midsummer Heads to LaMaMa ETC 11/3–7." *broadwayworld.com,* September 29, 2010. Available at http://www.broadwayworld .com (accessed August 27, 2011).

Célestin, Roger, Eliane DalMolin, and Isabelle de Courtivron, eds. *Beyond French Feminisms: Debates on Women, Politics, and Culture in France, 1981–2001.* New York: Palgrave, 2003.

Cornille, Sabine, Pauelette Soubeyrand, and Monique Surel-Tupin. "Woman Director: An Image to Create, a Role to Invent." *Theatre Women: For a Stage without Boundaries. Theatre Studies* 8 ["Metteuse en scène: une image à créer, un role à inventer." *Femmes de théâtre: Pour une scène sans frontiers. Études théâtrales* 8]. Edited by Philippe Ivernel, 41–61. Louvain-la-Neuve, Belgium: Centre d'études théâtrales, Université catholique de Louvain, 1995.

De Beauvoir, Simone. *The Second Sex.* Translated by H. M. Parshley. New York: Vintage, 1952.

Féral, Josette. *Directing and Acting: Interviews; Vol. 3, Women's Voices* [*Mise en scène et jeu de l'acteur: Entretiens; Tome III: Voix des femmes*]. Montreal: Québec Amérique, 2007.

Ivernel, Philippe, ed. *Theatre Women: For a Stage without Boundaries. Theatre Studies* 8 [*Femmes de théâtre: Pour une scène sans frontiers. Études théâtrale* 8]. Louvain-la-Neuve, Belgium: Centre d'études théâtrales, Université catholique de Louvain, 1995.

Jaques-Wajeman, Brigitte. E-mail interview. Translated by Kate Bredeson. December 20, 2011.

Miller, Judith Graves. *Ariane Mnouchkine.* Routledge Performance Practitioners Series. London and New York: Routledge, 2007.

Shakespeare & Company [blog]. "Ten Questions with Irina Brook." *Shakespeare & Company,* July 10, 2008. Available at http://www.shakespeare.org (accessed August 27, 2011).

Society of Dramatic Authors and Composers (SACD). "Theatre, Music, Dance: Where Are the Women?" ["Théâtre, musique, dance: Où sont les femmes?"]. Pamphlet. Paris: SACD, June 2012.

Surel-Tupin, Monique. "Uncensored and Uninhibited: Women's Worlds of Imagination." *Theatre Women: For a Stage without Boundaries. Theatre Studies* 8 ["Au-delà des censures et des interdits: L'imaginaire des femmes." *Femmes de théâtre: Pour une scène sans frontiers. Études théâtrales* 8]. Edited by Philippe Ivernel, 62–97. Louvain-la-Neuve, Belgium: Centre d'études théâtrales, Université catholique de Louvain, 1995.

 Germany

Ursula Neuerburg-Denzer

The history of women in German theatre is necessarily linked to the developments in arts and politics as well as the shifting nature of what has been perceived as Germany or Deutschland over the course of the last millennium. Within this unstable cultural and political conglomeration, the first two women to make names for themselves were Hrosvitha von Gandersheim (ca. 935–ca. 1002) and Hildegard von Bingen (ca. 1098–1179), recognized as the earliest women playwrights in Central Europe. Among professional practitioners, Friederike Caroline Neuber (1697–1760) takes a prominent position as impresario of her own troupe and radical reformer of theatrical practice at the time. We know little about professional women in the theatre during the later eighteenth and the nineteenth century when the role of the director became more defined. However, particularly since World War II the prominence of women directors has steadily risen, and at the start of the twenty-first century, many women worked professionally and increasingly took high-ranking positions as artistic directors of the large regional, city, and federal theatres.

Women's Rights: Historical Context

The role of women directors as well as the evolution of the women's movement itself is strongly linked to the political forces that shaped the changing German state. While women began to ask publicly for access to education during the eighteenth century, this right was not equally granted among the social classes. Under Frederick the Great of Prussia (1712–1786), a strong proponent of enlightenment absolutism, a few women gained special rights to study at Prussian universities. Similarly, the laws regarding the ownership of land or inheritance of property by women did not fundamentally change until the late nineteenth century, when under growing political liberalism the women's movement took a more distinct shape.

During the eighteenth and nineteenth centuries, the position of upper-class women improved, and many women ran salons, wrote, and published, albeit often under pseudonyms. Even the literary theatre men of the enlightenment like Goethe and Schiller, who helped a number of women to get published, perpetuated the idea of women as intellectually inferior beings. Influenced by political movements in France, during the early nineteenth century a number of women's groups linked to liberal church movements sprang up. But these movements were quickly extinguished in the conservative backlash following the failed German Revolution of 1848. Marked improvement for all women was only gained with the new German constitution of the Weimar Republic in 1919, which considered women as equals with the right to vote, to education, and to ownership of property. These new rights were diminished during the Third Reich. Hitler picked up the old slogan from the German empire, the three "K's," "Kinder, Küche, Kirche" (children, kitchen, church) as the proper place for women. Childbearing and rearing were of particular importance during the Third Reich, on one hand to create fodder for the expansive war machinery, and on the other as a means to enforce a sort of ethnic cleansing, by forbidding interracial (ethnic/religious) marriages and sterilization of "unfit" women and men. Ironically, that same war eventually brought more independence to German women: as their husbands, fathers, sons, and brothers were drafted, women had to join the workforce, manage their households, and become altogether more independent. After World War II, East Germany adopted the communist attitude toward woman's rights, which treated men and women as equals. The percentage of women gaining degrees in higher education skyrocketed in East Germany, while in the West it took decades for women to gain significant numbers both as students and as professors in the universities. While East Germany established free access to daycare and family planning, including abortion, West Germany had a school system with half days, thus forcing one parent—mostly mothers—to be at home in the afternoons. This pattern was continued after reunification, even though equality was granted under the law. Statistics from 2010 showed that only 14 percent of women with one child returned to work after giving birth, and only 6 percent of women with two children rejoined the workforce (Bennhold). In this climate, family planning and abortion rights remain a hotly contested issue.

In the reunited Germany, women have entered the job market and higher education in increasing numbers, but only in the twenty-first century have leading positions in politics, culture, and education become more commonly available to them. Despite the fact that in 2005 Germany elected a woman chancellor, Angela Merkel, there were hardly any women found in the top echelons of industry and business. According to a 2010 statistic, only 2 percent of executive committee members in the business world were women, compared with 14 percent in the United States and 17 percent in Sweden

(Bennhold). In the theatres, women directors were still paid several thousand Euros less for a directing job than their male counterparts.

Early Women Directors

In the mid-seventeenth century, women began to perform on Germany's traveling stages, and toward the end of the century Catharina Elisabeth Velten and Maria Margaretha Elenson were among the first woman principals heading their own companies. One of the pioneers in establishing a leading position for women in the theatre was the impresario, actor, playwright, and theatre reformer Friederike Caroline Neuber, who opened her own theatre in Leipzig in 1827. However, the theatre closed down after seven years due to a shift in funding because of governmental succession, and Neuber had to resume her life as itinerant player.

Friederike Caroline Neuber

While the role of the director as an implementer of an artistic vision only emerged in the late nineteenth century, the theatrical reforms of the eighteenth century set important impulses for this development. In German theatre history, the "Neuberin," as Caroline Neuber was known, is often considered to be one of the first impresarios whose work went beyond the mere managerial toward that of a director. The Neuberin collaborated with the playwright and theatrical reformer Johann Christoph Gottsched. Her troupe performed some of his plays, but also works by French classicists Pierre Corneille and Jean Racine. Despite the fact that the troupe also regularly performed the so-called Harlekinaden—shorter, comic plays that featured clown characters such as Hanswurst or Harlequin—Neuber felt strongly that a theatre that took itself seriously should refrain from these base comedic means of entertainment and should instead perform serious plays, written in or translated into High German. In 1737 she famously called for the banning of Hanswurst from the serious, educational theatre she wanted to promote. After repeated fights with the Hanswurst actor of her own troupe, she wrote her demand into the prologue to one of her plays, followed by a public burning of a harlequin effigy. Neuber and Gottsched's shared ideas planted the roots for a theatre reform movement during the eighteenth century that was epitomized in Johann Friedrich Schiller's essay from 1784, "The Theatrical Stage as Moral Institution" ("Die Schaubühne als moralische Anstalt"). From this viewpoint the theatre is not simply a place where an audience is entertained or emotionally purged; it is also where a national identity and the moral self-understanding of its growing bourgeoisie is shaped. The focus of this new theatre was the role of the individual within the family, so that even when a play was set within the nobility, the heroes and heroines were driven by their private concerns. Ironically, the changes Neuber initiated in the theatre erased the role of women as directors for the next two hundred years and anchored women's position as housewives and mothers more securely within the celebrated bourgeois household.

The remainder of the eighteenth and nineteenth centuries was dominated by male playwrights, directors, and dramaturges. Women achieved recognition as performers in theatre and opera, and some after retiring from stage life as teachers, but only after World War II did women emerge again as directors and in leading positions in the theatre.[1] In 1945, immediately following the end of the war, Jewish director and actor Ida Ehre (1900–1989) was appointed head of the Hamburg Kammerspiele, where she directed for four-and-a-half decades until her death. In 1949 actor Helene Weigel (1900–1971) and her husband Bertolt Brecht co-founded the Berliner Ensemble after returning to East Berlin with their family from years in exile. Weigel ran the company by herself after Brecht's death in 1956 and appointed Ruth Berghaus (1927–1996) as her successor. As one of East Germany's leading directors and strongest innovators in music theatre, opera, and theatre, Berghaus was able to work in both East and West Germany and freely cross the border that was closed to all but the most privileged citizens of the German Democratic Republic (GDR). Strong women of the theatre such as Ehre, Weigel, and Berghaus paved the way for the following generations of women directors in East, West, and the reunited Germany.

Dance Theatre

Although women directors were scarce during the Weimar Republic's intense artistic renewal, political activism, and relative gender equality, a new and radical dance movement emerged. This movement, which influenced the performing arts of the twentieth and twenty-first centuries worldwide, galvanized many creative forces in the performing arts. Early modern dance explorations were followed by the hybrid form of dance theatre, showing how women's creative forces were redirected from the word-heavy German theatre to the possibilities of physical expression. In the twenty-first century, the German theatre has embraced hybrid forms of all kinds and has become the stage of high emotion and multimedia, including music, movement, and dance as much as new technologies.

Beginning with expressive dance (Ausdruckstanz), inspired by the celebratory body culture of the early twentieth century, dancers began to dance barefoot. Mary Wigman (1886–1973) studied rhythmic gymnastics in Germany under musician Émile Jacques-Dalcroze and in 1913 moved to Switzerland to study with dance theorist Rudolf von Laban. Soon after she began to develop her own style of "absolute" dance, a movement of the body from within, performed with or without music, and sometimes only to the rhythm of drums. She titled her form of expressive dance "New German Dance." After World War I Wigman's career took off, and she became a major force in the development of modern dance throughout Europe as well as in the United States. Both Wigman's group choreographies and her solo dances stood out because of her unique movement style and her use of sounds and costumes, thereby challenging the traditional view of the woman performer.

Much of the positive vigor and reputation that was associated with pre–World War II Ausdruckstanz was compromised through the association of choreographers such as Laban and Wigman with Hitler's mass spectacles, as was the case with the pageantry of the 1936 Olympics in Berlin. Only a few choreographers maintained an unscathed standing after the war, and it was up to younger choreographers to regain world renown. Outstanding among them was Pina Bausch (1940–2009), who trained at the Folkwang School in Essen under Kurt Jooss, a founding figure of expressionist dance. While subsequently working in New York, Bausch was called upon to run the Wuppertal Opera Ballet at age twenty-nine. She renamed the company Tanztheater Wuppertal (Dance Theatre Wuppertal) and stayed with it until the end of her life. The German term "Tanztheater" (dance theatre) has become synonymous with Bausch's many world-famous pieces, such as *Rite of Spring* (*Das Frühlingsopfer*) in 1975; *Kontakthof* in 1978, 2000, and 2008; and *Palermo Palermo* in 1989. In Bausch's pieces, the dancers not only dance, they also speak, act, and feel. They tell bits of their life stories, which are restructured through fragmentation and repetition into pieces that have touched and excited audiences worldwide.

Choreographers Reinhild Hoffman and Susanne Linke, both born in the 1940s and students of the Folkwang School, each created unique works of dance theatre. Hoffmann, the artistic director of several ensembles, branched out to theatre direction and opera later on in her career. Linke became the head of several companies and, on occasion, collaborated with Hoffman. Both toured internationally and helped shape the current wave of dance theatre in Germany and elsewhere. Most notable among this next wave of younger choreographers is Sasha Waltz, who aside from running her own company and founding the Sophiensaele, a well-established performance space in Berlin, co-directed the famous Berlin theatre Schaubühne from 1999 to 2004. Among her best-known pieces is *Body* (*Körper*) in 2000, in which she dramatized the marketability of bodies and body parts. Similar to Bausch's work, Waltz's ensemble consists of performers who dance and speak. Her work, like that of the other dance theatre choreographers, bridges the gap between dance and theatre, and, to a degree, defies the separations of these genres.

Working Climate in the Twenty-First Century

Theatre in Germany consists of independent nonprofit theatres, private for-profit theatres, and a large and well-established system of publicly subsidized theatres that are funded by the state, city, and/or federal government. While financial support for the German theatre has become scarcer, a wave of women directors has swept the scene.

One measure of judging women's parity in the field is the number of women invited to direct at Theatertreffen, the prestigious annual theatre meeting in Berlin. From 1964 to 2011 the Theatertreffen invited a total of 470 productions, only thirty-four (7 percent) of which were directed by women. Out of these thirty-four, nine pieces were in the category of dance theatre; an additional four pieces at the Theatertreffen were directed by collectives that included one or more women. The woman director most featured at the Theatertreffen is Andrea Breth with nine invitations, followed by Karin Beier with four. The overall number of shows directed by women who were invited from 1980–2010 has not increased despite the growing number of women professionals: ten during the 1980s, twelve during the 1990s, and ten from 2000 to 2010. Several of the larger houses have been hiring women in the position of artistic directors, but there is still a long way to go, as demonstrated by a cycle of discussions during the 2011 Theatertreffen, inspired by Christina Haberlik's exhibit, "Directing Women" ("Regiefrauen"). Women directors, actors, and journalists debated at length the still-prevailing male dominance both in terms of financial remunerations as well as in sheer numbers of influential positions in Germany's well-funded theatre landscape.

Profiles of Contemporary Directors

Andrea Breth

Andrea Breth is one of the best-known directors in Germany since the mid-1980s. In addition to her invitations to the Theatertreffen, she has directed in some of the highest-ranked German-speaking theatres. Born in 1952 in a small town in Bavaria, Breth was raised in Darmstadt and began studying English and German at the University of Heidelberg in 1971. There she began work as a directing assistant in 1972. Instead of completing her academic training, in 1975 she followed one of her mentors—the director Peter Stolzenberg—to Bremen, where he became artistic director at the city theatre. In the same year, he invited her to direct her first professional production, Jevgeni Schwarz's *The Enchanted Brothers* (*Die verzauberten Brüder*). She simultaneously continued assisting the directors David Esrig and Christof Nel. When called to direct Gotthold Ephraim Lessing's *Emilia Galotti* at Berlin's Freie Volksbühne in 1980, the production flopped. Breth, who had been considered one of the young directing geniuses, went back to the drawing table, withdrew to Zürich, and worked there with a class of acting students on a two-semester project. She gained back her confidence and considered this to be one of her key learning experiences.

Breth has worked for long periods at established theatres and also as an independent director. From 1983 to 1985, after winning the director of the year award by *Theater Heute* magazine, she directed in Freiburg, and from 1986 to 1989 in Bochum; she subsequently worked for some years independently. From 1992 to 1997 she was part of the artistic directing team at the highly reputed Schaubühne in Berlin. From 1999 on, Breth has lived in Vienna, Austria, together with her partner, the actor Elizabeth Orth, and was resident director at Vienna's Burgtheater, one of the grandest German-language theatres. In addition to directing a play or two in Vienna each year she has spent time directing opera and working on projects in other cities.

Breth has been awarded numerous prestigious prizes for her direction. Her *Emilia Galotti*, the play that had flopped in 1980, garnered the coveted Nestroy award for best direction in 2003. According to theatre scholar Denis Leifeld, "*Emilia Galotti* is about 'Einfühlung' (empathy/feeling into) in the character, not about deconstruction or forced contemporizing. It is about the carnality and tangibility of the character. Breth shows great sensibility for the characters of the play in a poetic-realistic fashion."

Breth states that directing can only partially be learned. She suggests that one can acquire organizational skills, learn about lighting and other technical aspects of the theatre, and increase one's ability to read and truly comprehend a play. However, she believes that the most important skills a director needs—having imagination and the ability to lead others—cannot be learned. Critic Christine Dössel calls Breth's precise and sensitive readings and interpretations of complex dramatic texts a "subtle theatre of the human soul." Breth has returned repeatedly to certain authors, among them Anton Chekhov, Edward Bond, Heinrich von Kleist, and Friedrich Schiller. This has given her the reputation as a "classics" specialist, a categorization she strongly refutes. While she admits to being old-fashioned enough to like plays and linear stories in a theatre landscape that is usually more interested in devised plays, postmodern scripts, or radical adaptations, she points out that the material she works with indeed varies widely (Breth and Bazinger 87). In addition to the above-mentioned authors, she has successfully directed several comedies, contemporary plays, and operas, as well as a number of non-play-based projects, such as an adaptation of Fyodor Dostoyevsky's novel *Crime and Punishment* for the Salzburg festival in 2008.

Breth divides the work of directing a play into several phases. She begins by reading the text innumerable times and conducting as much research as possible. Then she develops her directorial approach and begins working with the set designer to create the world of the play. Work with other designers follows, with this collaborative research/design period taking about three months. After that, a first read-through with the actors takes place. At this rehearsal, not only the text is read out loud, but the directorial concept and the design are also introduced to the cast. This is followed by a two-month rehearsal period. She says: "There's also a lot of intellectual work before I start. And then it speaks in me, it happens to me. If it doesn't it's better to stop. My ambition pushes me to hunt for a play's soul. That's a real undertaking. But then when we rehearse I just have to forget it all again. I've got to be totally permeable to see what's going on, and to go about changing things carefully. But sometimes that doesn't work and I have to find another key, another way in. I run around the world with a huge bunch of keys" (Breth, Keim, and Wengierek).

In her contract negotiations, Breth has successfully demanded to have free choice of plays, of the cast, and of the amount of time she can spend on preparation and rehearsal. She has often been called a difficult and demanding director, but she insists on her precise work style, her in-depth analysis of the text, and her demands on the actors to deliver an intelligent and committed play.

Katharina Thalbach

Katharina Thalbach is the recipient of many prizes and awards in a variety of categories: stage actor, film actor, director of theatre, and director of opera. She thinks of
herself as someone who has grown up in a matriarchy. Thalbach was born in 1954 in
Berlin, East Germany, daughter of actor Sabine Thalbach and director Benno Besson.
A child of the theatre, Thalbach began acting as a four-year-old. After her mother's
early death, she was practically raised at the Berliner Ensemble, where both her parents
had worked. Weigel became her mentor and acting teacher and the defining character
in this matriarchy. Thalbach has never lost her Brechtian sensibilities and is known to
this day for her use of Brechtian distancing devices—often to comedic effect. In an
interview with Thalbach, theatre critic Irene Bazinger called it Brecht's "sensuality of
thinking," to which Thalbach replied: "I like sensuality of thinking—because thinking
is fun. Everything that is serious has comic edges, and vice versa: what is comical can be
deadly serious. Brecht, [Heinrich] Heine and Shakespeare already knew this. And they
entertained excellently—for three pennies!—very cheap but not stupid" (Bazinger).

Despite her great successes as a young actor at the Berliner Ensemble and the Volksbühne, Thalbach left the GDR in 1976 at age twenty-two with her partner, the playwright Thomas Brasch, and her daughter. In West Germany, Thalbach quickly made a
career as stage and movie actor. She made her directing debut in 1987 at the workshop
stage of the Schiller Theatre in Berlin. She directed Shakespeare's *Macbeth* in this small
and experimental space, and the production succeeded, introducing a new career for the
talented actor. In the late 1980s she directed plays such as Lessing's *Minna von Barnhelm*
and Shakespeare's *As You Like It* on the large mainstage. In 1990 she was invited to the
Theatertreffen with her production of Brecht's *Man is Man* (*Mann ist Mann*). She was
employed as a steady member of the ensemble as well as house director at Berliner
Stages, which included the Schiller Theatre and the Schlosspark Theatre until their
closures in 1993. A Berliner through and through, Thalbach has worked at the Maxim
Gorki Theatre and the Comedy Theatre at the Kurfürstendamm, but also in Hamburg
at the Thalia Theatre and other houses across the country. In 1997 she had her debut
as an opera director at the E-Werk in Berlin with Mozart's *Don Giovanni* and has since
directed opera in Basel, Cologne, Dresden, and at the Deutsche Oper (German Opera)
in Berlin. Among her many, varied projects, her joyful, sensual Shakespeare productions
are well known, as well her ability to use Brechtian staging elements such as signs and
song to great comedic effect.

Thalbach also has a reputation for her uncensored way of speaking. She projects
the image of the cheeky newspaper boy, wearing pants and a lopsided cap. However,
she is not a fervent defender of women's rights, instead stating that it is not gender
that determines a person's capabilities (Haberlink 97). On the other hand, one could
suggest that her own choice of playing the often-comedic versions of classic male roles

could be read as a feminist critique of this male-dominated business. She also chose to cast her 2009 production of *As You Like It* with an all female cast, playing the role of the fool Touchstone herself. Critic Dirk Krampitz commented, "No matter if bear, wrestler, nobility or burlesque dancer: director Thalbach lets only women play. Three hours of popular, coarse, great and grand theatre packed on a small stage."

Thalbach remembers that when she began her career, there were not many other working women directors; she recalls the Bavarian actor, director, and theatre manager Ruth Drexel, who like herself began her career at the Berliner Ensemble as an actor. However, Thalbach always had such an outstanding reputation that she might not have had to fight like other women in the male-dominated world of the German theatre. Possibly her upbringing in East Berlin, in the matriarchy of the Berliner Ensemble, lent her a perspective of gender equality that protected her from the chauvinism other women colleagues had to encounter. She considers the most important lesson learned from Weigel: an insistence on iron discipline, as well as respect and politeness toward her colleagues and collaborators.

Karin Beier

One of the most successful women in the German theatre of the early twenty-first century is Karin Beier, born in 1965 in Cologne. While she studied English at the University of Cologne, she co-founded with Elmar Goerden in 1986 an independent theatre collective called Countercheck Quarrelsome. For this group she directed nine radically adapted Shakespeare plays performed in English (Haberlink 122). She later abandoned her academic studies and worked as a directing assistant at the Düsseldorf Theatre. Very quickly, in 1989, she directed her first professional production, George Tabori's *The 25th Hour* (*Die 25. Stunde*). In 1994 she was invited to the Theatertreffen with her direction of *Romeo and Juliet* and again in 1996 with her direction of *A Midsummer Night's Dream*. In *Romeo and Juliet* she transformed the balcony scene into a trapeze act and cut the final reunion between Capulets and Montagues. This radical adaptation for a contemporary audience was highly successful in Düsseldorf, while Berlin's reviewers could not decide if Beier's play was a flop or the first steps of a future star director. *A Midsummer Night's Dream* opened the 1996 Theatertreffen, featuring a cast of fourteen different nationalities and staged multilingually; it was subtitled *A European Shakespeare* and again divided the critics.

These early successes, despite the mixed reviews, led to many high-profile work engagements in such cities as Hamburg, Cologne, Munich, and Zürich. Like Breth, she describes how the public's hunger for a new young directing talent put her under pressure to deliver. Different from Breth, however, she felt that a whole generation of young directors was missing, thus the desire for fresh directing blood was greater than in earlier decades. Beier, too, felt that older women colleagues such as Breth or the wonderful Elke Lang (1952–1998) had paved the way for her own generation. She didn't experience quite the same issues with sexism from technical staff and male colleagues

Elfriede Jelinek's *The Works,* directed by Karin Beier, Schauspiel Köln, Cologne, 2011. Photograph: Klaus Lefebvre

as they had, or the same need of having constantly to prove her competencies in areas not normally handled by directors, such as lighting.

Like Breth and Thalbach, Beier doesn't think of herself as a feminist or as someone who has to actively support women's issues. However, when looking over the list of directors she has hired since she has been the artistic director of the large city theatre in Cologne, she has consistently hired a number of young women directors, such as Jette Steckel, Katja Lauken, and Anna Viebrock, or sought out foreign colleagues, such as British director Katie Mitchell.

When hired as artistic director in Cologne in 2007, Beier became the head of one of the largest theatres in Germany. The theatre and the large opera of the Bühnen der Stadt Köln (Stages of the City of Cologne) employ together approximately 690 people with an annual budget of about fifty-six million Euros. During the 2009–10 season the theatre alone produced fifteen new works, hosted guest performances, and remounted several plays from its previous season (Steets 184–85). Despite her many organizational responsibilities, Beier directed two of the larger productions during that season: her highly acclaimed, all-female cast of *King Lear* and her radical adaptation of Ettore Scola and Rugero Maccari's 1970's neorealistic film script *Down and Dirty*, renamed *Ugly, Dirty, Bad* (*Die Schmutzigen, die Hässlichen und die Gemeinen*).[2]

Beier has put the Cologne theatre back on the national map. Some of the productions she has directed have been invited to the Theatertreffen, and by inviting companies such as the British-German company Gob Squad or the Sputnik Shipping Company from Budapest, Beier partakes in the move toward collective theatre making that is mirrored in the repeated invitation of theatre collectives to the Theatertreffen during the twenty-first century.

In her 2011 production of Elfriede Jelinek's three plays *The Works / On the Bus / A Fall* (*Das Werk / Im Bus / Der Fall*), Beier employed a number of theatrical means: her large ensemble, a full male choir, live music, and a gradually submerging stage. Jelinek's long prose pieces slowly reveal their thematic centers. All three deal with humanly caused catastrophes: the losses of life during the building of a giant dam in Austria using POWs and other forced labor during World War II in *The Works*; the collapse of a street in the middle of Munich, swallowing up a bus, caused by work on the sewage system in *On the Bus*; and the collapse of the Cologne Archive caused by the building of a subway tunnel in *A Fall*. Beier approached these pieces with metaphorical distance. Beginning with a choreography of pouring water that is at once laconic, poetic, and beautiful, the plays were set in an array of isolated office work stations spread out over the large stage, leftovers of a dysfunctional, meaningless business world. The three-hour evening ended with a primordial dance duet between two allegorical figures, water and earth, during which the whole stage, with the leftover office pieces, slowly became flooded with one foot of water. Beier directed her ensemble to deliver outstanding performances, full body commitment, and tight ensemble play, and combined in equal measure the strengths of her team of designers and performers. Critics described Beier's potent use of musicality as such: "The most important instruments of the performance are an extreme, but nonetheless highly developed, musicalization of all of the scenic and linguistic material—the effectiveness of which is due to the work of the composer and music director Jörg Gollasch—and Karin Beier's technically advanced, subtle art of scenic quoting" (Haas and Kirsch).

Another one of Beier's strengths lies in her capability of dealing with local politics. Against the city council's decision she stopped the planned destruction and rebuilding of the Cologne theatre in favor of a cheaper and faster solution: the renovation of the existing, architecturally protected building. She also successfully negotiated her change of position from Cologne to Hamburg, where she will take over the artistic direction of the Hamburg Theatre in 2013. Karin Beier is one of the forces in German theatre of the early twenty-first century, and one hopes that she will pave the way for more gender equality in the future.

▨ ▨ ▨

Since 2000 an increasing number of women directors have worked on Germany's small and large stages. It seems that work conditions have improved, and thanks to the successes of directors such as Breth, Thalbach, and Beier, women no longer need to prove their organizational and technical capabilities in the same way as during the 1970s and 1980s. Nevertheless, true equality in numbers and visibility for Germany's directing woman still seems to be far off.

Notes

1. Exceptions include Charlotte Birch Pfeiffer (1800–1868), a starring actor, playwright, and theatre manager, who led the Zurich theatre from 1837 until 1844; Ellen Franz (1839–1923), the third wife of Duke Georg II of Saxe-Meinigen and a former actor, who was instrumental in founding and training her husband's famous theatre troupe; and Luise Dumont (1862–1932), who co-founded and managed the Düsseldorf Theatre.

2. One of Beier's great feats is that she manages to leave the theatre at 4:30 PM every day to spend time with her child. This requires that she trust her team and give her staff members the room to act responsibly—a lateral style of management as opposed to a strictly hierarchical model.

Sources

Bazinger, Irene. "In Conversation: Katharina Thalbach; We in the East Had More Sex and More Fun." *Frankfurt General Newspaper* ["Im Gespräch: Katharina Thalbach; Wir im Osten hatten mehr Sex und mehr zu lachen." *Frankfurter Allgemeine Zeitung*], November 21, 2008.

Beier, Karin. Interview. February 26, 2011.

Bennhold, Katrin. "German Women: Stuck at Home." *International Herald Tribune*, June 29, 2011.

Breth, Andrea, and Irene Bazinger. *Free for the Moment* [*Frei für den Moment*]. Berlin: Rotbuch, 2009.

Breth, Andrea, Stefan Keim, and Reinhard Wengierek. "It's Poetry—Not Prattle." *Signand-sight: Let's Talk European*, September 1, 2005. Originally published in *Die Welt*, August 24, 2005. Available at http://www.signandsight.com (accessed December 16, 2012).

Dössel, Christine. "Dawn on the Boulevard: Emilia Galotti Newly Staged in Vienna." *South German Newspaper* ["Boulevarddämmerung. Neuinszenierung von Emilia Galotti in Wien." *Süddeutsche Zeitung*], December 23, 2002.

"Fifty Directors Working at German Theatres." ["50 Regisseure im deutschsprachigen Theater."] Goethe Institut, n.d. Available at http://www.goethe.de (accessed December 16, 2012).

Haberlink, Christina. *Directing Women: A Man's Job in Women's Hands* [*Regie-Frauen: Ein Männerberuf in Frauenhand*]. Munich/Leipzig: Henschel, 2010.

Hass, Ulrike, and Sebastian Kirsch. "Karin Beier's Staging of Elfriede Jelinek's 'Das Werk/Im Bus/Ein Sturz' in Cologne." *Prospero European Review: Theatre and Research*. Edition 2, 2011. Available at http://www.t-n-b.fr/en (accessed December 16, 2012).

Krampitz, Dirk. "Triumph for Thalbach's Shakespeare Women." *Berlin Newspaper* ["Triumph für Thalbachs Shakespeare Weiber." *Berliner Zeitung*], January 20, 2009.

Leifeld, Denis. Personal communication. November 6, 2011.

Steets, Bernd. *Theatre Almanac: 2009/2010 Season* [*Theateralmanach: Spielzeit 2009/2010*]. Kempten, Germany: Smidt, 2009.

 Great Britain

Adam J. Ledger

Great Britain is a country with a long history of both theatre and the women's movement. However, in a 2007 newspaper article Nicholas Hytner, artistic director of London's National Theatre (NT), claims that some male theatre critics simply cannot ignore the gender of women directors. Hytner claims that the critics write "misogynistic" reviews and are especially unfair to gay women directors (Hoyle). The critics refute this, but, as this chapter reports, the number of women directors remains disproportionally low in comparison to men. Yet women are beginning to occupy significant roles: one example is the director Jude Kelly, formerly the first artistic director of the prestigious West Yorkshire Playhouse, who became artistic director of London's Southbank Centre in 2005.

Historically, women have held positions of artistic or managerial leadership: for instance, the celebrated and colorful theatre manager Annie Horniman founded both Dublin's Abbey Theatre, along with Lady Augusta Gregory, as well as Manchester's Gaiety Theatre in the early 1900s, albeit with the help of a family fortune. In addition, Horniman is often credited with starting the British repertory theatre movement (Murphy). A century later, the first artistic director of the National Theatre of Scotland (NTS), formed in 2007, was a woman, Vicky Featherstone. In 2013 Featherstone became artistic director of London's Royal Court Theatre. To have a woman director at the helm of a major theatre is something that has not been matched by other large-scale, national institutions such as Stratford-upon-Avon's Royal Shakespeare Company (RSC). However, women directors have been influential throughout the twentieth century, running regional theatre companies as well as smaller, exciting theatre venues, and in the new millennium some of the most influential freelance directors in Britain are women.

Women's Rights: Historical Context

The women's movement gained significant momentum during the early twentieth century in Great Britain and led to changes in legislation. By fundamentally rejecting historical notions of "womanliness" within a deeply patriarchal society, women began to find alternative, more modern archetypes in such figures as Florence Nightingale (1820–1910), though she refused to identify herself with the emerging ideas of the women's movement. Many women were workers in agriculture or the rising industrial cities, yet had few rights beyond those granted by a father or husband. Since higher education and a profession were barred to women[1] as well as the ownership of property, the only option for many women became the pursuit of marriage, motherhood, and family life, certainly among the upper classes and even in the emergent middle classes.

By the middle of the nineteenth century an identifiable women's movement had been established, which argued against prejudice and for a fairer society. Its concerns encompassed healthcare and sex education, but much activism centered on the issue of women being granted the vote. Since Jeremy Bentham's 1818 book, *A Plan for Parliamentary Reform*, some men had also called for change. From 1894 women were allowed to vote only in local elections. The approaching twentieth century saw the establishment of several women's political groups pulled together by organizations like the National Union of Women's Suffrage Societies, which was formed in 1897 by Millicent Fawcett.[2]

Militancy followed, a feature that has dominated the history of suffragism in Great Britain. The Pankhurst family, which included Emmeline Pankhurst and her daughters Christabel and Sylvia, founded the Women's Social and Political Union (WSPU) in 1903 at their Manchester home. The WSPU's use of propaganda was creative and successful, and direct action was at first characterized by the breaking of windows, interruptions at political speeches, and members chaining themselves to railings. This earned the woman the derogatory label "suffragettes," and their tactics escalated into more violent episodes, such as bombings and major incidents of arson, causing many in the movement to disassociate from the more militant wing.[3] The organization suffered power struggles, especially around Christabel Pankhurst, but Sylvia Pankhurst moved in artistic circles and took steps to connect with working-class women. The most potent symbol of suffragism was Emily Wilding Davison, who died of injuries sustained while trying to pin the WPSU's colors to King George V's racehorse during the running of the 1913 Epsom Derby, thus becoming the martyr of the cause.

The start of the First World War resulted in a halt to direct militant action. This was a period that paradoxically would provide women with the opportunity to show they could operate heavy machinery in factories and work the land. In 1918 women were finally granted the vote in national elections, but only if they were at least thirty years old and married, owned property, or had a degree. Ten years later, the voting age was reduced to twenty-one—the same age as men at the time—and in 1928 and 1929 women Members of Parliament were elected.

Women served in the military during the Second World War, and the 1944 Education Act confirmed at least the principle of free education for all. Later, the 1960s saw the beginning of what has been termed Second Wave Feminism. This movement reacted in part to the 1950s facade of postwar domestic bliss. Feminism became fuelled by radical thinkers, philosophers, and feminists such as Australian Germaine Greer, whose influential book *The Female Eunuch* was published in 1970.

In 1975 the Sex Discrimination Act and Equal Pay Bill were passed, which gave women, at least in theory, legal and employment rights equal to men. Although many women have achieved positions of authority and influence in Great Britain, whether in the arts, business, or industry, balancing a career with the pressures of family life remains a topic of particular concern to many. Notwithstanding legislation, discrimination persists: according to a 2010 report cited by the Chartered Management Institute, senior-level women managers have seen their pay rise 2.8 percent compared to 2.3 percent for their male counterparts, yet an underlying pay difference of some £10,000 persists. Despite its history of sometimes radical feminism and legislative frameworks, Great Britain compares poorly to other European countries in this respect.

Early Women Directors

In order to make a career for themselves, several women directors combined entrepreneurial spirit with theatrical flair. The impact of Edith Craig (1869–1947) has been somewhat overshadowed by the memory of her famous mother, the celebrated actor Ellen Terry, and the legacy of her brother, the designer and theorist Edward Gordon Craig. Craig herself combined multiple roles as an activist in the women's movement—costumer, actor, and director—and founded the London-based Pioneer Players in 1911. The name of this prolific company is significant, as it focused on plays by women and works in translation.[4] As part of her activist work, Craig had earlier commissioned Cicely Hamilton's *A Pageant of Great Women* in 1910, which was performed throughout the country and proved a dynamic force in the establishment of the amateur theatre scene in Great Britain. Although living in a period of different attitudes toward sexuality, Craig did not hide her female companion, even living in a *ménage à trois* with a third woman later in life. Her personal and political ethics, as well as her artistic choices, have inspired recent research and books.[5]

Any survey of women directors in Britain must include the name Joan Littlewood (1914–2002), who founded Theatre Union with her husband, Ewan MacColl. The company was later renamed Theatre Workshop, which, after arduous touring, moved to the Theatre Royal, Stratford, London, in 1953. Theatre Workshop was characterized not only by its radical politics, but also by thorough preparation of actors and performance; Littlewood embraced the work of Stanislavski, Meyerhold, and Laban. Theatre Workshop devised work, introduced new plays such as the British premiere of Brecht's *Mother Courage* in 1955—directed by Littlewood in the lead role—and presented well-received

Edith Craig. Photo courtesy of National Trust at Smallhythe Place.

classical revivals to a tired British theatre scene. One of Theatre Workshop's most enduring pieces was its satire *Oh, What a Lovely War*, directed by Littlewood in 1963. Although the group received virtually no state subsidy, transfers to London's West End brought fame and income. However, the strain of work led to the end of Theatre Workshop by the early 1970s. Littlewood's life, work, and fierce personality are recorded in her own *Joan's Book*.

Mary Ann "Buzz" Goodbody (1947–1975) is likewise an example of a director who combined her political persuasions with her artistic choices. Following her activism connected to both communism and the women's movement of the time, as well as politicized theatre making, Goodbody became the first woman director to work at the RSC, an invitation she secured following success with a production at Scarborough's National Student Drama Festival (NSDF), which had transferred to the West End. At the RSC, Goodbody quickly built a reputation for radical interpretations of plays, often using simple staging and a focus on the ensemble or communal nature of performance. Goodbody helped start The Other Place, the RSC's small-scale Stratford venue, which was pulled down in 1990 as part of the RSC's redevelopment.[6] Since Goodbody committed suicide at the age of only twenty-eight, what she may have gone on to achieve can only be imagined. A director's award was established in her name at the NSDF.

Annie Castledine has been a champion of women in theatre. Castledine was artistic director of the Playhouse Theatre in Derby from 1987 until 1990, where she proved an invigorating if controversial figure, introducing reforms through her physical and visual aesthetics. Since the early 1990s, Castledine has pursued an eclectic career, directing at the Chichester Festival Theatre, for example, as well as within training and education. She has worked often with the highly regarded London-based Complicite company and maintained a collaboration with Annabel Arden, co-founder of Complicite. Several women directors cite Castledine as a particular influence and inspiration.[7]

Working Climate in the Twenty-First Century

Despite the male dominance of the large, national theatre institutions, women in Great Britain are directing in a full range of theatre venues, scales of production, and theatrical genres. Some, such as Phyllida Lloyd, have directed big, commercial productions. Women directors have been pioneers in artistic practice too, developing rigorous rehearsal approaches and innovative theatrical languages. These include Featherstone, who is closely allied to the development of new writing, and Castledine, who has particularly encouraged women's writing through development programs and her editorship of volumes of plays by women.

Smaller companies have provided a more politicized voice to women theatre practitioners. For example, The Women's Theatre Group began in London in 1973 and focused on portraying issues directly affecting women as well as an artistic policy of enabling women theatre practitioners to work. In addition to touring to regular theatres, the company toured to venues such as pubs, prisons, and factories. In the early 1990s the group changed its name to Sphinx Theatre Company. Though direct Arts Council funding ceased in 2007 and Sphinx's theatre work was reduced, the company has continued to be active in organizing seminars and debates around women in the arts and has its own large archive. Similarly, Foursight Theatre, formed in 1987 and based in Wolverhampton, maintained and developed a policy of educational and community activities alongside its production output. Essentially a company rooted in devising theatre, Foursight Theatre's performances tended to focus on women's historical biography in an often exuberant, physical, and theatrical style that can be seen as part of the Total Theatre movement in Great Britain.[8] Although Foursight, too, was a victim of funding cuts, these and other groups have been an important environment for women practitioners, away from the mainstream theatre, where they can typically work in a cooperative organization.

Since directing is already a demanding and competitive business in itself, reasons for gender imbalance in directing are not simple. A report by the Sphinx Theatre Company in 1984 found that around 12 percent of British directors were women, a figure that by 2006 had risen to 19 percent (Gardner "It's Time"). According to Sphinx's website, as of December 2010 approximately 25 percent of directors in Great Britain were women.

Author Helen Manfull begins her study of women directors by pointing out that another factor which seems to prevent shifts in employment patterns in directing is the traditional dominance by Oxford and Cambridge University graduates (xxii). Highly regarded British directors such as Peter Hall, Peter Brook, and Jonathan Miller are all graduates of Oxford or Cambridge, as are many of the succeeding generation, represented by the likes of Sam Mendes or Nick Hytner. But women, too, cannot deny their place in this apparent "old school tie" network: Katie Mitchell, for example, was president of the Oxford University Drama Society, and Josie Rourke (see below) studied at Cambridge.

In the early twenty-first century, alternative routes to training and entry into directing were established: universities increasingly developed practice-based, postgraduate courses in directing, as did drama schools. One of the co-artistic directors of London's innovative Gate Theatre, Carrie Cracknell, completed a master of arts in directing at the Royal Scottish Academy of Music and Drama and met her collaborator, Natalie Abrahami, at the 2004 NT Studio directors' course. Abrahami reports, "There were nine women and three men, so that shows how theatre is changing" (Gardner "It's Time").

Although a short survey by theatre critic Lyn Gardner in 2007 tends to be drawn to major London-based directors, it is important to note too that a new generation of women directors has found a focus around new writing: as well as Cracknell and Abrahami at the Gate, Featherstone ran Paines Plough, a London-based touring company specializing in new plays. It is intriguing to note that these smaller theatres or companies seem to foster collaboration between women and offer places where women can champion new voices. Although we should avoid generalizations, Gemma Bodinetz, the director of Liverpool Everyman and Playhouse Theatres, suggests, "Subconsciously, I suspect there is a female sensibility. I'd like everyone to think I'm nurturing, supporting and developing; those are probably more strongly female characteristics" (Gardner "It's Time"). In what has been seen as an important development for women directors, Josie Rourke, who was for some years artistic director of London's Bush Theatre, which specializes in new work, became artistic director of the Donmar Warehouse in London in 2012.

Profiles of Contemporary Directors

Deborah Warner

Like Mitchell, Deborah Warner had her own company, Kick Theatre Company, before working extensively for the RSC and later for the NT. She has won several awards for her directing and in 2006 was made an Officier de l'Ordre des Arts et des Lettres in France and Commander of the Order of the British Empire (CBE). In addition, Warner has worked extensively in opera, winning awards in 1998 for *The Turn of the Screw* at London's English National Opera.

Warner is known for her long-term collaboration with the actor Fiona Shaw, directing her in an emotionally hard-hitting production of Euripides's *Medea*, which appeared on Broadway, garnering Warner two directing awards in 2003. She also worked with Shaw, who played the title role in *Richard II*, at the NT in 1995. This production attracted the critics' ire; they liked Warner's direction but derided Shaw's Richard so much that critic Paul Taylor of *The Independent* sprang to their defense, writing, "The experience left me feeling that the invidiousness rampant in the critical reaction was well-nigh illogical. Fiona Shaw's dazzlingly discomforting impersonation of Richard is so integral to the thinking behind Deborah Warner's gripping, lucidly felt production that it would only make sense to like neither or both" (Taylor). Warner has also directed Shaw in projects such as T. S. Eliot's *The Waste Land*, which has toured around the world in a series of stagings since 1996; in an adaptation of *The PowerBook* by Jeanette Winterson at the NT in 2002; and in Brecht's *Mother Courage* at the NT in 2009.

It is Shaw who reveals something of Warner's rehearsal style, saying, "She's an odd sort of a director, in a way, because she tells you when you're down the wrong rabbit-hole, but infuriatingly doesn't tell you which the right one is, even when she knows: the point is to find it yourself. To an outsider, her rehearsals would look hugely time-wasting" (Christiansen). Shaw's observation suggests the space Warner gives to the actor's creative process in rehearsal.

Warner has also developed three site-specific projects, using empty buildings. In 1995 Warner's *St Pancras Project* used the vacant rooms of an abandoned hotel above London's St Pancras station. In an interview, Warner describes how she wanted to fill the empty space with "little hauntings, little strangenesses; sometimes you'd hear voices, sometimes you'd hear pianos playing, sometimes you would see figures flitting through. It was a joyous thing to work on. It of course interested me very much because it redefined theatre in some ways" (Tusa). Whilst actors were seen or heard briefly, no lines as such were delivered. Warner also decided that spectators should enter the building one by one at ten-minute intervals to emphasize an individual experience, and the possibility of creating "their own poem" (Tusa).

Phyllida Lloyd

Phyllida Lloyd is an example of a director who continues to work across a range of opportunities. Lloyd studied English at the University of Birmingham, graduating in 1979. She received honorary degrees from Birmingham and Bristol Universities and was awarded a CBE in 2010.

Reversing a trend in directing, in which work in theatre leads to film or television, Lloyd worked in television but then developed extensive experience in regional theatre. She has directed often at the RNT, though little at the RSC, and has become a notable opera director. Lloyd has also directed at London's Royal Court Theatre, where her 1992 production of John Guare's *Six Degrees of Separation* transferred to the West End.

In 1999 Lloyd directed the large, commercial production of the ABBA musical *Mamma Mia!* in the West End and, subsequently, the 2001 Broadway production and the 2008 movie version, starring Meryl Streep. All versions have been extraordinary successes: the stage version has simultaneous productions and tours internationally, and the film version became the highest grossing U.K. movie ever.

Lloyd is open to new ideas in rehearsals, which, as journalist David Benedict reports, "unseats certain actors who are happier with a more authoritarian approach. . . . [N]othing is sacrosanct, except possibly a text." She often surrounds herself with familiar collaborators, explaining to Benedict, "The rootlessness of the freelance world is not a thing I particularly thrive on, actually. It can be quite a lonely life. Preparing for big new adventures like Covent Garden with a team one knows is a great privilege and makes me feel marginally more secure." Lloyd's familiar team can share common understanding and mutual goals; she comments, "Perhaps we celebrate the same kind of theatre or we're aspiring to a common, indefinable something" (Benedict).

In 2005 Lloyd directed Schiller's *Mary Stuart* in London at the Donmar Warehouse. The production moved to London's Apollo Theatre, and then to New York's Broadway in 2009, where it ran simultaneously with *Mamma Mia!* Lloyd's production was nominated for seven Tony Awards and the *New York Times* praised the "crystalline intelligence" of this diverse director (Brantley). The review also reported something of the aesthetic of the production, stating, "Though *Mary Stuart* would seem to be made for a big pomp-and-circumstance production, the look here is hypnotically stark: black brick walls, austere minimalist furniture and outsize shadows that lend an even greater urgency to a show that relentlessly keeps you on the edge of your seat" (Brantley).

Lloyd is a particularly flexible director, clearly able to work across a range of genres and scales of production.

Katie Mitchell

Katie Mitchell has become one of the most notable and creatively daring women directors in Great Britain. She was an associate director of the NT in 2003 and often works in mainland Europe.

After graduating from Oxford University, Mitchell formed her own company, Classics on a Shoestring, and became an assistant director at the RSC, later leading Stratford's The Other Place. Mitchell has worked extensively at the NT and, despite her preference for classic texts, has strong connections with the Royal Court Theatre, the major venue for new playwriting in Great Britain. In 1991 she received a Time Out Award for directing and an *Evening Standard* Award for best director in 1996. She was awarded an OBE in 2009.

A feature of Mitchell's approach to directing is her professional development. In 1989 she received a Winston Churchill Memorial Trust award to study directing in Eastern

Europe, spending time with Poland's Gardzienice company, and director Lev Dodin in Russia, among others. She also set up training opportunities in London. From 2001 to 2004, Mitchell received a National Endowment for Science and the Arts award to undertake research into neuroscience, which relates to her interest in psychophysiological behavior on stage.

Mitchell's approach is outlined in her own book, *The Director's Craft*, a highly detailed, practical manual and discussion of directorial ethos. Mitchell uses Chekhov's *The Seagull* to lay out her methods, from early textual analysis to characterization and relationships and the staging of scenes. She explores managerial issues and dealing with technical rehearsals, as well as strategies for personal reflection after a production.

Mitchell's work is characterized by a highly detailed, imaginative, technical, and anthropological analysis of the play text, rooted in a Stanislavskian approach. Her methods include, for example, establishing fundamental facts and questions around the circumstances of a play, research, and analyzing scenes in terms of what she calls "events," when the situation and intentions for all characters change. Mitchell is also concerned with the influence of environment on human behavior. She often works closely with her designer, calculating room measurements, and establishing the quality of light, weather, or temperature in the play's location, sometimes by traveling to the actual place concerned. A detailed timeline of the play's "back story" is also drawn up. This precise investigation is used as the basis for early improvisations, in which the actors can explore character relationships and physical behavior.

A great appeal of Mitchell's work is her visual aesthetic. Mitchell has spoken of her interest in painting and dance, especially the work of the German choreographer Pina Bausch.[9] Social dance is a recurring, metaphorical motif in Mitchell's work, used, for example, by the chorus in Euripides's *Iphegenia at Aulis* at the NT in 2004. Dance class is also a regular part of Mitchell's company's rehearsals. For Caryl Churchill's adaptation of Strindberg's *A Dream Play* at the RNT in 2005, early rehearsals explored improvised dreamscapes, to create a fluid, sensuous production with comparatively few actors on the smallest of the NT's stages, where time and action became looped and distorted. Both of these plays also kept fragments of improvised speech in performance.

Despite her success and detailed work, Mitchell seems to court controversy (Delgado and Rebellato 318). Negative press reviews tend to focus on Mitchell's textual amendments and her auteur tendencies. Reviewing Mitchell's production of Martin Crimp's adaptation of *The Seagull* at the RNT in 2006, a production in which Masha told Medvedenko to "piss off," critic Michael Billington huffed that this was "director's theatre at its most indulgent." Mitchell's critics cannot quite square the British idea of authorial intention with what Mitchell would claim as her quest for theatrical clarity.

Since 2006, Mitchell has turned to what she calls "live cinema," which has also received a divided critical response. "Live cinema" incorporates large projection screens

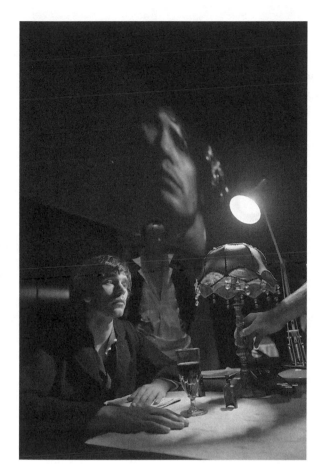

. . . some trace or her [sic],
directed by Katie Mitchell,
National Theatre, Lon-
don, 2008. Photograph:
National Theatre Archive/
Stephen Cummiskey.

into the staging, and actors create shots through live action and their own operation
of cameras. The technique can create beautiful images out of sometimes rough and
ready ingredients. Author Dan Rebellato evocatively describes how "[t]he work of
the audience became, in part, the movement of the eye, the performance structured
in many ways by the ocular movement between screen and stage. One observed the
beautifully realised images above but also the elaborately chaotic choreography of
the actor-technicians' work below" (Delgado and Rebellato 334–5). "Live cinema" has
implications for spectatorship and is ideally suited to the adaptation of novels, such as
Mitchell's production of Virginia Woolf's *Waves* at the NT in 2006. Her production
also used radio play techniques: the interplay of sensuous images, text, and sound
became an ideal solution to adapting an impressionistic work so concerned with time
and memory. Mitchell has also started to stage opera through "live cinema," such as
After Dido for the English National Opera in 2008.

Vicky Featherstone

As a stage director, Vicky Featherstone has been called "an inspiration" to other women directors because of her innovations (Gardner "It's Time"), notably around her work in new writing as director of Paines Plough from 1997 to 2005 and the diverse work she directed and programed at the National Theatre of Scotland (NTS).

Featherstone studied English and Drama at Manchester University and graduated in 1993. She worked in theatre and television, including an early period as assistant to artistic director Jude Kelly at the West Yorkshire Playhouse as part of the Regional Theatre Young Director Scheme. Among her prolific output at Paines Plough, Featherstone directed Sarah Kane's *Crave* and award-winning productions of Abi Morgan's writing, including *Splendour* in 2000. Featherstone continues to collaborate with Morgan.

The celebrated playwright Mark Ravenhill, who is also a literary manager at Paines Plough, describes Featherstone's rehearsals: "[She] creates an atmosphere where everybody feels they can riff and try things. Being unflappable and completely open to the unknown, she gives people that kind of confidence. You can see people relax and start to enjoy themselves when they work with her" ("Where the Art Is"). Featherstone's interest in new, ensemble-based work continued at the NTS, where her 2006 production with co-director Julian Crouch, *Wolves in the Walls*, was described as a "delightful, anarchically inventive exploration of the peculiar pleasures of fear" (Gardner "Wolves"). It is notable that this first production by the NTS (in collaboration with the theatre company Improbable) was, ostensibly at least, a piece for children.

Although Featherstone, like Lloyd, also directed a successful production of *Mary Stuart* for the NTS in 2006, she has staged performance that moves firmly away from her interest in text and new plays. For example, working with visual artist Stephen Skrynka, Featherstone created *Wall of Death: A Way of Life* in 2010 in collaboration with a motorcycle stunt team. *The Stage* found this "thrillingly visceral" (Dibdin). Going further, Joyce Macmillan in *The Scotsman* newspaper captured Featherstone's broader purpose, writing, "We should welcome Featherstone's efforts to explore and redefine the limits of the art-form for new times. Because exploration, in the end, is the essence of art; and with this imperfect but fascinating show, she demonstrates just how vibrant, and how thrilling, the process of discovery can sometimes be" (Macmillan).

The NTS's style proved physical and theatrical, with Featherstone's programming of, for example, the highly successful *Black Watch* in 2006 by Gregory Burke, a verbatim piece based on the Iraq war; and David Greig's version of *The Bacchae* the following year. Featherstone was listed in *The Stage* in 2008 as among the ten most influential figures in British theatre.

⸎ ⸎ ⸎

Although several women theatre directors maintain collaborative partnerships, an identifiable network of women directors in Great Britain has not been clearly established. As

Castledine says, "I don't think we talk together as much as we should, we women directors. It is possible to create an opportunity to do so but none of us will take that responsibility" (Manfull 174). Whether such a network is needed, and what its terms and purpose might be, remains uncertain. However, away from the mainstream theatre, a drawing together of women's skills and needs has been established through smaller companies.

Cracknell believes that "men have always called the shots in British theatre; it must have an effect on what is seen on our stages. It's time we women got a little more angry and petulant. If we don't like what we see, we should do something about it. But it is happening, and it is not just to do with theatre, but with the fact that, generally, women in society feel more able to express their opinions and take control of their lives" (Gardner "It's Time"). But of considerable concern is the lack of women directors from underrepresented sectors. Despite the brevity of this chapter's survey, what is clear is the dearth of women directors from the British Asian and Black communities;[10] this is true of male directors, too, but remains a very real challenge to and for women in the new millennium.

Notes

1. Oxford and Cambridge Universities admitted women from around 1880, although women could not actually graduate until some years later.

2. An organization in her name exists today. See the homepage of the Fawcett Society, http://www.fawcettsociety.org.uk.

3. Critics of the suffrage movement used the term "suffragette," coined by the *Daily Mail* newspaper.

4. Craig produced some 150 plays with the Pioneer Players.

5. See Cockin; Holroyd. See also the Ellen Terry and Edith Craig Database, http://www.ellenterryarchive.hull.ac.uk.

6. Two women profiled later in this chapter, Katie Mitchell and Deborah Warner, also directed at this intimate, experimental venue.

7. See Manfull; see also Gardner, "Power."

8. See the Total Theatre homepage, http://www.totaltheatre.org.uk.

9. See Giannachi and Luckhurst, 98, 100; see also Shevtsova and Innes for another interview with Mitchell.

10. In the United Kingdom, the term Asian does not represent Chinese peoples, although (for example) the Institute of Race Relations suggests the contemporary fluidity of some terms, as well as providing informative statistics. See http://www.irr.org.uk/statistics.

Sources

Benedict, David. "Arts: Together Wherever We Go." *Independent*, April 29, 1997.

Billington, Michael. Review of *The Seagull*, by Anton Chekhov. *Guardian*, June 28, 2006.

Brantley, Ben. "Must I Remind Your Majesty, Two's a Crowd?" Review of *Mary Stuart* by Friedrich Schiller. *New York Times*, Apr. 20, 2009.

Castledine, Annie, ed. *Plays by Women: Vol. 9*. London: Methuen, 1991.

———. *Plays by Women: Vol. 10*. London: Methuen, 1994.

Christiansen, Rupert. "Fiona Shaw's Double Life." *Telegraph*, May 10, 2002.

Cockin, Katharine. *Edith Craig (1869–1947): Dramatic Lives*. London: Continuum, 1998.

Delgado, Maria, and Dan Rebellato, eds. *Contemporary European Theatre Directors*. London: Routledge, 2010.

Dibdin, Thom. Review of *Wall of Death: A Way of Life*. *The Stage*, February 8, 2010.

Foursight Theatre. Available at http://www.foursighttheatre.co.uk (accessed December 16, 2012).

Gardner, Lyn. "It's Time We Got Angrier." *Guardian*, April 4, 2007.

———. "The Power Behind the Scenes." *Guardian*, April 4, 2001.

———. "The Wolves in the Walls." Review of *Wolves in the Walls*, based on the book by Neil Gaiman. *Guardian*, March 31, 2006.

Giannachi, Gabriella, and Mary Luckhurst, eds. *On Directing: Interviews with Directors*. London: Faber and Faber, 1999.

Holroyd, Michael. *A Strange Eventful History: The Dramatic Lives of Ellen Terry, Henry Irving and Their Remarkable Families*. London: Vintage, 2009.

Hoyle, Ben. "Dead White Men in the Critic's Chair Scorning Work of Women Directors." *Times*, May 14, 2007.

Littlewood, Joan. *Joan's Book: Joan Littlewood's Peculiar History as She Tells It*. London: Methuen, 2003.

Macmillan, Joyce. Review of *Wall of Death: A Way of Life*. *Scotsman*, February 12, 2010.

Manfull, Helen. *Taking Stage: Women Directors on Directing*. London: Methuen, 1999.

Mitchell, Katie. *The Director's Craft: A Handbook for the Theatre*. London: Routledge, 2009.

Murphy, Michelle. "Annie Horniman." *BBC News Manchester*, n.d. Available at http://www.bbc.co.uk/manchester (accessed July 15, 2010).

Petrook, Mike. "Equal Pay for Women Still 57 Years Away." *Chartered Management Institute*, August 19, 2010. Available at http://www.managers.org.uk (accessed January 6, 2011).

Shevtsova, Maria, and Christopher Innes. *Directors/Directing: Conversations on Theatre*. Cambridge: Cambridge University Press, 2009.

Sphinx Theatre Company. Available at http://www.sphinxtheater.co.uk (accessed December 18, 2010).

Taylor, Paul. "Second Opinion: Paul Taylor Defends Fiona Shaw's Richard II from the Baying Critics." *Independent*, June 14, 1995.

Tusa, John. "The John Tusa Interviews." Interview with Deborah Warner. *BBC*, n.d. Available at http://www.bbc.co.uk (accessed June 14, 2011).

"Where the Art Is—Vicky Featherstone." *The Stage*, January 28, 2005.

 Greece

Avra Sidiropoulou

Feminist theatre or "women's theatre" as such is not a Greek phenomenon. Albeit a European Union member state since 1980, due to its very unusual social and political circumstances, Greece has never experienced the activism of the booming feminist movements in the United States or countries like England, France, and Germany. Nevertheless, women's artistic activity in the country has been rising steadily; in the theatre women have occupied positions of power as producers or artistic directors of established institutions while stabilizing their status as artistic equals to men. In particular, despite the fact that the directing profession has been male-dominated throughout Greece's history, since the 1990s the large number of female artists working as freelance directors or in state-run, state-subsidized, or purely commercial theatres is clearly an expression of trust in women's artistic and managerial abilities.

Women's Rights: Historical Context

The beginnings of feminism in Greece are impressive. At the wake of the twentieth century, the dynamic presence of educated women from the Athenian upper-class society instigated a struggle for social and political reform in a variety of ways. The modern Greek state was founded in 1830, and by the end of the 1880s there were organized attempts to create a favorable climate for women. One of the pioneers was Kalliroi Siganou-Parren. A political activist, journalist, and playwright,[1] her major contribution was the establishment in 1887 of a women's press, called A Journal of Ladies (Efimeris ton Kyrion), and a women's club in 1888, called Women's Club (Leschi Kyrion). Because the matter of educating women was most pressing, in 1890 Parren established the Sunday School for Women and Girls of Lower Means (Scholi tis Kyriakis Aporon Gynaikon kai Korasidon tou Laou), paving the way to a more formal education for women. In the same year, Ioanna Stefanopoli became the first woman to be admitted as a student at the University of Athens in the School of Philosophy. In 1911 Parren also helped realize the Women's Lyceum Club (Lykeion ton Ellinidon), while in 1913 Avra Theodoropoulou, another pioneer in the women's cause, founded the club Women's Life (Gynaikeia Zoi). Significantly, in 1919 the Socialist Women's Club (Socialistikos Omilos Gynaikon) brought forth the issues of family equality, legalization of abortions, and the right to work, given that there were no labor rights to protect women and that vast inequalities prevailed in the work field.

The period between the two world wars was in fact a most dynamic era for the feminist movement in Greece, with women's clubs launched all over the country. What these groups demanded was basically the full recognition of women's place in society, with the women's right to vote present at the forefront of all claims. Not surprisingly, women activists met with major reactions from the press, the Greek Church, male politicians, and a portion of the female population, all of whom resisted a revised role for women and a new model of family and social equality. Although the Greek constitution granted women their first victory in 1927 by recognizing the equality of the two sexes by law, the actual conditions for women were anything but ideal. In fact, according to the statistics of the time, nearly 70 percent of Greek women remained illiterate (Loupa).

Despite the fact that Ioannis Metaxas's dictatorship in 1936 put a brief end to all attempts to further the women's cause, banning all women's clubs and restoring all traditional Christian and family values, World War II paradoxically empowered women's position. Several women actively participated in the Greek Resistance movement; more specifically, women guerrillas circulated their own pamphlets, addressing the population of women and trying to raise social awareness by forming more than 150 clubs in the Greek periphery. As soon as the period of the German occupation ended in 1945, these groups started to restructure themselves; however, their function was interrupted by the Greek Civil War, which lasted until 1949, putting an end to all activities. In fact, guerrilla women belonging to the Greek Left and rebelling in the mountains against the bourgeois state were led to prisons or sent off to remote islands of the Aegean Sea.

Things started to look up in 1952, when the Greek State finally passed a law that established women's full political rights after several years of irresolution. This was the period when women first gained access to traditionally male-dominated professions (such as law practice), also entering the Greek parliament, where they fought for women's equality, pitted against an overly distrustful and slow-moving society.

In 1967 another major event in Greek history stalled women's rights: the military coup of 1967 silenced most progressive voices, obliterating all signs of women's quests for social reform and allowing only charity organizations to exist. During the seven barren years that marked the rule of the military junta, a lot of Greek women affiliated with the Greek Left were imprisoned, tortured, or exiled. Ironically, while Greece was experiencing a painful revival of the Dark Ages, the rest of Western Europe and the United States celebrated a vibrant neofeminist movement, openly confronting major women's issues, such as self-definition, family empowerment, and sexuality. The revolutionary messages from abroad reached Greece belatedly, blurred, caricatured or distorted. Indeed, the term "feminist" or "feminism" to some extent continues to ring a negative tone. As Elizabeth Sakellaridou argues in her 2006 study *Contemporary Women's Theatre*:

> Undoubtedly, the Greek cultural situation, because of the very unique political circumstances, went straight from the proto-feminist to the meta-feminist period, and, as a result, the creativity of women lost the timeliness of the feminist movement. . . . The messages came all in a package from abroad, through the spreading of the foreign intelligentsia and the coming home of Greek intellectuals and artists who had been self-exiled in Western countries. In this respect, Greek women were involved in the feminist matters on a theoretical and symbolic level, through the doctrines of foreign experience, and the female creativity went straight to a meta-feminist viewing of the world, without being permeated by the spirit of social assertion and political activism. (318, my translation)

The restoration of the Greek republic in 1974 found women wounded and confused, rushing to catch up with the major developments that had already occurred in the West. A change in legislation, as well as in attitude within the family or workplace, now became imperative. Women organized themselves on university campuses, forming a type of "academic feminist movement" and voicing—often in writing—their condemnation of family violence, rape, and belittlement. Greece's act of joining the European Union in 1981 benefited the dialogue that had been taking place with feminists from other countries. The long-expected reformation of Greek family law in 1983, as well as the legalization of abortion in 1986, lifted many constrictions that held women captive in terms of social, economic, and cultural activity. Notwithstanding the challenges, women were now better prepared to claim their right to exist as equal partners to men in almost all fields of professional life, including the arena of theatre.

Early Women Directors

In the first half of the twentieth century Greek theatre was dominated by two rival star actresses, Marika Kotopouli (1887–1954) and Kyveli Andrianou (known simply as "Kyveli," 1887–1978), both of whom had a say in repertory, production, and casting choices; yet the directing profession in Greece remained male dominated up until almost the 1980s. Directing as a self-reliant discipline for women is a recent phenomenon, with the leap from acting to directing more common in the twenty-first century. This said, the actual beginnings of women's directing practice in Greece remain unexplored, and the exact number of contemporary women directors in the country is a matter of conjecture. The lack of information can be attributed in part to the fact that many women directors are self-employed or working in small-budget groups, which are not registered with the Greek Directors' Guild (Etairia Ellinon Skinotheton).

The 1990s marked a new era in the Greek theatre, particularly in the capital city of Athens, and the favorable wind blowing over the increasing number of theatre stages undoubtedly brought with it a broader change in the perception of women as partners potentially equal to men in the directing profession. The firm establishment of the Social Democrats in the Greek government, together with the country's developing economy, enabled the foundation of state-subsidized theatres in the Greek periphery. The result was an unprecedented flourishing of theatre practice; within the span of less than a decade, Greek theatre developed to the extent that in Athens, a city of approximately 4.5 million people, there could be more than three hundred theatre productions running at the same time. This clearly reflected the need for more directors, and women as well as men were recruited to meet the new demands.

Working Climate in the Twenty-First Century

There are several concurrent, subsequent, and/or complementary reasons that add to the establishment of women directors in Greece. For one thing, a hopeful economic climate bears with it a general investment in the arts, which in itself creates more positions to be filled, more opportunities for specialized education, and a trust in new cultural propositions. More specifically, having conducted graduate theatre studies in Europe and the United States, many young Greek women came into contact with more up-to-date directing and acting aesthetics. With a new confidence in themselves as artists, they subsequently returned to Greece, becoming actively involved in the theatre. Concurrently, it was only a matter of time for many women directors to emerge out of the plethora of semi- to fully professional experimental groups and the numerous state and private drama schools that have emerged since the mid-1990s. In addition, many women took advantage of the funding available to new forms of entrepreneurship, building their own theatres, which they also managed—producing, directing, and acting in the season's repertory. Finally, many women decided to combine the lonely practice of playwriting with the more communal nature of directing, staging their own plays. Given these shifts, one can see a bustling combination of disciplines: of actors, playwrights, and producers turning into directors. No doubt, this hybridized function of stage practitioners is also the consequence of the lack of an organized, higher-level education for directors within the Greek university system.

Women-Run Theatre Companies and Individual Voices

As already argued, women's directing in Greece became more visible near the turn of the twenty-first century. Despite the major economic crisis that hit Greece in 2010, people were still spending money on theatre—as audiences, but also as savvy entrepreneurs, investing money and time in an art that appears more popular than ever. More and more theatre spaces are sprouting up everywhere, and young women directors are just as active; although mostly self-employed, they manage their own production companies rigorously, often with little or no state subsidy. Many women-led groups secure for themselves a not-for-profit status, which allows them to apply for state funding. However, they remain mostly freelance, forced to move from one theatre space to another, seeking allegiances and co-production possibilities with more autonomous and financially viable establishments.

Other companies are more fortunate in this respect. Anna Kokkinou, a director, actor and producer, is an important voice in the contemporary scene, producing classics as well as experimental adaptations of literary texts, including an acclaimed 1993 production of Giorgos Vizyinos's *Figures from the Work of Vizyinos* (*Morphes apo to ergo tou Vizyinou*) at the elegant Sfendoni Theatre, which she runs herself.[2] A similar case can be made of Anna Vagena, who has managed her own space, Metaxourgio Theatre, since 1999, after having founded the state-owned Thessalikon regional theatre. Even though Vagena is mainly an actress, her directing work, focusing primarily on contemporary Greek plays or adapted material from Greek history and literature, has received strong critical and audience acclaim.

Like Vagena's company, Theatre at Colonus (Epi Kolono Theatre), led by Eleni Skoti, has become established by presenting an interesting international repertory that revolves around new writing, steadily attracting its own audience. In addition, Tatiana Lygari, also a producer, actor, and director, has channelled her creativity into a unique theatre space housed in a train wagon, The Train at Rouf (To Traino sto Rouf), where she often directs music and dance-informed pieces. Other women include Xenia Kalogeropoulou, an actress, director, and writer who runs the successful Door Theatre (Theatro Porta), where her company Little Door (Mikri Porta), established in 1972, also caters to the theatrical needs of children. In the second largest city of Greece, Thessaloniki, director Mona Kitsopoulou has been operating Diffraction Studio (Studio Parathlassi) since 1986. One of the fortunate few directors to work in her own space, Kitsopoulou made a name for herself as a cult figure in town, putting a touch of the "fringe" on the material she handles.

Despite the lack of a permanent base, there are several individual women's voices in the Greek directing scene today. The list of names of women who have in some capacity tried directing is lengthy, and history can only attest to how lasting the effect of their creative work will be. Some of these directors bring together their actor-director talent, like Lydia Koniordou, who has been particularly acclaimed in her work on Greek tragedy. Koniordou is an emblematic figure in the Greek theatre world, having worked extensively at the Greek National Theatre, where she directed the visually stylized productions of Sophocles's *Electra* in 1996, Euripides's *Ion* in 2003, and Greek poet Kostis Palamas's 1902 play, *Trisevyene*, in 2011. Maya Lyberopoulou is also highly respected among the members of the theatre intelligentsia. Counting almost fifty years in the theatre arena, Lyberopoulou, like Pateraki, belongs to a generation of women pioneers who helped form a distinct European aesthetic in Greek theatre practice. Although she has been working mostly as an actor, her directing credits— some during her time as artistic director of the Regional Theatre of Patras—include plays by Maxim Gorki, Carlo Goldoni, Yukio Mishima, and Bernard-Marie Koltes. Lyberopoulou's *Demons and Demonized* (*Demones kai Demonismeni*), a stage adaptation based on Fyodor Dostoyevsky's novel *Demons*, was produced at the Athens Festival in 2007.

What describes the directing practice of the younger generations is a sense of inter-disciplinarity. Combining a writer's and director's point of view, Elena Penga, whose work has also been informed by a British aesthetic and training, should be counted among the most promising voices of the Greek alternative scene. Of the same generation, director-playwright Avra Sidiropoulou, together with Persona Theatre Company (Kallitechniki Omada Persona), has been actively establishing artistic bonds internationally, as manifest in the productions of her plays *Clytemnestra's Tears* (*Ta Dakrya tis Clytemnestras*) in 2004—which was performed in a solo and tri-lingual version in Athens, Istanbul, and New York—and in 2009 *And God Said* (*Kai o Theos Milisse*), a play written in English and performed by two Turkish and one Iranian actor in Istanbul and Tehran. Like Penga and Sidiropoulou, other younger-generation women directors have been educated abroad and brought back to Greece a different artistic sensibility and innovative theatre forms. Notable examples include London-educated Elli Papakonstandinou, who has directed on both experimental and more mainstream stages in Athens, including the National Theatre of Greece (Ethniko Theatro), but who has also worked in London and the United States. Papakonstandinou's *ODC . . . after Homer* was featured at the Edinburgh Fringe Festival in 2002 and also traveled to the Opera of Cairo and to Princeton University. Similarly, some of the most representative younger directors, whose work is alternately produced in established repertory companies and more edgy spaces, include Athanassia Karagianopoulou, Katerina Evangelatou, Vicky Georgiadi, Aggeliki Darlasi, and Barbara Douka among others. Inclusion of every Greek woman director in this study would make the list of names unwieldy, but the exclusion of names is by no means indicative of the current state of women directing in contemporary Greece.

Profiles of Contemporary Directors

Roula Pateraki

In 1978, at a time when women directors were still a relatively rare phenomenon, Roula Pateraki, an actor-director, formed the theatre studio Review of Dramatic Art (Epitheorisi Dramatikis Technis) in Thessaloniki, which remained in full operation until 1985 and where she started to develop her own method of actor training. Pateraki holds a special place in Greek culture, a pioneering woman artist who has dared to experiment with the language and form of extremely demanding plays. Born in Thessaloniki in the north of Greece, she initially studied English—like many Greek directors—which also accounts for her affinity to stage masterpieces in the English language. In her early years as a director, she produced Tom Stoppard's *Travesties, Dark Crimes* (based on Rainer Werner Fassbinder's play *Bremen Freedom* and Michel Foucault's *Piviere Case*), an adaptation of Samuel Beckett's texts called *MultiBeckett 1,2,3*, Bertolt Brecht's *Lux in Tenebris*, and Henrik Ibsen's *Hedda Gabler*. However, Pateraki became especially established in the 1990s, in part by securing a solid theatre ensemble, the Dramatic Theatre of Roula Pateraki (Dramatiko Theatro Roula Pateraki). Her direction of Beckett's *Happy Days* in 1994, in which she also performed Winnie's role, caused a sensation among Greek critics and audiences alike, thanks in part to its exquisite visual environment.

Best known for her exacting work on the text, Pateraki has always been viewed as an enigmatic, phlegmatic, and highly intellectual persona; she likes to be constantly surprising in her eccentric choice of material, "entering the war and trying all different weapons" (Lazaridou). Particularly attracted to the great classics, Pateraki considers her work on *Hedda Gabler* and *Happy Days* to be perhaps the most representative of her directing method. She is also very fond of her 2010 production of James Joyce's unique play *The Exiles*, for which she structured the extensive material of the text through concrete directorial choices.

Pateraki's profound theatre experience makes her equally comfortable with large-scale works and black box monologue pieces. For that reason alone, it is difficult to classify her. Even though her reputation is that of an experimental-fringe artist, she has also directed for the National Theatre of Greece, as well as for commercial theatres. Over the years, Pateraki has developed four systems of actor training, which consist of specific physical and free-association acting exercises, based on the principle that in the theatre everything must be *embodied*. She believes that "the actor's body must be fully present in performance in order for the muscular and neurological system to relax" and the actor to attain that same "exciting innocence," which Pateraki herself experienced as a child actor (Pateraki). The director claims that there should be no analysis or psychological character buildup, because ultimately, these reinforce the body's submission to the tyranny of the mind. She has categorized these systems according to the material she handles each time; for example in her work on August Strindberg's *Chamber Plays—The Storm* and *The Pelican* in 1999—she applied what she calls an "anti-communicative" model, according to which each actor becomes an object of criticism by the spectators. As she provocatively claims, each major role by a major playwright carries within it a sense of autonomy, which therefore allows the actors to focus on themselves, rather than obsessively attempt to establish interaction with other performers.

Besides classics by Beckett, Ibsen, and Strindberg, Pateraki greatly favors the uncompromising plays of contemporary iconoclastic writers like Sarah Kane, Thomas Bernhard, and Krista Wolf, reworking them into solo form and bringing herself to the center of theatre praxis. In her treatment of Kane's suicide piece, *4.48 Psychosis*, Pateraki presented two different versions in 2002 and 2003, performing the part of the main character herself.[3] In both versions, she wished to capture the protagonist's anguished poetry, but in the 2003 production, through the mixture of logos and film, she reflected on the fundamental psychological split in the woman character, whose videotaped identity constantly undermines her live stage presence. Moreover, Pateraki's background in literature makes her an ideal interlocutor with works of fiction. Thus, in her stage renditions of Marcel Proust's *Days of Reading* in 2002, Krista Wolf's *Kassandra* in 2003, Thomas Bernhard's *Wittgenstein's Nephew* in 2003, and in Yannis Panou's *The History of Metamorphoses* (*Istoria ton Metamorphoseon*) in 2010, Pateraki engages in a fascinating dialogue with the culture of literature, embodying its dynamics and physicalizing the density of its language. Still, Pateraki's greatest dream is "[to] direct the history of the Peloponnese War," as told by ancient Greek historian, Thucidides (Pateraki). This fact alone testifies to the scope of her vision and epic-scale imagination.

Nikaiti Kontouri

Another admirer of the epic classics is Nikaiti Kontouri, one of the most professionally established women directors in Greece and a consistent collaborator of the main state theatres in the country. Such collaborations have afforded Kontouri the means to engage in large-scale stagings of Greek tragedy, including two productions at the National Theatre of Greece, *Medea* in 1997 and *Antigoni* in 2002, as well as *The Trojan Women* at the Municipal Theatre of Northern Greece (Kratiko Theatro Voreiou Ellados) in 2009. Notably, after its initial presentation at the ancient theatre of Epidaurus, *Medea* toured worldwide for more than three years, receiving critical acclaim. The production of the play was conceived in operatic terms, against an abstract set design by Giorgos Patsas, in which red and white dominated. Especially memorable were the ritualistic movement of the chorus and the spectacular last scene of the play, in which Medea is carried away in a flaming chariot to her grandfather, Helios.

Kontouri studied directing at Hunter College in New York City in the mid-1980s, and her theatre career began as an actor at various Greek theatres. However, in 1992 she made a sharp turn toward directing with the production of Patrick Süskind's *The Double Bass*. Since then she has worked steadily and exclusively as a director in state-funded as well as commercial theatres, both in Athens and the Greek periphery.

Although Kontouri's career seems ideal, it is not representative of the challenges Greek women directors face while struggling to win over the male producers and artistic directors who manage the financially healthy theatres in Greece. Returning to Greece after her studies in the United States at the beginning of the 1990s, Kontouri had the opportunity to contribute creatively to the establishment of a very promising repertory company, Notos Theatre Company (Theatro tou Notou), directing mostly experimental plays, such as Goethe's *The Brothers* in 1994 and Win Wells's *Gertrude Stein and a Companion* in 1993, among others. From then on, her directing projects multiplied and her reputation took off. At a time when money was still being invested in the theatre, Kontouri was fortunate enough to be employed in theatres that could support the productions of classics such as Molière's *Tartuffe* and Shakespeare's *Othello* in 1996, Frederico García Lorca's *Doña Rosita* in 1999, Ibsen's *A Doll's House* in 2001, and *Hedda Gabler* in 2004, all of which had high production budgets. At the same time, Kontouri also directed more contemporary works, such as Harold Pinter's *Betrayal* in 1996, Ingmar Bergman's *Scenes from a Marriage* in 2005, Martin McDonagh's *The Beauty Queen of Leenane* in 2008, and Shelagh Stevenson's *The Memory of Water* in 2000, collaborating with the crème de la crème of Greek actors.

On the whole, Kontouri's career has been extremely prolific. As she herself enthusiastically emphasizes, she loves to direct plays that have a strong plot-line and characters, and she is attracted to the contradictions and conflicts that make plays survive the passage of time. Being an experienced director, Kontouri tries to avoid repeated patterns in her work and comes to rehearsal fully prepared, spending a lot of time exploring the words and their meaning, because the meaning and the clarity of each reading are essential. She has also been successful at casting, which is something in which she invests, aware that her directing should never be too visible in performance. No matter what, she insists that she is open to her actors' suggestions, something that she learned to do when studying in the United States. In directing Donald Margulies's *Time Stands Still* in 2010 and Paula Vogel's *The Oldest Profession* in 2011 in Athens, Kontouri returned to her favorite American dramaturgy, through which she revisits her "own America" (Kontouri).

Angela Brouskou

Another one of the country's most idiosyncratic directors, Angela Brouskou also entered the world of theatre through acting, having been trained at the reputable Art Theatre Drama School (Dramatiki Scholi Theatrou Technis) in Athens in the beginning of the 1980s. As an actress she collaborated with several important Greek directors and continues to act, even though she is much more active as a stage director. Brouskou made a name for herself in directing classical plays with an edge, examining them from a clearly political point of view, as opportunities for unearthing the cultural circumstances both of the times in which those plays were written and of modern Greek culture. Her work as an actor, director, and theatre instructor is very much a product of intense experimentation with actors' methods and techniques, especially within Greek tragedy.

In 1993 Brouskou formed her own theatre company in Athens, Chamber Theatre (Theatro Domatiou), also founding her own acting studio, wishing to contribute to an in-depth exploration of the fundamental issues of theatrical representation and the understanding of how the body operates on stage. This is in keeping with her desire to change the theatre landscape in Greece; in fact, she laments the fact that there is very little training for directors and also that things are presently dominated by an all-consuming "reality-show" aesthetic, which has generated far too many theatre groups in need of a "quick fix" of celebrity. Brouskou contests the notion of directing as a mostly self-taught art and argues that because there is so little patience for studying in Greece, the sense of vulgarity and dispensability one observes in current theatre is only natural (Brouskou).

Thus seeking to reconsider the ethics of training and education in general, Brouskou's company, which is state subsidized, has over the years struggled to identify itself with experimental and alternative work, combining the visual element with unconventional acting forms. At the same time, the choice of material is instrumental; from its inception, the group has been dedicated to classics from the Western dramatic canon, as were productions of Molière's *The Misanthrope* in 1994, Jean Genet's *The Maids* in 1995, Strindberg's *Miss Julie* in 1997, and Euripides's *Medea* in 1999. In 2001 the company changed gears, staging an adaptation of the novel *Yes* (*Nai*) by Margarita Karapanou, one of Greece's most unique female voices, who redefined language, form, and subject matter in her fiction. That production established Brouskou as a distinct woman director in the country, daring to defy established theatre conventions in her work. Following in 2002, the production of Georg Büchner's *Woyzeck* and *Waiting . . . (something about hunger . . .)* in 2005, based on Beckett's *Waiting for Godot*, both further attest to the director's interest in exploring and reconceiving the great classics of the Western dramatic canon.

Brouskou's directing career has included productions of Sarah Kane's *Blast* in 2007 and Tennessee Williams's *A Streetcar Named Desire* in 2008, securing the director's access to the major cultural institutions of Greece such as the Athens Festival, for which she directed Sophocles's *Electra* in 2006. Similarly, the Athens and Epidaurus Festival gave her the opportunity to be one of the exceptionally few Greek women directors ever to present their work in the open-air ancient theatre with the production of Aeschylus's *Agamemnon* in 2008. Interestingly, for a company called Chamber Theatre, Brouskou's group succeeded in mastering the huge space of Epidaurus. Yet the performance of *Agamemnon* caused strong controversy among spectators and critics due to the director's revisionist outlook on the play. For example, the actor playing Agamemnon appeared in a sailor's cap, adorned with garlands that he collected during his travels in exotic lands. Although Agamemnon's cigar and whisky flask, as well as the watermelon that the messenger carried with him on his way back from Troy, may have irritated some, it was the treatment of the chorus that caused the greatest uproar. Depicted as a bunch of sycophants trying to please the state tyrant, they likened themselves to a cluster of dogs, licking up to their master. Several other elements in staging and characterization brought to the fore Brouskou's desire to reconsider the ways in which tragedy can be made relevant, namely, its dialectical relationship to contemporary society.

After *Agamemnon*, Brouskou took to large-scale theatre events, also working as a freelance director. For example, in 2010 she directed *Wonderland*, her adaption of Lewis Carroll's *Alice in Wonderland/Through the Looking Glass*, at Pallas Theatre, a newly restored, multipotential space, and in 2010 she directed Shakespeare's *Titus Andronicus*, produced by the National Theatre of Greece. In both productions Brouskou pursued

Shakespeare's *Titus Andronicus*, directed by Angela Brouskou, National Theatre of Greece, Athens, 2010. Photographer: Myrto Apostolidis.

Wonderland, adapted and directed by Angela Brouskou, Pallas Theatre, Athens, 2010. Photographer: Miltos Athanassiou.

her favorite themes of cultural violence, chaos, and the irrational, of things that are "spectacularly violent . . . just like our present reality," exploring the ways in which we are conditioned by society and our sexual identities (Spyropoulou). In fact, Brouskou is very much aware of how difficult it is for a woman director to make it in the male-managed directing world. She views the recent widespread euphoria regarding Greek theatre—as expressed in the large numbers of existing artists, groups, and productions—as overly optimistic and potentially dangerous, a product of an undigested, uncritical equation of the dramatic art with mass culture.

All three artists, Pateraki, Kontouri, and Brouskou have been fighting several battles in order to break through the male establishment of the directing elite in Greece. On an up-note, it is only a matter of time before the viable and potent current that has been forming since the 1980s starts to yield to a lot more women directors the critical attention, artistic recognition, and economic stability that they deserve.

Notes

1. Parren's play, *The New Woman* [*I Nea Gynaika*], was performed in 1907.
2. The production of *Figures from the Work of Vizyinos* was launched originally in 1993 but has been performed all over Greece and also in Europe, totalling more than 650 performances.
3. British playwright Sara Kane wrote *4.48 Psychosis* in 1998, a few months before committing suicide. The text is composed of lines unassigned to characters, allowing for great freedom in casting. In the first version, Pateraki is on stage alone, carrying the entire weight of the text herself, while in the later rendition, she interacts with her screened image, revealing the protagonist's mental and psychological dissolution.

Sources

Avdela, Efi, and Aggelika Psara, eds. *Feminism in Greece in the Years between the Wars* [*O Feminismos stin Ellada tou Mesopolemou*]. Athens: Gnossi, 1985.

Brouskou, Angela. Interview with Avra Sidiropoulou. November 14, 2010.

Kleftoyanni, Ioanna. "My Own Trojan Women Have a Name and a History" ["Oi Dikes mou Troades Ehoun Onoma kai Istoria"]. Interview with Nikaiti Kontouri. *Eleftherotypia*, August 6, 2009.

Kontouri, Nikaiti. Interview with Avra Sidiropoulou. October 16, 2010.

Lazaridou, Asteropi. "Theatre Is Cheaper Than a Restaurant" ["To Theatro Einai pio Ftino apo tin Taverna"]. Interview with Roula Pateraki. *To Vima*, October 24, 2010.

Loupa, Christianna. "The Struggle for Women's Vote" ["O Agonas gia ti Gynaikeia Psifo"]. *tvxs,* n.d. Available at http://tvxs.gr/news (accessed February 20, 2013).

Pateraki, Roula. Interview with Avra Sidiropoulou. November 12, 2010.

Patsalidis, Savas. *The 'Other' Theatre* [*To 'Allo Theatro*]. Athens: Tolidi, 1993.

Sakellaridou, Elizabeth. *Contemporary Women's Theatre* [*Synchrono Gynaikeio Theatro*]. Athens: Ellinika Grammata, 2006.

Spyropoulou, Maria Eleni. "We Are All Potentially Conspirators in Violence" ["Sti Via Eimaste Oli en Dynamei Symmetohi"]. Interview with Angela Brouskou. *City Press*, April 20, 2010.

Varopoulou, Eleni. *Theatre in Greece: The Tradition of the Modern 1974–2006* [*To Theatro stin Ellada: I Paradosi tou Kainourgiou 1974–2006*]. Athens: Agra, 2009.

Xiradaki, Koula. *The Feminist Movement in Greece* [*To Feministiko Kinima stin Ellada*]. Athens: Glaros, 1988.

 India

Erin B. Mee

In India, while there are professional and commercial theatres and companies in most cities, the majority of urban theatre is best described as amateur theatre in the economic sense with professional standards of performance and production, mounted in rented theatre halls by companies composed of theatre experts and enthusiasts who have other jobs to support them.[1] Most of these companies are run by a director-producer, actor-director-producer, or playwright-director-producer; only very rarely are freelance directors hired. In India, then, women directors run their own companies and produce their own work by necessity.

Since the 1990s there have been an increasing number of women directors and therefore an increasing number of women-run companies; women are also running important institutions such as the National School of Drama (NSD) in Delhi or the Rangashankara theatre in Bangalore, and chairing committees that choose productions to represent Indian theatre in state, national, and international theatre festivals. These women are asking important questions about what it means to be a woman director. Director-scholar Kirti Jain writes:

> Direction in theatre has been the privilege of men down the centuries. . . . Hence the entire notion of directing has been [defined and developed by them]. . . . It is very difficult to say if women's intervention had happened much earlier, would we have an altogether different notion about what a theatrical performance is meant to do—its relationship with the text, the actors and the audience? Is it possible that the expectations of the audience conditioned by a long tradition of theatre controlled by men, would have been completely different? And now, when women have started

working in this field, are they to fit into that tradition or can they create a theatre independent of the norms already set for centuries? Do the women feel the need for distinct norms of viewing and assessing? Will the audience accept their work as valid theatre? (151–52)

Director, scholar, and current director of the NSD in Delhi Anuradha Kapur asks: "Does a woman's language produce different narratives, stories, plots and characters? Another perception of time and temporality? An otherwise nuanced experience? Another sort of work process?" ("A Wandering Word" 6). An analysis of the work of women directors over the past twenty years shows they have questioned assumptions about gender, have complicated commonplace notions about what it means to be Indian, and have broadened ideas about what Indian theatre is, can be, or should encompass. Their contributions to contemporary Indian theatre exist in the overlapping realms of the political, the social, and the aesthetic: they reproduce the world as they see it.

Women's Rights: Historical Context

During the early Vedic period (roughly 1500–500 BCE), studies have suggested that men and women enjoyed equal rights and status. In the medieval period (roughly 550–1526 CE) child marriage, bans on widow remarriage, and the practice of *sati* (widow burning) reflected the lower status of women, although numerous women, including the poet-saint Mirabai, used their art to question these oppressive practices—proving that the fight for women's equality began quite early. The idea of powerful women in India is as old as the goddesses Durga and Kali, but the colonial period (1612–1947) brought to women's attention the ideas of democracy, equality, and individual rights, and women began to form organizations to promote women's rights. For example, women organized the All India Women's Education Conference in 1927, which focused on the education of women, and women ensured passage of the Child Marriage Restraint Act in 1929.

The anticolonial nationalist constructions of India that arose in the late nineteenth century and continued into the post-Independence period severely circumscribed women's social roles and movement. Partha Chatterjee traces the way the discourse of nationalism created a dichotomy between outer and inner which, when applied to daily life "separate[d] the social space into *ghar* and *bahir*, the home and the world" (120). Bahir belonged to the men, who had to make adjustments in their style of dress, their language, and their mannerisms in order to work with colonial administrators. "In the world," Chatterjee asserts, "imitation of and adaptation to Western norms was a necessity; at home, they were tantamount to annihilation of one's very identity" (121). Ghar, the home, became the domain of women, and it came to represent "one's inner spiritual self, one's true identity" (120). Mothers became the gatekeepers of "authentic" Indian culture and, as such, their purity had to be protected. As a result, their movement was circumscribed, and the presence of women on stage was seen as a transgression of respectability, a social prohibition that still operates to a large extent, particularly in smaller towns and villages.[2] Nonetheless, women played an active role in the fight for Independence: in Madhya Pradesh the Queen of Jhansi led a rebellion against the British and is considered a national heroine; in Manipur women led the first anti-British protests in the 1880s, went on to initiate several of the most successful anti-British protests of the twentieth century, and continue to agitate both for human rights and for women's rights; and in 1925 Sarojini Naidu was elected the first woman president of the Indian National Congress.

After India's Independence in 1947 the struggle for women's rights continued. In the 1970s protests against rape led to the introduction of rape as a category in the Indian Penal Code; and in Andhra Pradesh, Himachal Pradesh, Kerala, Tamil Nadu, and elsewhere women launched anti-liquor campaigns designed to keep income at home and curb domestic violence. In the 1990s foreign donor agencies enabled the growth of numerous nongovernmental organizations that specifically addressed women's issues. In 1993 the passage of the "Panchayat Raj" amendments to the constitution reserved 30 percent of seats in elected village councils for women. Over the years numerous laws to protect women, including the Equal Remuneration Act, the Prevention of Immoral Traffic Act, the Sati Prevention Act, and the Dowry Prohibition Act have been passed. In spite of this, women's rights vary greatly in different states: in Kerala 100 percent of women are literate, many have PhDs, and the matrilineal society allows women to inherit property, while the communist government ensures that there is less poverty in Kerala than elsewhere. By contrast, in Bihar women's literacy is extremely low, women do not inherit property, and poverty is widespread. In Tamil Nadu's cities women are well educated and share equal rights, while in some rural villages female infanticide and abortion still take place in spite of laws prohibiting such practices.

Early Women Directors

In the nineteenth century the British introduced modern theatre to Calcutta and Bombay in three ways: by touring productions to entertain their expatriate administrators, merchants, and soldiers; by supporting productions of English plays staged by the expatriates themselves in newly erected British-style playhouses; and by teaching English drama in Indian universities, where Shakespeare was presented as the apex of British civilization. In the mid-nineteenth century, urban middle-class intellectuals began to build their own proscenium stages, to translate English plays into Indian languages, and to write their own plays in the style of the modern European drama to which they were being exposed. The spread of English drama was part of colonizing Indian culture: it was designed not only to shape artistic activity but also to impose on Indians a way of understanding and operating in the world, and to assert colonial cultural superiority. The British introduced the proscenium stage to India, which changed the performer-audience relationship and the ways in which audiences participated in productions. They commercialized theatre going, turning theatre into a commodity rather than a community event related to annual harvests and religious occasions. Most significant, however, is that they introduced a conceptualization of theatre as dramatic literature, a construction that shaped the very definition of theatre and the aesthetics of the emerging modern Indian theatre. Modern theatre came to be defined in terms of plot-driven, psychologically motivated, realistic plays that stemmed from a single author. This definition of modern theatre also brought with it the notion of a director who is responsible for conceiving and realizing the production and coordinating all its aesthetic elements. Thus, the actor-manager of a genre such as *Nautanki*, a form of popular operatic theatre performed by women, gave way to the Western-style director.

One of the first women directors to gain nationwide recognition was Shanta Gandhi, a founding member of the Indian People's Theatre Association, which was formed in Calcutta and Bombay in 1942 to create revolutionary theatre using popular and mainly rural theatrical genres. From 1943 to 1947 Gandhi worked on dance-theatre productions such as *Voice of Bengal* in 1943, *Spirit of India* in 1944, and *India Immortal* in 1945. In 1968 she directed a famous student production of *Jasma Odan*, a story about *sati*, at the Meghdoot Open Air Theater in Delhi, incorporating techniques of *bhavai*, a genre of popular theatre from Gujarat. As such, she was an early pioneer of what later came to be known as the theatre of roots movement.

Because theatre was used to disseminate colonial culture and demonstrate colonial cultural superiority, it became a powerful tool with which to contest colonial authority both before and after Independence in 1947. After Independence a number of playwrights and directors turned to classical dance, religious ritual, martial arts, popular entertainment, and Sanskrit aesthetic theory—genres and theories marginalized by colonial theatrical culture—to see what could be used to create an "indigenous" nonrealistic style of production that could in turn define an "Indian theatre." This impulse became known as the theatre of roots movement, an effort to decolonize the aesthetics of modern Indian theatre by challenging the visual practices, performer/spectator relationships, and aesthetic goals of colonial performance. The roots movement sought new ways of structuring experience, new ways of perceiving the world, and new modes of social interaction that were not dictated by the values and aesthetics of the colonizers.[3]

The roots movement was primarily concerned with reflecting and constructing an "Indian" identity and therefore did not concern itself with women's issues. In 1989 the Sangeet Natak Akademi (SNA) funded a national theatre festival in Delhi designed to showcase modern Indian theatre as a unique phenomenon and as an "authentic" expression of Indian culture. Of the fifteen productions in this festival only one was directed by a woman—Vijaya Mehta, a director who began working in Bombay in the 1960s—and very few of the plays dealt with women's issues or presented the world from a woman's point of view because issues of gender were subsumed under issues of nationhood and the creation and promotion of a "national" culture. As Kapur said,

"Mehta was not concerned with the problematic of a woman's voice because to work was enough" (Interview).

In the 1990s women began to expand the basic question posed by the roots movement and to address women's issues and perspectives on the world. For example, B. Jayashree, Neelam Man Singh Chowdhry, Tripurari Sharma, Usha Ganguli, Veenapani Chawla, Gowri Ramnarayan, Tripurari Sharma, and A. Mangai began to use particular genres of traditional performance to question stereotypes about women and to explore gender.[4]

Although many women directors do not want to be categorized by their gender, both Amal Allana and Kapur agree that women have been responsible for freeing Indian theatre from the now-dated concerns of the pre- and post-Independence moment, and from the theatre of roots as the dominant stylistic answer to the questions "What is India / What is Indian theatre?" Kapur, Allana, and Zuleikha Chaudhari typify a group of women who are questioning almost all the assumptions of earlier work. The kind of theatre these women create is characterized by their methods of devising theatre rather than starting with text, by their use of nondramatic texts, by the nonlinearity of their productions, by the image-driven rather than text-driven nature of their work, and by their use of cross-casting and female impersonation as a way to examine gender and its acquisition and performance. Brecht has taught us that dramaturgical structure is political, and women directors in India are challenging the political and social assumptions underpinning traditional male structures.

Working Climate in the Twenty-First Century

In 1999 the NSD produced a nationwide theatre festival, or Bharat Rang Mahotsav (BRM), which is now the largest annual theatre festival in South Asia. Charting the number of productions directed by women in these festivals demonstrates the numbers of women receiving recognition for their work at the national level, although it is not a reliable way to measure the number of women working or the percentage of directors who are women (see p. 179). These figures show that women are clearly part of the Indian theatrical scene in ways they were not in the past; however, they also reveal that women are still not represented in equal numbers.

In March 2010 the NSD organized the first South Asian Women's Theatre Festival, with fourteen productions designed to showcase women's work and to address women's issues from a wide variety of perspectives. The festival included productions from Nepal, Myanmar, Pakistan, Afghanistan, Bhutan, Maldives, Sri Lanka, Bangladesh, and all over India. Amal Allana, chair of the NSD, wrote in her program notes: "In laying claim to herself, the woman begins constructing a new world, a new universe, a new image and identity of herself as she sees it. She questions her own desire, her own sexuality. And for all this the woman of today seeks to create a new language of articulation—one which she feels to be more truthful, more unbiased. She creates in the theatre, a theatre of sensual experience—not of intellectual debate, not of issues.

The number of women directing in festivals, 1999–2010.

Year	Total Number of Productions	Number of Productions Directed by Women
1999	32	7
2000	83	11
2001	85	10
2002	144	24
2003	87	12
2004	75	10
2005	56	5
2006	61	11
2007	53	11
2008	75	18
2009	63	11
2010	85	15

The woman reproduces the world as she experiences it" ("Introduction"). The festival included Allana's *The Actress Binodini*; *Sakubai*, a look at the life of a nanny; a Nepali adaptation of Ibsen's *A Doll's House*; an antiwar Pakistani adaptation of Aristophanes's *Lysistrata*; a Manipuri play about a woman who fights the atrocities committed against her tribe; and a retelling of stories from the *Ramayana* and the *Mahabharata* from the point of view of the female characters. Collectively, this work is important because it examines the world from new perspectives. The festival recognized, promoted, and validated the new work created by women directors.

Profiles of Contemporary Directors[5]

A. Mangai

A. Mangai is a Chennai-based director, a founding member of the street theatre group Chennai Kalai Kuzhu, and a professor of English at Stella Maris College. Mangai received nationwide recognition in 1991 for her production of *Battle for the Fodder* (*Theeni-p-Por*) and has gone on to use traditional performance in all of her productions since, including *Velavi* in 1998 and the more recent *Avvai*. Between 1993 and 1999 she coordinated Voicing Silence, an annual meeting dedicated to producing women's stories, perspectives, and performing art traditions.

Mangai's 1996 production *The Newborn* (*Paccha Mannu*) addressed female infanticide and the abortion of female fetuses. It was designed to be performed on the street in districts outside of Chennai where both are prevalent. The production began with members of the company, all dressed in red, parading through the village clapping, drumming, and singing, "listen to our story." When they arrived at an open space in the village center, Mangai announced the play to the surrounding crowd, inviting audience participation, interruption, dialogue, and questions. The company members assumed roles and began to enact a series of formative moments in a woman's life between birth and giving birth, using a handheld curtain, a drum, several bamboo sticks, and a bundle of cloth as their only set and prop pieces. *The Newborn* was structured around the lifecycle rituals of women in Tamil Nadu; Mangai's premise was that the restrictions of patriarchy are inscribed onto and embedded in the consciousness of girls and young women through these rituals of socialization. The rituals were not only the subject of *The Newborn* but its structure as well. Working in Tamil, Mangai and her actors "collected the songs and ritual practices of ceremonies conducted during puberty, marriage, and first pregnancy" (Mangai, "Cultural" 71). Then they rewrote and recontextualized them to re-present the experiences of women in the area. For example, Mangai placed a popular all-female puberty ritual in the play, but she changed both the lyrics to the ritual song, as well as the context in which it was performed: "The songs sung during this ritual speak of purifying a female body and casting off the evil. This mixed feeling of happiness and fear, pride and shame experienced during puberty seems to run all through our lives. We chose a traditional song describing each part of a woman's body from head to toe praying for purification. . . . The [lyrics were] changed to express the values of socialization implicated in that ritual. Restriction of free mobility and fear of safeguarding the virginity of the girl became the crux of the song" (Mangai, "Cultural" 71).

Mangai says the song and the ceremony both ultimately serve to imprison the girl, to end her freedom and to place her under the ever more watchful eye of her family. In Mangai's production the girl ended up boxed in by bamboo sticks, each wielded by a person shouting demands and opinions at her. In this way, Mangai literalized the way women get stuck in their gender roles through socialization, and her staging illustrated the ways in which women are complicit in perpetuating the patriarchal system by trapping their own daughters in certain traditional practices and roles. By turning the private rituals of women into public forums of debate, Mangai also focuses on genres that she says are "never recognized as performance" (Interview). The rituals are simultaneously the form, subject, and means of communication.

Her production *Manimekalai*, performed at the Bharat Rang Mahotsav in Delhi in 2002, was adapted from the eponymous second-century Buddhist epic. Under Mangai's direction Manimekalai refuses to acknowledge the chaste wife/courtesan binary, embarking on a journey of self-discovery to find an alternative way of defining herself. *Manimekalai* developed out of Mangai's collaboration with an all-female *kuthu* group—a genre of Tamil street theatre done with music and dance and usually performed by men—so that both form and subject challenged normative behavior for women.

Mangai continues to tell women's stories through women's ritual and performance, challenging typical gender roles by pointing out the ways in which gender is constructed and performed. *Avvai*, created in 2008, is based on the historical/mythical poet and flips traditional images, symbols, and representations of women to highlight gender construction. The central character, usually portrayed as old and celibate, is here depicted as a young, sensuous, creative woman.

Amal Allana

A graduate of the NSD, Amal Allana has worked with the Berliner Ensemble in Germany, studied noh and kabuki in Japan, and directed more than fifty-five plays in Hindi. She is founding artistic director of Theatre and Television Associates in Delhi and has been chair of the NSD since 2005. She started directing in Mumbai, but most of her work has been done in Delhi with TTA, and it is this work that earned her the 1998 Sangeet Natak Akademi Award for direction.

Allana says she didn't consciously address women's issues until she was in her fifties and began to play with cross-gender casting to explore and explode stereotypes about gendered attributes and behavior. For example, Kapur notes that in Allana's production of Brecht's *Mother Courage*, she "seeks to make gender mobile, as it were, by disturbing stereotypes. This she does by shifting and restructuring the elements of gender." By casting a man as Mother Courage "she reallocated the attributes of femininity and masculinity—passivity, patience, nurturing, sympathy, on the one hand; aggression, courage, bravery, single-mindedness and authority on the other—from a woman's 'role' to a man's 'body' and vice versa, and thus redefined them" (Kapur, "Reassembling" 11). In *Erendira*, her adaptation of Gabriel Garcia Marquez's novella *The Incredible and Sad Tale of Innocent Erendira and Her Heartless Grandmother* which opened in Delhi, Allana split the character of Erendira among eight actors to give body to her own experience of self, which, she says, is not homogenous (Allana Interview). One of the most striking scenes is set in a brothel, where her grandmother has sold her into sexual slavery, and where men line up to dance around the stage, grope her body, and then walk away without a backward glance. Erendira is yanked around like a rag doll, the dance a cross between a waltz and a polka set to relentlessly happy party music, which seems to mock her all the more. As each man leaves, she collapses, only to be pulled up again by the next man with just enough time to plaster a smile—or grimace—on her face before she is whisked away. Thus, Allana's production focuses on the relentless mistreatment Erendira endures because she is, as a girl and later a woman, devalued, while calling into question the ways in which monetary value is placed on lives.

Allana's 2006 Delhi production of *The Actress Binodini* (*Nati Binodini*) was adapted from the autobiography of a nineteenth-century prostitute-turned-actor who was one of the first women to perform on the public stage in Calcutta. Allana describes Binodini's autobiography as "a remarkable document as it is one of the earliest such accounts by

The Actress Binodini, created and directed by Amal Allana, National School of Drama, Delhi, 2006. Photographer: S. Thyagarajan. Photo courtesy Amal Allana and Theatre and Television Associates.

an Indian woman, which describes her coming into public life and having the courage to assert her independence and identity. . . . Staunchly opposed by a class and caste-ridden society that was unable to tolerate a 'polluted' woman donning the garb of either devi/goddess or Brahmin royalty on stage, Binodini was hailed and castigated in turn, making hers a dramatic and complex life" (Program). As director/auteur, Allana works with collage-like structure and imagery, collapsing past, present, remembered time, and stage time, weaving together numerous realities to demonstrate that moments lived on stage are as rich and formative as "real" events. We do not experience Binodini's life as a linear progression but as a series of emotional associations, and as shards of memory. Allana's work with the Berliner Ensemble and her interest in kabuki are visible in the dramaturgy, acting style, and physical approach to *The Actress Binodini*. Casting also plays into her production style, for Binodini is played by five actors: sometimes as an old woman watching or talking about her younger self, sometimes as a chorus of dancing selves, and once as a self that emerges from the wings to keep herself from reveling too deeply in the applause of her fans. In one extraordinary scene, four Binodinis struggle to play a role, experimenting with different gestures, dance moves, and emotions. Allana's work challenges traditional modes of presenting biographical material and apprehending the richness of human experience.[6]

Anuradha Kapur

Anuradha Kapur studied theatre in Leeds, England, has directed numerous productions in India, England, and Germany, and has taught and directed at the NSD since 1981. In 1989 she founded her own theatre company, Vivadi, along with a group of painters, musicians, writers, and video artists; and in 2007 she was elected director of the NSD.

Kapur's work is characterized by its multimedia nature; she does not incorporate other media into the theatre but brings different media together so that the theatre she creates is changed by the different dramaturgical structures, modes of spectatorship, and time-space relationships in those other media. She says her work is also concerned with "upsetting social and gender hierarchies" ("Reassembling" 10). Her 1997 production in Delhi of *The Job*, a one-woman show with an installation based on Brecht's short story of the same name, centered on a woman who impersonates her husband when he dies, and takes over his job in order to keep her children from starving. Kapur writes, "This play attempted to look at the repercussions of a woman becoming a man; its dangers and transgressions, and, in the context of the story, its disastrous consequences. For me it was especially important to consider this subversive masquerade as the reverse, or the negative, or the concept of female impersonation, as female impersonation continues to exist in India as an honored tradition" (11). Another production, *Sundari: An Actor Prepares*, first produced in Delhi in 1998, was developed from the autobiography of Jaishankar Sundari, a celebrated female impersonator who performed all over India between 1901 and 1931 and "became enormously popular, especially with women, for whom he became a sort of model, setting the style for everything from dress to deportment." Kapur writes, "The performance sought to investigate the enigmatic presence of the man-woman figure in the theatre, and the cross-gender fascination it has characteristically conjured in audiences. Even though the premise of female impersonation almost always rests on the idea of an essential femininity, its performance sought to emphasize that gender is actually constructed in practice, and that it is in fact encoded in demeanor, costume, manner and convention" (11).

In 2002 Kapur began working on *The Antigone Project*, a video-theatre collaboration with video artist Ein Lall about the brutal Hindu-Muslim riots in Gujarat, using some text from Brecht's *Antigone* interspersed with documentary footage of the riots and the filmed testimony of the victims. Kapur describes her working process for *The Antigone Project* in an interview: "We started working on the production . . . after the only state-sponsored riots in post-Independence Indian history, which happened in October, 2002. The scale of the riots, and the scale of the brutality was unparalleled. . . . Ein Lall and I began saying we have to do something to respond, and *Antigone* came to mind because the media coverage of the riots conveyed the attitude that the state has absolute right over the bodies of the dead, as well as conveying an attitude of enormous disrespect to the dead" (Interview). Antigone, in both costume (she wore a *burqa* without the *hijab*) and her positioning on a mound of sand, was a Muslim. She was the one affected, dispossessed, thrown out of Gujarat and the country, asked to leave, told she doesn't belong. When banished from her home and cast out into a cave in the wilderness, Antigone was immediately identified with the fate of thousands of Muslim families who were forced to leave their destroyed neighborhoods for refugee camps. "At the same time," says Kapur, "she is everyone who doesn't want this country to become a Hindu state" (Interview).

Kapur is keenly attuned not only to issues of gender, but to critical events in the contemporary world—which she examines onstage through painting, music, film, movement, and dialogue.

Zuleikha Chaudhari

Zuleikha Chaudhari is the daughter of Amal Allana and set designer Nissar Allana. She was born in Delhi but graduated from Bennington College in the United States with a degree in theatre direction and lighting design. She does not consider her work to be "feminist" in any way; she considers that to be the focus of a previous generation of women. Chaudhari describes her work as a "fragmentation of the linear structure of performance" and asserts that "an experiential relationship to the text is produced by structuring an environment where the performer creates a physical language which translates text into a series of visual registers" (Program, *On Seeing*).

Chaudhuri's 2008 production *On Seeing*—first performed in a Delhi art gallery, and later on various proscenium stages in Delhi and elsewhere—was one answer to a series of questions she had about how to articulate memory, experience, and what happens in the mind. "How does one chart or construct an emotional landscape? It's not about emotion, but the landscape. How do you convert words into images?" she asks (Interview). In *On Seeing* a performer moves in response to a sculptural installation of shifting fluorescent lights placed in an empty room. The spectator travels through the room and her perception of the space—and therefore of its meaning—changes based on the particular way performer, light, and spectator interact. Chaudhari writes: "The performer's presence is negotiated to integrate itself into and extend the visual language of the space . . . the performer's body assumes a life of its own; it becomes a sculptural object interacting with a space rendered dynamic" by both the changing lights and the movement of the spectators. She explains,

> For me performance and, more specifically, movement, functions less as a mimetic form to illustrate textual content, working instead to expand time so that a moment in a narrative is opened up to the possibility of multiple meanings and resonances. As a result, the visual story performed on stage, while based on and derived from the text, does not attempt to illustrate narrative content. Rather, it offers the viewer a series of visual experiences, which may relate obliquely and elliptically to the tex-

tual content, allowing the text and movement to coexist without necessarily always coinciding (Program, *On Seeing*).

Chaudhari's 2009 production in Delhi, *Some Stage Directions for John Gabriel Borkman*, explored Ibsen's *John Gabriel Borkman* as if it were a series of paintings: as if the audience were not seeing the relationships between the characters, who were isolated in pristine white cubicles surrounded by sheer plastic, but the relationships between the spaces they were in. She explored not the personal landscape of the characters but their physical landscape as well. Characters described their emotional states to one another and asked unanswerable questions about the future of the world.

Chaudhari has used her talents in both lighting design and conceptual direction to forge a unique style. Her 2011 production, *Propositions On Text and Space II*—a video and light installation at a Delhi art space called Project 88—was based on a play composed of fifty-one vignettes with forty characters. The program notes that Chaudhari intended to create a "relationship between the private unconscious emotional life of human beings and physical landscapes." Her installation "maps these spaces that are suspended between the real and the imagined. It eliminates the presence of the performer in performance and investigates the nature of a narrative in text, space and light" (Program, *Propositions*). Her experiments with the relationship between space and bodies have taken Indian theatre in new directions.

From the perspective of early 2012, it is clear that women have re-directed modern Indian theatre, and that their ways of working, ways of seeing the world, and ways of structuring experience are being recognized, thus opening up Indian theatre—and the society it reflects and constitutes—to a much wider range of experiences. In fact, these women can be said to have originated an avant-garde Indian theatre.

Notes

1. Some companies do manage to pay their members: they receive a substantial percentage of their income from ticket sales or from participating in national and international theatre festivals, and they often rely on corporate sponsorship. However, most companies rely on the limited funding available from the Sangeet Natak Akademi (SNA, the National Academy of Music, Dance and Drama) in New Delhi, on grants from the Ministry of Culture, and on state arts academies to fund their productions.

2. See Bhatia, 105.

3. See Mee, *Theatre of Roots*.

4. For information on Jayashree, see "Folk Forms and Contemporary Theatre: An Interview with B. Jayashree" in Subramanyam's *Muffled Voices* and Mee, *Theatre of Roots*. For information on Sharma and Ganguli, see Mee (all sources), Sharma, and Subramanyam's *Muffled Voices*.

5. Titles that are not attributed to another author may be assumed to be original, devised works.

6. See "Gender Relations and Self Identity: A Personal Encounter" in Subramanyam's *Muffled Voices*.

Sources

Allana, Amal. Interview. July 28, 2010.

———. Introduction to Program for the South Asian Women's Theatre Festival, National School of Drama. 2010.

———. Program notes. *The Actress Binodini* [*Nati Binodini*]. 2010, n.p.

Bhatia, Nandi. *Acts of Authority/Acts of Resistance*. Ann Arbor: University of Michigan Press, 2004.

Chatterjee, Partha. *The Nation and Its Fragments*. Princeton: Princeton University Press, 1993.

Chaudhari, Zuleikha. Interview. August 7, 2010.

———. Program notes. *On Seeing*. Bharat Rang Mahotsav. 2009, n.p.

———. Program notes. *Propositions on Text and Space II*. 2011, n.p.

Jain, Kirti. "In Search of a Narrative: Women Theatre Directors of the Northern Belt." *Muffled Voices: Women in Modern Indian Theatre*. Edited by Lakshmi Subramanyam, 151–64. New Delhi: Shakti, 2002.

Kapur, Anuradha. Interview. August 8, 2010.

———. "Reassembling the Modern: An Indian Theatre Map Since Independence." Program for the South Asian Women's Theatre Festival. NSD, 2010, 10–11.

———. "A Wandering Word, an Unstable Subject." *Theatre India* no. 3 (2001): 5–12.

Mangai, A. "Cultural Intervention through Theatre: Case Study of a Play on Female Infanticide/Foeticide." *Economic and Political Weekly* 33.44 (1998): 70–72.

———. Interview. June 25, 2002.

Mee, Erin B. "Contemporary Indian Theatre, Three Voices." *Performing Arts Journal* 19.1 (1997): 1–26.

———, ed. *Drama Contemporary: India*. Baltimore: Johns Hopkins University Press, 2001.

———, *Theatre of Roots: Redirecting the Modern Indian Stage*. Kolkata: Seagull, 2008.

Subramanyam, Lakshmi. *Muffled Voices: Women in Modern Indian Theatre*. New Delhi: Shakti, 2002.

 Ireland

Karin Maresh

Women have been directing for the stage in Ireland since the early twentieth century. They have found work and achieved critical and popular success in spite of the sometimes-volatile political situation and the conservative religious and social forces that have historically limited women's rights in both the Republic of Ireland and Northern Ireland.

Women's Rights: Historical Context

Although some in Ireland began to talk of a need for more equality between men and women by the early 1800s, no actual organized women's movement existed until the 1870s. The establishment of groups such as the Irish Women's Suffrage and Local Government Association coincided with a rising tide of nationalist and labor movements. In fact, the Irish struggle for independence from the United Kingdom throughout the nineteenth and early twentieth centuries influenced and affected all areas of Irish life, including women's rights and the development of a native theatre tradition in Ireland that from its beginnings involved women playwrights, actors, and directors. Unfortunately, struggle for independence strained the women's movement, forcing female and male participants to choose between fighting for freedom for their nation and fighting for women's rights. Finally, in 1918 women in the United Kingdom and Ireland of age thirty or older were granted the right to vote, and in 1922 the new Irish Free State, made up of twenty-six of Ireland's southern counties, granted suffrage to all adults older than twenty-one.

Following independence Ireland became a very conservative country with a government strongly influenced by the Catholic Church. For Irish women this meant living in a society that upheld the nineteenth-century Victorian ideals of a woman's role being solely that of wife and mother, as well as legislation that effectively barred women from serving on juries or maintaining employment in certain professions, like the Civil Service, after marriage. To this day the Irish constitution, adopted in 1937, contains two articles that articulate the Irish woman's support for the state by her work within the home.

By the early 1970s Ireland's desire to join the European Economic Community, as well as a burgeoning feminist movement in Ireland, led to changes in the Irish woman's status. In 1971 the Irish government set up a Commission on the Status of Women, which subsequently issued a report that made more than fifty recommendations and suggestions to eliminate gender discrimination in all public areas of Irish society. New legislation throughout the 1970s made it illegal for women to be barred from working after marriage and made it possible for married couples to obtain prescriptions for contraceptives. A conservative backlash in the early 1980s led to a constitutional ban on abortion, but progress continued, resulting in the legalization of divorce in 1995.

In the twenty-first century women in Ireland enjoy more parity with men in the workforce than they did in past decades, and two women, Mary Robinson and Mary McAleese, served (in succession) as president of Ireland from 1990 to 2011. However, women are still vastly underrepresented in the Irish parliament and senate, and as of 2007 their incomes on average were 87 percent of their male counterparts' incomes (Central Statistics Office 26).

Early Women Directors

Theatre in Ireland existed primarily as a British import prior to the final decade of the nineteenth century, when nationalist organizations began producing theatre for political and literary purposes. Many women took part as performers in these amateur productions, but it was not until the founding in 1904 of the first resident professional theatre in Dublin, which became known as the Abbey Theatre, that a few women began working as professional directors. The playwright Lady Augusta Gregory, one of the co-founders of the Abbey, Ireland's National Theatre, directed several productions there early in the decade beginning in 1910 in addition to essentially running the theatre's daily operations during that time.

Much as the new Irish Free State sought to limit the presence of women in public life, professional theatres in Ireland provided Irish women few directing or playwriting opportunities. Beginning with the 1940s, some women founded theatre companies, often in collaboration with a male colleague. During this time much of their responsibility involved management of the theatres—hiring of actors, helping with play selection, and the like—rather than directing productions. Two notable exceptions are Mary O'Malley, founder of the Lyric Theatre in Belfast, Northern Ireland, in 1951, and Ria Mooney, primary stage director at the Abbey Theatre from 1948 to 1963. O'Malley's Lyric Theatre, which started out as amateur productions directed by O'Malley in her own home, quickly became a vital part of the cultural scene in Belfast and established a reputation for producing new plays as well as literary classics that O'Malley believed deserved attention. Mooney, who gained directing experience at Eva Le Gallienne's Civic Repertory Theatre in New York City and at several prominent Irish theatres, maintained an exhausting schedule at the Abbey, directing between twelve and seventeen productions during each ten-month season. Yet she had little to no control over play selection or casting; that power remained in the hands of the all-male board of directors.

A few women in the last decades of the twentieth century found work as directors at high-profile theatres. Former Abbey actress Phyllis Ryan co-founded the independent Dublin company, Gemini Productions, becoming one of the most important producers of new plays in Ireland during the 1960s and 1970s, and in 1971 Lelia Doolan became the first person to hold the position of full-time artistic director at the Abbey Theatre. Other women, such as the five unemployed actresses who in 1983 founded Charabanc in Northern Ireland, created their own directing, performing, and playwriting opportunities when no others were available to them.

Irish women directors interviewed in 1989 noted that the Irish theatres with the largest budgets were "in the hands of men" who did not always take the work of women directors seriously (White 34). Brenda Winter, co-founder of Charabanc Theatre, observed that women "have to be ten times more efficient than a man in order to get taken seriously. And it doesn't stop, even after you're successful" (White 34). In fact, prior to the mid-1990s few women directed even a single production at the higher-profile theatres in Ireland. Some women, such as Fiona Shaw, began to find work in Ireland as freelance directors in the last decades of the twentieth century, but most found more success working with their own companies.

Working Climate in the Twenty-First Century

Some of the most successful directors in Ireland in the early twenty-first century are women, as evidenced by the four *Irish Times*/ESB Irish Theatre Awards handed out to women directors. Yet apart from Druid Theatre in Galway, the major commercial theatres in both the north and south of Ireland were still run by male artistic directors, including the National Theatre of Ireland (the Abbey) and the Gate in Dublin, as well as the Lyric Theatre in Belfast. Eschewing the "boys'" network long present in Ireland's major commercial theatres by founding or co-founding smaller, independent companies remains how most women directors get their start in theatre, and often where they remain. Economic and social factors have as much to do with this as a longstanding prejudicial belief that men are better suited to positions of power in any industry.

Although more women are directing for theatres like the Abbey and the Gate, the records of those theatres show that women directors are still in the minority. For example, of the nine productions appearing on stage between December 2010 and June 2011 at the Abbey, only three were directed by women. A 2008 government report containing Arts Council subsidies figures also suggests that male artists in Irish theatre continue to be trusted with more funding than women artists. According to the report, women working in Irish theatre receive almost as much Arts Council funding as men, 42 percent to 48 percent, but the average annual allocation to women is €4,392 less than that allocated to men (Central Statistics Office 37).

Profiles of Contemporary Directors

Garry Hynes

Arguably one of the most important directors, male or female, to come out of Ireland is Garry Hynes, who in 1998 became the first woman to win a Tony Award for best direction of a play. Hynes's work in theatre began in 1971 while she was still a first year student, when she joined Dramsoc, the student dramatic society of the University College Galway. Having little interest in being an actor, Hynes began directing for the society. Her first production for the group was Brian Friel's *The Loves of Cass Maguire*, and in 1975 her production of Paul Foster's *Elizabeth One* went to the Athlone Amateur Drama Festival. Theatre in the United States also shaped Hynes's knowledge and understanding of theatre when she spent the summers during her college years working in a New York City office. While there she saw innovative, nontraditional shows like the Performing Garage's production of Sam Shepard's *Tooth of Crime* and learned "that theatre could be made in small rooms" about young, ordinary people like herself (Orel).

After graduating with a bachelor of arts in English and history in 1975, Hynes, along with actors Marie Mullen and Mick Lally, created a summer theatre in Galway that subsequently became Druid Theatre, the first truly professional theatre outside of Dublin in the south of Ireland. Under Hynes's artistic directorship, Druid quickly made a name for itself with productions of classic Irish plays such as J. M. Synge's *The Playboy of the Western World* and the premieres of new plays such as Geraldine Aron's *Bar and Ger* and Tom Murphy's *Bailegangaire*, the latter of which starred the internationally renowned Siobhán McKenna in her last role for the stage. According to *New York Times* columnist Celia McGee, Druid's third production of *Playboy* in 1982 "is still remembered as a turning point for Synge's reputation and Ms. Hynes's with its emphasis on violence and sexuality" (4). The Druid company also toured its high-quality productions widely in Ireland, including to remote rural locations such as the Aran Islands, and to England, Scotland, and Northern Ireland.

Feeling the need to gain experience outside of Druid, Hynes began directing occasional productions for the Abbey Theatre in 1986, and between 1988 and 1989 she directed for the Royal Shakespeare Company (RSC) in Stratford and London as part of the RSC's endeavor to bring in women directors. In 1991 Hynes left Druid to accept the position of artistic director at the Abbey Theatre, which by the early 1990s was in dire need of modernization and reorganization. Despite directing successful productions for the Abbey and attempting to institute change there, Hynes left at the end of her three-year contract due to conflict with the theatre's board over the Abbey's future. She eventually returned to Galway and Druid.

Hynes's international career has taken off since returning to Druid, first as an associate director and then in her former role as artistic director in 1995. The following year, in connection with the Royal Court Theatre in London, Hynes directed the Druid premiere production of Martin McDonagh's *The Beauty Queen of Leenane*. After successful runs in England and Ireland, Hynes helped bring *Beauty Queen* to Broadway in 1998, where it earned her a Tony award for best direction. Since then Hynes has regularly directed in the United States and Ireland, splitting her time between Druid and theatres such as the Manhattan Theatre Club and Signature Theatre in New York City. Her success is demonstrated by the many honors she has received, including multiple nominations for the *Irish Times*/ESB Irish Theatre Award for best director and a win in 2002 for her production of John B. Keane's *Sive*, as well as a Joe A. Calloway Award for outstanding direction in 2009 for her production of McDonagh's *The Cripple of Inishmaan*.

Experimentation in production and the willingness to take risks, especially concerning play selection, are two of Hynes's greatest strengths as a director. For her a play, whether classic or untried, is "really a set of notes toward a performance, and each performance exists and is justified only in its own time" (Lavery E1). To a great extent Hynes's directorial process is rooted in the organic exploration of a play. Although a play based on a historical subject might necessitate some reading outside of the text, Hynes thrives on getting to know a play through close collaboration with actors and designers. It is within that collaboration that she believes the essence of theatre lies. According to Mick Lally, the late actor and co-founder of Druid, Hynes "never stops searching and delving and digging into a script. . . . You come along and think you have a scene grand, and she's there gnawing and scraping away at it to see if there are other nuances, and half the time she's right. She's very slow to give into satisfaction" (Foley 9). Getting actors on their feet—moving or at least standing with the potential for movement—as soon as possible in the rehearsal process is also very important for Hynes, as it more quickly breathes life into the text. She has also taken actors out of the rehearsal rooms to the real location of a play's setting, as she did for the 2004 Druid production of *Playboy*, in order to help the actors better understand the world of the play.

In 2005 the *Irish Times*/ESB Irish Theatre Awards recognized Hynes with a special tribute award for her work in Irish theatre. With thirty-five years of directing behind her, Hynes does not show signs of slowing down. Long ago she changed the landscape of theatre in Ireland by proving that high-quality, award-winning theatre can be done outside of Dublin. Druid continues to create two to three new productions every year, often touring them internationally, and in 2010 the theatre announced an exciting collaboration with the National University of Ireland, Galway that resulted in a Druid production and master classes for students. Part of Hyne's legacy also includes her discovery and development of the work of several new writers, including Martin McDonagh and more recently Enda Walsh, as well as the revitalization of stale Irish classics hampered by history. She proved this again in 2006 when Druid produced and toured all of Sygne's six plays in an eight-and-a-half-hour performance titled *DruidSynge*.

Lynne Parker

Like Hynes, Belfast native Lynne Parker has spent the better part of her career as the artistic director for a theatre she co-founded with college friends. Under Parker's leadership that theatre, Rough Magic, has grown into one of Ireland's leading theatrical organizations without losing its innovative edge.

During the summer immediately following her secondary education, Parker worked with the National Youth Theatre of Great Britain, where she says she "realized theatre was going to be more than just a hobby" (Manfull 5). Then, as a student at Trinity College Dublin, Parker joined Players' Theatre, the college's student drama society, which enabled her to explore, experiment, and gain experience with almost every area of theatre without fear of commercial or academic pressures. After finishing her studies, Parker, along with other Trinity alums, including the writer Declan Hughes, founded Rough Magic Theatre Company in 1984, in part because of the lack of opportunities for young theatre artists in Ireland at the time. In its first year Rough Magic created no less than seven productions and started building a reputation for producing the kind of contemporary international work that was absent from Ireland's stages. It was her successful production of Caryl Churchill's *Top Girls* in 1985 that garnered funding from the Irish Arts Council, thus giving Rough Magic a bit more security. Parker and her company also turned to new plays by Irish writers such as Parker's uncle, the acclaimed playwright Stewart Parker, and their own Declan Hughes.

In addition to her work for Rough Magic, Parker has directed for several other theatres, including Druid and Tinderbox in Ireland, 7:84 Scotland, and the Old Vic and Royal Shakespeare Company in England. She also served as an associate artist for the Belfast company, Charabanc, for which she directed a touring production of Lorca's *The House of Bernarda Alba* in 1993 that she set in the Irish midlands rather than Spain. That same year, Garry Hynes, then artistic director of the Abbey, invited Parker to direct there. Despite having little experience with verse or Greek drama at the time, Parker's directorial debut for the Abbey in 1993 was a new version of *The Trojan Women*, adapted from Euripides by Brendan Kennelly. The result was, in the words of *Irish Times* critic David Nowlan, "one of the most subversive manifestations of dramatic art that has been seen in recent times" for its portrayal of Troy's women as vengeful and unwilling to give in easily to their inevitable captivity rather than as the mournful victims of Euripides's play (11). Nowlan considered the production "well worthy of the stage of any national theatre" (11). Parker has directed more than ten productions at the Abbey, including Finegan Kruckemeyer's *The Girl Who Forgot to Sing Badly* in 2011.

For her efforts Parker has been honored with several awards, including a *Time Out* Award in 1992, the *Irish Times/ESB* Irish Theatre best director and best production awards in 2005 for her work on the Rough Magic hit *Improbable Frequency*, and an *Irish Times* special tribute award in 2009 for her contributions to Irish theatre. The year 2009 also marked the twenty-fifth anniversary of Rough Magic, which, under Parker's stewardship, continues to produce important theatrical work, as evidenced by its four *Irish Times/ESB* Irish Theatre awards for best production.

Parker values trusting her instincts and the kind of inspired ideas that can occur spontaneously in discussion with designers and in the rehearsal room with actors. She learned early on in her career not to do too much rehearsal preparation, such as preblocking, which can limit input from actors. She spends the first week of rehearsals helping the actors acclimate to the play and one another, giving them the freedom to play. Parker prefers to get things going in rehearsal "even if it's horrifically wrong," so the actors can react and perhaps rebel against it (Manfull 85). Collaboration is an essential part of any theatrical production for Parker. In fact, part of the reason she has remained committed to Rough Magic all these years instead of working solely as a freelance director is because "core collaboration [is] at the heart of Rough Magic" (Keating, "Rough" 9). Parker speaks of it as a "collective," a company built on collaboration between an ensemble of intelligent artists collectively sharing their passion for theatre with one another.

In 2010 Parker directed Oscar Wilde's *The Importance of Being Earnest* with American actress Stockard Channing as Lady Bracknell at the Gaiety Theatre in Dublin, as well as a new version of the Racine classic *Phaedra* for Rough Magic, which premiered at the Dublin Theatre Festival. Encouraging the work of the next generation has also been a priority for Parker. In 2002 Rough Magic started SEEDS, a mentorship program that trains, nourishes, and professionally stages the work of young artists including playwrights and directors.

Annie Ryan

Annie Ryan, founder of Dublin's The Corn Exchange Theatre Company, is a relative newcomer to Irish theatre compared to Hynes and Parker, and she brings to it a type of theatre based in improvisation and a "renegade version" of commedia dell'arte (*Corn Exchange*). Originally from the United States, Ryan began her career studying acting at Chicago's famed Piven Theatre Workshop. The focus on improvisation and theatre games there resulted in acting work in Chicago for Ryan, including her theatrical debut as Miranda in the 1987 Goodman Theatre production of *The Tempest*, directed by Robert Falls. Ryan also received training at New York City's Circle in the Square and at the Experimental Theatre Workshop at New York University's Tisch School of

Annie Ryan.
Photographer:
Paul McCarthy.

the Arts, from which she graduated in 1991. While still an undergraduate, Ryan joined New Crime Productions, the independent Chicago company co-founded by Piven Theatre Workshop alum John Cusack. New Crime Productions created a modern form of commedia performances first developed by companies in Los Angeles and France. It was there Ryan began working in the "highly percussive, emotive, physically charged, masked" style of theatre that has come to characterize much of her work (Ryan). She has also supplemented her early training by working with practitioners from Le Coq and the London-based Théâtre de Complicité.

Ryan's connection to Ireland began when she studied abroad as an undergraduate at Trinity College Dublin. While there she met many young artists, including her future Corn Exchange collaborator, Michael West, and began devising new productions with them during the summer of 1990. After graduation, Ryan relocated to Dublin in 1992 with the intention of looking for acting jobs, yet when she began teaching workshops in commedia and ensemble training she realized that she was more interested in sharing the techniques she knew with Dublin artists and audiences. Thus, in 1995 Ryan founded the Corn Exchange Theatre Company. At first the company performed in nightclubs, but with the start of the Dublin Fringe Festival in the fall of 1995, Corn Exchange had the perfect platform from which to launch their unique brand of theatre.

In the fifteen years since its inception, Corn Exchange has produced a variety of contemporary classics like *The Seagull* and *Cat on a Hot Tin Roof*, as well as new plays, several written by Michael West in collaboration with the company. Ryan believes that each play dictates the style of performance, but no matter the text almost all of Ryan's productions are non-naturalistic, and her early work with Corn Exchange often employed stylized, whiteface makeup. One production that both critics and audiences admired for its imaginative use of space was *Car Show*, first performed at the 1998 Dublin Fringe Festival. The piece consisted of four short plays performed separately in four parked cars, with two actors per car sitting in the front seats and three audience members sitting in the back. Helen Meany of the *Irish Times* noted that "the short plays offer us fascinating glimpses into other lives as we huddle in the back seat, eavesdropping" (15). Five years later Corn Exchange had even greater success with Maria Irene Fornes's *Mud*, changing the setting, as they often have with non-Irish plays, to Ireland. The play won the 2003 *Irish Times*/ESB Theatre Award for best production, and Ryan received a nomination for best direction. Her work was praised for "showing an instinctive feel for the rhythm of Fornes's succession of short, snapshot scenes and eking out the wry humour of the piece without detracting from its essential bleakness" (O'Toole 12).

By far Corn Exchange's greatest success occurred in 2010 with the production of Michael West's *Freefall*, which garnered *Irish Times* Theatre Awards for best new play for West and best direction for Ryan. The production, which Ryan and her collaborators spent almost a year preparing, involved actors playing multiple roles and literally becoming part of the set and sound design at times. After playing in Dublin, *Freefall* toured to Galway, Edinburgh, and Mexico, and finally ended the year with a run at the prestigious Abbey Theatre. Although not the first time Ryan's work was seen in Ireland's National Theatre—she had performed in a production of Brendan Behan's *The Hostage* in 1996 and directed Sam Shepard's *Fool for Love* in 1998—it was the first time Corn Exchange had been invited to play there.

Ryan does not like traditional, realistic stage sets, preferring a "clean, empty space" that does not "distract from the performer" (Ryan). She also tends to approach each rehearsal process in a nontraditional way. Eschewing the conventional "table talk" rehearsals, Ryan instead spends the first part of every rehearsal process leading actors through vocal and physical exercises in order to better connect the actors to their bodies and help them develop what Ryan calls an "articulate body" (Power 11). To this end, Ryan says, "We begin by washing the floor with water and tea towels, walking them, Japanese style (in downward facing dog), across the floor" (Ryan). Ensemble techniques from various training systems that guide the staging of the play, such as Le Coq, SITI Company's Viewpoints, and commedia dell'arte, are also a major component of Ryan's work with actors. "The idea here," says Ryan, "is that the ensemble are equipped to stage themselves. I want them to be empowered to make the strongest choices possible. . . . The training helps enormously in that we have a physical vocabulary for the staging" (Ryan). Input from the actors about their characters, the stage picture, and even the text is encouraged by Ryan, and many of the actors' ideas develop out of improvisation.

Despite significant funding cuts for Corn Exchange in subsidies by the Irish Arts Council in 2010, Ryan has continued work on various projects. In 2011 she and West co-created *Man of Valour*, a one-man "Commedia-esque treatment of a tax man gone renegade in post-boom Dublin" for the actor Paul Reid that resulted in numerous awards, including an *Irish Times* Theatre Award best actor nomination for Reid (Ryan). Additionally, *Freefall* toured internationally in 2011, journeying as far as Mexico. Future projects for Ryan and Corn Exchange include the development of some large ensemble pieces including a musical satire, *The Fall of the Second Republic*, and a modern take on Joyce's *Dubliners*, a collaboration with the National Theatre of Scotland. Ryan's explosive style of non-naturalistic performance in a country known for its literary tradition continues to garner her recognition and respect.

The number of women directors working in Ireland has grown over the last quarter century, as has recognition for their work by critics and mainstream commercial theatres. Although not all have risen to the same level of success as Hynes, Parker, and Ryan, women directors in Ireland are involved in creating and directing important and innovative theatre at every level of the profession.

Sources

Central Statistics Office. "Women and Men in Ireland, 2009." Central Statistics Office, February 2010. Available at http://www.cso.ie (accessed January 2, 2010).

Corn Exchange Theatre Company. Available at http://www.cornexchange.ie (accessed December 16, 2012).

Foley, Catherine. "Druid's Western Triumvirate Steal the Show." *Irish Times*, February 15, 2005, 9.

Grene, Nicholas, and Patrick Lonergan, eds. *Interactions: Dublin Theatre Festival 1957–2007.* Irish Theatrical Diaspora Series: 3. Dublin: Carysfort, 2008.

Keating, Sara. "Finding Their Balance in the Freefall." *Irish Times*, July 9, 2010, 13.

———. "Rough with the Smooth." *Irish Times*, March 7, 2009, 9.

Lavery, Brian. "Irish Masterpiece Returning to Its Bleak Home." *New York Times*, Mar. 17, 2004, E1.

Leeney, Cathy. "Garry Hynes in Conversation with Cathy Leeney." In *Theatre Talk: Voices of Irish Theatre Practitioners*, edited by Lilian Chambers, Ger FitzGibbon, and Eamonn Jordan, 195–212. Dublin: Carysfort, 2001.

Manfull, Helen. *In Other Words: Women Directors Speak.* Lyme, N.H.: Smith and Kraus, 1997.

Maresh, Karin. "Struggles for Recognition: The Women Artistic Directors of Ireland's Abbey Theatre." PhD diss., Ohio State University, 2002.

McGee, Celia. "Garry Hynes, an Irish Director, Arrives with 8½ Hours of Her Country-man." *New York Times*, July 2, 2006, 2: 4.

Meany, Helen. "Automobile Antics and Others: A Look at the Opening Shows of This Year's Dublin Fringe Festival." *Irish Times*, October 1, 1998, 15.

Middelton, Gillian. "Interview with Annie Ryan." *The Corn Exchange Theatre Company.* Available at http://www.cornexchange.ie, September 16, 2009 [blogpost].

Nowlan, David. "Subverting Ancient Greek Tragedy: *The Trojan Women*, Peacock Theatre." *Irish Times*, June 4, 1993, 11.

O'Toole, Fintan. "*Mud*, Project Arts Center, Dublin." *Irish Times*, September 3, 2003, 12.

Orel, Gwen. "Interview with Garry Hynes." *Celtic Café.com.* n.d. Available at http://www.celticcafe.com (accessed October 8, 2010).

Owens, Rosemary Cullens. *Smashing Times: A History of the Irish Women's Suffrage Movement, 1889–1922.* Dublin: Attic, 1984.

Power, Geoff. "Strike a Pose: Using Physicality to Bring Productions Alive." *Irish Times*, August 20, 2010, 11.

Ryan, Annie. E-mail message to the author. January 14, 2011.

White, Victoria. "Towards Post-Feminism?" *Theatre Ireland* 18 (April–June 1989): 33–35.

Wilmer, Steve. "Women's Theatre in Ireland." *New Theatre Quarterly* 7.28 (1991): 353–60.

# Kenya

Margaretta Swigert-Gacheru

It has only been since the 1990s that the directorial dynamism of Kenyan women like Mumbi Kaigwa, Mkawasi Mcharo Hall, and Caroline Odongo has been brought to light on the Kenyan stage. Before that, there were a rare few pioneering African women directors working from the 1970s—Janet Young from Gambia in West Africa and Mumbi wa Maina from the African Diaspora—who set high directorial standards for those who would follow. But it wasn't until after the 1985 United Nations International Women's Conference was held in Nairobi that Kenyan women began to come forward and seize the directorial baton. Women like Mshai Mwangola, Mueni Lundi, and Mkawasi Mcharo were among the first to emerge in the late twentieth century, laying the groundwork for Kenyan women to become some of the most prolific, innovative, and important directors in the country.

Women's Rights: Historical Context

In precolonial Kenyan societies, women were widely recognized as storytellers and dramatists who performed important roles as educators, teaching children around the family fire through the use of folktales, riddles, songs, and dances that deliberately conveyed moral, ethical, and cultural messages about how young people were meant to behave socially and in their personal lives (Kaigwa "A History"). However, under British imperial rule (1895–1963), indigenous cultural practices were shunned for being "bestial," "subhuman," and uncivilized (Elkins 97). A few women's organizations rose up in resistance to colonial rule and to the patriarchal practices introduced in the name of Christianity and the so-called "civilizing mission" of the colonizer. In the 1930s, for instance, women in the Presbyterian Church formed a group called Kia Ngo, meaning The Shield, aimed at challenging the patriarchy practiced by church elders (Kanogo Interview). As early as 1924 women created a wing of Kikuyu Central Association (KCA)—a group of Kenyan anticolonial activists—to ensure women's interests were well represented in the struggle for independence (Kanogo Interview).

Nonetheless, at the height of Kenyans' political resistance to colonialism, resistance which resulted in the British colonial government's declaring a state of emergency in 1952, women's activism was intentionally undermined with the formation of Maendeleo ya Wanawake the same year. According to Canadian feminist scholar Audrey Wipper, Maendeleo was explicitly formed to channel African women's energies away from political activism, especially from their working with the Land and Freedom Army (also known as the Mau Mau) and toward domesticity. The main focus of Maendeleo was teaching women to be good domestics, obedient wives, and self-sacrificing mothers. In essence, they were taught to be well satisfied with their subordinate status in society (Wipper 99–120).

In contrast, the women who worked as Mau Mau were a different breed altogether. Women like Muthoni Likimani and Wambui Otieno served the independence struggle primarily as spies, passing information to the freedom fighters in the forest. Women also found innovative means to pass food, clothing, and essential supplies through countless colonial checkpoints (Likimani 78–87). In spite of the vital role that women played in the struggle for independence, which was finally achieved in 1963, they continued to be subject to patriarchal practices even in postcolonial Kenya; for while independence brought equal rights de jure to both women and men, including the right to vote in 1919, women's and girls' access to education, employment, and even credit to conduct small business continued to be constrained by customary laws and traditions for decades.

Despite the discriminatory traditions, cultural strictures, and public policies premised on the notion that women are inferior to men, Kenyan women have excelled, especially since the United Nations (UN) declared the first women's decade in the 1970s. In 1985 when the UN held its international women's decade conference in Nairobi, the country itself went through an extreme mental makeover (Wa Gacheru, "African Renaissance"). The government was forced to address issues of gender equity for the very first time as the eyes of the world were focused on it. Since then women have made tremendous strides in the theatre arts as well as in many other disciplines and professions.

Early Women Directors

Decades before the UN came to Kenya to address issues of gender equity, European women were actively involved in stage productions. Even before 1952, when the British colonial government established the Kenya National Theatre in Nairobi, a number of amateur theatre groups were already up and running. All-white amateur groups like the Nairobi City Players, the Nanyuki Players, and the Mombasa Little Theatre Group were staging Western musicals, pantomimes, and light comedies to entertain exclusively expatriate and white-settler audiences. European women directors were rare, but actors like Petal Erskine, who had theatrical training in the United Kingdom, took the occasional stab at directing pantomimes, such as the pre-Disney version of *Alladin* for the Nairobi City Players at the Kenya National Theatre (Harragin-Hussy). Erskine also staged shows upcountry at the Nanyuki Sports Club (McCaffrey). However, even among expatriates, very few women directors came forward.

That reality did not change until 1970, when Annabel Maule, a British professional actor based in London, came to Kenya to work at the Donovan Maule Theatre (DM) in Nairobi with her British parents, Don and Molly Maule. Following World War II, Major Maule and his wife had come to Kenya to establish a repertory theatre, billed as "the only West End theatre" south of the Sahara. An only child, Annabel Maule grew up in England acting in plays her father directed, but when he went to war she remained in Britain to pursue her own theatrical career. It was only when he became ill in the late 1960s that she agreed to come to Kenya to manage the theatre and direct shows in his stead. Subsequently, she would also produce and perform in them as well. For nearly ten years, until 1979, she was a fixture on the Nairobi theatre scene, though her productions mainly catered to European audiences.

It was not long after Maule arrived in Kenya to direct everything from Shakespeare to Shaw that the first black African woman director arrived in Nairobi. Janet Badjian Young came from Gambia to Kenya via the United Kingdom, where she had studied at the Rose Bruford College of Speech and Drama in Kent. Upon arrival in 1973, Young immediately went to work as a drama advisor for the Nairobi City Council, teaching drama to Kenyan teachers and directing children's theatre for African youth. By so doing, she became the first African woman director to have a full-time job in the performing arts. Coincidentally, she was also the first African woman to integrate the previously all-white Nairobi City Players as well as the first black woman to direct productions at the Kenya National Theatre, such as the Langston Hughes musical *Tambourines to Glory*.

It was while casting *Tambourines* in 1976 that Young met an African American actor, Mumbi wa Maina. Trained at the American Community Theater of Harlem, wa Maina quickly became the star of the show, and in 1977, the two women co-founded Kenya's first progressive African theatre company, the Tamaduni Players. Based in Nairobi, the two devised innovative scripts, most notably one in which their Kenyan cast members researched and interviewed young impoverished street children. Crafting their stories into an eye-opening script, *Portraits of Survival* became one of the first authentically Kenyan contemporary shows to hit the local stage in the late 1970s. In addition, Young became a role model to countless Kenyans as she directed the Tamaduni Players in plays by Bertolt Brecht, Athol Fugard, Ola Rotimi, Okot p'Bitek, and Aristophanes. Meanwhile, wa Maina was also a trailblazer in Kenyan theatre, becoming the first black woman to direct plays and lecture in theatre arts at one of the country's top schools, Kenyatta University on the outskirts of Nairobi.

Both Young and wa Maina spawned a number of young women thespians who have gone on to become part of Kenya's current crop of leading women directors: Young mentoring Mumbi Kaigwa, one of the most dynamic women director-playwright-performers on the contemporary Kenyan stage, and wa Maina mentoring Mshai Mwangola, who was her student at Kenyatta University and who went on to direct plays both locally and overseas.

Working Climate in the Twenty-First Century

The training ground for practically all of Kenya's women theatre directors has been and remains the annual arts festivals, which were established during the colonial days but were subsequently indigenized once Africans took over festival leadership in the late 1970s. The influence of the Kenya Schools Drama Festival and Kenya Music Festival on young girls is incalculable. Since the 1980s, virtually all of Kenya's leading women directors, including Kaigwa, Mwangola, Mueni Lundi, Mkawasi Mcharo Hall, Ruth Kamau, Caroline Odongo, Millicent Ogutu, and Mbeki Mwalimu, have participated in either one or both of these festivals. Unfortunately, Mcharo Hall and Kamau moved abroad in the 1990s, but not before both had scored impressive records directing their own original scripts. Mwangola also moved away for further studies for more than a decade, returning in late 2007. Lundi, though directing briefly for Theatre Workshop Productions (TWP)—born out of the University of Nairobi's Literature Department—cultivated her directorial skills outside of Nairobi while working on "theatre for development" projects with CARE Kenya. However, while a number of Kenyan women directors moved out of the limelight near the turn of the twenty-first century, another crop of young women directors came onto the local theatre scene to challenge the male dominance that continued to hold sway over most Kenyan theatre companies.

The three women directors most active in Kenyan theatre as of 2012 include Kaigwa, who dared to go professional in 1999; Odongo, who has been a working director since the early 1990s; and Ogutu, who is the managing director of the Phoenix Players in Nairobi. All three have impressive records as stage directors, but the groundwork for their coming on the local scene was laid back in the 1970s and 1980s—when the first African women directors appeared and when the cultural climate opened up to a deeper appreciation of gender equity and the prospect of women taking leadership positions, not only as stage directors but also in the society at large.

While the impact of the 1985 UN Women's Decade Conference has been noted, two other historical factors played a vital role in shaping the historical context for the development of women working in Kenyan theatre. The first is the second Pan African Arts Festival (FESTAC) in Lagos, Nigeria, to which Kenya sent two important plays in 1976, one co-authored by Micere Mugo and Ngugi wa Thiong'o, *The Trial of Dedan Kimathi*. Mugo's play as well as her poetry and revolutionary prose have been a perpetual source of inspiration to many other Kenyan women poets, playwrights, and stage directors, including Mwangola and Kaigwa.

The other important factor in raising public appreciation of Kenyan theatre was the government's decision in 1977 to bulldoze the rural Kamiriithu People's Theatre just north of Nairobi as a heavy-handed means of censoring the immensely popular but politically provocative Kikuyu play by Marxist playwrights Ngugi wa Thiong'o and Ngugi wa Mirii, *I'll Marry When I Want* (*Ngaahika Ndeeda*). The destruction of the community theatre—which had been largely built with the labor power of rural women—dealt a devastating blow to Kenyan theatre at the time, but it also served to raise both global and local awareness of the vital role that popular theatre can play in the enlightenment and entertainment of the Kenyan public. The production set the bar not only for massive audience attendance but also for young Kenyans using theatre to rouse awareness of the urgent social concerns facing the country up to the present day (Bjorkman 94).

Several local theatre troupes also played their part in shaping the cultural landscape that allowed for the emergence of dynamic Kenyan women directors. Theatre Workshop Productions had a profound effect on a number of local women directors who got their initial opportunity to direct plays as members of TWP. Founded by two University of Nairobi lecturers, Dr. Opiyo Mumma and Gachugu Makini, TWP had both a professional and pedagogical orientation in that it aimed to train young Kenyan thespians through the workshop process in all aspects of the theatre arts, including directing, stagecraft, script writing, and acting. Encouraging members to rotate and train in all of these roles, TWP enabled women members like Mwangola and Mueni Lueni to gain experience in directing shows such as Derek Wolcott's *Moon on Monkey Mountain* and Oby Obyerodhyambo's devised play, *Drumbeats over Kirinyaga*.

A number of Christian theatre companies also inspired Kenyan women to get involved in theatre work. Both Mwangola and Mcharo directed Christian musicals with Mavuno Productions in Nairobi prior to their departure for further theatre art studies overseas. Mcharo's original scripting of the musical *Pambazuka* (*Arise*) was such a success that she was called to stage it before Archbishop Desmond Tutu and the All Africa Council of Churches in Addis Ababa. Lundi, Ogutu, and Odongo also got their first taste for drama while singing, acting, and stage managing dramatized Bible stories when they were still in primary school.

One of the most controversial theatre companies in Kenya is Phoenix Players, largely because it was born out of the ashes of the Donovan Maule Theatre. Like the DM, Phoenix originally focused on staging West End productions from the United Kingdom up until the late 1980s when its founder, James Falkland, finally recognized the need to indigenize his theatre and seek ways to appeal to Kenyan audiences and recruit Kenyan casts. His initiatives had many critics, but by "indigenizing" British scripts, starting with Gilbert and Sullivan musicals, he attracted young talents, including musicians and future stage directors like Odongo and Ogutu. What's more, he directed Kaigwa in several Shakespeare plays, invited Tamaduni Players to perform on his stage, and helped established an all-black Kenyan theatre company separate from Phoenix in Nairobi known as Muijiza Players, where Mwangola and Odongo both had opportunities to direct full productions. Perhaps the most important thing that Falkland did for Kenyan thespians was to prove that professional theatre could be an income-earning enterprise. By his example, he inspired women like Odongo, Ogutu, and Kaigwa to pursue theatre directing as a full-time income-generating occupation. "The ratio of men to women stage directors in Nairobi who are earning a living in the theatre is about three to one," said Eliud Abuto, founder of the Festival of Creative Arts (FCA), a popular Nairobi-based theatre group that often invites women directors such as Odongo and Mbeki Mwalimu to work with his troupe. "It isn't easy for any stage director to rely solely on theatre for survival in Kenya; but Nairobi does have a theatre-going public which doesn't seem to care whether the director is male or female. They simply want to be entertained and they will pay for a show that does that," Abuto added (Interview).

Profiles of Contemporary Directors

Mumbi Kaigwa

Kaigwa launched her career as a professional stage director in 2001, when she directed her own script, *The Voice of a Dream*, in Nairobi. Yet her directorial experience actually began at the age of fifteen at Limuru Girls School, where she directed an adaptation of Wole Soyinka's *Telephone Conversation* entitled *West African Sepia*. Her life on stage began even earlier when she acted in primary school plays and competed in a verse-speaking contest at a national music festival. By age ten, she was performing with her uncle Jagi in a local television version of Soyinka's *The Strong Breed*. Jagi enlisted her annually after that to act in University of Nairobi productions. Best known in Kenya as an actor who has performed in plays by everyone from Shakespeare and Ibsen to Ola Rotimi and Ntozake Shange, Kaigwa never formally studied acting, directing, or even scriptwriting, although she has attended numerous international artists' workshops and residencies. She says her best training was working with outstanding African stage directors, including Young, John Ruganda, David Rubadiri, Mhlangabezi ka Vundla, Seth Adagala, and John Sibi-Okumu (Kaigwa Interview). That training exposed her to various methods of directing. The one she says she draws the most inspiration from is Young's nurturing style of stage direction. Like Young, she takes care to work patiently with each of her cast members and never to rush a production: "Janet never put a show on stage until she felt clear that all the elements were working in accord with each other" (Kaigwa Interview). That same sort of intuitive sensitivity and professionalism is what has made Kaigwa a director with whom actors want to work. Her experience working with film and television directors has also broadened her perspective on various techniques of directing, but in her mind what's most important in directing is interacting with her cast and musicians to find what she calls "the individual music and rhythm" of the particular play on which her troupe is working (Kaigwa Interview).

What propelled Kaigwa into directorial work was the major decision she made in 1999 to leave her well-paid position as a Project Officer with the United Nations and do theatre work full time. According to Kaigwa, it was the decision of a lifetime, and it has been life transforming. It has also been a bit scary she says, but for her, the risk was worth it since working full time has allowed her to engage in all aspects of performance, from the writing, directing, and producing to the acting, dancing—with the Urban Bush Women of New York—and singing as well.

Kaigwa's directorial career took off shortly after she launched The Theatre Company (TTC) in Nairobi in 1999 and after she wrote her first script, *Voice of a Dream*. The first of three autobiographical scripts dealing with issues of identity, cultural authenticity, and other postcolonial concerns, Kaigwa found that directing followed logically from the scriptwriting, just as the second script followed necessarily from the first. *A Hook for Dreams* (*KigeziNdoto*) elaborates on themes touched upon in *Voice of a Dream*, the main difference being that *A Hook for Dreams* is a Kiswahili musical steeped in dance, drumbeats, and lyrical sounds. The show's success can be measured by the fact that after she wrote and directed the musical, she also managed to take it on two international tours: one to Europe in 2006 and another around East Africa in 2010.

The third script in the trilogy, *They Call Me Wanjiku*, is a one-woman production that Kaigwa directed and performed first in Canada at the University of Winnipeg, then in the United States at Dartmouth College, and finally at the City University of New York. The work reflects her own incredible odyssey from being Louise, the Anglophied African woman, to becoming a grounded and gutsy Kiswahili-speaking Kenyan woman fully conscious of her connection with Mau Mau freedom fighters, whose struggle she sees as unfinished and ongoing. In all of her writing and directing, Kaigwa has sought to dig deep into the soil of indigenous creativity and culture. Making choices to work closely with self-taught African talents while using local languages, indigenous instruments, and traditional dance, Kaigwa is consciously creating a new hybrid form of Kenyan theatre that draws upon the cultural wealth and resourcefulness of ordinary Kenyan working people.

While still with TTC, Kaigwa directed *Githaa*, a script she devised with her cast in Sheng, the polyglot language of urban Kenyans. In 2002 Kaigwa made another courageous choice to direct Eve Ensler's *The Vagina Monologues* in Nairobi at a time when usage of "the V-word" in public was strictly taboo. The production won her accolades, including a Woman of the Year award in 2003. Her work in Kenyan theatre has been widely recognized both locally and internationally, as when the Sundance Institute invited her first to Utah in 2003, then to the Kenyan Coast in 2011, to take part in its outreach programs for East African performing artists.

In 2008 Kaigwa left TTC to form a new entity, the Arts Canvas, which is both an online Kenyan arts calendar and archive as well as the umbrella under which she directs

Ariel Dorfman's *Death and the Maiden,* performed and directed by Mumbi Kaigwa, Arts Canvas, Nairobi, 2011.

her own scripts and those of established playwrights such as Ariel Dorfman's *Death and the Maiden* in 2011, Alan Bennett's *Talking Heads* in 2012, and Margaret Edson's *Wit,* also in 2012, all at the Phoenix Theatre.

Since the formation of the Arts Canvas in 2008, Kaigwa has taken more seriously her calling as a stage director. As the only Kenyan woman thespian who currently combines directing and playwriting with acting, her decision to take that courageous leap and go full time into professional theatre reflects both her passion and her determination to defy the odds that claim Africa has no funding for the arts and that African women can only have short-lived careers in theatre. It has been an uphill struggle for Kaigwa, but she has managed to successfully prove that there's a place for professional women directors in Kenya. In the process, she has also inspired many up-and-coming African women artists to be just as bold and artistically ambitious as she is.

Caroline Odongo

The only Kenyan woman director who has theatrical credentials that come anywhere near to Kaigwa's is Caroline Odongo. Like Kaigwa, Odongo formed her own theatre company in Nairobi. In 1998 along with her playwright husband Cajetan Boy, she established Et Cetera Productions, through which she not only directs and acts but also produces plays on the Kenyan stage. Also like Kaigwa, she nurtures new theatrical talents, including young women directors like Mbeki Mwalimu, with whom she has co-directed several plays for the Festival of Creative Arts (FCA) at the Alliance Francaise in Nairobi, including *Disturbia* in 2011.

Odongo's trajectory into theatre was slightly different from Kaigwa's. Performing solo verse recitals in primary school and singing in the annual Kenya Music Festival, Odongo also belonged to the debate club, which may be one reason she holds her own so well in a Kenyan theatre world, which is still largely male dominated. She acted in plays at Moi Nairobi Girls School, but unlike Kaigwa, Odongo did not discover her affinity for theatre until she was a first-year student at the University of Nairobi in 1989. She was accompanying a friend to watch the first musical she had ever seen, *Joseph and the Amazing Technicolor Dreamcoat*, directed by Ian Mbugua, a protege of Falkland. "I was hooked from that moment on," recalls Odongo, who was studying economics at the time (Odongo). Falkland had already begun staging multiracial productions at Phoenix Theatre, but Odongo was introduced to Phoenix Players just at the moment when Falkland had actively begun to Kenyanize Gilbert and Sullivan musicals. She watched *A Kenyan Mikado* in 1990 and got a part in the chorus of *A Kenyan Gondoliers* in 1991. Content at the time just to watch Falkland direct, she was working backstage as well as acting in the chorus by 1992 when he co-directed the first Kenyan musical devised by Joy Mboya, Susan Gachukia, and George Mungai, called *Changing Generations*.

While still at university in the early 1990s, Odongo was quick to split her time between her studies and her work for Phoenix. Upon graduation, she devoted herself full time to apprenticing with Falkland, the man she says inspired her to be a stage director. "He helped me understand the power of the director. It's the power to create something out of nothing, to create characters out of thin air," said Odongo, who stages ten shows a year on average. "Someone once told me being a director is like getting a glimpse into being a god!" (Odongo). While reveling in that sense of directorial power, Odongo is never overbearing with her cast, but she does have a very clear sense of what she wants from them and spends hours working with character development. Since most of the scripts she directs are by Kenyans about social issues that affect ordinary Kenyans' lives, she defines her aesthetics in terms of how closely her productions can come to reflecting the mood and spirit of people's everyday experience.

In 1993 Falkland helped establish an all-Kenyan theatre company in Nairobi committed to promoting HIV/AIDS awareness, called Muijiza Players. Straight away, he invited Odongo, who had been stage managing at Phoenix for months, to come on board as Muijiza's project coordinator, which she did for the next four years. It was during that time that her directorial powers were sharpened as she took charge directing a series of original one-act plays by Kenyan playwrights like JPR Ochieng Odero and Cajetan Boy. Muijiza Players started off with twenty Kenyan cast members who staged AIDS-awareness plays all over Kenya, in schools, churches, factories, and corporate offices as well as on the downtown Nairobi Muijiza Theatre stage. The response was overwhelming but the funding was inconsistent, so the cast dropped by half after a year.

For Odongo, Muijiza proved to be a perfect training ground for testing her skills as both a producer/project coordinator and director, the role she fell in love with from the moment she first saw *Joseph* in 1989. Once Muijiza shut down in 1997, Odongo joined several theatre-for-development, nongovernmental organizations (NGOs) in succession, including the Nairobi-based Sanaa Arts Promotions, with whom she again went out into the community, only this time to devise and direct innovative AIDS-awareness plays together with students and other community members.

Throughout the 1990s, Odongo kept her hand in Phoenix Players, finding time either to stage manage, act, or direct plays like Boy's *Family Ties*, Oby Obyerodhi-ambo's *The Striped Leopard*, and Paul Njoka's *Three Blind Mice*. She was gaining a name for herself as one of the few Kenyan directors who concentrated on staging scripts by Kenyan playwrights.

Shortly after Muijiza Players died, in 1998, Odongo joined hands with Boy to form Et Cetera Productions, which would serve as a platform both for staging Boy's myriad scripts and giving her chances to direct.[1] Odongo credits Falkland as her mentor and main source of inspiration. "He taught me the value of discipline, punctuality and consistency. He also taught me how to see the creative potential in everyone" (Odongo). Odongo says she also valued the way he lived, moved, and breathed for the theatre, which is what she does herself.

From 2005 to 2010, Odongo primarily directed plays with FCA, and it was through FCA that she was able to direct new shows at a pace unmatched by any other Kenyan thespian. However, in early 2011, she recommitted herself to putting her formidable energies back into Et Cetera. It is unlikely that she will leave FCA altogether, however, since she had an abundance of successful runs with them, staging both Kenyanized versions of British and American comedies and original Kenyan plays.

Millicent Ogutu

One of the most courageous and resourceful women directors in Kenya is a young lawyer who fought hard using all her legal skills and persuasive powers to save the Phoenix Theatre from demise not once but twice in 2009. Millicent Ogutu had never planned to make the performing arts a full-time profession, but as the current managing director of the Phoenix, she combines stage directing with all the other aspects required to keep the Phoenix alive.

Having been introduced to theatre in primary school at age twelve, Ogutu acted in Nativity plays and helped her teacher stage manage. She went on to join the Drama Club at Pangani Girls School, where her plays invariably won awards at the Kenya Schools Drama Festival. But it was seeing the Mbalamwezi Players come to Pangani in 1999 and

Millicent Ogutu

stage John Ruganda's powerful play *The Burdens* that compelled her to rethink her whole life course. Up until then, her goal had been to go to law school, but the fire that began burning inside her once she saw Ruganda's poignant play turned her life upside down.

"I got into a big debate with my dad since he wouldn't hear of my giving up my law studies for the stage, but I figured out how to do both," said Ogutu who managed to juggle her love for the theatre with her law studies at Moi University in Eldoret, Western Kenya, starting in 2001. "I'd come home every end-of-term and spend three months at Phoenix, doing everything from stage management to ticket sales and acting," recalled Ogutu.

Upon graduation in 2004, when she officially became an advocate of the High Court of Kenya, Ogutu made a radical decision: she didn't start up a law practice or join a thriving law firm in Nairobi as she easily could have done. Instead, she chose to take a job updating the membership files at Phoenix. She made herself immediately indispensable, not only because she was prepared to do "the donkey work" of the day-to-day running of the theatre. She also brought a sense of discipline and professionalism to the Phoenix that had practically disappeared since the departure of Falkland. "I'm very focused when I'm directing, and I love working closely with my cast members on character development, especially to help them find and then fine-tune their character. We do a lot of exercises, both physical and mental, in order to feel at ease while a production develops organically," she said (Ogutu).

Ogutu didn't actually begin directing plays at the Phoenix until 2005. Before that, she was mentored by Mungai and to a lesser degree by Falkland. Favoring Mungai's more personable, engaging style of directing to Falkland's, which she says she found more aloof and impersonal, Ogutu nonetheless followed Falkland's taste in stage productions. She initially directed only British scripts such as Alan Ayckbourn's *Snake in the Grass* in 2005 and Simon Gray's *Just the Three of Us* in 2006. But after she saved the theatre from its imminent demise in 2009, her sense of aesthetics broadened to the point where she began directing a wider variety of plays, such David Mamet's *The Winslow Boy* in 2009 and Federico Garcia Lorca's *House of Bernarda Alba* in 2011. Yet even these shows had been London West End productions before they were staged by Ogutu in Nairobi at the Phoenix.

It is only since her return from maternity leave in 2011 that she has begun scheduling plays at the Phoenix that appeal more directly to local audiences, featuring scripts by Kenyan playwrights such as John Sibi-Okumu and Oby Obyerodhiambo. "I want to put on plays that resonate with Kenyans and reflect aspects of their everyday lives," she explained (Ogutu). In this regard, Ogutu is starting to cultivate an aesthetic that is more akin to that of both Kaigwa and Odongo, both of whom are consciously blending their Western training with indigenous issues, ideas, and cultural artifacts to create a new hybrid style of contemporary Kenyan theatre.

While all of the Kenyan women directors profiled above are making immense contributions to Kenya's thriving theatrical culture, all have had to deal with the dilemma of having both a professional and a personal life. All feel a passionate commitment to theatre. At the same time, each one insists that one reason there are so few women directors in Kenya is because many women find the demands of family life to be incompatible with those of the stage. Yet in the case of all these women, it's their persistence as well as their passion for the stage that has enabled them to put other considerations aside and make stage direction their top priority. And while all our Kenyan women directors have been steeped in Western theatrical traditions, all are involved in creating hybrid forms of African theatre that do not only draw upon Western genres and forms of stagecraft; they are also striving to reflect social realities of everyday Kenyan life, aiming to make theatre not only engaging and entertaining but enlightening and socially relevant as well.

Notes

1. It was shortly after Et Cetera took off that Falkland decided Phoenix Theatre was on the verge of financial collapse and recommended it be shut down. He met stiff resistance from Kenyan thespians, but rather than debate the point, Falkland simply quit, and within months he passed away.

Sources

Abuto, Eliud. Interview. June 22, 2011.

Bjorkman, Ingrid. *"Mother, Sing for Me": People's Theatre in Kenya*. London: Zed, 1989.

Elkins, Caroline. *Imperial Reckoning: The Untold Story of Britain's Gulag in Kenya*. New York: Holt, 2005.

Harragin-Hussy, Robin. E-mail message. November 29, 2011.

Kaigwa, Mumbi. "A History of Kenyan Theatre." Presented at Nairobi Museum Society's "Know Kenya" course, Nairobi. 2003.

———. Interview. June 9, 2011.

Kanogo, Tabitha M. *African Womanhood in Colonial Kenya: 1900–1950*. Oxford: Curry, 2005.

———. Interview. August 11, 2011.

Likimani, Muthoni G. *Passbook number F.47927: Women and Mau Mau in Kenya*. London: Macmillan, 1985.

Maule, Annabel. *Theatre Near the Equator: The Donovan Maule Story*. Nairobi: Kenway, 2004.

McCaffrey, Vanessa. E-mail message. November 29, 2011.

Odongo, Caroline. Interview. June 6, 2011.

Ogutu, Millicent. Interview. June 22, 2011.

Wa Gacheru, Margaretta. "Phoenix Players Rises from Ashes." *Saturday Nation* 9 (July 2011): 59.

———. "The African Renaissance and the African Woman Artist as Heroine: The Kenyan Case." Presented at the UNESCO-International Stone Sculpture Symposium, Kisii, Kenya. August 1, 2011.

Wipper, Audrey. "The Maendeleo ya Wanawake: The Co-optation of Leadership." *African Studies Review* 18.3 (December 1975): 99–120.

 Mexico

Ileana Azor

translated by Emilia Ismael

In Mexico, the history of theatre directing by women is a relatively recent phenomenon. Nonetheless, the work of women directors in the last half of the twentieth century and into the twenty-first exhibits the quality and diversity of their work throughout the country and, in many cases, internationally.

Women directors have founded and directed independent theatre companies, and they have also engaged in the commercial sphere as well as in dramaturgy and acting. However, the most significant aspect about these artists is that their approaches vary widely, both in terms of style and themes, forming a rich and creative landscape.

Women's Rights: Historical Context

In the southeastern Mexican state of Yucatán, a group of women anarchist teachers in 1870 organized, around the teacher and writer Rita Cetina Gutierrez, a group known as La Siempreviva (Emanuelsson). One of their goals was to create a school for girls. Benito Juarez, as governor of Oaxaca, had stated that he was in favor of the issue of equal education in his proposals in the 1850s.

In 1905 the *Women's Newspaper* (*Periódico de las Mujeres*), a paper with a clear socialist tendency, first appeared along with other social manifestations such as the miners' strikes of Cananea, in the northern state of Sonora. All of these events marked the start of the preparatory stage of the Mexican Revolution of 1910.

Two feminist congresses were held in Yucatán in 1916, and a year later President Venustiano Carranza, as part of the revolutionary movement, recognized the rights of married women, allowing them to have their own voices at court and to manage their own estates, decisions which until then had been solely in the hands of their husbands. That same year, during the preparations for the Revolutionary Constitution Convention, women demanded the right to vote and to be elected to public office. However, the members of the convention argued that women had no political experience, and so they rejected the proposal.

In the next decades women workers were at first shunned from labor unions, then accepted as union members but with salaries that fell below their male counterparts' for the same duties and hours. Unions did not become their advocates until almost midcentury.

In 1936 women who supported President Lazaro Cardenas demanded suffrage, but the president did not comply. Women's right to vote did not become a reality in Mexico until 1953. According to feminist historian Francesca Gargallo, it was not the result of organized feminist movements, but rather a concession from the state, which wanted to be seen as modern and similar to the European and United States models of democratic progress (Emanuelsson).

Once voting rights were established, women ceased street demonstrations (Emanuelsson), but, according to Francesa Gargallo, in the 1960s the second wave of feminism emerged and a series of demands by feminists coalesced, all of them political or economic in origin. For example, some women writers addressed themes in their own experiences, and many women enrolled in universities, challenging patriarchal patterns. The feminism of the 1960s, as a women's liberation movement, was basically focused on the urban middle class. It consisted mainly of educated sectors—college students and other women who had experienced legal discrimination.

A crucial shift for women in the poorer class occurred in the 1960s as well. Factories called *maquila* emerged as a means of cheap labor on the Mexican side of the United States border and employed many women. Maquila women also began working for transnational companies in appalling working conditions and received poor pay. The mass incorporation of women into the labor force meant that many women became the main source of family income, or at least the stable source.

Mexican historian and women's studies researcher Ana Lau declares the 1970s produced a "new feminist wave" in Mexico, when the middle class women increased their politicization (14). The magazine *fem* was founded, and middle-class women were demanding changes in the national constitution. At this stage, the first petitions to eliminate the laws that made abortion illegal were made to Mexico's parliament and congress (20). This demand still remains a matter of ideological and legal debate in the country, except in Mexico City, where the local congress approved it. In the agricultural sector the women's movement was just beginning in the 1970s. Spouses and partners of male union members and representatives of women farmers began to protest unequal working conditions, but the police ultimately repressed them. By the 1980s feminists tried to put into practice the action plan of the National Front for the Liberation and Rights of Women, founded in 1979. The plan included voluntary maternity leave, daycare services, and the fight against sexual violence in all of its forms, as well as discrimination in the workplace (23).

The next stage of feminism in Mexico developed with the arrival of the journal *Feminist Debate* (*Debate Feminista*) in the 1990s. Mexican women attempted to become part of the country's political life with their proposals of "alliance and conversion" (Lau 15). In the labor force, Mexican women who arrived at the Mexico/U.S. border became part of the exploited women's workforce that peaked in the 1990s.[1] Labor rights and other entitlements disappeared. Young women worked from dawn to sunset for miserable salaries without personal security.[2] This situation with women on the Mexico/U.S. border involved drug cartels and other male criminal behavior resulting in the murder of approximately six thousand women and girls in Mexico between 1999 and 2006 (Emanuelsson).

Although it appears that multiple feminist ideals started to decay in Mexico in the early twenty-first century, there remains a movement of women field workers—including indigenous women—and fisherwomen's organizations. Many of their members are women who provide the main support for their family households, which are among the country's poorest and largest.

Since the 1990s women's study classes and seminars in universities across the country have focused on gender studies and have debated gender issues. According to journalist Miriam Ruiz, thirty-five university programs focused on gender studies in 2010. In the social, economic, and political sectors, a struggle for egalitarian treatment of women continues.

Early Women Directors

Women stage directors began with the work of Luz Alba, the artistic name for performer Henrietta Levine Hauser, of Mexican origin but born in Arizona in 1913. During her career as a director, Alba directed in both the United States and Mexico. She came to Mexico City for the first time as an actor in 1935. Beginning in 1942, Alba worked there as a theatre teacher and director for ten years, then went to San Francisco, California, where she founded an acting academy.

A student of Martha Graham, Benjamin Zemach, and Max Reinhardt during her years in California, Alba acted in film and graduated in 1932 from the School of Theatre Arts at the Pasadena Community Playhouse (Ceballos 7). With the group Mexican Theatre of Art (Teatro Mexicano de Arte) she directed Oscar Wilde's *Salomé* in 1944 at the Palace of Fine Arts in Mexico City. A year later, also in Mexico City, she directed Ibsen's *A Doll's House*. Four years later she co-founded the Theatre of the Reform (Teatro de la Reforma) in Mexico City, together with the Japanese director Seki Sano and the Spanish actor Alberto Galán.

In 1949 Alba directed Jorge Villaseñor's *The Woman in White* (*La mujer de blanco*) at the Molière Room in Mexico City, with the group Autonomous Student Theatre of

Mexico (Teatro Estudiantil Autónomo de México). She returned to the United States where she directed and co-created—with Tamara Garina and Ronn Marvin—*Angels and Clowns* in 1950 for the Pasadena Community Playhouse; she went on to direct the premiere in Mexico City at the Esperanza Iris Theatre a year later (Obregón 58). That was the end of Alba's short but significant career as a director. She brought to the stage female characters of high social status and introduced an "open style," with homosexual dancers and nude actors, thereby confronting the most established patriarchal and theatrical model of her times. Also well known was her work with young actors who would later become prominent, as well as her preoccupation with prison audiences at Islas Marias Federal Prison in Nayarit, Mexico (Ceballos 7). Despite her innovations, not all critics recognized her affiliation with the best of experimental theater.

Another outstanding figure is that of Nancy Cárdenas (1934–1994). She was a fellowship student of film and drama at Yale University in the United States from 1960 to 1961, disciplines that she continued to study in 1961 at the Film Studies Center and the Center for Polish Language and Literature, both in Lodz, Poland. She graduated from the National Autonomous University of Mexico (Universidad Nacional Autonoma de Mexico, UNAM) in 1965, where she was also awarded a doctoral degree in 1968. She was a student of Fernando Wagner, Rodolfo Usigli, Allan Lewis, and Luisa Josefina Hernández. Her debut as a director in 1960 was with Brecht's *Mr. Puntila and His Man Matti* in Mexico City. In that same decade, she was intensely involved in the student movements of 1968, which led to her imprisonment.[3]

In the next decade Cárdenas directed plays with innovative themes, such as the acceptance of homosexuality in Mart Crowley's *The Boys in the Band*, produced in Mexico City in 1974. That same year she founded the first Mexican homosexual organization, Homosexual Liberation Front (Frente de Liberación Homosexual, FLH), and a year later she co-wrote—with the renowned Mexican writer Carlos Monsivais—the "Manifesto in Defense of the Homosexuals in Mexico" ("Manifiesto en Defensa de los Homosexuales en México"). Her directing credits of the 1970s included Paul Zindel's *The Effect of Gamma Rays on Man-in-the-Moon Marigolds* staged in Mexico City in 1970, which earned her the Theatre Critics of Mexico Association (Asociación de Críticos de Teatro de México) award.

Cárdenas came out as a lesbian in a televised interview in 1973, and in the late 1970s and early 1980s she directed a theatrical trilogy that addressed lesbian relationships more deeply (Obregón 60). Produced in Mexico City, the plays included an adaptation of Colette's biography *Claudine at School* (*Claudina en la escuela*) in 1979, Reiner Werner Fassbinder's *The Bitter Tears of Petra von Kant* (*Las amargas lágrimas de Petra Von Kant*) in 1980, and her own text, *The Day We Walked on the Moon* (*El día que pisamos la luna*) in 1981. These productions took her through a significant road of thematic exploration more focused on didactic issues than on a search for artistic excellence. The productions that became her professional epitaph, all of which she wrote herself, were: *Sexuality 1*, about men's bisexuality; *Sexuality 2*, about women's bisexuality; and *AIDS . . . that's life* (*Sida . . . así es la vida*), all produced in Mexico City in 1988. Her emphasis was on divulging and denouncing pressing issues. Her death in 1994 left unfinished the production of her theatre piece *I Love the Sexual Revolution* (*Yo amo la revolución sexual*).

Another early stage director was Marta Luna, who studied theatre direction at the School of Theatrical Art (Escuela de Arte Teatral), in the National Institute of Fine Arts (Instituto Nacional de Bellas Artes, INBA), and obtained bachelor and master of arts degrees in the same discipline at the Theatre School of Charles University in Prague in the 1960s. She directed Brecht's *The Threepenny Opera* in 1977 in Mexico City, where she continued to direct works from Mexican playwrights, including Emilio Carballido's *The Clockmaker of Cordoba* (*El relojero de Córdoba*) in 1978, Hugo Argüelles's *The Ritual of the Salamander* (*El ritual de la salamandra*) in 1981, Victor Hugo Rascón Banda's *Voices on the Threshold* (*Voces en el umbral*), and Elena Garro's *San Angel Stop* (*Parada San Ángel*), both in 1993. Luna has been a professor of acting and theatre direction at several Mexican institutions and also for Televisa TV. She has received numerous awards and fellowships in recognition of her professional career in Mexico and Prague. As of 2009 she had directed more than 120 professional productions for the stage.

Working Climate in the Twenty-First Century

Modern theatre buildings and funding in Mexico have been fundamentally supported since the mid-twentieth century by governmental organizations. Other structures that support theatre arts are linked to the training of actors in different universities and schools around the country. For example, by the 1970s the Mexican Institute for Social Security (Instituto Mexicano del Seguro Social, IMSS) had built more than seventy theatres throughout the country (Aguilar 19).

Commercial theatre is also run by enterprises such as OCESA (Operators of Entertainment Centers/Operadora de Centros de Espectáculos S.A.), which, along with producing mass events, brings Broadway productions to Mexico and very often finances national productions of successful works from Europe, Latin America, and the United States. Although women are generally not hired to direct and produce large commercial productions, women who work in national financing organizations such as the National System for Arts Creation have begun to support quality projects directed by women and to award scholarships to young women directors. Sandra Félix, one of the women directors with the most visible presence on the stages of Mexico City in the early twenty-first century, has received financing from state and national institutions. In a 1999 interview she stated, "Although there are more women in areas like stage direction, scenography, and lighting than I suppose have existed for a long time, there still persists some discrimination towards women in these areas . . . especially towards the youngest. Being young, women, and directors, is still viewed as 'weird' even if there are now many female directors" (Riquer, "Theater"). Despite the increasing numbers of women directors in the early twenty-first century, there is still a smaller percentage of women than men.

Profiles of Contemporary Directors[4]

Jesusa Rodríguez

Jesusa Rodríguez studied from 1971 until 1973 at the University Theatre Center of the UNAM but she did not graduate. Instead, she followed director and Professor Julio Castillo, with whom she learned about scenography and theatre direction. Her directing career began in the 1980s when Rodríguez founded the group The Divas (Las Divas) with Liliana Felipe—composer, singer, and also her domestic partner—with the aim of following a personal staging style that included Mexican theatrical traditions.

In 1983 Rodríguez directed *Donna Giovanni* for The Divas in Mexico City, based on the comic opera of Mozart and Lorenzo Da Ponte. With an all-female cast that had no singers, she proposed a "theater sung in old span-ita [Spanish and Italian]," a "complex thematic treatment . . . representing one of the most masculine archetypes of all times" (Obregón 60). In this parody, Leporello is the dramatic axis, and the cast of women assumed different characters and alternated performing the role of Don Juan. Sensuality, eroticism, plasticity, and unlimited freedom from a women's standpoint gave a twist to one of the greatest icons of western masculinity.

Since the 1990s Rodríguez has directed and/or performed texts of a diverse nature. Sources for inspiration include poets such as Sor Juana Ines de la Cruz and Marguerite Yourcenar, as well as tent theatre (*carpas*), cabaret, and political testimony. Her inspiration from Shakespeare is evident in *How Is the Night Going on Macbeth?* (*¿Cómo va la noche Macbeth?*), which she directed in 1980 in Mexico City and reworked there twenty-two years later. The production in 2002 was a parody, drawing an analogy with the new presidential couple, Vicente Fox and Martha Sahagún. The use of Catholic icons, so appreciated by the new governmental party—the National Action Party— provoked many polemic reactions in the audience, presenting a leftist view about a watershed moment.[5]

With Felipe, Rodríguez restored the theatre The Chapel (La Capilla) and co-founded the cabaret The Habit (El hábito) in Mexico City. She performed and directed more than 320 shows at The Habit between 1990 and 2000. In 1997 she directed a version of Sor Juana Inés de la Cruz's poem as a chamber opera, *First Dream* (*Primero Sueño*), which she continued to revise as director and actor until its definitive version in 2009 in Mexico City. Rodríguez has a very personal dialogue with this poem, her mother's favorite—and she has performed it herself in various countries throughout North and South America. Rodríquez creates a unique theatrical approach in which humor is mediated by other aesthetic strategies, such as her tribute to the role of poetry as a mechanism for understanding a critical social reality. In *First Dream*, the sonority of the baroque words, the video images, and the music composed by her sister, Marcela Rodríguez, combined with the chiaroscuro-style lighting designed by Juliana Faesler to provide an atmosphere for philosophical thinking.

Examining the power behind Rodríguez's work, scholar Roselyn Constantino writes:

> Jesusa chooses to represent the leading roles for women, which are not all "good" women. . . . She revives mythical women, converted in myths, famous and anonymous. . . . She elucidates the real consequences of the institutional mechanisms designed to invade, penetrate and violate the individual and collective body. Jesusa Rodríguez is a fearless woman with deep convictions and commitments; she artistically and politically practices the act of raising the voice; she intervenes and participates fully in the creation of new modes of existence. Her work process is collaborative; through her collective The Divas she teaches to the new generations.

Rodríguez has received numerous awards, scholarships, and honors from organizations like Montreal's Festival of the Americas in 1989, the Guggenheim Fellowship in 1990, and the Rockefeller Foundation Fellowship from the Arts and Humanities Program for the period 1994 to 1997. National critics and international producers consider Rodríguez one of the most prominent women of the Mexican stage. In 2001 Tim Weiner of the *New York Times* wrote, "When Jesusa Rodríquez is on stage, on camera, in the streets protesting her latest outrage—she may be the most powerful woman in Mexico" (A4). However, due to her irreverence and critical approaches she has repeatedly experienced censorship of some of her shows.[6]

In addition to her directing and awards, Rodríguez has shown her commitment to the problems of farm workers. From 2001 to 2004 she taught seventeen workshops on empowerment for indigenous women and female farmers, and four workshops in masculinity in eighteen different states around Mexico. The talented Mexican dramaturge, the late Jorge Kuri, considered Rodríguez's ability to address political topics with a great sense of humor, stating she "has formed a school already with branches, of a theater that found its prestige at the beginning of the 20th century." Through her theatre, Rodríguez has made an important social impact on the "escapist comfort that globalization sells to us" (Kuri 60).

Juliana Faesler

Born in Mexico, Juliana Faesler—a director, scenic, and lighting designer, and the daughter of a scenographer—earned the advanced diploma in theatre design at the Central Saint Martins School of Arts in London in 1994. She was also a student of Julio Castillo, Hector Mendoza, and Ludwig Margules, three of the most renowned figures of Mexican theatre direction. She has been awarded with several distinctions as a director and stage designer.

Faesler's work is characterized by research based on the symbolic synthesis of the different elements that compose the scenic fact. In 1996 Faesler co-founded the group The Theatre Machine (La Máquina de Teatro) with actor Clarissa Malheiros. The Theatre Machine creates theatre as a means of expressing their thoughts, ideas, and history.

As a director, Faesler works with words, movement, gesture, and visual image in her interdisciplinary theatre. She has directed professional productions for UNAM, ranging from the dance company Quiatora Monorriel's *Do You Hear Orestes?* (*¿Qué oyes Orestes?*) in 2006 to Shakespeare's *A Midsummer Night's Dream* in 2008. In *Do You Hear Orestes?*, she investigated what happened to the children of lost civilizations like Troy, Baghdad, and Tenochtitlan. This evocative production included an Orestes baby doll, built with plastic bottles that actors filled with water, sand, and garbage. She also cross-gender cast a young male dancer as Iphigenia and a male actor with beard and mustache as Helena. In terms of representing character, Faesler states, "I don't talk too much about characters with actors, we talk more about impulses, subtexts, in general" until actors gradually come to an understanding of character (Faesler 49). It was interesting that during each production Orestes asked a person in the audience, "What can I do? I have to kill my mother?" and nobody ever prevented the murder (Faesler 47–48).

Some of Faesler's directed works include pieces she has written or adapted herself, including her 2001 free adaptation from Mary Shelley's novel, *Frankenstein, or The Modern Prometheus,* (*Frankestein o el moderno Prometeo*), and her version of Villiers D' Isle-Adam's novel *The Future Eve* (*La Eva Futura*) in 2003, both produced in Mexico City. In these pieces she investigated new definitions of life, the future, scientific curiosity, love, and fear of solitude, with multimedia explorations. She explains, "My shows usually are determined by . . . a defined space, scores of movements very tested, and accurate lighting . . . however we never had a final story board before the end of the work, we never knew how the next passage would develop" (Faesler 53).

From 2007 to 2010 in Mexico City, she directed a trilogy, which she also wrote, dedicated to reflections on the bicentennial of the independence of Mexico: *Nezahualcóyotl* in 2007, *Moctezuma II, the Dirty War* (*Moctezuma II, la guerra sucia*) in 2009, and *Malinche/Malinches* in 2010. With these works she reactivated pre-Hispanic culture and values—the contradictions; the encounter with opposites; and the links to things inexplicable, such as the origins of Mexican culture—revealing that Mexico is a country as paradoxical as it is grandiose.

Raquel Araujo

Raquel Araujo graduated from UNAM in 1988 when she founded and directed the professional group, Slit Theatre (Teatro de la Rendija) in Mexico City. She collaborated in 1993 with the filmmaker and sculptor Oscar Urrutia and reached her maturity as director-author with Slit Theatre shows like *Horizon of Events* (*Horizonte de sucesos*) in 1998 and *Oval* (*Óvalo*) in 2001.

In 2002 Araujo moved to Yucatán, where she created the Department of Theatre of the Institute of Culture (Departamento de Teatro en el Instituto de Cultura de Yucatán) and the Performing Arts Research Center (Centro de Investigación de las Artes Escénicas). Her work is particularly connected with shows where body art, closely related to performance, constructs a spectacular dramaturgy—from the biographies of its creators, from gesture, and from an interaction with nature.

Araujo's international collaborations have resulted in various shows, such as Sterling Houston's and Raquel Araujo's *The Temperature of Love* in 2003, a production with Jump Start Performance Company in San Antonio, Texas. She explains, "In three weeks I had to write, to rehearse, to produce and to direct the mise-en-scène. It was a bilingual play, two full performances. A chicano version in an open space. . . . Then, in 2005 we presented a second version in the Peon Contreras Theater, in Merida, Yucatán, for a young audience who usually do many things simultaneously, now in Spanish and with changes in the plot and with a new title: *Heat* (*Calor*)" (Araujo 105–6). She adds, "As a stage creator I have the need to create several angles in the plot or in the characters that complement each other. . . . We let the characters reach their emotional springs through body contact. . . . In *Heat* the action is built through superimposed short cuts. . . . I like to work from the beginning with scenographic elements" (107).

With the Colombian Itinerant Theatre of the Sun (Teatro Itinerante del Sol) created by Beatriz Camargo, Araujo directed and wrote the project *Just Like from a Dream We Suddenly Arouse* (*Sólo como de un sueño de pronto nos levantamos*), which had the support of Iberoescena in 2007 in Colombia. Among the other productions she has written and directed at national and international festivals are *Chejovian Emblems* (*Viñetas chejovianas*) in 2009 and *Multiple Medea* (*Medea múltiple*) in 2010. She has presented work in other countries such as Argentina, Brazil, Indonesia, Japan, and the Philippines.

Concepción León Mora

Concepción León Mora, born in Mérida, Yucatán, studied folklore beginning in 1981 and six years later began an acting program at Mexican Institute for Social Security (IMSS) in Merida, Yucatán. In 1992 she began teaching theatre pedagogy workshops for children, and from 1994 to 2001 taught stage movement. Since 1995 she has created theatre as author and director, departing from very diverse points of view, including anthropological research, personal testimonies, cinematographic structure, revalorization of regional culture, and the rescue of Mayan rites. In addition, she has worked to disassemble the artistic canon of the Yucatán Regional Theatre, in which music, lyrics, idioms, popular songs, and dialogues are popular with the audience.

Yucatán, a predominantly indigenous state with a high percentage of women as heads of families, still reports significant violence, discrimination, and lack of health and education rights for women. All these constitute a source for the theatre work of León, work that is inundated with international, local, and pop music. Also included are popular voices in the blunt and ironic humor of domestic employees and "the help," the legends of herbalists, the experiences of young migrants to the United States, or the relationships among female family members. At the same time, her work is imbued in mythical and ritualistic universes that share an audience.

An actor, director, dramaturge, and pedagogue, León has traveled with her work, both as a solo artist and with her group Sa'as Tun (Light Stone), which she founded in 2005. Her productions have taken her to Argentina, Peru, Spain, the United States, and several states in Mexico. Inspired by and focused on women, she has published and premiered more than twenty shows as an actor and director, all of them in Yucatán. For example, *Mestiza Power* in 2005 was a well-known play about three mestizas women, sellers whom León met and interviewed in the most important *tianguis* (popular market), in Merida.[7] *Tolok Paradise* (*El paraíso de la iguana*) in 2006 explored Mayan legends based upon anthropological research by Silvia Terán and Christian Rasmunsen in Xoquen, a little town in Yucatán, where a commissary had to deal with complaints about magic from Xoquen neighbors between 1999 and 2004.

The Huiras of the Papakal Mountains (*Las Huiras de la Sierra Papakal*) in 2009 was another three mestizas' story in which the women go to a friend's wake. When the wake is revealed as a fake, the friends debate about the political and artistic situation in Mexico. At the end, they decide to create a band, playing typical music from the north of the country, in order to "salir adelante," meaning to do well for themselves.

León is a director who usually focuses her work on actors' performances, including dance and musical performances. She begins with a reading and a debate about the play before starting improvisation sessions. Next, the music is a very important element to build the show, and actors bring in costume proposals. Her methods of creating and directing theatre have been successful, for her performance works are recognized for their excellence and originality by cultural institutions, critics, and the audiences in Mexico and beyond.

⊞ ⊞ ⊞

The women profiled in this chapter, along with others,[8] are only a few of the women stage directors in Mexico, but they do offer a diverse display of aesthetic approaches and tendencies that emanate from historical theatre, musicals and cabaret, action-art, and regional theatre. In this mosaic of women stage directors one can see that directors in Mexico are part of the cultural mainstream and also are involved in the experimentation and awakening of critical and once silenced voices that will no longer remain quiet.

Notes

1. Since 1994 the Zapatista army in Chiapas, on the Mexico/Guatemala border, has been an advocate of women's rights. When women began to organize, it resulted in an increase in associations of women mestizo farm workers.

2. Among the Mexico/U.S. border towns, Ciudad Juárez represents the height of Mexican femicide, where the impunity of women's rape and murder is, sadly, internationally high. See also Diana E. H. Russell on femicide.

3. In October 1968 there was a government massacre of students and citizens protesting in Mexico City.

4. Many directors in Mexico include a research process in their work, which can involve writing their own theatre pieces.

5. After seventy years of the Revolutionary Institutional Party in power, the National Action Party won the 2000 election.

6. Colombian researcher Gastón Alzate writes of the 1988 production of *The Council of Love*, a satire of Bavarian society: "Jesusa Rodríguez's group was the target of threats, theft of equipment and costumes, and they could only finish their season under the protection of police patrols stationed outside of the Shakespeare Forum where the play was being presented" ("Political Dissidence").

7. *Mestizo/a* denotes a person of mixed race, usually of European and Native American ancestry.

8. Additional women directors include Claudia Cecilia Alatorre, Julia Alfonso, Socorro Avelar, María Alicia Martínez Medrano, Aurora Cano, Maribel Carrasco (children's theatre), Perla de la Rosa, Lorena Maza, Ana Francis Mor, María Morett, Silvia Peláez, Claudia Ríos, Susana Robles, Lydia Margules, Susana Wein, and Iona Weissberg.

Sources

Aguilar Zinser, Luz E. "Splendors and Miseries of IMSS. Social Security: A Right on the Verge of Extinction?" *Cat Step* ["Esplendores y miserias del IMSS. La seguridad social: ¿Un derecho en extinción?" *Paso de Gato*] 1 (2002): 19–22.

Alzate, Gastón. "Political Dissidence: Jesusa Rodriguez and Liliana Felipe." *Visual Archive of Scenic Arts* ["La disidencia política: Jesusa Rodríguez y Liliana Felipe." *Archivo Virtual de Artes Escénicas*], 2002. Available at artesescenicas.uclm.es (accessed March 13, 2011).

Araujo, Raquel. "Simultaneousness in *Heat* Visual Constructions." In *Un/weaving Scenes: Dismounting; Creation and Researching Process* ["La simultaneidad en la construcción visual de *Calor*." En *Des/tejiendo escenas: Desmontajes; Procesos de investigación y creación*], edited by Ileana Dieguez, 105–10. Mexico City: INBA/Universidad Iberoamericana, 2009.

Ceballos, Edgar. *Basic Encyclopedic Dictionary of Twentieth Century Mexican Theatre* [*Diccionario enciclopédico básico de teatro mexicano Siglo XX*]. Mexico City: Escenología, 1998.

Comas Medina, Andrea. "Maquiladoras in México and Their Effects on the Working Class." *Globalization: Monthly Journal of Economics, Society and Culture* ["Las maquiladoras en México y sus efectos en la clase trabajadora." *Globalización: Revista Mensual de Economía, Sociedad y Cultura*], 2002.

Constantino, Roselyn. "Introduction." *Inconvenient Women: Social Memory, Politics, and Women's Performance in Mexico*. N.d. Available at http://hemi.nyu.edu (accessed March 13, 2011).

Emanuelsson, Dick. "Mexican Women: Politics and Revolution; Women's Social and Feminist Movement in Latin America" ["Mujeres mexicanas: Política y revolución; Movimiento social de mujeres y feminista en Latinoamérica"]. *ARGENPRESS*, 2006. Available at http://argenpress.info (accessed March 3, 2011).

Faesler, Juliana. "The Theater Machine." In *Un/weaving Scenes: Dismounting; Creation and Researching Process* ("La Máquina de Teatro." En *Des/tejiendo escenas: Desmontajes; Procesos de investigación y creación*), edited by Ileana Dieguez, 41–54. Mexico City: INBA/Universidad Iberoamericana, 2009.

Gargallo, Francesa. *Latin American Feminist Ideas* [*Ideas feministas latinoamericanas*]. Mexico City: University of Mexico City, 2004.

Kuri, Jorge. "New War, New War." *Cat Step* [*Paso de Gato*] 1 (2002): 60.

Lau, Ana. "The New Mexican Feminist Movement." In *Feminism in México, Now and Then* ["El nuevo movimiento feminista mexicano." En *Feminismo en México, ayer y hoy*], edited by Eli Bartra, Anna M. Fernández Poncela, and Ana Lau, 11–36. Mexico City: Universidad Autónoma Metropolitana (UAM), 2000.

Molina, Silvia. *Encounters and Reflections* [*Encuentros y reflexiones*]. Mexico City: National Autonomous University of Mexico (UNAM), 1998.

Obregón, Rodolfo. "Feminine Genealogy." *Conjunct* ["Genealogía femenina." *Conjunto*] 145/146 (2007–2008): 56–62.

Riquer, Sonia. "Actresses, Dramaturges, Directors Break with the Masculine Domain in Theatre" ["Actrices, dramaturgas, directoras rompen el predominio masculino en el teatro"]. Part I. Interview with Carmen Montejo, Sabina Berman, and Juliana Faesler. *La Journada en linea*, 1999. Available at http://www.jornada.unam.mx (accessed January 8, 2011).

———. "Theater Is an Instrument to Know Reality" ["El teatro es un instrumento para conocer la realidad"]. Part II. Interview with Jesusa Rodriguez, Sandra Felix, and Berta Hiriart. *La Journada en linea*, 1999. Available at http://www.jornada.unam.mx (accessed January 8, 2011).

Ruiz, Miriam. "Mexican Feminism Would Have to Be Much More Combative: Luz Elena Gutiérrez" ["El feminismo mexicano tendrá que ser mucho más combativo: Luz Elena Gutiérrez"]. *CIMAC News,* 2010. Available at http://www.cimac.org.mx (accessed March 3, 2011).

Russell, Diana E. H. "Definition of Femicide and Related Concepts." *Femicide in Global Perspective* ["Definiciones de feminicidioy conceptos relacionados." *Feminicidio: Una perspectiva global*], edited by Diana E. H. Russell and Roberta A. Harmes, 73–96. Mexico City: UNAM, 2006.

Weiner, Tim. "Pummeling the Powerful, with Comedy as Cudgel." *New York Times*, June 15, 2001, A4.

 Pakistan

Claire Pamment

Women stage directors in postcolonial Pakistan (1947–) have played active roles in college and amateur theatre circuits, which have provided important avenues for experimentation in the absence of theatre training academies and university courses. Ironically, it was in the late 1970s, when new discriminatory laws against women were enforced, that women directors began to come into the spotlight. Some women actors took up direction in the emerging popular comedy theatre. Others, in reaction to the new laws, created a political theatre. As such, women directors in Pakistan reflect an exciting diversity of approaches in challenging both theatrical innovation and women's rights.

Women's Rights: Historical Context

The first phase of the women's rights movement emerged during pre-partition Pakistan and was led by colonial missionaries with the support of members of the Indian elite in the nineteenth and early twentieth centuries. Together, they implemented moral reforms and advocated women's education to restrict cultural-religious practices they deemed oppressive, such as *sati* (the sacrificial burning of widows), child brides, dowry law, prohibitions of widow remarriage, *purdah* (literally, veiling), and polygamy. They also chastised the *tawaifs* (courtesans) and *devadāsīs* (temple dancers), whom they derogatorily dubbed as "*nautch* girls," meaning dancing girls. Although elite women had participated in the colonial schools and colleges set up in the nineteenth century, traditionally only the courtesans and temple dancers were the beneficiaries of a broad education, which had included reading, writing, singing, dancing, and other arts (Srinivasan 165). Through the anti-nautch movement, circa 1893–1947, the once-respectable and educated courtesans and temple dancers were explosively targeted. They were declared ordinary prostitutes, and a leading missionary of the movement, Jenny Fuller, notes that these women were to be pushed "outside of decent society" while their arts were to be "redeem[ed] and rescue[d]" by elite girls and housewives (136, 130). The ramifications of these reforms are reflected in the scorn assigned to early actresses, and similar stigmatization continues to assert prejudice over contemporary female dancers and comediennes of the popular Punjabi theatre.

Education and political participation of women played an increasingly critical role in the early twentieth century through the nationalist movement that was to lead to the creation of Pakistan. Early female role models of the Pakistan movement included elite, educated women, who variously took up important political and educational positions in the new nation-state. Crusader for women's rights and politician Begum Ra'ana Liaquat Ali Khan set up the All Pakistan Women's Association (APWA) in 1949, a charity for women's welfare that continues to be an important lobbying body for social and legal reforms (see Mumtaz and Shaheed).

From the relatively emancipated position that women had experienced in the early decades of Pakistan, conditions suddenly changed after General Zia-ul-Haq overthrew the elected Zulfikar Ali Bhutto's Pakistan People's Party government in 1977, imposing martial law and assuming the post of president from 1978 to 1988. Under Zia's governance, Prime Minister Bhutto was sentenced to hanging and Sharia law (Islamic jurisprudence) was imposed. The new laws were highly discriminatory against women, especially the Hudood Ordinance, which blurred the distinction between adultery and rape.[1] In a strict period of media censorship, theatre activity in colleges was suppressed, women were banned from singing or dancing in public forums, and female television actors and presenters were forced to cover their heads. In protest against the political dictatorship and particularly the discrimination against women, female activists united in 1979 under Tehrik-e-Niswan (The Women's Movement) in Karachi, and in 1983 under the larger umbrella of the Women's Action Forum (WAF), which formed cells in Pakistan's major cities. The WAF asserted considerable pressure on the government to repeal a number of its cases against women by protesting against discrimination and violence against women. Tehrik-e-Niswan and WAF both used performing arts as part of their campaigns, spearheaded by prominent theatre directors and practitioners such as Sheema Kermani, Farrukh Nigar Aziz, Madeeha Gauhar, Huma Safdar, Nasreen Azhar, and Sania Saeed.

Conditions for women's rights improved after General Zia's regime, but even under the governments of 1988–1989 and 1993–1996, headed by Pakistan's first woman prime minster, Benazir Bhutto, the ordinances remained in place, though they were rarely enforced. In the early twenty-first century the influence of Islamist parties grew further, with conservative elements often targeting women through honor killings, bombings, and threats to girls' schools. In addition, they desecrated advertisements featuring women and issued threats to performing artists. Even during the apparently liberal government of General Musharraf—which amended the Hudood Ordinance with the Women's Protection Bill and encouraged women in politics, professional careers, education, and the performing arts—in 2002 the police conducted extensive raids in the popular Punjabi theatres, leading to the arrest and prosecution of a number of female artists who were declared to be promoting obscenity. Patriarchy remains strong, and gender proves to be interconnected with other forms of social exclusion. The status of women differs across class, regions, and the rural/urban divide due to uneven socioeconomic development and the impact of tribal, feudal, and capitalist social formations on women's lives (Bari ix).

Early Women Directors

The role of the modern director, as derived from Euro-American theatre practice, is a relatively recent development in South Asia, where the actor-manager model remained dominant until the early to mid-twentieth century. Notable women managers included Iqbal Begum (?– c. 1980) and Baali Jatti (1938–1997) of the *nautanki* (operatic theatre) and popular variety show theatres that traveled in urban and rural localities in the Punjab (Saeed and Nayyar). One of the first women theatre directors to be working outside the confines of the colonial dramatic clubs was from Sweden. Sigrid Kahle had studied drama in Sweden and was posted in Karachi during her husband's diplomatic service between 1952 and 1957. Within weeks of their arrival she put out an advertisement in the newspapers asking for collaborators in forming Pakistan's National Theatre. While these aspirations proved too ambitious, she began activity on a smaller scale. Actors from the local amateur Group Theatre approached Kahle to direct Patrick Hamilton's *Gas Light*, because they wanted to prove their worth in the English theatre of Pakistan. She agreed to direct as long as their next play together would be in Urdu. However, the Urdu play never materialized because the chairman of the Group Theatre showed distaste at a foreign lady's influence over its dramatics. Such postcolonial identity politics continued to challenge Kahle's work.

Founding the Karachi Theatre, a new semi-professional group in 1953, Kahle directed a variety of genres and styles of drama from European and American theatre to successful acclaim. This led to a trilogy of Urdu plays, of which she co-directed Krishen Chandra's *Outside the Inn* (*Serāi ke Bāhar*) in 1954, earning Kahle a mixed response from the press. She explained, "The absurdity was that the Westerners wanted an Eastern Theatre and the Easterners a Western Theatre!" (Kahle 86). Conforming to expectations for a more Western theatre, *Antigone* was the last play she directed in Pakistan in 1956, performed in Karachi and Lahore. She also played the title role.

While male directors were staging professional productions from the mid-1950s in the urban centers, women directors continued to be relegated to the colleges and semi-professional circuits. Kinnaird College for Women in Lahore had a very active drama society, run by its history teacher and later vice principal Leela Najmuddin from the 1940s to the 1970s. Farrukh Nigar Aziz (1928–2005) acted in Najmuddin's society as a student and founded the Alpha Players in Lahore in the 1960s, a group that was composed of volunteer thespians, many of whom evolved as established professionals. Aziz also became the first woman director to bring her plays into the Lahore Arts Council, which was controlled in part by the government (Ahmad 151). While directing principally from the classic English theatre canon, she also provided a forum for new work to be developed for the stage.

Perin Cooper, born in 1942, is another of Najmuddin's protégés; after graduation from college she began acting in the professional theatre of the Lahore Arts Council's plays. She joined Kinnaird's faculty of literature in 1965 and became staff advisor to the college's Najmuddin Drama Society with her directorial debut of Shaw's *Pygmalion* in 1972. She injected modernist plays into the college's classical repertoire, along with devising new work with the students. Cooper continued her involvement with the professional theatre, mostly as an actor, but in the 1970s she also began to direct plays for children, a first in Pakistan's history.

Ironically, it was in the harsh era of Zia's martial law that the first professional women theatre directors began to emerge. Naheed Khanum, born in 1960, entered theatre as a child star, acting in the state-controlled Lahore Arts Council plays in the 1960s. She began directing Urdu comedies in the late 1970s and by the 1990s was one of the few established women directors and writers of the comic Punjabi Theatre. This theatre developed in the late 1970s out of popular forms inherent in the traveling Parsi and nautanki theatres and comic improvisations of the *bhānd*.[2] These forms indigenized the colonial-style drawing-room comedies that had been prevalent in the early Arts Council's plays. Samina Ahmed, born in 1947, is another important practitioner who worked closely with the Arts Council, becoming its deputy director of programs between 1981 and 2000. At the Arts Council she founded the Alhamra Puppet Theatre in 1986, organized drama festivals, and directed a number of plays, including the 1992 production of Shoaib Hashmi's *Gurya Ghar*, an Urdu adaptation of Ibsen's *A Doll's House*.

In Karachi, actor Yasmin Ismail (1950–2002) set up Grips Theatre in 1979, modeled on the German children's and cabaret theatre of the same name. She began working on English translations of Grips's plays, which were staged at Karachi's Goethe Institute. Bringing out a strongly physical vocabulary, expert comic timing, and a live orchestra of piano, tabla, guitars, and a singing cast, Ismail created a popular theatre, which was targeted principally toward children. From the mid-1980s she began collaborating with the journalist Imran Aslam, who became the in-house writer for the company, adapting and writing original bilingual (Urdu-English) plays fueled with sociopolitical relevance. Ismail groomed a close-knit team of actors, and with support from the Goethe Institute and ticket sales, she developed one of the longest surviving theatre companies in Pakistan, producing on average two new productions a year. The cabaret style and playful bilingual form that the company had established through the children's plays led to additionally charged political content for an adult audience in a new genre of revues that Grips began staging in 1995.

Working Climate in the Twenty-First Century

The working climate in contemporary Pakistan for all theatre makers is challenging. Without regular state subsidy or university theatre courses in the public sector, but instead a discouraging atmosphere of expensive hall rental fees, entertainment tax (except in the capital), and cumbersome censorship procedures, it is difficult to sustain a profession in theatre. Within these limitations, three types of theatre have struggled to survive.

The parallel theatre is a movement that began in 1979 in political protest against General Zia's martial law, discrimination against women, and as an alternative to the commercial trends of the arts councils. Feminist directors of the parallel theatre, such as Sheema Kermani and Madeeha Gauhar, developed small teams of committed individuals working on a semi-professional basis through the financial support of international donor agencies. This model inspired the creation of a number of other parallel groups. While such funding has been necessary for these groups' survival, some critics claim that it has led their recent work toward "depoliticized" social terrains of modernizing agendas "such as health campaigns, birth control, or campaigns against discrimination against women" (Mundrawala, "Shifting" 5).

The comic Punjabi theatre has succeeded in producing the only regular commercially sustainable theatre, which is run exclusively from popular patronage. Its center is in Lahore, and it has spread across many cities of Pakistan, also traveling to other countries with large Punjabi-Pakistani communities. Driven by the monopoly of the male producer, who works to the demands of a mostly male audience, many critics argue that this theatre projects sexist portrayals of gender (Safdar 142). While its audience, performers, and producers are principally men, women directors like Naheed Khanum and Aasma Butt have managed to penetrate this commercial field.

A new brand of English-language farces and musicals—occasionally including Urdu adaptations and originals—developed in 2002, continuing the trends of college and amateur dramatic activity, now supported by big budgets drawn from multinational sponsorship. Directors in these theatres have been mostly male, commissioned by male producers with business contacts. Women directors have recently started entering this field, often by forming their own companies and doubling as producers.

Profiles of Contemporary Directors

Sheema Kermani

Spurred to theatre through political resistance, Sheema Kermani creates work with a strong feminist and class angle, which often includes a highly physical style. Along with Grips Theatre, her theatre company Tehrik-e-Niswan (The Women's Movement), founded in 1979 in Karachi, is one of the oldest groups in the country.

Kermani's initiation to the performing arts was through dance training at the Ghanshyam's Centre, Karachi, in childhood. Returning to Karachi after completing a foundation course in fine arts at the Croydon College of Art in the United Kingdom in 1972, Kermani soon became involved with leftist and feminist politics, first setting up Tehrik-e-Niswan as an adult literacy center for women workers that aimed to draw them into the trade unions. Tehrik-e-Niswan began to organize various cultural events, seminars, and conferences to attract a wider participation of women. In one of these gatherings, the Indian author Amrita Pritam's *Distances of Pain* (*Dard Kay Faaslay*), a compilation of short allegorical stories about oppressed women, was presented as a dramatic reading (Mundrawala, "Shifting" 106). Tehrik-e-Niswan decided to work the same material into a theatrical production at a new women's shopping center in Karachi in 1981, marking Kermani's directorial debut. Its reception prompted many invitations from political

Sheema Kermani

activists and trade union workers to bring plays into their areas, ultimately transforming Tehrik-e-Niswan into an activist theatre group (Mundrawala, "Shifting" 107).

Kermani subsequently directed *Distances of Pain* at the Pak-American Cultural Centre auditorium in Karachi with a new cast of known television actors and an extended audiovisual design, including recorded sound to enhance mood and a slide show interspersed into the scenography (Mundrawala, "Shifting" 113). This crossover between community and more formal, proscenium theatre has been a central preoccupation in Kermani's work. She explains, "We started our theatre of agitation and propaganda . . . but from the beginning we have tried to raise it to a high artistic level. Along with this we have worked at both levels—reaching out to uninitiated audiences—both Urdu speaking and English speaking" (Mundrawala, "Shifting" 109).

Kermani's next major play with Tehrik-e-Niswan was *Woman* (*Aurat*) in 1982, written by Safdar Hashmi, the communist playwright of the Indian People's Theatre Association. The play dramatizes instances of oppression in the life of a woman, in a rites-of-passage cycle. In this production Kermani was influenced by "*Nautanki*, local and folk traditions . . . Asian traditions of story telling and dance [and] . . . Brecht's theatre for entertainment and instruction" (Mundrawala, "Shifting" 110). The production was well received for its "fascinating blend of forms" (Niazi 54), although some reviews criticized the play's propagandist feminist polemics (Marker 4). This production was first performed in the Mutahidda Mazdoor Federation (United Laborers' Federation), and has had more than three hundred stagings to community audiences in the outskirts of Karachi and in rural Sindh in nontheatre venues, as well as in urban proscenium theatres.

Kermani is also an accomplished dancer who has traveled internationally with her work. After the general elections of 1988, when Benazir Bhutto became Prime Minister, Kermani proceeded to India to study Bharatanatyam, Odissi, and Kathak dance from renowned teachers (Kermani). Her research into South Asian dance and the Indus Valley civilization culminated in her choreographing a cycle of major dance-theatre pieces that have been performed at various venues in Pakistan: *The Song of Mohenjodaro*, a classical ballet that traced ancient dance history; *Aaj Rung Hai*, a tribute to Muslim musicians and dancers; *Indus and Europa* (in collaboration with the French group K Danse), a modern ballet, and *Peace Dreams*, which are both attempts at evolving a unique hybrid style; and *Raqs Karo,* featuring contemporary dance based on the poetry of feminist Pakistani poetess Fahmida Riaz. Kermani has produced a number of committed dance students through both her independent practice and as the choreographer and artistic director of the Pakistan National Performing Arts Group in Karachi from 2002 to 2007.

Kermani selects material for her productions that lends itself to choreography, music, and possibilities of interpretation (Kermani). She has brought to life the writings of Beckett, Buchner, Chekov, Aristophanes, J. B. Priestley, Franca Rame, Vikram Seth, Surendra Verma, and poetesses Fahmida Riaz and Attiya Dawood, in adaptations, translations, and original plays. Kermani's productions demonstrate a variety of forms and styles, from the dance-drama played out against a highly visual set in *Long Live the Jungle* (*Jungal, Jungal Zindabad*) in 2001, based on a poem by Vikram Seth; to the highly stylized movement and physical comedy of *There Will Be No War* (*Jang Ab Nahin Hogi*) in 2002, based on Aristophanes's *Lysistrata;* to the realism of the docudrama *After All, Why?* (*Aakhir Kyun?*) in 2005, collectively created and based on case studies of women killed in the name of honor. She describes a strongly egalitarian ethos in the rehearsal room, where "workshops and improvisations are very much the process of all my productions combined with much background research about theme and character" (Kermani). Asma Mundrawala, who has been associated with Tehrik-e-Niswan since 1997 as a performer, designer, and director, describes Kermani as being extremely open to letting ideas from the ensemble feed into production in an "organic fashion" (Mundrawala Interview). In addition to directing, Kermani often also acts in the company's productions.

Madeeha Gauhar

Similar to Kermani, Madeeha Gauhar entered theatre through sociopolitical activism against the military dictatorship of the 1980s and directs work for her own company, Ajoka Theatre (Today's Theatre) in Lahore. Her work has addressed the complex contemporary issues of fundamentalism, bonded labor, censorship, honor killings, and discriminatory laws against women, through "blend[ing] traditional theatre forms with modern techniques . . . to provide entertainment which has a social relevance . . . and thus contribut[ing] to the struggle for a secular, humane, just and egalitarian society in Pakistan" ("Ajoka Theatre").

Gauhar became particularly active with theatre during her student years, marking her directorial debut as president of Najmuddin Drama Society with Federico García Lorca's *The House of Bernada Alba* in 1975. While pursuing her master's in English literature at Government College Lahore, she became president of their Dramatic Club and directed Jean Paul Sartre's *Men without Shadows* in 1980. After graduation, Gauhar joined the WAF protests in 1983 with her politically active mother and sister, and all were briefly jailed. Exploring other modes of activism, she began to present short dramatic skits at the WAF meetings in Lahore (Mundrawala, "Shifting" 118).

In 1984 Gauhar joined together with college friends and activists to launch the theatre company Ajoka with her production of Indian writer Badal Sircar's *Procession* (*Michhil*) under the Urdu title *Jaloos.* The play revolves around rediscovering a collective voice of political protest. Sircar's notion of a "Third Theatre" that blends folk and Western forms was a great inspiration to the development of Gauhar's production aesthetic, as well as her politics. Since the government would not allow such political work in their auditoriums, the play was performed on her mother's lawn, with audiences seated in the round, so that actors could interact with audiences. A reviewer from the *Star* newspaper noted, "To an audience sickened by the steady dose of drawing room farces,

Jaloos revealed the possibilities of the stage as a powerful medium of entertainment and sociopolitical criticism" ("Ajoka Theatre").

Gauhar earned her master of arts in theatre studies from Royal Holloway College in London in 1985, where she directed Badal Sircar's *Stale News* and wrote a dissertation on Western influences in Indian theatre. Returning to Lahore in 1985, she resumed work with Ajoka, directing an Urdu adaptation of Brecht's *Caucasian Chalk Circle*, again by Sircar. In this production, she began to consciously draw upon traditional forms, most notably nautanki's synthesis of song, dance, and live musicians, also evoking Brechtian narration devices through the comic interludes of bhānds (Erven 165).

From the late 1980s a wave of original plays was injected into the company's repertoire, written by Shahid Nadeem, who became the company's in-house writer and Gauhar's husband. The first of his many contributions included *The Acquittal* (*Barri*), which focuses on the effect of the Hudood laws on women from diverse class strata, staged in 1987. This new phase marked the end of General Zia's military regime and the birth of Ajoka's community theatre, in which plays from the repertoire traveled from villages to streets within the Punjab and beyond, at the invitation of political organizations (Mundrawala, "Shifting" 126).

Ajoka occasionally receives commissions from development agencies, but mostly the company stages work in Lahore, which then travels to other venues and specific communities on the invitation of government and nongovernment organizations (Mundrawala, "Shifting" 123). An Ajoka actor describes that the company's working methodology is to decide on a contemporary issue that Nadeem converts to dramatic material, which Gauhar usually directs (Naseem Abbas). However, Gauhar has also staged adaptations from writers such as Ibsen, Brecht, and Saadat Hasan Manto, as well as works by contemporary playwrights such as Intezar Hussain. Like Tehrik-e-Niswan, Ajoka has a semiprofessional structure.

One of Gauhar's most celebrated pieces is Nadeem's *Bulha*, which was first staged in 2001, and has been performed extensively in Pakistan, as well as in India, the UK, Iran, and the USA. *Bulha* is a biographical rendering of the most vibrant Punjabi poet and Sufi of the 18th century, Bulleh Shah. The work examines his rebellion against materialism and orthodoxy, which Gauhar states, "carries a powerful message about peace and tolerance" ("Ajoka Theatre"). Gauhar's production evokes popular Islam in a Punjabi-Urdu musical theatre, with live performances of Sufi devotional music, dance, and Bulleh Shah's poetry, which a local critic describes as a "favourite with its qawwali recitals that punctuate its climactic passages" (Nosheen Abbas).

A keen campaigner for cross-border harmony and regional peace, Gauhar has organized several festivals with Indian theatre groups in Lahore, and she regularly stages her plays in India. Gauhar was awarded the Medal of Excellence (Tamgha-I-Imtiaz) for her contribution to art and culture of social commitment by General and President Musharraf in 2003, and in 2006 she received the Netherlands' Prince Claus Award for her outstanding contribution to culture and development.

Aasma Butt

In contrast to Gauhar and Kermani, Aasma Butt directs primarily commercial comedy through her company, Dolphin Communications. Her style is characteristic of the popular Punjabi theatre, drawing upon the improvisational skills of professional performers.

Aasma Butt describes that she was "just an ordinary housewife" before she entered theatre. With a passion for the performing arts, she enrolled in a one-year acting diploma program in 1994, run by the Pakistan National Council of the Arts in Islamabad. Drawing upon this network of artists she established her company in Islamabad the following year, hiring directors and performing herself. Within a year she began directing plays with her debut of Shahid Naqvi's *Pinni*. Produced as part of a youth festival in the state-controlled Liaquat Hall in Rawalpindi, the production won awards for best actress, best director, and best playwright.

In her short career, Aasma Butt says that she has produced an astonishing one hundred stage productions, mostly as a director, but occasionally also as a writer and actor (Interview). With a rapid turnaround of work, she usually spends one week rehearsing each play. Since the actors use improvisation, usually based on a stock repertoire of local character types, the director's work is principally to ensure that the actor stay within the parameters of the situational comedy and maintain energy and comic timing. Aasma Butt states that the greatest hurdles come in the preparatory stages of casting, to ensure that she has the right team for each production. She has worked with a core

Aasma Butt

group of some twenty regular actors from Islamabad and Rawalpindi, but she also utilizes the talent from other cities for guest roles. At the centre of her aesthetics are the indigenous forms of bhānd and nautanki, which she describes as "the basics of theatre everywhere" (Interview). The bhānd mode provides the actors' comic improvisations and spontaneity, while the nautanki lends itself to story structure, and interlude music and dance sequences.

Keen to develop a theatre idiom beyond comedy, in 2009 Aasma Butt staged Arshad Chahal's *Shah Hussain the Faqir* (*Shah Hussain Faqir Saeen Da*), dramatizing the legends of the sixteenth-century Sufi saint, accompanied with music, dance, and poetry. She received recognition as best director in 2007 at the Punjabi Drama Festival Delhi, where she staged her own play, *The Arrogant Girl* (*Uchchiyan Mijajan Wali*). In this play a romantic relationship between a feudal lord and a humble nautch girl turns sordid when the hypocritical lord tries to assert his high-class positioning. While the play is a comic treatment of class and gender warfare, by using popular-Sufi dance and music, Aasma Butt blended a spiritual layer into her production aesthetics. With these Sufi connotations, the dance of the stigmatized nautch girl becomes a metaphor for transcending mundane authority and in the process subversively teases at contemporary restrictions against popular dancers. The play was praised by one Indian reviewer for its blend of "wit and wisdom" (Bajeli).

Aasma Butt's theatre is performed in the commercial, proscenium theatres in Islamabad, Rawalpindi, Lahore, and Gujranwala, and she has also taken her work to Singapore, Dubai, the United Kingdom, and India. Her production company also organizes musical evenings and concerts, broadening both her talent pool and revenue. While much of her work is sustained through ticket sales, she has also been able to acquire financial support from local businesses and multinational companies.

Nida Butt

Like Aasma Butt, Nida Butt (not related) produces commercial theatre, but in the English language, and more recently in Urdu. She is a lawyer by training and profession, as well as a self-taught performer and director with a passion for dance and musicals. Since 2006 she has introduced the "razzle dazzle" of the American Broadway musical to the Pakistani stage with large casts and big budgets (Isani).

She launched her directing debut with Mel Brooks' musical comedy *The Producers* in 2006 through her family-run production company, Made for Stage, which was founded in the same year in Karachi. However, it was in directing, choreographing, and performing in *Chicago* in 2008 that she made her mark. Despite indigenous musical theatre traditions, the trend of Western musical theatre in Pakistan had featured lip-synched performances to backing tracks. Nida Butt set new standards with *Chicago* by introducing a singing and dancing cast, a live jazz band, edgy choreography, and high production values. *Chicago* ran to packed houses in Karachi for ten nights, prompting

Nida Butt in *Mamma Mia!*, directed by Nida Butt, Karachi and Lahore, 2010.

its return in 2009. Because the Karachi Arts Council cancelled her booking a week before the opening night in favor of another production, she constructed a temporary theatre consisting of lounges, makeup rooms, seating for 450, and a stage. Despite these challenges, she returned to the stage with a successful production of *Mamma Mia!* in 2010, which played in Karachi and Lahore and was described by one critic as the "theatrical extravaganza of the year in Karachi, just like *Chicago* was before it. . . . She's putting musicals into the limelight . . . and forging the all important links between theatre, fashion, celebrity and music that thespians aren't doing" (Kamal). In January 2010 Nida Butt was selected for the Arts Presenters Program, a theatre internship, at the John F. Kennedy Center for Performing Arts in Washington, D.C.

Nida Butt claims to be a taskmaster in the rehearsal room. While the average rehearsal time for English theatre tends to be one month, hers can stretch to four in bringing the various components of dance, song, and acting together with large casts of up to fifty amateurs who are often untrained. In 2010 Nida Butt and her fiancé, the musician Hamza Jafri, opened the MAD (Music Art Dance) performing arts school in Karachi. The school offers classes in the performing arts by day and a performance venue at night, grooming new talent and showcasing new work. Nida Butt and Jafri in 2011 collaborated on an original Urdu musical *Karachi: Never Give Up* (*Haar Na Mano*), set in the impoverished Sindh province of Lyari, which is also the stronghold of the current Pakistan's People's Party government.

▦▦ ▦▦ ▦▦
▦▦ ▦▦ ▦▦

As seen historically from the actor-manager model, amidst male-dominated production and financial networks, women directors in contemporary Pakistan are forging creative ground through establishing their own theatre companies. In the amateur, semi-professional, and commercial theatres, they are playing important roles in bringing new aesthetics to the stage, and many are giving an important voice to gender activism.

Notes

1. Enacted in 1979, The Hudood Ordinance is considered Islamic law by its supporters, but it has raised considerable controversy in Pakistan and abroad for its harsh penalties and has largely been criticized for its policies that oppress women.

2. In contemporary Pakistan, bhānds are comic duos who perform in the ritual forum of weddings, offering incisive and improvisatory wit, with a tendency to debunk sociopolitical authority through jibes and disclosures (Pamment "Mock Courts" and "Sufi Wise Fool").

Sources

Abbas, Naseem. Interview with Shamshir Haider. 2005. N.p. Unpublished manuscript. December 23, 2005.

Abbas, Nosheen. "Ajoka's Bulha City's Perennial Favourite." *Dawn.com.* April 11, 2009. Available at http://www.dawn.com (accessed May 25, 2011).

Ahmad, Nazir. *50 Years of Lahore Arts Council.* Lahore, Pakistan: Sang-e-Meel, 2000.

"Ajoka Theatre." *Ajoka Theatre Online,* 2010. Available at http://www.ajoka.org.pk (accessed January 10, 2011).

Bajeli, Diwan Singh. "Feudal Lords from Lahore." *The Hindu,* September 14, 2007. Available at http://www.hindu.com (accessed December 16, 2012).

Bari, Farzana. "Women in Pakistan: Briefing Paper." Asian Development Bank, 2000.

Butt, Aasma. Interview. October 16, 2010.

Erven, Eugène van Erven. *The Playful Revolution.* Bloomington: Indiana University Press, 1992.

Fuller, Marcus B., Mrs. [Jenny]. *The Wrongs of Indian Womanhood.* Edinburgh, Scotland: Oliphant, Anderson and Ferrier, 1900.

Isani, Aamna Haider. "A New Kind of Theatre: Nida Butt Breezes In with All That Jazz." *The News.* March 1, 2009. Available at http://jang.com.pk (accessed January 5, 2011).

Kahle, Sigrid. "Theatre in Pakistan 1952–1957. A Personal Experience with the Historical Background." *Transactions Vol. 1,* 63–100. Istanbul: Swedish Research Institute, 1987.

Kamal, Muniba. "Mamma Mia! Here They Go Again!" Review of *Mamma Mia!,* by Nida Butt. *The News.* October 18, 2009. Available at http://jang.com.pk (accessed January 4, 2011).

Kermani, Sheema. Interview. November 10, 2010.

Marker, Aban. "Strong Messages of Black and White." Review of *Aurat* by Sheema Kermani. *The Star,* June 24, 1982, 4.

Mumtaz, Khawar, and Farida Shaheed, eds. *Women of Pakistan: Two Steps Forward, One Step Back*. Lahore, Pakistan: Vanguard Books, 1987.

Mundrawala, Asma. Interview. March 30, 2011.

———. "Shifting Terrains: The Depoliticisation of Political Theatre in Pakistan." PhD diss. University of Sussex, 2009.

Niazi, Samarah. "Major Boost for Serious Drama." *MAG* 1–7, July 1982, 53–4.

Pamment, Claire. "Mock Courts and the Pakistani Bhānd." *Asian Theatre Journal* 25.2 (2008): 344–62.

———. "The Sufi Wise Fool Syndrome in the Performance Mode of Bhānds." *Sohbet* 2 (2011): 62–70.

Saeed, Fouzia, and Adam Nayyar. *Women in Folk Theatre*. Islamabad: Lok Virsa, 1991.

Safdar, Huma. "The Representations of Women in Commercial Theatre." In *Engendering the Nation-State*, vol. 2, edited by Neelam Hussain, Samiya Mumtaz, and Rubina Saigol, 139–45. Lahore: Simorgh, 1997.

Srinivasan, Doris M. "Royalty's Courtesans and God's Mortal Wives: Keepers of Culture in Pre-colonial India." In *The Courtesan's Arts: Cross Cultural Perspectives*, edited by Martha Feldman and Bonnie Gordon, 161–81. Toronto: Oxford University Press, 2006.

"Theatre." *Tehrik-e-Niswan*. Available at http://www.tehrik-e-niswan.org.pk (accessed December 10, 2010).

Poland

Magda Romanska

The issues facing women directors in Poland were always connected to the history of Poland's liberatory struggle—first, under partitions, then, under Nazi and Soviet occupations. Although historically Polish theatre has gained worldwide renown predominantly thanks to its male directors such as Tadeusz Kantor and Jerzy Grotowski, Poland today has a thriving and influential cadre of young women directors, who have gained renown and respect in Poland and abroad.

Women's Rights: Historical Context

In 1772 Poland was partitioned by the Russian Empire, Kingdom of Prussia, and Habsburg Austria, which divided the Polish Commonwealth among themselves. In 1795 after two more partitions, Poland ceased to exist as an independent nation. It did not regain its statehood until 1918, following World War I. Because of its long legacy of partitions, the early Polish feminist movement has always been connected to national liberatory struggle. Positivism, the late-nineteenth-century progressive socio-cultural movement, considered women's education and work outside of the home to be necessary for the survival of the Polish nation. The ethics of equal access to work and knowledge allowed for a relatively pluralistic social structure. On military ground, many women fought alongside men in various national uprisings. In addition to the Positivist and militant strains, deeply rooted Polish Catholicism, Polish Romanticism, and a long-established system of nobility created an idealized image of a Polish woman, respected and worshiped foremost as a mother (stemming from the Madonna figure) whose domain was to protect and safeguard the Polish home and national values of

"God, Honor, and the Country" (Walczewska 10). As a result of all of these factors, Polish women received their full voting and elective rights the same year as the country gained its independence, a tacit acknowledgement of their contributions to the national struggle during the 123 years of partitions.[1] However, despite visible progress, the two visions of Polish womanhood—the militant, working woman and the "Polish Mother"—remained in tension.

Following World War II, the rise of communism and the Soviet regime changed gender relations in Poland: the Communists saw social relations primarily through the prism of class struggle. In that context, the new image of a socialist working woman, who was simple, healthy, able to work side by side with men, and contributed equally to the common, brilliant socialist future, contrasted with the prewar image of a "bourgeois" woman of leisure, who was portrayed as hysterical and weak. With the spread of state-owned kindergartens and preschools, women were given equal access to the workplace, and the concept of a stay-at-home mother basically disappeared from the Polish landscape. As most society was, on some level, engaged in some form of resistance against the Communist regime, once again the image of a "Polish Mother" came to the forefront: she was now both a working woman and a stereotypical Polish mother who stood guard over family, national, and religious values; she was often engaged in some form of subversive political activity, while at the same time being primarily responsible for the survival of her family. Since the Communist regime greatly undermined the sense of Polish masculinity, day-to-day existence under the system was a combination of matriarchal and deeply misogynistic tendencies, with women shouldering the entire burden of housework and childrearing activities while maintaining their position as equal or sometimes the only breadwinners. Regardless of their complex position within the family structure, women were equally present in the workforce, getting the same pay for the same work. Though they had more difficulties gaining recognition and promotion, women had a relatively strong social and cultural position despite the deeply misogynistic tendencies of the Catholic discourse that continued to dominate much of Polish family life.

Early Women Directors

During the nineteenth and early twentieth centuries, despite the progress that Polish women were making on other fronts, theatre and art remained a male domain. Though women playwrights such as Gabriela Zapolska and Felicja Kruszewska made their mark on Polish theatre, women directors were virtually absent. One of the early women directors was Lidia Wysocka (1916–2006), a theatre and film actor, theatre director, and costume designer. Her most notable productions were staged after World War II and included Stuart Engstrand's *Springtime in Norway*, produced in 1949 in Szczecin, and Aleksander Fredro's *Husband and Wife*, produced in 1959 in London. The situation in Polish theatre changed significantly after World War II. As Polish theatre critic Wojciech Szulczyński noted, "The communists privileged the Polish theatre, never stinting it money or other means" (499). Although initially theatre was thought to be a useful tool of socialist propaganda, it soon became a tool of subversion. Classic texts gained new meaning, and playwrights and directors developed a peculiar coded language to talk about present concerns while escaping the omnipotent and omnipresent state censorship. During the postwar period, two women directors marked the strongest presence: Lidia Zamkow (1918–1982) and Krystyna Skuszanka (1924–2011).

Zamkow studied drama at the National Institute of Theatre Arts (Państwowy Instytut Sztuki Teatralnej, PIST) in Warsaw and at the State Academy of Drama (Państwowa Wyższa Szkoła Teatralna) in Łódź—now the Aleksander Zelwerowicz State Theatre Academy. She started her career as an actor and throughout her career continued acting and directing simultaneously. She directed her first show, Bolesław Prus's *Error* (*Omyłka*) in 1948 at the Polish Military Theatre (Teatr Wojska Polskiego) in Łódź. The production was praised by critics for the skillful construction of grand group scenes (Fik 195). In her later years Zamkow directed at a variety of Polish theatres. Some of her most notable productions include Maxim Gorky's *Barbarians* in 1953 at The Coast Theatre (Teatre Wybrzeże) in Gdańsk; Friedrich Dürrenmatt's *The Visit* in 1958, Shakespeare's *Macbeth* in 1966, and Stanisław Wyspiański's *The Wedding* in 1969, all at the Juliusz Słowacki Theatre (Teatr im. Juliusza Słowackiego) in Cracow; and Bertolt Brecht's *Mother Courage and Her Children* in 1962 followed by Albert Camus's *Caligula* in 1963 at the Old Theatre (Narodowy Teatr Stary) in Cracow.

Having started her career during the heyday of Socialist Realism, Zamkow, like other Polish artists of that time, had to struggle against the prevailing socialist aesthetics. In 1956 Zamkow said that most of the plays she directed were chosen by the theatre management (Fik 195). Her own personal style, however, was eventually given a chance to flourish in the mid-1950s. In 1953 Stalin died, and Khrushchev came to power. Three years later, Khrushchev denounced Stalinist atrocities, and the period referred to as The Thaw, or Polish October, began as the Communist Party loosened its grip on the country's political and cultural life. In the spirit of the times, Zamkow's 1954 direction of Viesvolod Vishnevsky's *An Optimistic Tragedy* in Gdańsk at the the Coast Theatre was praised for its "realistic, unsentimentalized image of Russian Revolution" (Fik 196). Similarly, Zamkow's 1956 production of *Romeo and Juliet* at the Polish Army Theatre (Teatr Domu Wojska Polskiego) in Warsaw tackled Shakespearean text through the prism of contemporary social and political problems of Polish youth. Like many Polish directors of her generation, during the years 1956 to 1959, Zamkow wanted to make theatre that would engage both social and political reality of the moment. Since then, her plays began sharing a common theme: one's struggle against an idea, a political force, or a society (Fik 197). Although her staging continued to be subtly political, Zamkow was primarily interested in directing classics, since they allowed for ambivalence, and she generally avoided grotesque and farce because they remained politically too hazardous, although they eventually came to dominate Polish playwriting of the post–1956 era. She did, however, direct a number of notable productions in the expressionist style, including Dostoyevsky's *Dream* and Camus's *Caligula* in 1963 at the Old Theatre; an adaptation of Kafka's *America* in 1968 at the Juliusz Słowacki Theatre; and Tolstoy's *Resurrection* in 1969 on the Stanisław Wyspiański stage at the Silesian Theatre (Stanisław Wyspiański Teatr Śląski) in Katowice (Węgrzyniak 443). Thanks to her bold and grand reinterpretations of classics, Zamkow is considered, next to Krystyna Skuszanka, one woman auteur director who was able to develop her individual artistic style under challenging political circumstances.

After studying at the Old Theatre Studio, Skuszanka graduated in 1949 with a degree in Polish literature from the University of Poznań. Three years later she received her directing diploma from the National Institute of Theatre Arts in Warsaw and made her directorial debut with Władimir Bill-Białocerkowski's *Sztorm* (*Storm*) at the National Theatre (Teatr Ziemi Opolskiej) of Opole. The production, with set design by Kantor, was unconventional by the norms of that time, which was dominated by Socialist Realism. In 1955 Skuszanka became an artistic director of the People's Theatre (Teatr Ludowy) in Nowa Huta, a working neighborhood of Cracow, where, as French theatre critic Raymonde Temkine noticed, she "made an avant-garde theatre which has been able to attract the workers" (17). That year Skuszanka worked with Kantor again on her production of Shakespeare's *Measure for Measure* at the National Theatre in Opole. At that time, Jan Paweł Gawlik, a renowned Polish theatre critic, wrote of her work: "Skuszanka always focuses on one theme of the drama that she considers the most important, and she develops it, even while disregarding all other possibilities. This bold theatrical shortcut, invention, creativity and monumental vision are the most important elements of her newly evolving artistic style" (Fik 201). In *Measure for Measure,* Skuszanka was trying to make a political statement, and she focused on the issue of power and dictatorship (Fik 202). In 1972 she took a job as an artistic director of the Juliusz Słowacki Theatre, while also teaching at the Cracow Theatre School. In addition, along with her husband, she was an artistic director of the National Theatre in Warsaw from 1983–90. Unlike Zamkow, Skuszanka began her career at the twilight of Social Realism, and she always directed at "her" theatres as an artistic director, which gave her more political and artistic freedom (Fik 200). Skuszanka's most notable productions include Juliusz Słowacki's *Balladyna* in 1956 and Shakespeare's *The Tempest* in 1959, both at the People's Theatre in Nowa Huta; Adam Mickiewicz's *Forefather's Eve* in 1962 at the Polish Theatre (Teatr Polski) in Warsaw; and Słowacki's *Kordian* at the Drama Theatre (Teatr Dramatyczny) in Wrocław in 1962.

Although Skuszanka also focused on classics, particularly on works by Shakespeare and Polish Romantics, she did not stray away from contemporary Polish drama. She always wanted to "reference the Polish national tradition, but choosing works which would ring true and alive to the contemporary society, often touching on painful and controversial issues" (Fik 202). Following the 1956 October Thaw, several Polish playwrights began creating an absurdist language that tackled both transnational, existential themes and specifically Polish political and cultural issues. Skuszanka staged some of those works, including a 1967 production of Mrożek's *Enchanted Night* for the Polish Television Theatre. Skuszanka's style, even in her work on classics productions became more abstract, often involving metatheatrical elements of "theatre within theatre." For example, her 1966 version of *As You Like It* at the Polish Theatre (Teatr Polski) in Wrocław, took place on an empty stage with one gold bush of mistletoe (Fik 204).

Working Climate in the Twenty-First Century

Following the 1989 Round Table talks that ended the forty years of communist regime in Poland, the Polish theatre—always entangled in one way or another in the political struggle—suddenly was left in an ideological vacuum. At the same time, with the economic turnover to the free market, the state sponsorship of the theatres was significantly curtailed, leaving many of them to their own devices as far as funding was concerned. In October 1989, during the general meeting of the Association of Artists in Warsaw's Polish Theatre, it was acknowledged that during the communist period, theatre depended financially on government. "Suddenly, in free market conditions, the artists felt lost" (Udalska 167). As well-known Polish scholar Halina Filipowicz said: "Who needs the stage for political expression when public debate has moved to the parliament and the media?" ("Polish" 70)

Culturally, during the 1990s, as a country in transition between the communist rule and capitalism, Poland became a battlefield between religious and liberal groups. Catholicism's overly repressive rule following the fall of communism clashed with the freedom of expression and the influx of the Western (particularly American) culture, with its morally lax attitude toward the female body and sexuality. On the crossroad between the traditionally Catholic-centered mentality of the old Poland and the newly emerging class of women unwilling to submit to it, Poland came to represent a larger, global paradigm shift in the politics of sex and representation. Many women became bitterly disappointed with the direction of the country, becoming nostalgic for socialism, often referred to as a period of "gender innocence."[2] Despite the obstacles, or perhaps because of them, the transitional period of the 1990s included small political victories. In 1989 Izabella Cywinska, theatre director and critic, became the first Minister of Culture. As Filipowicz wrote in 1992, only a decade earlier Cywinska had been imprisoned for one of her politically engaged productions ("Polish" 76). Another victory for women occurred in 1992 when Hanna Suchocka became the Prime Minister in the government of President Lech Walesa. Unfortunately, during the 1990s, no theatre was willing to discuss "the issues that have dominated public discourse: abortion, the reinstatement, by governmental decree, of religious instruction in public school, the promotion of Christian values on public radio and television" (Filipowicz, "Demythologizing" 124). The function of political and social commentary was relegated to performance art and multimedia art, which saw its Polish renaissance during that decade of transition.

The turbulent 1990s, however, proved to be fertile ground for a new crop of young women theatre directors of the so-called transitional generation. The years 2001 through 2003 saw directorial debuts of many young women directors, some of whom eventually came to establish themselves as leaders of Polish theatre.[3] Interestingly, nearly all of the shows directed by Polish women directors during the first decade of the new millennium were written by foreign men and were lacking in the traditional Polish canon that once constituted a foundation of Polish theatre. This tendency might have been a general syndrome of uncritical fascination with the Western culture that dominated the transitional decade. It may also testify to certain absorption of the patriarchal mode of storytelling and fear—fear on the part of women directors—of being labeled feminist and relegated to the margins of Polish culture. Nonetheless, Polish women directors work at top theatres in the country, gaining international recognition and earning many of the country's highest theatre awards. They appear to thrive in the post-communist world, although perhaps their successes are not yet fully on their terms.

Polish Performance and Video Art: Post-1989

The transitional climate of the 1990s was a fruitful ground for the number of artists—mostly filmmakers, performance artists, and video artists—to pursue the paradoxes and ironies of the Catholic discourse vis-à-vis gender difference and sexuality. Women performance and visual artists such as Katarzyna Kozyra, Alicja Zebrowska, and Dorota Nieznalska caused scandals by either mocking or shocking the Polish public opinion with radical juxtapositions between the sacred and the profane. Much of Kozyra's work entertains the issues of gender, power, and violence. Her 1999 short video, *Men's Bath House* (*Łaźnia męska*), filmed in Budapest in a men's bath house, is influenced by Jean Auguste Dominque Ingres's painting *The Turkish Bath* and a 1995 photograph titled *Bonds of Blood* that focuses on the Yugoslavian conflict and depicts two sisters' mutilated bodies lying under religious symbols of Catholicism and Islam. In addition, her video performance and photo series, *Lou Salome*, shown in Rome at Teatro di Cani in 2005, features femme fatale Lou Salome driving a buggy through Vienna's Schwarzenberg Palace drawn by Friedrich Nietzsche and Paul Rée, who are dressed as men-dogs undergoing training at the hands of their dominitrix. Kozyra's most monumental multimedia-performative project yet, *Art Dreams Come True*, performed during the years 2003 to 2006, is a surreal landscape of mythical and modern iconography. The main heroine, Berlin-based drag queen Gloria Viagra, is an actor and Kozyra's alter ego, who is both Madonna and dildo-wearing transvestite desperately trying to weave in a coherent self-image from fragmented pieces of her postmodern identity (Kireńczuk 18–22).

Profiles of Contemporary Directors

Anna Augustynowicz

Born in 1959 in Dębica, Anna Augustynowicz studied theatre at Jagiellonian University and directing at the Ludwik Solski State School of Theatre (Państwowa Wyższa Szkoła Teatralna im Ludwika Solskiego, PWST) in Cracow, graduating in 1989. While at PWST, she studied with Krystian Lupa, a well-known, award-winning Polish director who is considered the patron of the new post-1989 directing wave. In 1992 she became an artistic director of the Modern Theatre (Teatr Współczesny) in Szczecin. In this position, as one of the first Polish directors, she began introducing a number of new European plays onto the Polish stage, tackling difficult social themes with bold theatrical gestures. Her directing style is often characterized as naturalistic, risky, and brutal. The critics also refer to it as "dirty," "meaty," "visceral," "bodily," and "physical" (Żółkoś 73). Augustynowicz is also credited as one of the first Polish directors to use video and other multimedia techniques widely in her productions. She also introduced a new style of adaptation, updating a number of classics, including those from traditional, national Polish repertoire. Her adaptations attempt to reflect contemporary issues and sensibilities.[4] Augustynowicz's work has been honored with many awards at Polish and European theatre festivals. In 1996 her all-male production of Witold Gombrowicz's *Iwona, Princess of Burgunda* was awarded a directing prize at Opole's Theatre Confrontations: Polish Classics (Opolskie Konfrontacje Teatralne: Klasyka Polska). The production has been judged as a harbinger of a new wave in Polish theatre, a signpost of the new post-1989 generation. Augustynowicz "ranks among Gombrowicz's most important contemporary interpreters" (Augustynowicz and Semil 70). The Polish theatre critic and scholar Rober Cieślak wrote that by cross-dressing her actors, Augustynowicz was able to trigger other theatrical processess that revealed new dimensions of Gombrowicz's text. Transgendered aesthetics enhanced the focus on form. Another Polish critic noted that Agustynowicz's adaptation "is dynamic, full of bitter humor, with its own rhythm and fascinating atmosphere" (Liskowacki). In 2007 Augustynowicz received the top prize for her staging of Wyspiański's *The Wedding* at the National Competition of Stagings of the works of Stanisław Wyspiański (Ogólnopolski Konkurs na Inscenizację utworów Stanisława Wyspiańskiego). One critic noted that Augustynowicz's version of *The Wedding* captures the essence of Wyspiański's play: the anxieties over Polish national identity at the crossroads: "With simple black and white aesthetics, subtle music and rhythmical acting, the director asks questions about the future and national identity of the Polish nation: where are we coming from, who are we, where are we going?" (Wójcicka). Another critic pointed out that Augustynowicz's version of *The Wedding* "goes beyond theatre, reframing the issues touched on by Wyspiański into a new modern context. It's an important and wise meeting with an incredibly complex work" (Dolega). For her radical and critically acclaimed adaptations of Polish classics, Augustynowicz received the Passport of *Polityka Weekly*, which cited her artistic boldness and sensitivity to modern issues as two most significant accomplishments.

Iwona Kempa

Born in 1967 Iwona Kempa graduated with a degree in Theatre Studies from Jagiellonian University in 1992 and studied directing at the State School of Theatre in Cracow, graduating in 1996. She debuted as a director in 1994 at the Universal Theatre (Teatr Powszechny) in Łódź with a production of *Quartet* by Bogusław Schaeffer. Combining quasi-theatrical and quasi-instrumental elements, *Quartet* was so successful that during the 1990s it was staged by practically every Polish theatre. In 1996 Kempa began working in Toruń at the Wilam Horzyca Theatre (Theatre im. Wilama Horzycy), where she directed *Caricatures* (*Karykatury*) by Jan August Kisielewski. For this production she received the Bohdan Korzeniewski Prize, awarded to young directors by the magazine *Teatr*. Her other productions in Toruń included Beckett's *Endgame* in 1998; *Two and Half Billion Seconds*—based on Beckett's five one-acts—in 2006; and Martin McDonagh's *The Lonesome West* in 2002. All three productions received critical acclaim, with *The Lonesome West* winning the Minister of Culture and Journalist Awards.

Kempa is mostly interested in contemporary drama, and she directed a number of Polish premiers of international hits, including McDonagh's *The Cripple of Inishmaan* in 1999 at the Wrocław Contemporary Theatre (Wrocławski Teatr Współczesny), Zoltan Egressy's *Portugal* in 2004 at the Polish Theatre in Poznań, and Neil LaBute's *The Shape of Things* in 2003 at the Polish Theatre in Bydgoszcz. Her production of *Portugal* was met with critical acclaim, with one of the Polish critics writing, "Iwona Kempa is never sentimental, always looking at her characters with a somber eye, seeing their poses and pretenses for what they are. Kempa knows how to balance the proportions. In today's theatre, where everyone's falling for cheap tricks of extreme emotions—love or hate—looking at things in their true proportions is a real feast" (Sieradzki). Zoltan Egressy, the author of the play, praised Kempa for a perfect balance between pathos and grotesque (Maćkiewicz). The production also won a number of awards, including the 2004 directing award at the IV Festival of Contemporary Drama "Reality Represented" in Zabrze. Kempa's productions of classics include Chekhov's *Seagull* in 1999 at the Jana Kochanowskiego Theatre in Opole, Carlo Gozzi's *The Love of Three Oranges* in 2002 at the Contemporary Theatre in Wrocław, Büchner's *Woyzeck* in 2003 at the Wilam Horzycy Theatre in Toruń, Brian Friel's *Dancing at Lughnasa* in 2006 at the Theatre Academy (Akademia Teatralna) in Warsaw, and an adaptation of Ingmar Bergman's *Scenes from a Marriage* in 2008 at the Juliusz Słowacki Theatre. Kempa chooses productions that combine humor with irony, violence, pathos, and the grotesque, focusing on carefully crafted emotional range and subtle study of characters.

Maja Kleczewska

Maja Kleczewska was born in 1973 in Warsaw. She graduated with a degree in psychology from Warsaw University and a degree in directing from the State School of Theatre in Cracow. She was an assistant of Krystian Lupa and Krzysztof Warlikowski, internationally known Polish theatre directors. Her 2000 directorial debut, *Jordan* by Anna Reynolds and Moiry Buffini, staged at the Juliusz Słowacki Theatre, won her immediate critical praise.[5] Kleczewska's productions analyze the psychology of the characters and their motivations, showing lonely and lost heroes who are unable to adapt to their world and eventually end up either going insane or committing a crime. The central theme of Kleszewka's work is crime, murder, and violence. Her direction is rough and unsentimental. Polish theatre critic Łukasz Drewniak even calls it, "manly and brutal in the way it portrays the world" (111). Kleczewska's most acclaimed production was Shakespeare's *Macbeth*, staged in 2004 at the Jan Kochanowki Theatre in Opole. The production combined Shakespearean language with modern aesthetics of pulp fiction movies. Peter Rieth poignantly summarizes the impact of the production, explaining,

> Kleczewska's *Macbeth* takes the ostentatious step of making Shakespeare's witches— weirder. Rather than witches, the drama unfolds with what appear to be two transvestites and a prostitute. Such an opening salvo may initially be regarded as an application of stereotypically modern crassness to an ancient classic, but Kleczewska's apparent genius lies in the fact that she recognizes modernity as effectively crass, thus transmutating Shakespeare's "weirdness" from an acknowledgment of the mystic frontiers of Fortuna into a representation of modern decadence. This very transmutation is essentially the foundation for the plays' dialectic regarding the possibility of tragedy and the question of farce.

In Poland, the production provoked scandal, because, as Jacek Wakar, a Polish theatre critic pointed out, it "features sex and violence similar to a Tarantino movie."

Agata Duda-Gracz

Agata Duda-Gracz is a theatre director and designer. Her father, Jerzy Duda-Gracz is considered one of the greatest contemporary Polish painters. Born in 1974 in Cracow, Duda-Gracz graduated with a degree in art history from the Jagiellonian University in Cracow and studied directing at the State School of Theatre in Cracow. She worked on more than twenty productions either as a director, scenic designer, or costume designer at theatres in Kalisz, Cracow, Lódź, Warsaw, and Wrocław. She began her career with the production of *Cain* by George Byron, staged at the Witkiewicz Theatre in Zakopane in 1998. Other notable productions include her direction at the Theatre Academy of Dramatic Arts in Crocow of Karl Büchner's *Woyzeck* in 1999 and Jean Genet's *Balcony* in 2004; her direction at the Juliusz Słowacki Theatre of Vailland's *Abelard and Heloise*

Michel de Ghelderod's
Galgenberg, directed by
Agata Duda-Gracz, Juliusz
Słowacki Theatre, Cracow,
2007. Photographer:
Marcin Wegner.

in 2002 and Camus's *Caligula* in 2003; Shakespeare's *Othello* in 2009 at the Jaracz Theatre in Łodź; *Father*, based on a short story by Oscar Tauschinski, in 2010 at the Juliusz Słowacki Theatre; and Giacommo Puccinni's *La Boheme* in 2011 at the Grand Theatre (Teatr Wielki) in Poznań.

Duda-Gracz designs costumes and scenography for her own shows as well as for other shows, and she has won a number of awards for her designs, including a Ludwig Award for the set of *Abelard and Heloise*. In 2009 she was awarded a Golden Laurel for her Mastery of Arts, an award given by the Polish Culture Foundation in Cracow. She is often called a "visionary" due to her larger than life, symbolic, and rich visual imagery. Her productions are often compared to those of Józef Szajna and Kantor, two of Poland's most renowned theatre directors who began their careers in visual arts. Duda-Gracz's breakthrough production was *Galganberg*, a collage of texts by Michel de Ghelderode, staged in 2007 at the Słowacki Theatre in Cracow. The production has

Michel de Ghelderod's *Galgenberg*, directed by Agata Duda-Gracz, Juliusz Słowacki Theatre, Cracow, 2007. Photographer: Wojtek Jankowski.

been hailed as her best show yet, earning critical accolades. Most recently, Duda-Gracz has been staging productions not only of her own design but also for which she writes her own texts, as with *Apocalypsis: A Short History of Marching*, staged at the Słowacki Theatre in Cracow in 2011. Critically acclaimed for its visual and ritualistic aspects (the viewers were sitting in church-like pews), the production marked a new direction in Duda-Gracz's career; however, like her previous productions, it was called "strong" and was filled with haunting images of violence and sexuality.

In the first decade of the twenty-first century, the number of women directors in Polish theatre grew exponentially, with the Grand Theatre in Poznań announcing that its 2011 season would be devoted solely to women directors and the Stara Prochoffnia Theatre in Warsaw organizing "women only weekends" for their women audiences. The new generation of women directors is not afraid to take risks and tackle difficult subjects on both small and grand scales.

Notes

1. For example, Roza Pomerantz-Meltzer was the first woman elected to the Polish parliament in 1919 as a member of a Zionist party.

2. In 1994 Katherine Verdery warned that the Western scholars "should be especially attentive to how nationalist politics [in post-Communist Eastern Europe] integrates gender, what alternative forms of national imagery will be offered and by whom, and how the politics around issues like abortion will produce distinctive forms of democracy and capitalism in which nation and gender are intertwined in novel ways" (255).

3. Some of them include Maja Kleczewska, Aldona Figura, Grazyna Kania, Agniesza Glińska, Monika Strzępka, and Olga Lipinska.

4. Her directing repertoire at the Contemporary Theatre (Teatr Współczesny) in Szczecin includes Stieg Larsson's *Chief* (*Naczelny*) in 1993 and *Brothers and Sisters* (*Bracia i siostry*) in 1995, Clare McIntyre's *Beware of Pity* (*Bez czułości*) in 1995, Werner Schwab's *People Destruction or My Liver Is Senseless* (*Moja wątroba jest bez sensu, albo zagłada ludu*) in 1997, an adaptation of Ben Elton's *Popcorn* in 1999, Marius von Mayenburg's *Parasites* (*Pasożyty*) in 2001, Mark Ravenhil's *Polaroids* (*Polaroidy*) in 2002, Alan Ayckbourn's *Comic Potential* (*Komiczna siła*) in 2003, an adaptation of Eric-Emmanuel Schmitt's novella *Oscar and the Lady in Pink* 9 (*Oskar i pani Róża*) in 2004, Gérald Sibleyras's *L'inscription* (*Napis*) in 2005, and Wyspiański's *The Wedding* (*Wesele*) in 2007. Her work for other theatres includes Witold Gombrowicz's *Ivona, Princess of Burgunda* (*Iwona, księżniczka Burgunda*) for the Old Theatre in Cracow in 1997; Catherine Anne's *Agnes* for the Wilam Horzyca Theatre (Teatr im. Wilama Horzycy) in Toruń in 1997; Sergi Belbel's *After the Rain* (*Po deszczu*) for The Coast Theatre (Teatre Wybrzeże) in Gdańsk in 2000; and at Warsaw's Universal Theatre (Teatr Powszechny) Naomi Wallace's *One Flea Spare* (*Tylko ta pchła*) in 2000, Bernard-Marie Koltès's *Return to the Desert* (*Powrót na pustynię*) in 2004, and in 2006 Shakepeare's *Measure for Measure*. Her two shows Catherine Anne's *Agnes* in 2000 and Krzysztof Bizia's *Toxins* (*Toksyny*) in 2002 have been filmed by the Polish Television Theatre.

5. Other notable productions include Hugo von Hofmannstahl's *Electra* (*Elektra*) in 2001 at the Cyprian Norwid Theatre (Teatr im. Cypriana Norwida) in Jelenia Góra, David Harrower's *Knives in Hens* (*Noże w kurach*) in 2002 at the Juliusz Słowacki Theatre, Ken Kesey's *One Flew Over Cuckoo's Nest* (*Lot nad kukułczym gniazdem*) in 2002 at the Szaniawski Theatre (Teatr im. Szaniawskiego) in Wałbrzych, Chekhov's *The Seagull* (*Czajka*) in 2004 at the Cyprian Norwid Theatre, George Büchner's *Woyzeck* in 2005 at the Wojciech Bogusławski Theatre (Teat im. Wojciecha Bogusławskiego) in Kalisz, Shakespeare's *Midsummer's Night Dream* (*Sen nocy letniej*) in 2005 at the Old Theatre in Cracow, Racine's *Phaedre* (*Fedra*) in 2006 at the National Theatre in Warsaw, Sara Kane's *Blasted* (*Zbombardowani*) in 2007 at the Old Theatre, Peter Weiss' *Marat/Sade* in 2009 at the National Theatre, and Elfried Jelinek's *Babel* in 2010 at the Polish Theatre in Bydgoszcz.

Sources

Augustynowicz, Anna, and Małgorzata Semil. "A Facelift for the Soul: On Directing Gombrowicz." *Theater* 34.3 (2004): 70–77.

Cieślak, Robert. "Trans-Mission." ["Trans-Misyjność"]. Proceedings of "Trans-Polonia" conference, organized by City Theatre, Gombrowicza in Gdynia, October 23, 2010. *Dialog* 12.12 (December 16, 2011).

Dolega, Aneta. "This Is Poland." *Szczecin Courier* ["A to Polska właśnie." *Kurier Szczeciński*] 183, September 22, 2007.

Drewniak, Łukasz. "Tsunami of Youth." In *Public Strategies, Private Strategies: Polish Theatre: 1990–2005* ["Tsunami młodości." In *Strategie publiczne, strategie prywatne: Teatr polski: 1990–2005*], edited by Tomasz Plata, 102–19. Izabelin: Świat Literacki, 2006.

Fik, Marta. *Thirty-Five Seasons: Polish Theatre in 1944–1979* [*Trzydzieści pięć sezonów: Teatry dramatyczne w Polsce w latach 1944–1979*]. Warsaw: Wydawnictwa Artystyczne i Filmowe, 1981.

Filipowicz, Halina. "Demythologizing Polish Theatre." *TDR: The Drama Review* 39.1 (Spring 1995): 122–29.

———. "Polish Theatre after Solidarity: A Challenging Test." *TDR: The Drama Review* 36.1 (Spring 1992): 70–89.

Kireńczuk, Tomasz. "Princess Catharina and Thirteen Dreams" ("Królewna Katarzyna i trzynaście snów"). *Didaskalia* 76 (2006): 18–22.

Liskowacki, Artur D. "Ivona in the World of Fashion." *Szczecin Courier* ["Iwona w świecie mód." *Kurier Szczeciński*] 187, September 25, 1996.

Maćkiewicz, Marcin. "Conversation with Zoltan Egressy." *Gazette* ["Rozmowa z Zoltanem Egressym." *Gazeta Wyborcza*] 136, July 12, 2004, 7.

Rieth, Peter. S. "Tragedy & Farce in Kleczewska's Macbeth." *e-teatr.pl*, April 11, 2005. Available at http://www.e-teatr.pl (accessed November 1, 2011).

Sieradzki, Jacek. "Postsocialist Mishmash." *Cutout* ["Jaja popegeerowskie." *Przekrój*] 27, July 4, 2004.

Szturc, Włodzimierz. "These Brave Productions." *Theatre Notebook* ["Te odważne inscenizacje." *Notatnik Teatralny*] 16–17 (1998): 33–39.

Szulczyński, Wojciech. "Review: 'Forefather's Eve: Twelve Improvisations.'" *Theatre Journal* 48.4 (December 1996): 499–503.

Temkine, Raymonde. *Grotowski*. Translated by Alex Szogyi. New York: Avon, 1972.

Udalska, Elenora. "Polish Theatre after 1989." *Canadian Slavonic Papers* 39½ (March–June 1997): 167–79.

Verdery, Katherine. "From Parent-State to Family Patriarchs: Gender and Nation in Contemporary Eastern Europe." *East European Politics and Societies* 8.2 (1994): 225–55.

Wakar, Jacek. "Kleczewska's Most Radical Play to Date." *Dziennik* 117, May 28, 2008, n.p.

Walczewska, Sławomira. *Ladies, Knights, Feminists: Gender Discourse in Poland* [*Damy, rycerze, feministki. Kobiecy dyskurs emancypacyjny w Polsce*]. Cracow: eFka, 1999.

Węgrzyniak, Rafał. "Directing. Enacting." In *Theatre Spectacle* ["Reżyseria. Inscenizacja." *Teatr. Widowisko*], edited by Marta Fik, 425–59. Warsaw: Instytut Kultury, 2000.

Wójcicka, Magda. "Anna Augustynowicz' Black Wedding." *Here* ["Czarne Wesele Anny Augustynowicz." *Tutej*], May 12, 2008. *e-teatr.pl.* Available at http://www.e-teatr.pl (accessed February 1, 2012).

Żółkoś, Monika. "On the Surface of the Body, That Is to Say, Inside. 'Ivona' in the Theatre of Anna Augustynowicz." In *The Speaking Body: Gombrowicz's Ivona, Princess of Burgunda* ["Na powierzchni ciała czy w środku 'Iwona' w teatrze Anny Augustynowicz." In *Ciało mówiące. Iwona, księżniczka Burgunda Witolda Gombrowicza*], 73–87. Gdańsk: Słowo, Obraz, Terytoria, 2001.

 Romania

Diana Manole[1]

Women started directing professionally in Romania only at the end of the
Second World War, and their number increased very slowly. During the communist
dictatorship, from 1947 to 1989, very few women were accepted into the country's
only bachelor of arts program in stage directing and even fewer worked after graduation. After the fall of communism in 1989, Romanian mainstream theatre remained
male-dominated, although more women pursued professional directing, working for
state- and city-subsidized repertory theatres but often founding small, private companies
and/or freelancing in Romania and abroad.

Women's Rights: Historical Context

For centuries, Romanian women were traditionally destined to be wives and mothers, while legally being treated as minors. The first pleas for emancipation occurred at
the end of the nineteenth century, when the first Romanian women earned university
degrees and founded feminist associations and magazines. At the 1898 Reunion of
the Women's League from Iași, Eliza Popescu was the first to plead for the Romanian
women's right to vote, later supported by the other societies.

However, only the increase of women in the workforce after the First World War
determined changes in the constitution with the inclusion of partial suffrage in 1923
and the stipulation of women's right to vote in 1938. The 1946 Election Law ratified
gender equality, followed by the first general elections in the same year, the results
of which were falsified by the Romanian Communist Party (RCP), leading to the

proclamation of a popular republic with a sole political party under the control of the Soviet Union. During the 1947–1989 communist regime, men maintained their privileged position despite the official politics of gender equality. The communist regime's duplicity became even clearer in 1966, when an anti-abortion law was enacted, exposing the official treatment of women as "baby-makers" and causing the deaths of more than ten thousand women from illegal abortions (Betea 251). By 1987 women held 34 percent of the Great National Assembly[2] membership—five out of the forty ministries—and women held only two of twenty-one seats, for 9.5 percent of the RCP Executive Bureau (Scutaru). Women continued to receive lower salaries for the same work and struggled with the surviving patriarchal mentalities of almost the entire society and especially of men in power, who considered women the only ones responsible for housework and childrearing.

Early Women Directors

At the beginning of the nineteenth century, Princess Ralu Caragea initiated the transformation of a ballroom into the first theatre house in Bucharest. Here, the St. Sava School's students presented the first performance in Romanian in 1819 (Masoff, *Midnight* 247–49). Despite its start under feminine auspices, until the end of the Second World War, Romanian professional theatre limited women's presence to acting and founding private companies, for which they hired male directors. The first bachelor of arts in stage directing was established in 1950 at the Theatre Institute in Bucharest, which was later called the Institute of Theatrical and Cinematographic Arts (IATC) and after 1989 the I. L. Caragiale National University of Theatrical and Cinematographic Arts (UNATC). Earning this degree soon became the primary avenue to becoming a stage director and working professionally. Although a small number of women finished their degrees in stage directing before the end of communism in 1989, most gave up working in professional theatre after graduation.

All arts and media suffered from the communist regime's drastic political oppression and censorship. In 1948 the government expropriated all private companies and opened several national and municipal theatres across the country, where "propaganda replaced art" (Runcan 222). Taking advantage of the short period of relative freedom that followed Stalin's death in 1953, the newly founded Young Directors' Circle denounced the lack of professionalism that dominated Romanian theatre. In a 1957 public report, the organization asked for artistic freedom and professionally trained artistic directors instead of the usual police informants appointed by the communist government (Runcan 270–82). After Nicolae Ceaușescu delivered a pivotal speech in 1971 that focused on communist and socialist reform, political oppression and censorship increased again. Theatre productions underwent several previews with state censors, who often required significant changes or banned shows that even remotely criticized the regime or did not conform to the socialist realist style. Stage directors who did not want to leave the country or obey the official requirements took refuge in classical, mainly Russian, drama, and/or chose to work in smaller cities or at IATC, where censorship was less drastic. However, the more daring directors were persecuted, some even imprisoned or exiled, and occasionally were required to direct propagandistic theatre productions.

Marietta Sadova (1897–1981) is the first Romanian woman whose work as a stage director is documented. A famous actor in the interwar period, she started directing in 1945. Although she had been a sympathizer of the Iron Guard, a Romanian fascist organization, Sadova became an active supporter of communism at the end of the Second World War. After the new regime rose to power in 1947, it rewarded her public display of loyalty, allowing her to direct at the most important theatres in Bucharest— the National, Bulandra, and Nottara—and to tour internationally. However, when she returned from a tour in Paris in 1956, Sadova was arrested and sentenced to three years in prison because she brought home a few books written by banned Romanian intellectuals living in exile (Handoca).

When released and "rehabilitated," Sadova was allowed to continue her work and directed the only performance ever attended by Ceaușescu and his wife (Masoff, *Between* 321).[3] This production, *The Sunset* (*Apus de soare*) by Barbu Ștefănescu-Delavrancea, successfully opened at the inauguration of the new Grand House of the National Theatre in Bucharest in 1973 and remained a model for historical theatre in the next decades. She also directed classical works, including two plays by Anton Chekov in Bucharest in 1959: *The Seagull* at the National Theatre and *The Cherry Orchard* at the Municipal Theatre (Teatrul Municipal). In both productions, Sadova renounced the officially accepted naturalist stagings and instead poetically portrayed the Russian aristocracy, causing politically subservient critics to label them as ideologically misguided (Bratu 22–34).

With more rebellious beginnings, Sorana Coroamă-Stanca (1921–2007) was the only woman director who signed the 1957 report of the short-lived Young Directors' Circle. In the same year, her poetic staging of Arthur Miller's *The Crucible* at the C. I. Nottara Theatre was consistent with the Young Directors' innovative principles and was praised by a few courageous theatre critics. From 1959 to 1965, Coroamă-Stanca was banned from theatre and public life for political reasons. After her official "rehabilitation" she continued staging classical texts, but also directed and even wrote a few propagandistic texts, such as *An Evening of Dance* (*Seară cu dans*), a stereotypical praise of communist morality and values (Ghițulescu 18–19). Despite her occasional political compromises, Coroamă-Stanca made an important contribution to Romanian theatre and was recognized after the fall of communism through the Romanian Theatre Union (UNITER) lifetime achievement award in 1999 and with an honorary doctorate from the George Enescu Arts University in Iași in 2005.[4] Throughout her fifty-nine-year career she directed more than 190 shows for the most important Romanian professional theatre companies, as well as television productions and radio dramas.

Among the stage directors who chose teaching as their main career path, Sanda Manu, born in 1933, became one of the most revered Romanian theatre professionals. During a career that has spanned more than five decades, she has directed more than 120 theatre and television productions at IATC/UNATC in Bucharest and at professional theatres all over Romania, but also in Germany and the United States. In a theatre culture that has primarily praised visual and allegorical shows, she has distinguished herself through the deeply touching realism of her productions and her belief in the actors' ability to communicate and embody "theatrical signs" without stage artifice. According to theatre historian Ileana Berlogea, Manu was an adept at "what she called 'intensive directing,' based on truth, on the discovery of the emotional and psychological mechanisms of the human actions" (qtd. in Ghiţulescu 541). She was awarded the UNITER awards for excellency in 1992 and lifetime achievement in 2008, as well as an honorary doctorate from UNATC in 2009.

Although with a less publicly celebrated career, Nicoleta Toia (1941–2003) was one of the few women directors who successfully worked in theatres all over the country, choosing to stay away from the heavily censored capital, Bucharest. She directed more than eighty shows, most of them at the National Theatre in Iaşi, where she was head director from 1980 to 1990, a position very few women held during communism. Although generally leaning toward realism, she also experimented with elements of Romanian popular culture, especially in the mythical portrayal of voivode Ştefan cel Mare Delavrancea's *The Sunset*, which she directed three times between 1972 and 1991. In these productions, Toia intensified the play's poetic aura by including popular songs, legends, and folk dances.

Despite the official politics of promoting the cultures of ethnic minorities, directors of non-Romanian ethnicity remained very few and mostly unknown during the communist regime. As an exception, Hungarian-Romanian Ildiko Kovacs (1927–2008) achieved national and international recognition in puppet theatre and received numerous awards. She directed more than one hundred shows that included adaptations of fairytales as well as works by Shakespeare, Cervantes, and Ionesco. In her productions, Kovacs employed a total theatre style, using pantomime, special effects, live music, and actors who manipulated but also interacted with puppets. Her politically challenging direction of Alfred Jarry's *Ubu Roi* at the Cluj National Theatre in 1980 was banned because of the similarities between the Ubus and the Ceauşescus (Damian).

Although Romanian theatre was heavily censored by the communist government, its live nature helped it secure a higher degree of freedom of expression compared with other visual and literary genres. Taking advantage of their direct relationship to the audience, numerous actors and directors included subversive political innuendos that escaped scrutiny or were sometimes tacitly tolerated by the censors (Popescu 121).

Working Climate in the Twenty-First Century

After the violent fall of the communist regime in 1989 and Romania's integration into the European Union in 2007, special laws and agencies meant to protect women's rights were created despite the absence of a cohesive feminist movement. However, during the first two decades of democracy, gender inequality persisted. Fewer women than men graduated from technical schools and universities, worked after graduation, or held management and political positions (Scutaru). In addition, women's average salary nationally was significantly smaller than men's, by 17.6 percent in 2003, as the majority worked in lower-income fields (Scutaru).

Because freedom of speech was abruptly achieved in 1989, theatre temporarily lost its dominant role of subversively expressing collective protests and, subsequently, some of its social and political relevance (Popescu 178–212). By the end of 2010, however, it regained its appeal, especially in Bucharest, where most theatre productions were sold out in advance. The number of stage directors grew, mainly as a result of new under-graduate and graduate programs in stage directing, but most women who earned a degree in directing after 1989 opted for more stable and/or better-paying jobs. Among those who continued directing, only a few were hired as associate directors and even fewer as artistic directors for the state- and city-funded theatre companies that survived the political transition. Most women directors chose to found small companies and/or freelance in Romania and abroad. While the younger generation did not feel that they were discriminated against because of their gender (Cărbunariu, Mărgineanu), most mature women directors, such as Nona Ciobanu, still believed that stage directing was "a man's world" in Romania (qtd. in Welsh).

A quick examination of the UNITER awards might explain the different opinions, showing that women directors have received mainstream recognition at the beginning of their careers, but have been marginalized once they become professionals. For ex-ample, while a few women won awards for student production and debut, no women directors were nominated in the UNITER best show and best director categories from 1996 to 2009, despite winning other national and international awards.

Profiles of Contemporary Directors

Cătălina Buzoianu

Until the beginning of the twenty-first century, Cătălina Buzoianu remained the only Romanian woman director who shared mainstream box-office success and artistic rec-ognition with her internationally renowned male colleagues. She directed more than one hundred productions and earned the most important national awards several times, before and after the regime change, including the UNITER awards for best director in

Cătălina Buzoianu.
Photographer:
Nadia Mosanu.

1994 and 1996, and lifetime achievement in 2001, as well as a number of international distinctions. After finishing a bachelor of arts in stage directing at IATC in 1970, she worked as a director for the National Theatre in Iași and the Youth Theatre in Piatra Neamț. From 1979 to 1985, she held the position of head director at the Mic Theatre in Bucharest and then transferred as a permanent associate director to Bulandra Theatre, where she remained until her official retirement. In addition, Buzoianu has consistently worked for other theatre companies in Romania and abroad. She has further left her imprint on Romanian theatre through her work at IATC/UNATC from 1975 to 2008, teaching and mentoring some of Romania's most innovative contemporary directors.

During Ceaușescu's dictatorship, Buzoianu's productions were subject to ruthless political censorship because of their daring character. For example, in 1975 she adapted and directed Ecaterina Oproiu's *Interview* (*Interviu*), a collection of real-life interviews with women from different social categories, at Bulandra Theatre. The performance was framed as a television show, produced by a fictional divorced and heartbroken female reporter. Although it was subsequently performed for ten years and was invited to a festival in Germany, the production initially went through seventeen official previews, during which lines were censored and two characters were cut because they contradicted the propagandistic image of the happy Romanian woman (Malița 152). Buzoianu's subsequent productions at the Mic Theatre encountered similar difficulties, as they were among the most aesthetically innovative and politically daring productions of their time. Some of the most famous were Luigi Pirandello's *Let's Dress the Naked* in 1979, and her adaptation of Mikhail Bulgakov's eponymous novel *The Master and Margarita* and Witold Gombrowicz's *Ivona, Princess of Burgundia*, both in 1980.

An eclectic director, Buzoianu has explored many styles and genres, from realism to absurdism, and from dance theatre and puppet theatre to opera. As theatre historian Mircea Ghiţulescu notes, one of Buzoianu's goals seems to have been "not to produce theatre without text, as it is now fashionable [in Romania], but to make theatre out of any text" (103). Consistent with her interest in theatre anthropology, Buzoianu developed and directed some of her adaptations in the places of origin of the source texts, exploring the past and present relationships between the written word and the culture that generated it (Modreanu 56). For example, in 1997 Miguel de Cervantes's *Don Quijote* was created and then performed in La Mancha, Spain.

Despite their great variety, all Buzoianu's shows display the characteristics of her unique, highly visual, ironic, and playful directing style. Her work on each production usually starts with a two- to three-week workshop, during which she guides the actors to improvise particular aspects of the play and/or of a space, in the case of site-specific shows. The subsequent rehearsals last up to two months and focus on creating the show's structure and style, as a synthesis of what was already discovered (Buzoianu).

According to Buzoianu, writing, directing, and touring with the *Odyssey 2001* (*Odiseea 2001*), in 2001, has been one of her most interesting professional and personal experiences. Her script focused on Homer's description of Odysseus's trip home at the end of the Trojan War, but it also brought together some of the most important world myths, using selections from the *Orphic Tablets* and *One Thousand and One Arabian Nights*, as well as major authors such as Euripides, Dante, Omar Kayyam, and Albert Camus. As theatre critic Cristina Modreanu notes, the show's modular structure resembled "a giant puzzle, a dictionary of founding fathers," coordinated by an ironic character whose identity shifted from Zeus to Abraham, Tiresias, and Dante (69). After opening at Bulandra Theatre in Bucharest, it took part in a Mediterranean tour to several countries on board a Romanian military training ship, replicating Odysseus's main stops. With the help of local actors, the *Odyssey 2001* was adapted, translated, and performed for the audience in each country where they stopped, culminating with a final multilingual show at the last stop in Brăila, Romania (Buzoianu).

Having a spectacular career of more than forty years and raising two children, sometimes breastfeeding them during rehearsals, Buzoianu contradicts the common prejudice that a woman has to choose between art and family. She states, "directing is not a matter of being a man or a woman; it's a matter of resilience" (Buzoianu).

Nona Ciobanu

Nona Ciobanu is one of the most successful Romanian stage directors of her generation. She graduated in the 1990s and combined the professional choices made by her colleagues before and after the fall of communism, working both in Romania and abroad. In 1995 she earned a bachelor of arts in stage directing at UNATC and between 1993 and 1996 participated in several international workshops in directing, set design, Japanese butoh theatre, and cultural management. In her second year of studies, Ciobanu made her directorial debut with a childlike adaptation she wrote of a Romanian folktale, *Youth without Old Age and Life without Death* (*Tinerețe fără bătrânețe și viață fără de moarte*), which was successfully performed at the Bulandra Theatre in Bucharest and internationally.

In 1994, while still a student, Ciobanu was hired as a permanent associate director at the Mic Theatre. Her first professional production, Carlo Gozzi's *The Love for Three Oranges*, won the award for debut at the 1994 UNITER Gala, as well as the best director awards at the I. L. Caragiale National Theatre Festival in Bucharest and at the 1995 Image-Theatre Festival in Satu-Mare. Ciobanu also successfully remounted it in 2004 at La Jolla Playhouse in San Diego, California, where reviewer Charlene Baldridge described her directorial style as "pure, amusing, and refreshingly offbeat."

Searching for a place "outside the system" (Welsh) for her more experimental productions, together with actor and designer Iulian Bălțătescu, her long-time collaborator, Ciobanu founded the Toaca Cultural Foundation in Bucharest in 1996, which has supported young artists and interdisciplinary projects, including some of her own. For example, Ciobanu's *Orpheus: or, How to Undress Your Feathers* (*Orfeu sau cum să te dezbraci de pene*) opened at the 2005 East Meets East Festival in Cambridge, England, then played at other theatres and festivals in Romania and abroad, receiving enthusiastic reviews. Although it was based on her selections from poems and a novel by Gellu Naum, the performance did not rely on the spoken word. Theatre critic Anna Carey of the *Irish Times* described it as "a production of astonishing beauty and grace," writing, "Is Nona Ciobanu's retelling of the Orpheus myth a play, a dance piece, a poem, a puppet show or a video installation? The answer is all of the above" (Carey).

In 2008 Ciobanu coordinated *Pilgrim towards the Centre* (*Pelerin spre centru*) for the 2008 Puzzle Project, initiated in Romania under the auspices of the European Year of Intercultural Dialogue. It consisted of a video installation by Ciobanu and Slovenian artist Peter Košir and a production of Shakespeare's *The Tempest*, which she adapted and directed. In her powerful ritualistic version, Prospero and Miranda were the only speaking characters; Ariel and Caliban were both performed by an African-French dancer, and the other characters were suggested through music by a Syrian band (Zirra 22). Ciobanu continued her collaboration with Košir with *Hopscotch*, a multimedia performance and video installation produced in Ljubljana, Slovenia, in 2010. The show also included live music played on a traditional Persian fiddle and choreography based on the whirling rituals of Sufi dervishes.

Over the years, Ciobanu developed a personal creative strategy. Before beginning rehearsals, she likes to define clearly the production's main ideas, and together with designer Bălțătescu to search for the best and simplest images to represent them. She also prefers to cast actors who can freely improvise during the first stage of a production, inspiring her "in getting the depth of the literary material" on which they are working. Towards the end of the process, she edits the findings, selecting what is essential and shaping the final version of a production (Ciobanu). Her shows have gained Ciobanu international recognition as "a director who views theatre as a place for poetic transformations" (Welsh). Although they are usually based on a written script, the text is only a starting point for creating performances that are mainly visual.

Gianina Cărbunariu

Gianina Cărbunariu is one of the most successful Romanian women playwright/directors to emerge at the turn of the twenty-first century. She finished a bachelor of arts in Romanian and French in 2000 at the University of Bucharest, and at UNATC she received a bachelor of arts in stage directing in 2004, a master's degree in playwriting in 2006, and a doctorate in theatre in 2011. She has also participated in several international workshops and was artist-in-residence at the Royal Court Theatre in London in 2004 and at Lark Theatre in New York in 2007.

Cărbunariu openly believes in the director as the author of the show and in directing as an act of personal creation (Popovici 105). To avoid the rigid working conditions and prejudices of mainstream theatres, which still favor well-established, authoritarian, and usually male directors as well as classical plays, Cărbunariu chose first to direct and sometimes write independent small-budget experimental shows for alternative companies (Cărbunariu). In 2002 she became a co-founder of dramAcum—meaning "drama now" but also "drama how"—a theatre organization based in Târgu Mureş, Romania, that has actively promoted young writers through translations and a national drama contest. Among other dramAcum winners, Cărbunariu worked on *Sado Maso Blues Bar* with the playwright Maria Manolescu over several years, and in 2007 directed it at the Foarte Mic Theatre, the studio theatre of the Mic. As theatre critic Iulia Popovici described it, the show unified the city and theatre spaces, with pedestrians glancing through the theatre's uncovered windows at the show but also at the paying audience, who, in turn, acknowledged the street as part of the performance (119).

When she develops her own texts, she usually relies on improvisation and casts the same actors she worked with as colleagues at UNATC. She actively involves them in her creative process, "sharing ideas, exchanging experiences connected with the chosen theme" and often "changing things until the last day of rehearsals and even after the opening night" (Cărbunariu). Originally workshopped during her 2004 residency at the Royal Court Theatre, *Kebab* tells the story of a teenage girl who moves to Ireland in hopes of a better life, is forced into prostitution by her so-called boyfriend, and is killed when she gets pregnant. Cărbunariu directed it in Bucharest under the title *mady-baby.edu*, but the show was banned from Act Theatre while still in rehearsal because of its content and language, and it eventually opened at the Foarte Mic Theatre in 2004. Although most of the Romanian theatre professionals and critics ignored it, *mady-baby.edu* was invited to several international festivals and nominated for the best foreign performance in the Festival des Theatres des Ameriques in 2008 by the Montreal

English Critics Circle. Cărbunariu bitterly notes the paradox: "I was lucky enough to work abroad and I didn't depend on the Romanian theatre system to get recognition for my work. Usually, they had to accept this recognition."

She is also interested in theatre that is based on real events. Produced by the Yorik Theatre in Târgu Mureş in 2010, *20/20* was a fictional re-enactment of the violent ethnic conflicts between Romanians and Hungarians that took place in the same city twenty years earlier. Based on more than seventy documentary interviews, Cărbunariu developed the multilingual script through a workshop organized with Romanian and Hungarian artists, then wrote the final version alternating Romanian, Hungarian, English, and French, with one scene mixing all four languages, and directed it in an interactive style. The production toured the region, and each show was followed by public discussions, giving the spectators the opportunity to share their personal memories of the events. *20/20* earned the 2010 best performance award from the International Association of Theatre Critics in Romania (AICT) and the special prize and the Rivalda Prize at the 2010 Pozst—the Hungarian National Theatre Festival.

According to theatre critic Corina Oprea, the physical and psychological brutality of Cărbunariu's productions is an attempt to draw attention to the problems of her generation, the so-called "survivors in blue jeans, warriors, fighters for their life and for their place in the world."

Ana Mărgineanu

Ana Mărgineanu is another woman director who often writes or collates the texts of her productions and is one of the co-founders of dramAcum. She earned a bachelor of arts in stage directing at UNATC in 2002 and participated in the Lincoln Center Directors Lab in New York City in 2007. Mărgineanu became very successful after her directorial debut with *Garbage* (*Deşeuri*), based on texts by Matei Vişniec, which was produced at the Luni Theatre in Bucharest in 2001. The production won the best show award at the Mangalia Hop Gala for Youth in Romania and was nominated in the debut category at the UNITER Gala.

Mărgineanu's work has been showcased in Romania and Russia, as well as in major European cities and New York City, where she has been hailed by critics for her inventiveness and creative use of multimedia, attention to detail, and ability to bring the best out in her actors. During rehearsals, she strives to make the company members "feel like they are all creators, rather than executants" (Mărgineanu). Thematically, her productions are very diverse. Some have ironically explored the perception of the communist regime twenty years after its fall—as in her dramatic collage *89, 89 . . . Hot after '89* (*89, 89 . . . fierbinte după '89*), performed at the Foarte Mic Theatre in 2004, while others have dealt with the transformation of local traditions under the influence of Western consumerism and mass media, as in Vera Ion's *Vitamins* (*Vitamine*) at the same theatre in 2005. Mărgineanu also addressed more general aspects of the human condition when directing Ştefan Peca's romantic comedy *The Sunshine Play*, which opened at the Dublin Fringe Festival in 2005 and received the best play award in the 2006 Relationship Drama category at the London Fringe Festival, as well as the Romanian Critics Award in 2007.

The relationship with the audience is the main focus of Mărgineanu's aesthetics: "I always search for new ways to communicate with the potential viewers of my work. It is as much about the subject I am going to present next, as the way I will be presenting it." Using interactivity, she treats spectators "not only as observers but also as participants [who] are 'tripping' into the shows perceived as experiential journeys" (Mărgineanu). Relevant for these beliefs, *The Blind Trip* was a multimedia theatre collage she directed for "Which Direction Home," an international festival showcasing nine productions inspired by Homer's *The Odyssey* at New York's LaGuardia Performing Arts Center (LPAC) in 2010. Based on Mărgineanu's concept, *The Blind Trip* consisted of five ten-minute performances, each written by a single different playwright from Romania or the United States, performed by more than twenty actors in five different rooms at LPAC. One at a time, a blindfolded audience member was guided from place to place, allowed at any time to take off the blindfold, and thus end his/her theatrical journey. As Mărgineanu stated, the voluntary lack of vision and the ability to choose between staying and leaving forced each spectator to redefine his or her perception of the world, but also to accept that we continuously make decisions because "we cannot have it all, but we are not aware of this" (qtd. in Lee).

Like other Romanian stage directors of her generation, Mărgineanu is also interested in documentary theatre. *Only the Best about Romania* (*Despre România, numai de bine*) was a series of performances developed in collaboration with Peca, each inspired by the stories, myths, and legends from a single Romanian town and aiming to present its inhabitants with an outside perspective of themselves. The first production, *5 Miraculous Minutes in Piatra Neamţ* (*5 minute miraculoase în Piatra Neamţ*) won the best show award at the 2010 Romanian Comedy Festival (FestCO) in Bucharest. It took place simultaneously in three different apartments that coexisted on stage, enacting the stories of the disillusioned inhabitants in a style that ironically combined realism with musical comedy, dance routines, and cartoon-inspired moments.

Despite persisting patriarchal mentalities and the usual lack of resources for new play development and experimental theatre at the start of the twenty-first century, many Romanian women directors have continued to attend and give workshops, participate in festivals, and direct a large range of shows, from innovative stagings of classical texts to multicultural and multimedia documentary productions, slowly strengthening their position in national and international professional theatre.

Notes

1. Special thanks to Nadia Moşanu of the Romanian Cultural Institute for her extensive research support.

2. From 1948 until December 1989 the Great National Assembly (Marea Adunare Naţională; MAN) was the equivalent of the parliament in Romania during communism.

3. "Rehabilitation" was the exoneration of a person after being politically and/or criminally prosecuted, usually without basis. In Romania, political rehabilitations began after Stalin's death in 1953.

4. Established in February 1990, Uniunea Teatrală din România (UNITER) is a professional, nonpolitical, nongovernmental, and nonprofit association of Romanian theatre artists, offering the most prestigious awards in Romanian mainstream theatre.

Sources

Baldridge, Charlene. "Lugubria Light." Review of *The Love of Three Oranges* by Carlo Gozzi. Turbula, Autumn 2004. Available at http://www.turbula.net (accessed June 8, 2011).

Betea, Lavinia. "The Outlawing of Abortions (1966–1989) as a Fact of Social Memory." In *The Daily Life in Communism* ["Interzicerea avorturilor (1966–1989) ca fapt de memorie socială." In *Viaţa cotidiană în communism*], edited by Adrian Neculau, 244–63. Iaşi and Bucharest: Polirom, 2004.

Bratu, Horia. "Chekhov and Chekhovism." *Theatre Magazine* ["Cehov si cehovismul." *Revista Teatrul*] 4.2 (1959): 22–34.

Buzoianu, Cătălina. Telephone interview. December 20, 2010.

Carey, Anna. "First Nights, Second Week: A Look at What Is Happening in the Dublin Fringe Festival." *Irish Times*, September 9, 2005.

Cărbunariu, Gianina. E-mail message to the author. January 4, 2011.

Ciobanu, Nona. E-mail message to the author. June 12, 2011.

Damian, Horaţiu. "How a Puppet Show Was Banned." *The Transylvanian Paper* ["Cum a fost interzis un spectacol de păpuşi." *Foaia transilvană*]. Available at http://www.ftr.ro (accessed February 27, 2011).

Ghiţulescu, Mircea. *The Book of Artists: Romanian Contemporary Theatre* [*Cartea cu artişti: Teatrul românesc contemporan*]. Bucharest: Redacţia Publicaţiilor pentru Străinătate, 2004.

Handoca, Mircea. "Unpublished: Preface to *The Forbidden Forest* by Mircea Eliade." *Literary Romania* ["Inedit: Prefaţă la *Noaptea de Sânziene* de Mircea Eliade." *România Literară*]. November 1–17, 2006. Available at http://www.romlit.ro (accessed December 30, 2010).

Lee, Felicia R. "Theater for Audiences of One." *New York Times*, July 27, 2010: C1.

Maliţa, Liviu, coordinator. *Theatrical Life during and after Communism* [*Viaţa teatrală în şi după communism*]. Cluj: Efes, 2006.

Mărgineanu, Ana. E-mail message to the author. January 6, 2011.

Masoff, Ioan. *Between Life and Theatre* [*Între viaţă şi teatru*]. Bucharest: Minerva, 1985.

———. *The Midnight Actor* [*Actorul de la miezul nopţii*]. Bucharest: Cartea Românească, 1974.

Modreanu, Cristina. *The Director in Checkmate* [*Şah la regizor*]. Bucharest: Editura Fundaţiei Culturale Române, 2003.

Oprea, Corina. "Gianina Cărbunariu—Staging the Newspaper Facts." *The International Artist Database*, 2007. Available at http://culturebase.net (accessed December 30, 2010).

Popescu, Marian. *The Stages of the Romanian Theatre, 1945–2004: From Censorship to Freedom* [*Scenele teatrului românesc, 1945–2004. De la cenzură la libertate*]. Bucharest: UNITEXT, 2004.

Popovici, Iulia. *A Theatre at the Curb* [*Un teatru la marginea drumului*]. Bucharest: Cartea Românească, 2008.

Runcan, Miruna. *Theatricalization and Re-theatricalization in Romania: 1920–1960* [*Teatralizarea şi reteatralizarea în România: 1920–1960*]. Cluj Napoca: Eikon, 2003.

Scutaru, Codrin. "The Politics of Equal Opportunities between Men and Women in the Social Inclusion." *The Committee against Poverty and for Social Inclusion* ["Politicile pentru egalitatea de şanse între bărbaţi şi femei in cadrul incluziunii sociale." *Comisia anti-sărăcie şi promovarea incluziunii sociale*]. SC MEDIAUNO SRL, March 6, 2002. Available at http://www.mediauno.ro (accessed February 21, 2010).

Welsh, Anne Marie. "'Oranges' Gets Juiced Up in an Avant-Garde Staging at Playhouse." Review of *The Love for Three Oranges*, by Carlo Gozzi. *San Diego Union-Tribune*, September 19, 2004.

Zirra, Ioana. "Minimalism and Metaphysics." Review of *The Tempest* by Shakespeare. *Literary Romania* ["Minimalism şi metafizică." Cronică la *Furtuna* de Shakespeare. *România Literară*], November 21–28, 2008. Available at http://www.romlit.ro (accessed December 30, 2010).

 Russia

Maria Ignatieva

Since the emergence of the directing profession in Russia, and under the great influence of the first directors of the Moscow Art Theatre (MAT) such as Konstantin Stanislavsky and Vladimir Nemirovich-Danchenko, the director was viewed by actors and society in general as the most powerful individual in the theatre and in the company—the guide who shared a great vision with a team of followers. Although there were several women directors in the thirties and forties, until after the death of Stalin in 1953 the profession in general was not associated with women. This prejudice is deeply rooted in the society, and even in the twenty-first century directing is predominantly a male profession.

Women's Rights: Historical Context

The changes in women's rights in Russia are inextricably linked to the political changes of the twentieth century. The Russian Revolution of 1917, which toppled the Russian Empire, was followed by a civil war won by the Bolsheviks. In 1922 the Soviet Union, or the Union of the Soviet Socialist Republics (USSR), was formed, and it existed until 1991—the year modern-day Russia was recognized by the international community.

The early-twentieth-century Russian feminists were inspired by the emerging international women's movement. Usually fluent in several languages and well traveled, Russian women were familiar with the fight for suffrage and with feminist writing. There is no doubt that Chicago's International Women's Congress in 1893 became a model for the First All-Russian Women's Congress (Pervyi Rossiiskii Zhenskii S'ezd), which was held in St. Petersburg in 1908.

In the first constitution of 1918 the equal rights of all citizens were manifested in the Russian Soviet Federative Socialist Republic. In the 1930s the Soviet Union proclaimed the complete victory of socialism after completing the industrialization and collectivization of its economy; at that time, women became a major part of the workforce. Soviet propaganda promoted images of new Soviet women in films: as factory and collective farmworkers, teachers, communist leaders, and even airplane pilots. Massive involvement of women in various aspects of Soviet life was interpreted by society and presented to the outside, hostile, capitalist world as true emancipation. Thus, the idea of the feminist movement itself was interpreted by the official propaganda as women's struggle for their rights in the capitalist society. As Rochelle Goldberg Ruthchild wrote in *Equality and Revolution*, "The history of Russian feminist activism and victories were made invisible and inconsequential, to be rediscovered largely after the fall of the USSR" (249). The 1936 constitution, also known as the Stalin constitution, emphasized in article 122: "Women in the USSR are accorded equal rights with men in all spheres of economic, state, cultural, social and political life. The possibility of exercising these rights is ensured to women by granting them an equal right with men to work, payment for work, rest and leisure, social insurance and education" (USSR "1936"). However, the inequality of men and women is obvious in the wording itself: women "are accorded" these rights, which are being "granted" to them. The USSR Constitution of 1977 stated that women and men have equal rights in the USSR, and thus had "equal access with men to education and vocational and professional training, equal opportunities in employment, remuneration, and promotion, and in social and political, and cultural activity" (USSR "1977"). Since the communist paradise was achieved on paper, "the idea of separate organization of women formally constituted within the communist movement was therefore seen as divisive, diversionary and, hence, politically unacceptable" (Ruthchild 121). Therefore, the feminist movement began to be revived only after 1991. By 1999, more than six hundred women's organizations were registered by the Ministry of Justice. According to the 2011 statistics available through the Moscow City Department of Culture, 60 percent of jobs—including both creative and administrative positions in theatres and museums—were occupied by women, with a median age of thirty-nine years. Although only fourteen women were listed as artistic directors, this number is much higher for women directors in various fields, including children's theatre, religious theatres, folk theatre, and even the Animal Durov theatre—a theatre in which animals perform. However, the Russian feminist movement in general is in the process of finding its voice and paths in the rapidly changing political, social, economic, and cultural circumstances of twenty-first century Russia.

Early Women Directors

The first Russian women directors emerged from the First Studio of the MAT, where Stanislavsky, Leopold Sulerzhitsky, and Evgeny Vakhtangov taught the first version of the Stanislavsky System and directed according to it. The First Studio, which became the MAT II in 1924, created a unique group of the first Russian women directors, who often worked together as a team, inspiring and supporting each other. This group included Serafima Birman (1890–1976), Sofia Giatsintova (1895–1982), and Lidia Deykun (1889–1980). These three women developed professional and personal bonds, which they preserved throughout their lives. Among them, only Birman established herself as a noted director. A character actor with a strong tendency toward expressionistic forms and the grotesque, Birman became a recognized teacher of the Stanislavsky System. Although her first directorial attempts were not successful, as she described in her memoirs, Stanislavsky encouraged her to continue directing (Birman 149). In 1923 Birman directed her first independent production of a play by Alexei Tolstoy, *Love is the Book of Gold* (*Lubov—Kniga Zolotaya*) at the First Studio of the MAT. Despite the bad reviews, *Love is the Book of Gold* was performed sixty times to full houses. In 1934 at the MAT II, Birman directed *The Spanish Curate*, by J. Fletcher and Phillip Massinger. Although the actors were reviewed positively, the play was criticized by the press for its thematic estrangement from the Soviet agenda. As a director, although portraying on stage the psychological motivations of her characters' behavior, Birman always tried to recreate the author's reality rather than real life.

In 1936 the MAT II was closed. Birman was offered the position of actor and director in the Theatre of the Moscow City Trade Union Council or MOSPS (Teatr imeni Moscovskogo Oblastnogo Soveta Professional'hykh Souzov), which was renamed the Mossovet Theatre in 1938. There, in 1936, Birman directed Maxim Gorky's play *Vassa Zheleznova* and played the leading part of Vassa. The show was not a success with either audiences or critics. From 1938 to 1958, Birman worked as an actor and director at the Leninskogo Komsomola Theatre in Moscow, where she was reunited with Giatsintova and Ivan Bersenev, her friends and colleagues from the First Studio. Among her most successful productions there were Leo Tolstoy's *Live Corpse* (*Zhivoi Trup*) in 1942 and Edmond Rostand's *Cyrano de Bergerac* in 1943. After 1959 Birman worked in the Mossovet Theater; she directed her last show, J. B. Priestley's *Mr. Kettle and Mrs. Moon*, in 1962 at the Moscow Theatre of Drama and Comedy (Moscovsky Teatre Dramy I Komedii). Despite her lack of critical acclaim as a director, Birman's work certainly influenced the theatrical process of the time and paved the way for the future involvement of women. Her style—the condensed realism, highly selective details, and sculpturesque poses and gestures of the actors—was influenced by the Stanislavsky System and her work with Vakhtangov and Michael Chekhov. Birman always defended the high ethical values of theatre, believing in its exceptional educational, civic, and cultural role for humanity.

The first Russian woman to be recognized as a professional director was Maria Knebel (1898–1985). She was trained by Michael Chekhov and Stanislavsky, and the MAT became her alma mater. As theatre critic Pavel Markov wrote, Knebel and the well-known male directors "took upon themselves the noble mission of expanding and deepening the theatrical methods of Stanislavsky and Nemirovich-Danchenko in the contemporary world" (582).

In 1918 Knebel started her studies of acting at Michael Chekhov's Studio in Moscow. From these first classes, she was able to rationalize and accept the creative differences between Stanislavsky, Nemirovich-Danchenko, and Michael Chekhov's interpretations of the origins of acting and directing. In her own pedagogical practices, Knebel successfully unified the best of all three. This miraculous clarity in understanding the Stanislavsky system in its variations, without any dogmatism, made Knebel a world-renowned pedagogue who taught several generations of actors and directors.

In 1921 Knebel became a member of the Second Studio of the MAT, and from 1924 to 1950 she worked as an actor and director of the MAT. A brilliant character actor, Knebel started her career as a theatre director in 1935 at age thirty-seven, and she co-directed several plays with Nikolai Khmelev at the Ermolov Theatre in Moscow. In 1936 Stanislavsky invited Knebel to become one of the teachers in his Opera-Dramatic Studio (Operno-Dramaticheskaya Studia) in Moscow. While teaching there, Knebel continued her studies with Stanislavsky on his new approach, which was called Active Analysis: actors improvised their characters and the situations from the play, gradually building the ensemble and discovering the wealth of meanings.

In 1950 Knebel was fired from MAT because her rehearsal method, based on the Active Analysis, contradicted the earlier Stanislavsky approach to acting known as the Method of Physical Actions, which was the method accepted there at the time. The same year, Knebel became a director at the Central Children's Theatre (Tsentral'nyi Detskii Teatr) in Moscow, and from 1955 to 1960 she was its artistic director. Inna Solovyova wrote that Knebel "demonstrated a will of the theatre builder [as if] it were inherited from Nemirovich-Danchenko—[viewing] theatre as a mutual home and a place for creativity" (*Moscow* 89). Besides directing herself, Knebel invited young authors and directors to the theatre, raising a new generation of theatre directors, and she found the nondogmatic use of the Stanislavsky System—and its improvisational nature—as her perfect tool. It was her policy that the Central Children's Theatre should become the center for experimental staging in the last quarter of the century.

The death of Stalin in 1953 and the Thaw—the partial reversal of censorship from the mid-1950s through the early 1960s—brought cultural transformations to the Soviet Union. At that time Anton Chekhov's *Ivanov* was a very unpopular play: the main character indirectly threw a bad light upon the intelligentsia and their hopes for the better future of the Soviet state. In 1954 at the Pushkin Theatre in Moscow, Knebel directed *Ivanov*, and despite the reluctance of the actors to start rehearsals, Knebel made the show a great success. Among other outstanding productions directed by Knebel were Chekhov's *The Cherry Orchard* (*Vishnevy Sad*) at the Central Theatre of the Soviet Army (Tsentral'ny Teatr Sovetskoi Armii) in Moscow in 1965 and Ostrovsky's *Talents and Admirers* (*Talanty I Poklonniki*) at the Mayakovsky Theatre in Moscow in 1969. Knebel wrote several books, including *Nemirovich-Danchenko Teaches Directing*, *My Life*, and *The Poetry of Pedagogy*. From 1932 until her death in 1985, Knebel taught directing in the State Institute of Theatre Arts (Gosudarstvennyi Institut Teatral'nogo Iskusstva,

GITIS) in Moscow and led master classes at various theatre schools in the USSR and abroad. In one of her books, Knebel wrote: "I have realized that I am capable of [emotional] merging with actors while they are in the process of creation, and everything they experience I feel as if it all were happening to me. Until now, the understanding of someone else's soul and our togetherness in the process of working on the role are the most joyful elements that this profession has given me" (298).

Natalia Sats (1903–1993) has been credited as the creator of children's theatre in the Soviet Union (van de Water 45–46). In 1917 Sats graduated from the musical college named after Skriabin in Moscow. Upon the recommendation of Stanislavsky, the fifteen-year-old Sats was appointed the director of the children's section of the theatre and music department of the Moscow Soviet City Council in 1918. She initiated the foundation of the first children's theatre, which was transformed into the Central Children's Theatre in 1936. From 1920 until 1937, Sats was its artistic director. Among the productions for children which she directed there were *Robinsons from the Altai* (*Robinzony s Altaia*) in 1928 and *About Dzuba* (*O Dzuibe*) in 1931, both written by Sats, and *The Golden Key* (*Zolotoi Kluchik*) in 1936, written together with Vladimir Korolev. The productions were fairy tales, politicized and filled with propaganda. With enthusiasm, Sats used theatre as an instrument of ideological education of the young Soviet citizens. In 1937 Sats was arrested as a member of the family of an enemy of the people and sent to the Gulag. Upon the termination of her labor, she was released but not permitted to return to Moscow. Thus, she resided in Alma Ata, where she founded the Kazakh Theatre for Children and Youth (Kazakhsky Teatr Dlia Detei I Yunoshestva) and where she served as artistic director between 1944 and 1950. There she directed *Twelfth Night* by Shakespeare in 1947; *The Two Captains* (*Dva Kapitana*) in 1948, based on Veniamin Kaverin's bestseller; and *The Young Guard* (*Molodaia Gvardia*) in 1948, based on Alexander Fadeyev's novel.

Sats's directorial style was straightforward and nonmetaphorical: she viewed theatre as an educational institution where characters expressed strong feelings and were involved in confrontations with each other, and where, after overcoming difficulties, evil was punished and justice restored. In 1958 Sats returned to Moscow, and in 1965 she founded the Musical Theatre for Children (Detsky Muzykal'nyi Teatr), the first of its kind in the world. The new theatre's goals were to bring the art of opera, ballet, and music to children. Sats received numerous awards, including the USSR State Prize in 1972, People's Artists of the USSR in 1975, Lenin's Prize in 1982, the Hero of Socialist Labor Medal in 1983, and the Lenin Komsomol Prize in 1985 (*Russian* 416).

Working Climate in the Twenty-First Century

After the final collapse of the USSR in 1991, the Russian Federation was established as an independent democratic republic, with a market economy and a plural party system. The economy underwent a radical change from a highly centralized structure where the private economy played a minimal role to a decentralized economy with a vast private sector. The state theatres, however, remained subsidized, although every theatre sought out sponsors, donors, and additional income—for example, renting out corners of theatre buildings for cafes and bookstores is a typical source of such revenues. As theatre critic John Freedman wrote, "The notion of crisis—perhaps the single most repeated word in Russian theatre in the first half of the 1990s—infected the general psyche. In some ways, one might argue that Russian theatre began recreating itself from scratch after the Fall of the Wall" (5). In the subsequent twenty years, Russian theatre reached new heights in playwriting, directing, and acting, re-establishing the names of women directors who worked during and after the collapse of the USSR, and introducing new names.

Profiles of Contemporary Directors

Galina Volchek

Born in 1933, Galina Volchek is an actor who graduated from the MAT School-Studio in 1955 and became one of the founding members of Moscow's Sovremennik Theatre in 1956. There, in 1961, she directed her first production, William Gibson's *Two for the Seesaw*. The show was a great success and stayed in the repertoire for more than thirty years. In 1966, at the Sovremennik, Volchek directed *An Ordinary Story* (*Obyknovennaia Istoria*), based on Ivan Goncharov's nineteenth-century novel, and received the State Prize for this production the following year. *An Ordinary Story* portrayed the transformation of a romantic youth into a cynical grownup, and it was thematically close to Volchek's generation, who witnessed the political shift from the Thaw to stagnation under Leonid Brezhnev's regime. In 1972 the troupe asked Volchek to become the artistic director of Sovremennik, which was approved by the Ministry of Culture of the Russian Federation and the Moscow Administration of Culture. Volchek was the first Soviet director invited to stage a production at an American theatre in the midst of the Cold War: Mikhail Roshchin's *Echelon*, which Volchek directed in Houston, Texas, in 1978, upon the invitation of the Alley Theatre's artistic director, Nina Vance.

Volchek has always been an artistic advocate for lost, forgotten, and under-appreciated women of the twentieth century, during World War II, in the Gulags, or in the Soviet daily routine, with its moral and social degradation. She has been recreating women's lives in the style of condensed realism, portraying them and the circumstances of their existence with the utmost social and historical truthfulness. However, she never allows audiences to forget that they are in the theatre, constantly breaking the fourth wall. Volchek has often used the alienation effect, allowing the actors openly to step in and out of character. This device was used with particular success in the production of Mihkail Roshchin's *Hurry to Do Good Deeds* (*Speshite Delat' Dobro*), directed in 1981. Out of kindness and compassion for a provincial girl, who had tried to kill herself, a man brings her home to Moscow. The good deed jeopardizes the life of his family and brings desperation into the life of the girl, this time over being undereducated, uncultured, and unworthy. During the performances, the actors sat in chairs onstage, openly becoming their characters when it was time for them to participate in a scene, and then returning to their chairs afterward, as actors. The show had the effect of a docudrama, as if anticipating the theatrical experiments to come at the end of the twentieth century.

Volchek feels it is her duty to bring the tragic pages from the history of the Soviet Union and the world onto the Sovremennik stage. For example, her direction of *Into the Whirlwind (Krutoi Marshrut)* is dedicated to the victims of Stalin's repressions. Based on the first part of the autobiographical book written by Evgenia Ginsburg, the production tells the story of a young journalist arrested in 1937, who spends the next eighteen years in the Gulag. In a dry, nonsentimental manner, with limited scenery and props, the show portrays the lives of eighteen women who accidentally found themselves locked away for many years in one place.

A clever and gifted artist, Volchek is also a born leader. Her success as an artistic director of one of the best Russian theatres is explained by the fact that she has always been preoccupied with the perpetual renewal of the theatre. She updates the Sovremennik's running productions with new actors. She also has invited several young directors, among them Nadezhda Chusova, and has given them a chance to work in the theatre with the most prominent Russian actors.

Ludmila Roshkovan

Born in 1938, Ludmila Roshkovan graduated from the Stanislavsky Theatre Studio in 1959 and from the Lenkom Theatre Studio in Moscow as an actor in 1961, and from GITIS as a director in 1965. In 1974 Roshkovan created the Theatre-Studio Chelovek in Moscow. She repeated several times in various interviews, "A man who suffers has always been my personal theme." As Freedman also noted, writing about the twenty-fifth anniversary of the Chelovek Studio, "This tiny house, whose name means 'human' in English, was a pioneer of underground theater in the Soviet Era and a standard-bearer of the powerful, though short-lived theatre-studio movement in the later 1980s when small, independent studios responded quickly to the rapidly changing social, political, and theatrical climate" (9).

From the very first productions of the Theatre-Studio Chelovek, Roshkovan clashed with Soviet authorities: her production of *Vladimir Mayakovsky*, which she created from Mayakovsky's poetry, letters, and diaries, was banned from public performances in 1976; and another production, Enn Vetemaa's *Requiem for Harmonica (Rekviem dlia Gubnoi Garmoniki)*, was also banned in 1982. Roshkovan's uncompromising portrayals of Mayakovsky's life in the former, or the events of the spring of 1944 in Estonia in the latter, did not agree with the opinions of the officials.

Zigzags, written and directed by Ludmila Roshkovan, Chelovek Theatre-Studio, Moscow, 2010. Photographer: Alexander Ivanishin.

Although Roshkovan's theatrical style has changed during her thirty-five years of work, it has remained nonrealistic. She has created her shows in poetic, expressionistic, and postmodernist styles, not submitting to Socialist Realism and not appreciating realism in general. Among Roshkovan's favorite playwrights are Fernando Arrabal and Slawomir Mrozek; Roshkovan also directs her own adaptations and dramatic compositions, such as *Zigzags* (*Zigzagi*) in 2010 at the Theatre-Studio Chelovek. The play is about Alexander Pushkin, Russia's most beloved poet, and it revolves around two of Pushkin's lifelong obsessions: women and cards. Not only did the little stage with a table on wheels and a few chairs became the acting space, but also the walls, windows, and the ceiling. Roshkovan interpreted the expression "drives up the wall" litcrally, for Pushkin's obsessions make him climb up the walls and hang there at any price. Even after his marriage, the poet is confronted by his demons: women dropping from the ceiling wrapped in large white cocoons. Not only do the cocoons create a phallic metaphor, but also the fabric from which they were made—a white stretchy gauze—gives the feeling of the eternal web, in which the poet's soul is trapped. As the famous literary

Zigzags, written
and directed by
Ludmila Roshkovan,
Chelovek Theatre-
Studio, Moscow,
2010. Photographer:
Alexander Ivanishin.

historian and critic Alla Marchenko accentuated, "Roshkovan does not belong to the Russian realistic theatrical tradition. She thinks in poetry" (Marchenko). Roshkovan has remained faithful to the ideals of the theatre-studio movement: a small space, a limited audience, and the experimental nature of performances. She welcomed the seeming disappearance of censorship, but essentially continued to lead her studio in exactly the same manner as she had before.

Genrietta Yanovskaya

Over the past quarter-century, critics and juries of both domestic and international festivals have named Genrietta Yanovskaya as the leading woman director of contemporary Russian theatre. Born in Leningrad in 1940, Yanovskaya was not accepted to the Leningrad State Institute for the Study of Theatre, Music and Cinematography (LGITMIK) on her first try and thus became a radio technician. After having worked as a radio specialist in north Russia, she returned to Leningrad, and this time she was accepted as a student director to the class led by the legendary Bolshoi Drama Theatre (Bol'shoi Dramatichesky Teatr) director, Georgy Tovstonogov. She graduated in 1967. Soon thereafter, she realized how difficult it was to find a job in a professional theatre, being both a woman and a Jew. Needing to support herself and her family, and being married to Kama Ginkas, another Jewish professional director who was often unemployed, Yanovskaya knitted for a living. From 1970 to 1972, Yanovskaya worked at the Krasnoyarsk Theatre for Young Audiences (Teatr Yunogo Zritelia), where she directed William Gibson's *The Miracle Worker* in 1970 and Moliere's *Scapin's Deceits* in 1971. Since the first days of her directing, Yanovskaya has directed plays of various genres, from comedy and farce to melodrama and tragedy.

From the mid-1970s until the mid-1980s, not being able to find a permanent position, Yanovskaya directed various plays in different Russian theatres; among the most famous was Irina Grekova and Pavel Lungin's *The Widow's Ship* (*Vdovii Parohod*) in the Mossovet Theatre in 1983.

Her big break came after President Mikhail Gorbachev's announcement of Glasnost and Perestroika as the new policy of the USSR. In 1986 she was named the artistic director of the Moscow Theatre for Young Audiences (Moskovskii Teatr Unogo Zritelia [MTIUZ]). Unlike Sats, who firmly believed that the role of children's theatre was in preparing good Soviet citizens, or Knebel, who viewed theatre for children as a humanistic, artistic, and cultural liberation for young spectators and young theatre practitioners, Yanovskaya did not have any particular agenda for young audiences. At the time when she accepted the offer, she was a mature director who wanted to be the leader of her own theatre and to produce meaningful shows of high quality. Theatre scholar Manon van de Water wrote that Yanovskaya is "clearly a director for older youth, or adults" (156).

Yanovskaya's 1987 staging of *Dog's Heart* (*Sobach'e Serdtse*), based on Mikhail Bulgakov's censored novel and adapted by Alexander Chervinsky, became an overnight success at the Moscow Theatre for Young Audiences. The story is about doctor Preobrazhensky, who performs a surgery on a dog, Sharik, and turns the canine into a man. By the end of the story, Sharikov—a drunken womanizer, liar, and thief—denounces his creator, and Preobrazhensky turns him back into a dog. Yanovskaya created the fantastic and yet highly ironic environment of golden idols and the Egyptian chorus from Verdi's opera *Aida* among which Preobrazhesky lived. The artificial beauty of his world was contrasted by the proletarian angry crowds, pieces of paper flying around the stage, throbbing lights, and revolutionary songs. Allusions of all kinds were incorporated into the show: the performance was highly contextualized, and the audience was challenged to recognize the hints, the symbols, and the allegories. Professor Preobrazhensky was portrayed as an idealistic thinker whose dreams and hopes contributed to the chaos and destruction that followed his experiment—a parallel to Lenin and the 1917 October Revolution. The production became a legendary page in Soviet theatre of the times of Perestroika.

Ten years later, in 1996, Yanovskaya started to rehearse *The Storm* (*Groza*) by Ostrovsky, which premiered at the Theatre for Youth in 1997. The story—about a merchant's wife who falls in love and ultimately confesses her adultery and drowns herself—is part of the Russian classical theatre repertoire. In her production, Yanovskaya toppled the traditional interpretation of the play, in which Katerina's love affair becomes the rebellious act against the rigid and suffocating merchant's life. In Yanovskaya's interpretation, the main character, Katerina, became a naïve girl coming of age. Instead of an image of the wide Volga and vast Russia that people customarily associated with the play, Yanovskaya and the designer, Sergei Barkhin, created a little creek in the middle of the stage, placing two mirrors stage left and stage right. Anything that was out of the ordinary became doomed in this claustrophobic Russian souvenir reality: that was Yanovskaya's response to the Russia of the day.

Yanovskaya likes to change the genres of plays, which helps her to reach radical reinterpretations of them. Thus, she staged a 2001 production of Agatha Christie's *Witness for the Prosecution* at the Moscow Theatre for Young Audiences as a musical, wrapped in the stereotypical images of England as they appeared in literature and film, and yet the show became the image of the naturalistic blood battle at the end, purposely violating the conventions of a musical and gaining the quality of wrestling. Yanovskaya's successful shows prove that her creativity needs to be connected to the pulse of the surrounding life: her best productions are the ones that express the brewing pains of the society and the struggles of the day in her highly metaphorical masterpieces.

Nina Chusova

Born in 1972, Nina Chusova received her master of arts in acting in Voronezh State Theatre Institute and in 2001 graduated as a director from the Russian Academy of Theatre Arts (RATI) in Moscow. In the ten years following her graduation from RATI, Chusova directed more than twenty productions in Moscow and all over Russia, including in the repertory theatres, small noncommercial and large commercial theatres in Moscow, and elsewhere in Russia. She is well paid, in demand, and chooses the scripts and the theatre companies in which she directs. She also writes her own adaptations. Following in the Russian directorial traditions, Chusova takes the liberty to change, reformat, and edit texts. Thus, in 2003, she used a new translation of Shakespeare's *A Midsummer Night's Dream*, which she renamed *The Wild Night's Dream* (*Son v Shaluiu Noch'*), to direct at the Pushkin Theatre in Moscow. She moved the setting to Africa and incorporated African rituals, masks, and puppetry in the production. She also abridged the text almost by half.

Chusova's actors work in the expressionistic manner, never in psychological realism. One of her favorite authors is Nikolai Gogol, and she appreciates both his prose and plays. Thus, at the Moscow Pushkin Theatre she directed Gogol's *Vii* in 2003. Chusova placed the story not in the folkloric setting of the Ukrainian myth but in a contemporary sauna, where people were passionately involved with demons and spirits. She presented the audience with Gogol's mysticism, shown through light and sound, but also through the naked passion of the actors. As a director, she completely turned her back on the naturalistic or realistic traditions of Russian theatre. Theatre for her is the expression of her own vision and her hyperbolic fantasies, influenced by the play, which is often presented in a fragmented, postmodernistic approach. As Chusova pondered in one of her interviews, "When do you cross the line from good into evil? What is faith? What does it mean to trust words? All my characters are always lost, and sometimes they have to die before they understand" (Sellar and Ross 144).

Among her productions are Ostrovsky's *Storm* at the Sovremennik in 2004, Moliere's *Tartuffe* at the MAT in 2004, and Gogol's *Inspector General* (*Revizor*) at the Mossovet Theatre in 2005. In 2009 Chusova opened her own theatre in Moscow—Nina Chusova's Liberated Theatre (Svobodnyi Teatr Niny Chusovoi), which premiered in 2009 with *The Portrait* (*Portret*), based on Gogol's short novel. There is no director in Russian theatre at the beginning of the twenty-first century who has created a more controversial critical response than Chusova. One critic writes, "Chusova belongs to the group of non-professional harakiri directors who are encouraged by every new success as a signal to do even less in their next shows" (Sokoliansky). On the other hand, the newspaper *Kommersant* wrote that "Nina Chusova . . . is taking the highest rankings," and she has received several Russian and International theatre awards (Dolzhansky).

In a 2005 interview Chusova stated, "I really think it's a man's job. I used to resist it, but I realize now that it really is male" (Sellar and Ross 144). This conviction, or rather prejudice, has been toppled throughout the twentieth and early twenty-first century, and, ironically, Chusova was one of the women directors who greatly contributed to the re-evaluation of the profession, which has no gender.

Between 1987 and the end of the twentieth century, former Soviet citizens revised their "previous assumptions about the rights, duties and powers of the individual vis-à-vis the state and about the nature of the society" (White 211). The women directors in the Soviet Union and new Russia have always presented their audiences with original ideas, fresh interpretations of classical and new plays, and with a variety of theatre forms and genres. They have expressed themselves through the art of theatre and have greatly contributed to all the positive changes that have taken place in Russia in the last ten years of the twentieth century and the first ten years of the twenty-first. The situation continues to shift, as more and more women directors are included in the theatrical process. As Eugenia Kuznetsova, the head of the Literary Department of the Sovremennik Theatre, said in 2011, "Twenty-first century theatre belongs to women" (Kuznetsova).

Sources

Baigell, Renee, and Mathew Baigell. *Peeling Potatoes, Painting Pictures.* New Brunswick, N.J.: Jane Voorhees Zimmerli Art Museum and Rutgers University Press, 2001.

Birman, Serafima. *The Path of an Actress [Put' Aktrisy].* Moscow: VTO, 1962.

Bridger, Sue. "Something Unnatural: Attitudes to Feminism in Russia." In *Feminism and Women's Movement in Contemporary Europe,* edited by Ana Cento Bull, Hanna Diamond, and Rosalind Marsh, 118–31. New York: St. Martins, 2000.

Dolzhansky, Roman. "Interview with Nina Chusova." *Kommersant,* August 8, 2003.

Freedman, John. "Russian Theatre in the Twenty-First Century." *Theater* 36.1 (Summer 2006): 5, 9.

Knebel, Maria. *All My Life [Vsia Zhizn].* Moscow: VTO, 1967.

Kuzhetsova, Eugenia. Interview. December 21, 2010.

Leach, Robert. "Revolutionary Theatre, 1917–1930." In *A History of Russian Theatre,* edited by Robert Leach and Victor Borovsky, 302–24. Cambridge: Cambridge University Press, 1999.

Marchenko, Alla. Interview. December 21, 2011.

Markov, Pavel. *Diaries of a Theatre Critic (Dnevnik Teatral'nogo Kritika). About Theatre (O Teatre).* Vol. 4. Moscow: Iskusstvo, 1977.

Moscow Art Theatre: 100 Years Vol. 2. *[Moskovskii khudozhestvennyi teatr: Sto let].* Edited by Smeliansky. Moscow: Izdatelst'vo Moskovsky Khudozhestvennyi Teatr, 1998.

Russian Dramatic Theatre: Encyclopedia [Russkii Dramaticheskii Teatr: Entsiklopediia]. Moscow: Nauka, 2001.

Ruthchild, Rochelle Goldberg. *Equality and Revolution.* Pittsburgh: University of Pittsburgh Press, 2010.

Sellar, Tom, and Yana Ross. "Art Is Not for Fear: Russia's New Directors in Conversation." Interview with Nina Chusova. *Theater* 36.1 (Summer 2006): 142–44.

Sokoliansky, Alexander. "Chef-d-oeuvre after Chef-d-Oeuvre." *News Time [Vremia Novostei],* May 23, 2005.

USSR. "1936 Constitution of the USSR; Chapter X." *Bucknell University Russian Program,* 1996. Available at http://www.departments.bucknell.edu/russian (accessed January 7, 2012).

USSR. "Constitution of 1977." *Constitution Society,* n.d. Available at http://www.constitution.org (accessed January 14, 2012).

van de Water, Manon. *Moscow Theatres for Young People: A Cultural History of Ideological Coercion and Artistic Innovation, 1917–2000.* New York: Palgrave Macmillan, 2006.

White, Anne. "New Mothers' Campaigning Organizations in Russia." In *Feminism and Women's Movement in Contemporary Europe,* edited by Ana Cento Bull, Hanna Diamond, and Rosalind Marsh, 211–12. New York: St. Martin's, 2000.

South Africa

Marié-Heleen Coetzee
and Lliane Loots

[O]ne of the few profoundly non-racial institutions in South Africa is patriarchy
. . . Patriarchy brutalizes men and neutralizes women across the colour line. At
the same time, gender inequality takes on a specifically apartheid-related character; there is inequality within inequality . . . some are more unequal than others.
—Albie Sachs

Judge Albie Sachs's words allow us to step into the minefield that is gender
in South Africa. When looking at how women theatre directors have shaped and continue to shape a theatrical landscape, it becomes imperative to understand gender as one
of the most invidious domains of oppression within a South African context. Often,
when we imagine the landscape of South Africa's history, the political understanding is
overwhelmingly one of race and the apartheid legacy; however, Sachs offers a reminder
that all power struggles are interconnected and gender remains the most prevailing.

Women's Rights: Historical Context

Narrating a history of women theatre directors in South Africa requires an understanding of the multiplicity and interconnectedness of the power dynamics underpinning South African society. Power operates primarily around the collisions of
nationalism, race, class, and gender, and it is framed against the backdrop of historical
white privilege. The constantly renegotiated and rewritten contemporary histories of
South Africa have dominantly focused on nationalist and race revision. Women's voices,

however, remain relatively marginalized or co-opted in the re-telling of the history of South Africa and its theatre.

Although feminist scholar Lizbeth Goodman laments that South African women directors are few and far between, there has, in fact, been a very long history of women theatre directors who assisted in shaping the landscape of South African theatre of the twenty-first century—a history that is still to be fully explored and recorded. South African women theatre directors, more so than their male counterparts, seem to have simultaneous and multiple professional roles, primarily as actor-playwright-director-producer, to maintain visibility. This multiplicity of roles reflects women's attempts to claim a right to control their own artistic voices, thereby representing an alternate identity that is both powerful in agency and beautifully theatrical.

There are key periods in South African history that reveal women fighting for their rights and redefining their place in theatre that have had a profound influence on the development of theatre and women directors. One such period developed after the white minority Nationalist Party came into power in 1945: the Apartheid Separate Development Policies, dictating the geographical residence of black Africans and denying their rights to vote, own land, or travel without passbooks.[1] The second of these periods is the 1950s, which marked the intensification of the anti-apartheid passive resistance campaign and saw the writing of the first women's charter in Southern Africa. This culminated in the 1956 women's pass law march in Pretoria where women across race, class, and language divisions demonstrated peacefully against the imposition of pass laws on South African black women.[2] This vocal show of solidarity among women made visible issues that women specifically faced under apartheid, primarily the profound understanding of the "double oppression" faced by black women in terms of both race and gender.

With the growing awareness that resistance was possible, many theatre makers working outside of mainstream government-funded spaces realized that theatre was a cultural weapon. Protest theatre emerged more fully as a genre in the late 1960s, and its roots lay in protest marches that allowed ordinary citizens to voice their opposition. Despite years of protest in various arenas, it was only in 1994, with the release of Nelson Mandela and the unbanning of the African National Congress, that black women were finally allowed to vote in South Africa.

Early Women Directors

Temple Hauptfleisch states that early South African theatre history is steeped in an Afrikaner nationalist and British colonialist history, yet it is also indebted to a precolonial, indigenous performance heritage ("Beyond" 181). Indigenous modes of theatrical performance—including storytelling, praise poetry, and dancing—were practiced as an integral part of indigenous cultures' social and spiritual practices long before the colonial era. However, these forms were largely dismissed as quasi-theatrical or as tourist attractions. Imported British colonial theatre acted as an instrument of cultural dominance and an expression of imperialist ideals from the late 1700s onward. By 1910 South Africa's British theatre heritage was so entrenched that it formed the basis for the country's theatre practice until deep into the twentieth century (Hauptfleisch, "Beyond" 181). African (or black) theatre, on the other hand, found its home in townships. It drew on eclectic roots, lacked financial resources, and followed a path of separate development.[3]

The Depression of the 1930s and notably the Second World War left the theatre enterprise in the hands of white women[4] who directed many of the amateur and semi-professional groups that dominated white South African theatre until the mid 1900s (Hauptfleisch *ESAT*). These women—similar to their later counterparts—took on multiple roles in theatre, including acting, playwriting, and producing. Notably, most of these women also left behind an extraordinary legacy as teachers in high schools and professors in universities.

In 1947 the first state-funded theatre organization came into being: the National Theatre Organisation (NTO). The NTO advocated for the empowerment of professional white theatre based on the British model. It served to engineer white nationalism by forging bonds between white Afrikaans and English speakers and by excluding black Africans (Kruger, *Lights* xxv). Despite the NTO's aim at white nationalist propaganda, the somewhat progressive theatre administration at times employed racially mixed casts playing to racially mixed audiences. The two first directors of the English and Afrikaans sections of the NTO were women: Leontine Sagan (1890–1974) and Anna Neethling-Pohl (1906–1992).[5] Born Leontine Schlesinger in Hungary, Sagan studied at the theatre school in Berlin under the German theatre director Max Reinhardt from 1911 to 1912 and started her directorial career in 1928 in Berlin. She defied the male-dominated world of directing in Central Europe in the 1920s, where she established herself as a prominent director. Sagan was active in the development of professional theatre and the NTO in South Africa, as well as in cultural development programs. Her 1940 production of Emlyn Williams's *The Corn Is Green* toured to black townships, and between 1939 and 1943 she trained African students in dramatic arts. Many of her protégés played important roles in anti-apartheid theatre (Kruger, "Lights"; Hauptfleisch *ESAT*).[6]

Neethling-Pohl is legendary for her role in developing Afrikaans theatre and was influential in founding and running a number of theatre societies. She was the recipient of many awards for her work in amateur and professional theatre both as an actor and director. She became a member of the first board of the NTO and was the first director of its Afrikaans section. In 1952 she was the main director of pageants for Cape Town's Van Riebeeck Festival, celebrating Afrikaner nationalism (Hauptfleisch *ESAT*).

The mid-1950s in South Africa marked the hesitant beginning stages of theatre as a means of political intervention. By the 1970s many artists sought to overtly engage with South Africa's politics through theatre, transcending a largely colonial theatre legacy. Although women's voices were marginalized in favor of male-driven narratives, the Space

Theatre in Cape Town and the Market Theatre in Johannesburg were hubs of resistance, offering women access to performance venues (Hauptfleisch, "Unwilling" 55).

Protest theatre of this period generally took the political line of showing how a system such as apartheid victimized the black man living and working in South Africa. Thus, while opposing a racist apartheid system, it tended to marginalize gender issues and foreground race and racism (Loots 142). Anti-apartheid plays were often performed at the expense of silencing women's voices—both in terms of performance and directing—and often dismissed the specific plight of (black) women under apartheid as secondary to the "real" struggle. Some seminal exceptions are the work of Phyllis Klotz, profiled below, and Gcina Mhlophe, who was born in KwaZulu-Natal in 1959 and had a remarkable international career as a storyteller, actor, playwright, and director. Mhlophe's theatrical career started in the 1980s at the height of the two apartheid States of Emergency. Her play, *Have You Seen Zandile?*, which she directed in 1986 at the Market Theatre, became a seminal South African play based on her own life story. Also known as a freelance author and storyteller, Mhlophe was resident director at the Market Theatre between 1989 and 1990.

Juxtaposed with the politically conscious Klotz and Mhlophe was Taubi Kushlick (1910–1991), who had a successful career spanning almost sixty years during which she served "the commerce of theatre . . . to a degree not before experienced" ("Taubi"). Her directorial work leaned strongly toward staging works from the British, European, and, later, American traditions. She became well-known for her numerous popular productions around Belgian singer/composer Jacques Brel, for example *Jacques Brel Is Alive and Well and Living in Paris*, staged in the Chelsea Theatre in Johannesburg in 1972.

As South Africa moved into the 1990s, the growing political climate was one of the inevitable demise of white minority rule and the end of the apartheid state with the African National Congress. Banned and jailed political activists were freed with the approaching democracy—eventually made reality in 1994 when Nelson Mandela became president. However, with this political change, the concepts of "blackness" began to be more openly scrutinized, with primarily the Diaspora Indian community asking profound political questions around their sense of belonging. Classified under the apartheid state as "Indian" and relegated to the identity status of black and therefore lacking any political rights, this "Indian" South African voice has a history of using theatre as a weapon to speak of both the Diaspora and the prevailing race and economic conditions of living in South Africa. In addition, patriarchy often continued to relegate Indian women into domestic roles, making it very difficult for them to step out of their social/religious conditioning. It is in this context that Dr. Muthal Naidoo and Saira Essa impacted the landscape of South African theatre. As staunch political activists, both Naidoo and Essa used their own Diasporic Indian identities as political weapons to challenge the apartheid state in their educational theatre practice. Both saw their work banned or censored.

Naidoo began her theatre work in the 1960s with the Durban Academy of Theatre Arts and one of its offshoots, the Shah Theatre Academy in Durban. A doctoral Fulbright scholar in the late 1960s and early 1970s, Naidoo returned to Durban in 1976 to teach high school. Her sympathies with the 1980s school boycotts ended her government teaching career, and she began slowly pursuing a theatre career full time as a playwright and director. Her work has been hailed as particularly important as it began to mediate the very fraught politics of identity among ideas of Indian-ness, African-ness, and what it means to be South African. She is regarded as one of the forerunners of "Indic Theatre"—theatre with issues emerging from and relating to the South African Indian experience (Bose). Some of Naidoo's seminal works, which she wrote and directed, include *Of No Account* in 1982, *We Three Kings* in 1992, and *Flight from the Mahabarath*, also in 1992, most of which premiered in Durban.

Essa founded the Upstairs Theatre in Education Company in Durban in 1980, but the former apartheid system censored Essa and her company's work. She is perhaps best know for her politically charged directing of John Blair's and Norman Fenton's *The Biko Inquest*, first performed in Durban at the Laager Theatre in 1985.

Also opening up the schisms in the concept of blackness are the voices of South Africa's colored population. "Colored" is an old apartheid category for South Africans born of mixed race descent—not black, white, or "Indian." Much like their Diasporic Indian counterparts, a large colored community was denied voting, social, and economic rights under white Afrikaner apartheid. Although "colored" has been understood as racially derogative, some feminist theatre activists have re-claimed the term as a celebration of a heritage that official history has often written out. Durban-born Lueen Conning (now Malika Ndlovu), is an example of such a colored woman director. She both wrote and directed her seminal 1996 play, *A Coloured Place*, which redefined a post-apartheid genre of political theatre that began to make feminist connections between autobiography, theatre, and re-representing self on stage. Both directorially and in the writing, Conning links a political history of racial pain to a present context of increased gender-based violence through mixed media. Conning lives and works in Cape Town, where she is very active in community-based theatre and performance poetry.

The 1990s further marked a noticeable shift in theatre toward narratives covering a wide variety of issues, ranging from gender equality to identity politics. A proliferation of art festivals came into being, allowing women more platforms to present their work. The 1994 Grahamstown National Arts Festival, for example, hosted 110 fringe productions, of which women directed over a third (Pietersen 47).

Mhlophe noted in 1996 that the situation for women in theatre had not changed much since the 1980s. In addition to women finding a voice in theatre and struggling for better roles, she states, "above all, it means earning some kind of respect among one's male counterparts, fighting sexual harassment and being looked down upon as a cheap woman by one's own community" (Blumberg, "En-gendering" 50).

Working Climate in the Twenty-First Century

Very few women, past or contemporary, have emerged who can claim their role as theatre director as a singular career/artistic path.[7] The multiplicity of roles that women theatre directors take on has become an almost iconic South African notion. Perhaps this multiplicity is gender-specific and primarily defined by access to funds, for theatre remains a resource-poor arena. With state theatres receiving most of the funding in the apartheid years, it was an almost impossible task for other theatre complexes to access funding to produce work, especially for anti-apartheid theatre. In South Africa, private or business funds to arts and culture are not tax exempt, and it is very difficult to get business involved in the arts. Added to this, most theatre spaces are still owned and run by men, so women are doubly marginalized in accessing resources. A notable exception is director Janice Honeyman.

Profiles of Contemporary Directors

Janice Honeyman

Multi-award winner Janice Honeyman is arguably the most widely known pantomime director in South Africa, operating within a network of male South African pantomime producers. Born in 1949 in Cape Town, she works as a freelance stage and television director and is known for large-scale, large-budget productions of opera, pantomime, and musicals. She obtained her diploma in speech and drama from the University of Cape Town. Honeyman spent her early career as associate director of Performing Arts Council Transvaal (PACT) from 1988 to 1993, then in the unprecedented capacity of artistic director in 1993 and deputy executive director in 1996 of the famous Civic Theatre in Johannesburg. She resigned from the Civic in 2000 to focus on a freelance directing career and also became associate director at the Market Theatre. She has acted as ad hoc director for numerous venues including the Royal Shakespeare Company, the Windybrow Theatre, the Playhouse Theatre, and the Nico Malan Theatre (Hauptfleisch *ESAT*).

Despite aligning strongly with the commercial theatre enterprise, much of Honeyman's work interrogates the complex and often contradictory fabric of South African society. Some notable contemporary works of this kind include John Kani's *Nothing But the Truth* in 2002 and 2010 at the Market Theatre; her stage adaptation of A. H. M. Scholtz's novel *Just Take It/Help Yourself* that premiered in 2002 at the Oude Libertas Amphitheatre in Stellenbosch; Athol Fugard's *Booitjie and the Oubaas* at the Baxter Theatre in Cape Town in 2006; her stage adaptation of Chris van Wyk's childhood memoirs *Shirley, Goodness and Mercy* at the Market Theatre in 2007; and Ben Elton and Andrew Lloyd Webber's *The Boys in the Photograph* in the Nelson Mandela Theatre in Johannesburg as part of the 2010 FIFA Soccer World Cup. Besides directing works from the Western canon, she also re-imagines canonical works into African idiom—a notable example being Shakespeare's *The Tempest*, first performed at the Baxter Theatre in 2009. The production used African ritual, imagery, notions of magic, mythology, music, and dance. According to Honeyman, the production "explores colonialism, paternalism, the master/servant relationship, corruption—trickery and plotting—reconciliation and forgiveness, and most of all the appropriation, not only of land, but also of cultural and religious beliefs" ("Tempest"). Much of Honeyman's work thus shows a political consciousness.

Phyllis Klotz

Phyllis Klotz's theatre career began in an educational capacity, with her training in the 1960s to be a teacher. With the infamous 1976 Soweto School riots, Klotz was eager to be part of what she calls "moving . . . towards a democracy. I would use theatre and combine my education qualification to teach, [to] raise issues in schools on the Cape Flats and black townships in South Africa. I had heard of an organization called Theatre for Youth, which did Theatre in Education programmes in the schools. I joined the organization and they gave me my first opportunity to direct" (Klotz).

Klotz never studied directing but says it was something that she just felt drawn to: "I loved directing and putting my own devised pieces together. I have never attended any directing course but learned as I went along. I read a lot and saw as much theatre as I could when the opportunities came along" (Klotz).

In 1988 Klotz and her artistic and life partner, Smal Nadaba, formed the now famous Sibikwa Arts Centre, located just outside Johannesburg. Sibikwa is one of South Africa's premiere community arts centers and is instrumental in the continued training of actors, directors, dancers, and arts administrators. Her collaborative process of workshopping or devising[8] and allowing the actors' real life stories into the script and directing choices models the democratic and feminist process of making theatre. She says of her directorial approach:

> In rehearsal I like the actors to feel that they are free to contribute to the whole . . .
> to tease things out, discuss, and debate. I like the cast to prepare extensively for
> the play and thoroughly research the subject matter and issue. I insist that the cast
> prepare physically for the play and do one hour [of] movement everyday, combined
> with voice rehearsal. The actors need to be physically fit and finely tuned, because
> my work is physical and fast paced. One has to remember that the content of the
> play will always inform the context of the work. (Klotz)

One seminal example of devised protest theatre directed by Klotz is *You Strike the Woman, You Strike the Rock* first performed in 1986 in Johannesburg at the Market Theatre. It is an example of protest theatre produced, directed, and devised by women, about women under apartheid. The uniqueness of this play lies in the fact that a group of primarily black women were not afraid to voice gendered concerns when it was considered divisive for women to speak of sexism instead of the "larger" evil of racism in society. Even today, the play is often re-staged and performed as a reminder of women's stories.

Lara Foot Newton

Lara Foot Newton, born in Pretoria in 1967, has won many awards as theatre director, playwright, and producer. She earned her bachelor of arts (Hons) in dramatic art at the University of the Witwatersrand in 1989 and her master of arts from the University of Cape Town in 2007 (Hauptfleisch *ESAT*). Winner of the Standard Bank Young Artist of the Year Award in 1995, she also received the Rolex Award in 2004, allowing her to work with director Sir Peter Hall in London. She is widely recognized as one of South Africa's most prominent and prolific directors. After freelancing for a number of years she became one of the youngest resident directors of the Market Theatre in 1996. From 1998 to 2000 she served as associate artistic director at the Market Theatre, and between 2004 and 2007 she took on the job of resident director and dramaturge at the Baxter Theatre in Cape Town (Hauptfleisch *ESAT*). She became the first woman artistic director of the Baxter Theatre and is committed to developing new indigenous work. Besides directing works from prominent South African, European, and American playwrights, she began collaborating on new work as a writer and director. Some of her directorial works include her play *Solomon and Marion*, first staged at the Baxter Theatre in 2011; co-created works such as the award-winning *Karoo Mouse*, produced by the Baxter Theatre in 2007; her stage adaptation of Zakes Mda's *Ways of Dying*, first staged at the Market Theatre in 2000; and *Tshepang—The Third Testament*, which had its world premiere in Amsterdam in 2003. Much of her work explores violence against women, child rape, and elements of societal support for such abuse. In this context, hope and redemption are thematic trends in her work. For Foot Newton, directing assists in understanding humanity in a different way and in seeing how people affect each other (Rolex).

Her work often follows the trend in South African theatre to co-create work. This co-creating extends to writing, designing, devising, and directing processes. Her directorial style is influenced by Barney Simon, Peter Brook, and Peter Hall.[9] Foot Newton's directing is characterized by imaginative and image-laden storytelling and is highly stylized, symbolic, evocative, emotional, and often physical. Foot Newton also often writes her plays and develops them from page to stage in collaboration with others. At the start of the theatre-making process, she works with a scenographer to visualize the central directing concept. She identifies the challenges that face all theatre makers in South Africa with a lack of funding and platforms for staging new work (Rolex).

Foot Newton founded the Barney Simon Young Directors and Writers Festival at the Market Theatre as well as a project called Masambe in 2004. The project aims to translate exceptional plays into South Africa's eleven official languages and tour the translated productions to communities around the country, performing them in the preferred language of the community.

Warona Seane

The new millennium has seen the rise of young black women directors,[10] many of whom are finding theatrical spaces to voice powerful messages. Actor, scriptwriter, director, and theatre maker Warona Seane is one of the country's leading black theatre practitioners. Born in 1974, she earned her performers certificate at Trinity College through the Cape Academy of Dramatic Arts in 1995 and her performance diploma in speech and drama from the University of Cape Town in 1999. Seane made her directorial debut at the National Arts Festival in Grahamstown in 2000 with her workshop-created theatre-work, *Sacred Thorn*, which interrogates the culturally sensitive issues surrounding female circumcision.

When Seane tried to present her work at established theatres, she was told that the problem was that her work was "art," leading her to find alternative theatre venues (Seane "Interview"). Seane found that the main challenges for women directors in the country are finding performance space and a lack of trust in women as directors. As she stated in 2010: "It always feels as though someone opens the door for a female

Warona Seane

theatre maker; the expectation is that she will enter and under-prepare the meal. When the meal comes out a delicious and nutritious feast it always seems to take the gate-keepers by dizzying surprise. As long as we understand that someone else's perception of our competence does not immediately render us incompetent and we continue to soldier on, the quiet revolution will become a sensory din altering the sector" (Seane, "Women" 12–13).

In directing already scripted work, Seane prefers to work with material with which she has a visceral response upon reading. Her own work centers on female sexuality and violence against women. Seane acknowledges the collective process of making theatre, scripted or not, explaining, "My successes often come within rehearsal rooms when I realise that the cast chosen is the only one ordained to tell whatever tale we are telling at that time and that the tale insisted upon this moment to be told. Because of this, each piece I have directed has been a success for me and all these successes accumulating to make me overstand [sic] that I am a director. Each time I try new forms of expression artistically and these impact on my growth as a human being" ("Interview"). Seane's direction of Danai Gurira's *Eclipsed* at Johannesburg's Windybrow Theatre in 2010 became an artistic focal point for her as she felt that it was relevant to Africa at the time. She explains that this production caused her to "stand as a creative artist and realise the importance of maintaining and remembering the seed that fuels an idea and never losing sight of it until the necessary steps have been exhausted" ("Interview"). Her own acclaimed work, which she also has directed, includes *We Are Here* in 2010, *Mute Echoes* in 2007, and *Yes Medem* in 2004, all of which premiered at the National Arts Festival in Grahamstown.

Napo Masheane

Another leading black theatre practitioner is Soweto-born Sotho cultural activist, actor, playwright, poet, producer, and director Napo Masheane, who has made her mark on both international and national stages. A founding member of Feela Sista! Spoken Word Collective in South Africa, she is also the co-director of the international organization Colour of the Diaspora and the director of her own company, Village Gossip Productions in Johannesburg.

Masheane was exposed to African literature, poetry, and music from an early age and started her theatre career in 1998 as an actor in Ola Rotimi's *The Gods Are Not to Blame* at the Windybrow Theatre. It was also the first play that she directed as her final project in the speech and drama division of the Federated Union of Black Artists academy (FUBA) in Johannesburg in 1999, where she was the only woman majoring in directing. Realizing that the theatre offers women more than acting or performing opportunities, she developed herself further as a playwright and a director by making her mark in a "world that does not make it easy for women to own/tell their stories" (Masheane).

Following a collaborative creative process, Masheane's poetry and plays strongly express the voice of a black South African woman. She finds inspiration in the work

Fire (*Mollo*), performed and directed by Napo Masheane, Joburg Theatre, Johannesburg, 2010. Photographer: Moeketsie Moticoe.

of other South African women directors such as Yale Farber and Warone Seane. Masheane aims to use her work to rewrite history and to foreground notions of joy and healing, spirituality, and sisterhood (Telima "Napo"). Much of her collaborative work interrogates "female perceptions of self-worth and body image," notions of beauty, and female sexuality (Telima "Review"). This is evident in her works such as *Fat Black Women Sing* at the Market Theatre in 2008, *Mollo—the Woman in Me* at the Joburg Theatre in Johannesburg in 2010, and *Bubbly Bossoms* at the South African State Theatre in Pretoria in 2010. *Fat Black Women Sing* borrows its title and some of its contents from Caribbean poet Grace Nichols's 1984 collection *Fat Black Woman's Poems*, in which the poet criticizes Western notions of beauty. Masheane added text, Afro-jazz singing, music, and an African perspective to the poems and their thematic content by providing a humorous yet critical look at female beauty and body size as well as the subjugation of African women in the interests of culture or tradition (Thurman).

She considers herself an activist for women's issues (Telima "Review") and aligns herself with the thinking of American author and feminist bell hooks in foregrounding the notions of voice and agency in her work. She states, "There are stories untold by us . . . stories that we share when we plait each other's hair or when we cook and gossip during family gatherings . . . stories that seem hard to leave our kitchen tables. And theatre has allowed me to give these stories names and voices. . . . I keep taking a leap of faith in telling stories that are true reflections of my community and life" (Masheane). Furthermore, she follows the trend of collectively devising work:

> Most of the plays I have directed are either written by me or revised in collaboration with other artists. And as the script develops or takes shape I start to see the characters, the set, and props and how lighting can fill the mood. But I don't like planning ahead when it comes to the actual blocking of actors. I choose to follow intuition and journey with the actor—I listen to actors off stage. When they are having coffee or chatting during lunch. I study their behavior, personal traits and body language. I watch their reaction to things. . . . I pay attention to the way they use their voices and language. And when we get to the rehearsal room, I remind them of what they did or said when they were off stage and ask them to present that world on stage for the audience to witness. (Masheane)

Masheane identifies the challenges facing women directors as finding work, resources, and funds, and explains, "Somehow it feels like as a woman director you are always developing even when you work twice as much." In Masheane's experience, the South African theatre landscape has been dominated by white theatre practitioners and black men, with black women being "oppressed as people who have no voice when it comes to writing or directing" (Masheane).

Masheane's words come as a prophetic ending and bring us full circle back to Sachs's quote that frames this chapter. By placing women theatre directors back into a performance history and by identifying the context in which these women work, we are reminded of the fact that the "struggle" is never over. While the political climate continues to shift, the regulation around what Sachs calls a "gender inequality taking on a specific apartheid-related character" seems to be a prevailing oppression (53). That women theatre directors have been forced into taking on a multiplicity of roles to survive in a performance industry is, indeed, testament to this oppression. But, like all opposition, this has also started a theatrical legacy in which many women directors unquestioningly take on the roles of administrator, writer, actor, and director—perhaps a legacy that has allowed for, and continues to allow for, a rich growth of talent.

Notes

1. White South African women obtained the vote in 1930.

2. The pass laws prohibited black men and women from entering a white-zoned area unless they were in possession of a pass book that designated them as workers (usually domestic) in these apartheid-defined white enclaves.

3. See Loren Kruger's *The Drama of South Africa: Plays, Pageants and Publics Since 1910*. London: Routledge, 1999.

4. Women such as Marda Vanne, Gwen Francon-Davies, Dame Margaret Inglis, Truida

Louw, and Dr. Hermien Dommise helped shape the early theatrical landscape in South Africa (Kruger, "So" 54; Hauptfleisch *ESAT*).

5. See Kruger's biography of Sagan (*Lights and Shadows*, 1999).

6. Special thanks to Temple Hauptfleisch for prepublication access to his encyclopedia.

7. Multiple-award-winning director Yale Farber (Standard Bank artist of the year, 2003) may perhaps be one of the few exceptions at this stage of her career.

8. "Devising" refers to the collaborative creation of a new work in rehearsal.

9. Barney Simon is a South African playwright, theatre director, and co-founder of the Market Theatre.

10. Notable upcoming black women directors include the Standard Bank Young Artist prize winners for theatre Ntshieng Mokgoro in 2009 and Princess Zinzi Mhlongo in 2012.

Sources

Blumberg, Marcia. "En-gendering Voice, Staging Intervention: Constructions of Women in Contemporary South African Theatre." PhD diss., York University, 1996.

———. "Revaluing Women's Storytelling in South African Theatre." In *South African Theatre As/And Intervention*, edited by Marcia Blumberg and Dennis Walder, 137–46. Cross/Cultures 38. Amsterdam: Rodopi, 1999.

Bose, Neilesh. *Fitting the Word to the Action: An Ethnographic Journey into Theatre.* Indic Theatre Monograph Ser. 4. Durban: Asoka Theatre, 1997.

Goodman, Lizbeth. "Drama in South African Theatre during and after Apartheid." *Contemporary Theatre Review* 9 (1999): 5–26.

Hauptfleisch, Temple. "Beyond Street Theatre and Festival: The Forms of South African Theatre." *Maske und Kothurn* 33.1–2 (1987): 175–88.

———, ed. ESAT - *The Encyclopaedia of South African Theatre, Film, Media and Performance.* Available at http://esat.sun.ac.za (accessed February 20, 2013).

Hauptfleisch, Temple, Anja Huismans, and Juanita Finestone. "Unwilling Champion: An Interview with Reza de Wet." *Contemporary Theatre Review* 9.1 (1999): 53–63.

Klotz, Phyllis. E-mail message to Lliane Loots. March 10, 2011.

Kruger, Loren. "So What's New? Women and Theatre in the 'New South Africa.'" *Theatre* 25.3 (1995): 46–54.

———, ed. *Lights and Shadows: The Autobiography of Leontine Sagan.* Johannesburg: Witwatersrand University Press, 1996.

Loots, Lliane. "Re-remembering Protest Theatre in South Africa." *Critical Arts* 11.1 (1997): 142–52.

Masheane, Napo. "Interview." E-mail message to Marié-Heleen Coetzee. February 28, 2011.

Pietersen, Dudley. "Patterns of Change: Audience, Attendance and Music at the 1994 Grahamstown Festival." In *Women, Politics and Performance in South African Theatre Today* 2, edited by Lizbeth Goodman, 45–51. Amsterdam: Harwood Academic, 1999. Also available in *The Contemporary Theatre Review* 9.2 (1999).

Rolex Mentor & Protégé Arts Initiative. "Protégé Lara Foot 2004/2005." *Rolex Mentor & Protégé Arts Initiative,* 2005. Available at http://www.rolexmentorprotege.com (accessed July 29, 2011).

Sachs, Albie. *Protecting Human Rights in a New South Africa*. Cape Town: Oxford University Press, 1990.

Seane, Warona. "Interview." E-mail message to Marié-Heleen Coetzee. March 3, 2011.

———. "Women in Theatre: A Q and A with Warona Seane." *Windybrow News* 1.1 (2010): 12–13.

"Taubi, Kushlick 1911–1991." *South African History Online*. Available at www.sahistory.org .za (accessed December 10, 2010).

Telima, Tiisetso. "Napo Masheane: A Storyteller by Nature." *Arts Review* [online], July 22, 2009. Available at http://www.artsreview.co.za (accessed January 20, 2011).

———. "Review: Napo and the Indigenous Orchestra." *Mail & Guardian*. Mail & Guardian Online, December 31, 2009. Available at http://www.mg.co.za (accessed January 20, 2011).

"The Tempest." *Cape Town Today.* Cape Town Today.co.za, November 30, 2010. Available at http://www.capetowntoday.co.za (accessed July 29, 2011).

Thurman, Chris. "Review: The Fat Black Women Sing." February 28, 2009. Available at http://www.christhurman.net (accessed November 20, 2011).

 Taiwan

Iris Hsin-chun Tuan

Women started directing theatre in Taiwan in the 1980s. Although women directors are accepted in the social environment in Taiwan—which emphasizes equal opportunities for everybody—in practice, men have the advantage of being hired for big-budget, commercial productions and for getting government funding for large exhibition performances.

Women's Rights: Historical Context

The history of women's rights in Taiwan is inextricably linked to its history and governance. At the end of the nineteenth century, Taiwan was given to Japan by the Ching (Qing) Dynasty in China after China's defeat in the Sino-Japanese War of Imperialism. After being colonized by Japan from 1895 to 1945, the Kuomintang (KMT) government, also known as the Chinese Nationalist Party, recovered Taiwan. In 1949 the KMT retreated to Taiwan after it was defeated in a civil war by the opposition political party, the Chinese Communist Party.

Theatrical aesthetics and politics combined in the Little Theatre Movement, which proliferated after the lifting of thirty-eight years of martial law in 1987. With an increase in the migration of people back to Taiwan after completing their studies in the United States and Europe, the Little Theaters in Taiwan began to be steeped in feminism during the 1990s. Compared with the women's movement of the 1960s and 1970s in the United States—which focused on women's emancipation, equal pay for equal work, gender, and sexuality—the feminist movement of the late twentieth century in Taiwan highlighted postcolonialism, gender, and race under the Chinese patriarchy and under conservative Confucianism. Despite these differences, Taiwan is influenced more by the Western first-world feminisms than by third-world feminisms.[1] In Taiwan the status of women in the twenty-first century is satisfactory in the general sense of equal pay for equal work, but there is still an invisible glass ceiling for women in some high-level vocations according to the "Statistics of Women's Labor" compiled by the Council of Labor Affairs in Taiwan.

Early Women Directors

In the 1980s women directors began to emerge by staging very small productions that were often performed for free at schools and in small venues. However, after the Little Theatre Movement in the 1990s, more women began to direct productions that sold tickets to the public. In the last two decades of the twentieth century, women performers in the Lan Ling Theatre—a famous experimental Taiwanese troupe staging Spoken Drama (Hua-Ju) in Taipei—began to direct. These women included Ling-Ling Chen, Zun-Yu Liu (formerly known as Chin-Min Liu), and Wan-Jung Wang. Chen, after directing two successful productions in public, including *Old Wind Town* (*Chiu Feng Cheng*), was invited to teach in the Department of Theatre at Taipei National University of the Arts in 1986.

The major obstacles of early women directors were financial problems, insecure incomes, and poor theatre environments. Other pioneering women directors included Hsiao-Te Wang, Chi-Mei Wang, Ting-Ni Ma, and Li-Li Yang. Hsiao-Te Wang began her directing and playwriting career in theatre in the 1990s, but she has directed more for film and television in the first decade of the twenty-first century. Her works depict the "ordinary" or "everyday" people in society and comment on human nature in a bright, optimistic perspective. In contrast, Chi-Mei Wang, a director, playwright, and retired university scholar, emphasizes the issues of indigenous peoples and social justice. Her theatre pieces include *Dancer AYu* (*Dancer Tsai Zui-Yu*), for which she both directed and performed at the National Theatre in Taipei in 2004. *Dancer AYu* presented a woman dancer's life and creations, even though oppressed by the White Terror—a period of martial law from 1949 to 1987 in which some 140,000 Taiwanese were jailed or killed based on their opposition to the KMT. Ting-Ni Ma, after directing Shakespeare's *A Midsummer Night's Dream*, also began teaching in the Department of Theatre at Taipei National University of the Arts in 1986.

Working Climate in the Twenty-First Century

Most of the production work available to women directors in Taiwan has been small, avant-garde, and experimental, although some women stage performances in medium-sized theatres. The play genres staged are often tragedy and tragicomedy, and the cast size is small, usually below ten. The venues include café basements, little theatres, schools, community halls, historical sites in the open air, city and county cultural centers, the National Experimental Theatre, as well as the National Theatre, though only a few recognized women are lucky enough to be able to direct large commercial productions with big budgets.

Unfortunately, there are no studies recording the actual number of professional women directors in the workforce. There is no professional union for stage actors and directors, only one for movie actors. According to directors Wan-Jung Wang and Yu-Hui Chen, a rough estimate of the number of professional women directors in the workforce in 2011 would be fewer than twenty, with an estimated ratio of women to men directing as 1:5. The possible reasons for such a discrepancy are social concepts, economic reality, family burden, childrearing, and the Chinese patriarchy.

Profiles of Contemporary Directors

Ruo-Yu Liu[2]

Ruo-Yu Liu began working in theatre in her late twenties and soon became known as a performer. She was a leading actor with the Lin Lang Theatre Workshop before turning her attention to creating theatre and directing. In the early 1980s Liu earned her master of arts in performance studies at New York University and then received grants to go to the University of California, Irvine, to study for one year with Polish director Jerzy Grotowski. She learned from Grotowski that it is important to listen carefully with your heart. After watching one of her assigned performances, Grotowski pointed out that Liu was a "westernized Chinese woman," meaning that she performed more with her intellect, from Western artistic training, rather than with her intuition, from Eastern artistic training. Liu reflected upon that evaluation and sought to find more meditation and intuition from her native Eastern culture. She brought her American learning experiences back to Taiwan, where she continued to work as a director and playwright.

In 1988 Liu founded her performance group, U-Theatre, which has become one of Taiwan's premiere music theatre companies. Under Liu's direction, U-Theatre began by "embracing folk customs" and performing "on the streets and in front of temples" (Kao). In 1993 Liu invited drum master Chih-chun Huang to join the group, bringing the influence of Buddhist principles and meditation to their daily practice. Liu explained, "Over the next five years the U members learned to be introspective and examine who they really are . . . to relieve themselves of worldly concerns and find peace of mind" (Kao). Huang and Liu have created a new performance aesthetic by working in tandem. Journalist Leanne Kao reports, "Since his arrival, Huang has been creating the movements and music for the group, while Liu modifies and organizes his creations into theatrical forms." The group practices tai chi, meditation, and drumming as preparation for rehearsals.

Among U-Theatre's well-known works are *The Sound of Ocean*, *Meeting with Vajrasattva*, and *The Dandelion Sword*. In 2010 Liu and her U-Theatre cooperated with American theatre director-auteur Robert Wilson to stage the world première of *The Grand Voyage 1433* at the National Theater in Taipei, for which Liu wrote the script. U-Theatre has committed to a variety of performance endeavors, such as Walking Around Taiwan, Flowers Expo in Taipei in 2010–11, and the opening and closing of the Sports Games in Zhen-Hua County in 2011. The troupe has been invited to perform in many international cities, such as Avignon, Berlin, and Auckland. Liu has received the Cultural Award of Taiwan for her work.

Ying-Chuan Wei

As an avant-garde feminist director, Ying-Chuan Wei stages her productions mainly in small experimental and medium-sized theatres and has directed more than forty works. She earned her bachelor of arts in 1989 in the Department of Foreign Languages and Literatures at the National Taiwan University (NTU) in Taipei, where her undergraduate education was influenced deeply by western literature. Eventually, Wei obtained a master of arts in 1996 from the Educational Theatre Department of New York University in New York City. Her first endeavor in theatre began in 1984 as a playwright, director, and performer for an English class project. Her career in directing began soon thereafter, in 1985, when she formally wrote and directed her first production, *Letter to Godot*. It was produced by the NTU to welcome college freshmen and played at the NTU theatre, which accommodates eight hundred people.

Wei was one of the founders and the artistic director of Shakespeare's Wild Sisters Group (SWSG), established in the summer of 1995. The name of the troupe is inspired by a fictional character in Virginia Woolf's book, *A Room of One's Own*, and refers to liberating women's talents from the oppression of patriarchy. Without limiting SWSG to conventional aesthetics, Wei emphasizes the experimentation of new theatricality, such as focusing on bodily movement with no dialogue. Under Wei's solid foundation, the directors and performers in SWSG create original theatrical works by taking materials from a variety of art forms. SWSG has been invited to many cities around the world, including Beijing, Berlin, Busan, Hong Kong, Kobe, Macau, New York, Paris, Shanghai, Singapore, and Tokyo. Wei's legacy of an idiosyncratic directing method has made SWSG an important venue for staging productions about lesbians, gender, and feminism.

As both playwright and director, Wei completed a piece in repertory entitled *Blossoms in Wonderland* for the Flowers Expo in Taipei in 2010–11. In collaboration with Diabolo Dance Theatre and SWSG, she spent two years preparing for the Flowers Expo theatre production, which combined the elements of drama, dance, diabolo (a spool juggled on a string between two sticks), picture books, and more. *Blossoms in Wonderland* played 207 performances, breaking a record for performances in Taiwan.

In terms of her working methods, Wei wants to try any type of theatre without limitation. She likes to improvise with performers to create the work together, stating, "Improvisation and interactivity are inspirational in theatre, no matter [if] it's between director and actors, or performers and audiences" (Wei). Compared with daily life, Wei finds theatre offers much more freedom to express herself.

Yu-Hui Chen[3]

Most of Yu-Hui Chen's big productions have been staged in the National Theatre in Taipei. She is a novelist, correspondent, director, and playwright, who travels around Europe and currently resides in Germany. She is also the European special correspondent for the Taiwanese newspaper, *United Daily News*.

Chen studied acting in 1984–85 at the International Theatre School Jacques Lecoq in France, participating with different theatrical groups, including Théâtre du Soleil in France and La Mama Experimental Theatre in New York City. Chen earned a master of arts in 1988 and a D.E.A. in 1996 in history and literature at École des hautes études en sciences sociales.[4]

Like many directors, Chen began her career as an actor before turning to directing. Her first professional acting job was in the summer of 1983, with performances touring Spain. The following year, Chen began her directing career in New York City with an Off-Off Broadway production of *Act without Words* (*L'act sans parole*), adapted from the original play by Samuel Beckett. Due to this successful experience, Chen continued to direct productions when she was in Taipei, including a 1985 production of *Act without Words* at the National Theatre, which set a new record for continuous production. Chen began to be invited to direct large productions. For example, as both director and playwright, she staged several productions at the National Theatre in Taipei: *Autobiography* in 1986; *The Story of 1937* in 1987; *A Year without Summer* (*Mei Hsia Tien Te Na Nien*) in 1988, adapted from a story by Rainer Maria Rilke and Lou Andreas-Salomé; *Cinderella* in 1989, based on Jerzy Grotowski's piece; and *Wish You Happiness* in 1991.

Chen's most noteworthy production is her direction of her own script, *Phantom of the Opera* (*Xi-Ma-Yi*, literally *Theatre Ant*) in 1991 at the Taipei Cultural Center.[5] According to Chen, the production was reviewed by the *Wall Street Journal* in Asia as one of the most excellent Chinese stage performances. The music was composed by Ming-Chang Chen to explore new ideas for the traditional Taiwanese Opera. It also brought out a musical wave of crossover from traditional Taiwanese opera to pop music. Associate Professor Yu-Shan Huang at Tainan National College of the Arts commented: "This theatre music was for the first time a combination of rock and opera, which is a major innovation in the Taiwan Pop music field, and also a major innovation on the stage" (Chen).

Chen taught in the Department of Theatre Arts at the Chinese Culture University (CCU) in Taiwan in 1986 and again in 1991 while she directed her play *Phantom of the*

Opera. As the playwright and director, Chen cooperated with the Council for Cultural Affairs in Taiwan to direct *Main Road* (*Tai Lu*) in 1986, during the time she was teaching at CCU. Chen later established the performing arts group U-Theatre with Ruo-Yu Liu and directed *A Year without Summer*, but after some months she decided to focus instead on her writing career and quit U-Theatre.

Mazu's Bodyguards (*Hai Shen Chia Tsu*), produced at the National Theatre in 2009 and based on Chen's own novel, was her last engagement as both playwright and director. The media commented that this performance was one of the ten best shows in 2009, and theatre critic Zi-Mou Zou stated: "Through a totally free method, Chen transforms the whole big theatre into [a] personal space, . . . the literariness and magic surrealism is just part of the performance. The music is supportive, the performers' acting strengthens the show's emotions, and the images also provide a role of commentator. . . . The free transition of the stage is spectacular and effective. This is a complete work faithful to the author's consistent creative style" (Chen).

The productions Chen directed emphasized the innovative relationship between the form of theatrical expression and the content of the script. She has enjoyed the excitement of meeting high artistic standards while playing to sold-out houses. Chen likes her productions filled with strong visuals and theatrical tension. She focuses on the expression of literature in the scripts and particularly wants to show the dramatic conflict. In Chen's theatre career, the most painful aspect is that she was never able

Mazu's Bodyguards, written and directed by Yu-Hui Chen, National Theatre, Tapei, 2009. Photo courtesy of Yu-Hui Chen.

to create an acting ensemble; whenever she directed a production, she had to retrain people each time, starting from scratch.

Chen is the only woman stage director who crosses the boundary between literature, news, and theatre in Taiwan. For example, *Men Wanted* (*Personals*), published in 1992, is one of Chen's bestselling books. The Ping Fong Acting Troupe adapted the book as a stage script, and it became one of the best-selling scripts in Taiwan. The script has been performed in New York, Los Angeles, and Moscow, and in 1998 it was adapted into the film scenario *The Personals*, winning the Asia-Pacific Film Festival in 1999. Chen also writes performance reviews for *Performing Arts Review* magazine in Taiwan. As an international curator of performing arts, she scheduled many important directors, choreographers, and performing arts troupes for the National Theatre of Taipei's festival, The Window of the World.

Hui-Ling Chou

Hui-Ling Chou is a director, playwright, and educator exploring issues of gender and sexuality in her work. Most of Chou's productions have been staged at the Taipei Cultural Center.

Chou got her bachelor of arts in the Department of English from Fu Zen University in Taipei in 1986. During Chou's undergraduate studies there, she directed Ron Hart's *Lunch Girls* in 1984 and Euripides's *Hippolytus* in 1985. At college, Chou also designed the costumes for *Fiddler on the Roof.* She earned her master of arts in performance studies at New York University (NYU) in 1989, followed by her doctorate in performance studies at NYU in 1997. In 1998 she started teaching in the Department of English at National Central University in Chungli, with a specialty in performance studies and a focus on culture/gender/transgression.

Her direction of feminist pieces includes work with the group Creative Society in the past decade, especially from 2000 to 2004. Creative Society's goal is to create "new works concerning and/or reflecting Taiwan's society and experience" by focusing on artistic innovation over commercial success (Creative Society).

Chou's aesthetic method applies the style of American director Robert Wilson's Theatre of Image, though she also borrows from German choreographer Pina Bausch—particularly from Bausch's dance-theatre piece *Carnation*, with Tanztheater Wuppertal. For example, in the mise-en-scéne of *A Photo Album of Memory*, which she directed in Taipei in 2002, Chou made a vivid impression on the audience through her use of flowers on the ground. She displayed photos, both dispersed on the stage and through the use of transparent glass rooms illuminated with strong, colored lights to emphasize the unforgettable memories within the characters' minds.

Chou represents the issue of multiple gender identities through theatricality in her original play, *I Want You before Sunrise* (*Tien Liang I Chien O Yao Ni*), which she directed in 2000 in Taipei Cultural Center.[6] In the play, set at a party, a gay man has sex with a straight woman director on a sofa while their two friends witness in a surrealist milieu. Another play dealing with gender and sexuality was Wei-Jan Chi's *De ja vu*, which Chou directed at the Novell Hall for Performing Arts in Taipei in 2003. The play deals with the male gaze and the concept of a woman as a sex toy. Exposing sexuality on the Internet in *Click, My Baby* (*Click, Pao Pei Erh*), which she wrote and directed for Creative Society at the Taipei Cultural Center in 2004, Chou explores the issues of childbirth, sexuality, and new forms of relationships conducted via the Internet. In the play one of the characters puts in an order for semen and receives it the next day via courier, but an embarrassing problem arises when she finds out that the sperm donor is her sister's husband. All three of these productions examine the female body as something more than just a reproductive machine.

Gender and sexuality also played a part in Chou's 2009 production *He Is My Wife, He Is My Mother* (*Shao Nien Chin Chai Nan Meng Mu*), adapted by Chou from the short story written by the seventeenth century author Lee Yu. Staged at the Taipei Cultural Center, this story depicts the social phenomenon of some men—including married men—who adored young fair boys, a practice which was popular and allowed in the southern provinces in the late Ming and Chin Dynasties in China. Chou skillfully subverted the conventional meanings of sex/gender by casting the role of the young boy with a female performer to create multilayered interpretations for the audience. Act II of the play examines homophobia, communism, and the White Terror, creating an interchange of gender and politics with multiple significations.

Presenting gender and sexuality as unfixed and as combined in different ways, Chou presents keen satires of marriage and love in her work. She questions the traditional binary opposition between the two sexes. Furthermore, she also challenges the binary division of heterosexuality and homosexuality. According to Chou, she does not preset her vision for a production before creating a work because she thinks that each work's aesthetic is different, and she discovers each one in rehearsal. She tries to complete each work to its fulfillment and does not sacrifice the work's maturity for experimentation (Chou). For example, Chou does not force the performers to perform fixed, regulated, and routine movements. Instead, she allows the performers to develop their own body movement in their interaction during the rehearsals.[7] By occasionally inviting other directors to collaboratively direct a production, Chou achieves her goal of exploring multiple directing styles. Chou's legacy is in her ideas of representing the multiple dimensions of culture, gender, sex, and identity in feminist theatre, which she asserts is not about love, but eroticism.

Wan-Jung Wang

Wan-Jung Wang's productions have been staged in a wide array of venues, ranging from the professional theatre of New York City to community centers and museums in Taiwan. She earned master of arts degrees in theatre at the Chinese Culture University in Taiwan and at Indiana University in the United States. She also earned a master of fine arts in directing in 1997 from the New School for Social Research in New York City, where she was trained in Stanislavski's methods. In 2007 Wang obtained her doctorate in applied drama of theatre studies at Royal Holloway, University of London. She also began teaching that year as an assistant professor in the Department of Drama Creation and Application at the National University of Tainan in Taiwan. Outside of school, Wang also participated in the training of performers and directors at Taipei's Lan Ling Theatre, one of the most important experimental theatre groups in Taiwan in the 1980s. Her training extends to techniques from the American avant-garde, improvisation, group collaboration, and the physical training of Grotowski.

From the beginning, Wang aspired to direct original plays and to present contemporary, contested social issues to arouse debate and give a modern interpretation to ancient texts. In 1997 she founded an experimental, feminist theatre group in Taipei called The Singing and Rocking Women (Ta Yao Niang Chu Fang), for which she directed six productions and produced three original plays. In 2008 Wang had to disband the group, for her personal and professional life was mostly in Tainan.

Wang's first professional directing project in Taiwan was *Wild Vision* (*Yeh Jen Feng Ching*), written by Wang and produced in Ping Fong Little Theatre in Taipei in 1998. The play addressed issues of multiple sexualities using metaphors of plants as different types of lovers' relationships. Since her professional debut, Wang has directed continuously in Taipei.[8] Her productions examine varied topics, such as a moral dilemma in the metropolis and the struggle of Peking Opera actors in a modern society.

As a stage director, Wang takes on original works that tackle urgent social issues or issues about women's various struggles in life. Her interest has shifted mainly to devising original, applied drama performance and collaborating with university students or community theatre workers.[9] According to Wang, she synthesizes what she has learned in professional theatre and experimental theatre into the applied theatre projects that she directs. She describes herself as an eclectic director who uses whatever she needs to help actors derive creative and productive fruits from rehearsals (Wang Interview).

Wang particularly loves the interactive techniques in applied drama and drama education to get the most out of audience participation and to empower the audience to have a say as participants. For example, in 2009 Wang directed *The Country Farmer Enters into the City of God*, which is a Taiwanese museum theatre piece set in the historical site of the South Gate of Tainan during the Ching Dynasty. The play was performed for primary school children at the heritage site as environmental theatre and was infused with interactive activities between the dramatic scenes of the play, depicting how a country farmer deals with social injustice imposed upon him and how he could solve the crises one by one. All of the major crises were designed as interactive opportunities for the children in the audience to express their views in order to help the characters to solve their problems. The children had heated discussions about these touchy legal, social, and moral issues; their decisions aided their understanding of the differences of social customs between the past and the present and helped them appreciate the value of the heritage site in their city. Wang thinks this kind of applied drama project has a strong social and educational value (Wang Interview).

Another example of Wang's applied drama is the community performance *Sisterhood Bound in Yuan Ze Flower*, which Wang devised in 2008 with the local community elders in Tainan to combat domestic violence, using techniques from the forum theatre of the Brazilian director Augusto Boal to arouse public debate and participation. The performance toured ten rural and remote community centers and evoked many responses and discussions among participants about this taboo issue. The other area of Wang's creation in applied drama is the oral history performance that she devised with her undergraduate and graduate students in the Department of Drama Creation and Application at the National University of Tainan. Wang and her students created four productions telling stories based on colonial history and memory of the elderly population: *The Taste of Mango* and *The Sound of Flower Blossom* in 2008; *Hello, Grown-Up* in 2009; and *Wow Youth!* in 2010.

Wang calls her aesthetic as a director eclectic and interactive. She engages the actors and participants to think and feel personally about the issues, circumstances, and relationships they are exploring at the moment. Wang encourages her actors to use any kind of theatre with which they are familiar to perform their stories, rather than imposing any particular style on them. She asks them to use everyday activities, objects, and physical rituals and to transform the stories into theatrical signs and language. Wang also employs techniques of Boal's Theatre of the Oppressed as well as techniques of community theatre, such as Basic Integrated Theatre Arts Workshop (BITAW) to inspire the actors and participants to create with their own bodies, voices, and experiences.[10] As a director, she finds the collaborative process is genuinely mutually beneficial for creating plays that are owned by all the participants. This interactive and collaborative method echoes to the founding spirit of theatre: to share, communicate, and own the collaborative artwork together as a community (Wang Interview).

Wang wants to continue her research in applied drama and theatre to further record, explore, and develop the methods, theories, and praxis of applied drama so as to pass it on to the next generation. She also wishes to expand her research field into the Chinese-speaking communities in Asia, including Hong Kong and Singapore, and to explore differences and similarities in methods and practices as well as the social impact and significance of performance. If possible, Wang would like to devise and direct more plays concerning women's rights and issues and to advocate for women's creativity, expression, and connection. Her advice to future generations is simple: "Any blows you suffered will be your best guide to the next phase of your life, which you never dreamt of. Continue to work, share and enjoy your work to your best. Keep up your faith and good work" (Wang Interview).

While successes such as those of Wei, Chen, Chou, and Wang are uncommon in Taiwan, women stage directors continue to struggle for recognition and admiration in the local arena as they strive to set good examples to future young global talents.

Notes

1. For more on postcolonialism and feminist theory, see Gayatri Chakravorty Spivak's essay "Can the Subaltern Speak?".

2. Former name: Chin-Min Liu. In the press, her name may appear as Liu Ruo-Yu or Ruo-Yu Liu.

3. Also known as Jade Y. Chen.

4. In France, a DEA is a one- to two-year degree between the master's and doctorate.

5. Chen explains that *Theatre Ants* was the nickname for the leaders or the managers of ancient Chinese opera troupes. Chen loved this name very much, but for the English name she borrowed the title *Phantom of the Opera* because she thinks the two plays have a lot of similarities (Chen).

6. The play's title in Chinese means *I Want You, I Want You Not.*

7. Based on author's observation in 2004.

8. Wang's directing credits in Taipei include *The Angels in the Night* (*Hei Yeh Tien Shih Hsin Shou Hsiang Lien*) and *The Tragic Comedy of Po Pi Liao* (*Po Pi Liao Ching Chun Pei His Chu*), both in 1998; *The Trilogy of Burglars* (*Tao Tsei San Pu Chu*), *The Match of the Mouse*, and *The Kingdom of IC* (*Lao Shu Chu Chin Yu I.C. Wang Kuo*) in 1999; and *The Legend of Life* (*Sheng Ming Chuan Chi*) in 2000.

9. Applied drama or applied theatre employs theatre techniques as a tool, not necessarily for art or entertainment, but to address issues. Often, applied drama is incorporated into classrooms, hospitals, prisons, or other communities to help address personal or social concerns.

10. Basic Integrated Theatre Arts Workshop is a system of dramatic devising strategies used and developed by the Philippines Educational Theatre Association (PETA), one of the most significant and influential people's theatre associations in Asia. It includes multiple and interdisciplinary art forms employed in the devising process, such as poetry, music, dancing, singing, drawing, local performing strategies, improvisation, and folk art. It aims to inspire all the participants to express their feelings, ideas, and experience with their local artistic forms and expressions in community settings.

Sources

Chen, Yu Hui. Personal interviews. February 12, 15–16; March 2–4; June 18, 2011.

Chou, Hui Ling. Personal interview. June 6, 2011.

Creative Society. "The Theatre Group of Creative Society." *Creative Society,* n.d. Available at http://creative.indextw.com (accessed March 23, 2011).

Falls, Siam. "Drumbeats of Wisdom." *The Nation*, August 15 2011.

Kao, Leanne. "Peace in Motion." *Taiwan Review*, December 1, 2004.

Liu, Ruo-Yu. Untitled speech. *TEDxTaipei*. YouTube, August 23, 2011.

Spivak, Gayatri Chakravorty. "Can the Subaltern Speak?". In *Can the Subaltern Speak? Reflections on the History of an Idea*, edited by Rosalind C. Morris. New York: Columbia University Press, 2010.

"Statistics of Women's Labor." *Council of Labor Affairs,* n.d. Available at http://www.cla.gov.tw (accessed May 17, 2011).

Tuan, Hsin Chun (Iris). *Alternative Theater in Taiwan: Feminist and Intercultural Approaches.* New York: Cambria, 2007.

Wang, Wan Jung. "An Exploration of the Aesthetics of an Oral History Performance Developed in Classroom." *Research in Drama Education* 15.4 (November 2010): 563–77.

———. Personal interviews. February 12, 14–16; March 6, 9–10; June 8, 2011.

———. "The Subversive Practices of Reminiscence Theatre in Taiwan." *Research in Drama Education* 11.1 (February 2006): 77–87.

———. "Transgressive Local Act: Tackling Domestic Violence with Forum and Popular Theatre in 'Sisterhood Bound as Yuan Ze Flowers.'" *Research in Drama Education* 15.3 (August 2010): 413–29.

Wei, Ying Chuan. Personal interviews. February 13–14; March 8, 11; June 7, 2011.

United States of America

Anne Fliotsos and Wendy Vierow

Women have been directing professionally in the United States for more than a century, though making a living as a professional director has remained a challenge for most. When Julie Taymor and Ireland's Garry Hynes swept Broadway's Tony Awards for direction in 1998, it signaled a new era, for no woman director had ever won a Tony Award in directing up to that point.[1] Although hundreds of women direct professionally in American theatre in the twenty-first century, the majority are at small- to medium-sized theatres; very few earn the large salaries and prestige that Broadway theatre can secure. However, not all women aspire to the commercial theatre of Broadway.

Women's Rights: Historical Context

The obstacles facing women directors in the United States are interwoven with the history of women's rights. Today, women directors still face challenges encountered by their early predecessors but have also made progress as they gain recognition in the profession.

When the United States became a country at the end of the eighteenth century, women had few rights. They could not vote and were excluded from most educational institutions and professions. In addition, married women had no legal or property rights.

The beginning of the women's rights movement grew from women's fight for abolition in the 1820s. By the next decade women became active in moral reform, speaking out against prostitution, double standards, and the exploitation of women. A pivotal point was The Women's Rights Convention in Seneca Falls, New York, in 1848, where a Declaration of Sentiments called for equality between men and women as well as women's suffrage. The suffragists, who were sometimes imprisoned or committed to asylums, were the "first wave" of the feminist movement. With their persistence, women received the right to vote in 1920.

Although white women could now vote freely, many African Americans in the South were restricted by Jim Crow laws, state legislation that limited their rights. Racism caused a rift in the women's movement between women of color and white women, who often created "objective" feminist agendas without regard to race, class, or culture.

During the Great Depression of the 1930s, women were discouraged from working and taking jobs from men. However, the arrival of World War II posed problems for the United States, which needed workers to manufacture supplies. The government created a propaganda campaign to encourage women to work, but by the end of the war, women were forced to take lesser paying jobs and relinquish their positions to men. Society continued to encourage women to stay home and protect their families from communism during the Cold War of the 1950s.

The idea that women find fulfillment at home was questioned during the 1960s, leading to the second wave of feminism, which grew out of the fight for civil rights. In 1965 an advocacy group was born called the National Organization for Women (NOW), which fought for issues ranging from the right for girls to have equal opportunities in sports and educational programs to the current battle for the passage of the Equal Rights Amendment (ERA), which would guarantee equality regardless of sex.

Frustrated by the agendas of white, middle-class feminists, the third wave of feminism gained strength in 1992 when Rebecca Walker published an article entitled "Becoming the Third Wave," urging activism. The third wave stressed the interconnection of women's issues to class, race, and sexual orientation and continues to fight for women's rights in a multicultural society.

Early Women Directors

In the 1800s, the lack of women's rights affected American women directors. American women gained a foothold into directing through their work as theatre managers, often co-managing with their husbands. One such co-manager was Minnie Maddern Fiske (1865–1932), who began her career as an acclaimed actress and later became a producer and playwright, directing and acting in her own productions. By the end of Fiske's career early in the twentieth century, fewer than 5 percent of Broadway plays were directed by women (Housely 107).

In the early twentieth century, the role of the modern director emerged on the commercial stage. However, most women directors were relegated to staging productions in educational institutions, little theaters, and other amateur venues away from Broadway. Like Fiske, these women directors were often playwrights, actors, or managers.

The 1920s brought prosperity to the United States and more freedom for women with the right to vote. The multi-talented Eva Le Gallienne (1899–1991) paved the way for the Off Broadway and regional theatre movements that emerged later in the century. Her Civic Theatre was an affordable repertory theatre in Manhattan, where she produced, directed, and performed. Later in her career she continued to promote theatre beyond Broadway when she joined director and performer Margaret Webster (1905–1972) and producer Cheryl Crawford (1902–1986) to form the American Repertory Company, dedicated to staging classic plays.

Webster started out as an actress in England but came to the United States during the 1930s to direct Shakespeare's *Richard II* on Broadway. Critics applauded her innovative and fresh staging, and Webster went on to direct numerous Shakespeare productions and other plays. In 1943 her direction of *Othello* broke racial grounds with actor Paul Robeson, who was the first African American to play Othello on Broadway. Later in her career, she formed the Margaret Webster Shakespeare Company, which included an interracial cast and toured Shakespearean productions to high schools.

While Webster had much success on Broadway, other women directed plays at their own theatres and became pioneers of the regional theatre movement, which gained strength during the second half of the twentieth century. One leader of the movement was Margo Jones (1911–1955), who had directed on Broadway but founded a professional repertory theatre in her home state of Texas. Her new Dallas theatre, Theatre '47, presented classics and new plays and updated its name annually to reflect the current year. Jones directed productions on the theatre's arena stage by budding playwrights, such as Tennessee Williams and William Inge. Nina Vance (1914–1980) worked under Jones in 1939 and learned many skills for her future roles as producer and director. The same year Jones's Theatre '47 opened, the Alley Theatre with its arena stage opened under the direction of Vance in Houston, Texas. Also following in Jones's footsteps was Zelda Fichandler, co-founder of Washington, D.C.'s Arena Stage, which opened in 1950.

Although some women directed in their own theatres, finding freelance directing work was challenging for others. After World War II, the attitude that women should stay at home affected employment for women directors on Broadway. Historian Helen Housely states that from 1945 to 1950 women directed about 11.6 percent of Broadway productions, but from 1951 to 1961 they directed only 2 percent (112).

In the 1960s and the decades that followed women directors struggled for work. During this time, directors from different backgrounds and cultures made an impact. African American directors such as Vinnette Carroll (see sidebar) directed works that were influenced by African ritual and other traditions. Feminists such as Maria Irene Fornes from Cuba explored experimental and feminist theatre. In addition, performance artists such as Meredith Monk blended different genres and media.

Vinnette Carroll

Given the racial upheaval and push for representation in the 1960s and 1970s in the United States, it is not surprising to find a wave of pioneering women directors of color during that era, including Vinnette Carroll (1922–2002). Over the course of her career Carroll earned numerous awards and became associated with the gospel-inspired song-plays she created, injecting a unique aesthetic into the American theatre. Biographer Calvin A. McClinton writes, "[Langston] Hughes may have coined the term 'gospel song-play' but it was Carroll who developed the style and paved the way for a distinct Black American Musical" (75). She created performances drawing from ritual, music, and dance, infused with a strong sense of spirituality, proclaiming, "I want to show Black people that there's dignity and beauty in our art" (George D9).

Born in New York City but also raised in Jamaica, Carroll's family fostered a love of the arts in her from an early age. After high school she studied psychology, earning her bachelor of arts at Long Island University, a master of arts at New York University, and completing doctoral work at Columbia University before turning her attention fully to theatre.

Carroll never aspired to be one of the first African American women to direct on Broadway, yet that became her legacy.[2] She began her theatrical career as a performer and studied acting at Erwin Piscator's New School of Social Research in New York City, which strongly influenced her directing style thereafter. Directing Langston Hughes's gospel song-plays *Black Nativity* and *The Prodigal Son* in the 1960s in New York City helped launch Carroll's career as a director. She became the director of *The Prodigal Son* at Hughes's request, taking the place of a previous director, and made the production her own by cutting chunks of dialogue and replacing the original cast with her own breed of performers who could act, sing, and dance.

In 1968 Carroll's career took an important turn as she helped found the Urban Arts Corps in New York City and became its first artistic director. It was there she met composer/performer Micki Grant, who became her collaborator on a series of original pieces, including *Don't Bother Me, I Can't Cope* and *Your Arms Too Short to Box with God*, both of which earned Broadway runs in the 1970s and garnered Carroll acclaim as a director and creator. Carroll continued to work on new gospel song-plays throughout her career, but when she reached her sixties, she semi-retired in Ft. Lauderdale, Florida, where she founded the Vinnette Carroll Repertory Company in the early 1980s.

Although Carroll's accomplishments are many, her intent was not so much on commercial success, but on the work itself. The actual business of theatre was extremely challenging and painful to her at times. She explained, "There are so many problems a black artist has to face. Yet you can't let it dominate your work, because it's so immobilizing. When I said I wanted to direct, I was told I'd have to take a third off the show's budget because I'm black, and a third off because I'm a woman. And I said, 'I'm gonna do a helluva lot with that other third'" (Dolan 17). Ultimately, Carroll's spirit of determination helped her survive the business and bring a more diverse aesthetic to Broadway and Off Broadway stages.

Working Climate in the Twenty-First Century

Despite improvements, women directors continue to struggle for steady work and recognition. Until 1998, no woman director had been awarded a Tony Award, Broadway's coveted honor. That year, Garry Hynes and Julie Taymor were awarded Tonys for best director and best director of a musical. However, women directors are still in the minority when working professionally. Full membership of women in the professional union, the Society of Directors and Choreographers (SDC), was approximately 22 percent in 2010, the same percentage as at the end of the last century (Jonas 8). According to the U.S. Department of Labor, a profession including less than 25 percent women is "untraditional" for women (Norman). In a field with mostly men, this makes networking opportunities for work challenging.

In addition to networking, women face other hurdles as directors. Directing requires leadership, and there is a prejudice that men are better leaders than women, limiting directing opportunities for women. Sometimes, a woman's collaborative style of directing is seen as weak, but when a woman is authoritarian she may be considered too domineering. Producers, who are mostly white men, do the hiring, and statistics show that they tend to select directors who are men (Vierow, "Women" 103–4). Some producers are hesitant to give women productions to direct with large budgets. One study found a relationship between high production budgets and a scarcity of women (Jonas 3). An additional study showed that the majority of women directors are limited by the genres of plays they are hired to direct and the types of theatres in which they direct (Vierow, "The Status" 9).

Another factor that limits some women's opportunities is the need to balance a family and a career. Many women directors with children are not willing to spend a long time away from home. Directors such as Fichandler and others solved the problem by working as artistic directors in their own theatres, where they could direct plays in one location. In addition, women directors who create productions at their own theatres have a better chance of making it on Broadway by transferring their productions there.

Profiles of Contemporary Directors

Elizabeth LeCompte

Tackling the challenges of directing during the 1970s and beyond, Elizabeth LeCompte works in the area of experimental theatre and creates her multimedia works Off Broadway in New York City.

Born in Summit, New Jersey, in 1944, LeCompte graduated in 1967 with a bachelor of science in fine arts from Skidmore College in New York. Three years later, she joined the Performance Group in New York City as a graphic designer and painter. She became the assistant director of the collective environmental theater group, where she gained skills as a performer, director, and manager.

From 1975 through 1980 LeCompte and other members of the Performance Group began working Off Broadway on a trilogy called *Three Places in Rhode Island*, which included autobiographical elements of group member Spalding Gray. LeCompte and Gray co-directed the first two plays of the trilogy, but LeCompte took over full direction for the last play and the epilogue, which won her an Obie (Off Broadway) Award for her direction. The trilogy contained sounds, images, deconstructed text, film, and a controversial taped conversation of a psychiatrist recorded without the doctor's knowledge.

In 1980 LeCompte and other members of the Performance Group formed the Wooster Group in New York City, with LeCompte as the artistic director and stage director. The group began collaborating from 1981 to 1987 on another trilogy, *The Road to Immortality*, winning awards and causing more controversy than the first trilogy. Building on components of their previous works, the group also incorporated the use of television monitors featuring the performers and live telephone calls. The trilogy resulted in legal threats from the Thornton Wilder estate as well as playwright Arthur Miller, regarding the experimental use of their plays.

Throughout the next decade LeCompte continued to direct Wooster Group productions, including two Eugene O'Neill plays and the award-winning *House/Lights*, based on Gertrude Stein's *Dr. Faustus Lights the Lights*. In his review of the 1999 production, Ben Brantley of the *New York Times* wrote, "The ways in which 'House/Lights' carries out the confusion of flesh and technology, of self and the projected image, are often breathtaking" ("A Case" E1). Another multiple award winner was the 2002 production of *To You, The Birdie! (Phèdre)*, based on Jean Racine's *Phèdre*, which included a male actor speaking many of Phèdre's lines into a microphone.

Most Wooster Group productions take years to develop and become part of the company's repertoire, which are presented throughout the United States and abroad. To cast productions, LeCompte selects performers from within and outside of the company and may have performers play multiple parts as well as different genders, races, or ages. When beginning work on a piece, LeCompte may show the group an image and use game structures or tasks during rehearsals. She explains, "I say to the actors, 'You have information to present to the audience, and you are responsible for a clear imparting of this information.' That's giving them a mental task, so they can get through the persona thing without coloring it emotionally" (Mee 147). LeCompte's direction grows out of the work done by the performers during rehearsals, which are taped. She pays great attention to detail and arranges unlikely materials together, such as a modern video and a classic text, to allow the viewer to create new meanings.

LeCompte works closely with the company, selecting material from rehearsals for the final production. She believes that the strength of theatre lies in the interaction between the production and the audience (Kelly 1). In addition to the experimental use of technology, movement, and sound, LeCompte's legacy lies in her challenge to viewers to create individual meanings from the production.

Julie Taymor

Julie Taymor's theatrical background is extremely varied, including acting, mime, puppetry, and design. Born in Newton, Massachusetts, a suburb of Boston, in 1952, she became interested in theatre and puppetry as a child, self-producing plays in her backyard and performing in Boston. At age sixteen she graduated high school early and studied mime and mask work with Jacques LeCoq in Paris. Upon returning to the United States she enrolled in Oberlin College in Ohio, where she focused on folklore and mythology and also performed with Herbert Blau's experimental group, Kraken. Taymor also trained with such well-known experimental companies as the Open Theatre and the Bread and Puppet Theatre, and she gained new insights into theatre while traveling abroad on fellowships in the early 1970s. While in Indonesia, Taymor started her own theatre company, Teatr Loh, and in 1974 created, designed, and directed her first major work, *Way of Snow*, a trilogy employing masks and puppets.

Returning to New York City, Taymor became known for her ability to tell stories visually, usually incorporating masks and puppets that she designed herself. Among her many inventive productions, Taymor earned positive reviews from New York critics for

Disney's *The Lion King*, directed by Julie Taymor, Broadway, New York City, 1997. Photographer: Joan Marcus/Photofest.

her direction of Shakespeare's *The Tempest* and *The Taming of the Shrew* in the 1980s, but it was *Juan Darien: A Carnival Mass*, that garnered attention from prestigious award committees. Part passion play, part folktale, the piece was based on a short story by Uruguayan writer Horacio Quirogà. Imagery and music were the prime means of communicating the tale, as the spoken text was in Spanish and Latin. The imaginative Off Broadway production won Taymor an Obie Award for directing in 1988, and a subsequent 1996 Lincoln Center Theatre production earned five Tony Award nominations, including best musical. *New York Times* critic Mel Gussow reflected, "She has grown from being an imaginative scenic designer and puppeteer into a conceptual director with a fabulist's view of the mythic possibilities of theater" (3). Taymor not only directed but also designed the masks and puppets, co-designed the costumes and scenery, and co-wrote the book with her partner, Elliot Goldenthal.

Disney's Broadway production of *The Lion King* in 1997 catapulted Taymor into an international league of directors. In conceiving the stage production, Taymor emphasized the magical, theatrical elements of *The Lion King* as well as its African roots, explaining, "It all goes back to the earliest form of theater, which is the shaman. . . . You watch the shaman put on a mask and transform himself. And the audience is allowed to participate in that simple power of transformation" (Richards G01). This transformational aesthetic is carried into her depiction of the characters, for the audience simultaneously sees the human performer and the animal character being performed, a theatrical device she calls the "double event." In conceiving the stage version, Taymor highlighted the rituals of birth, death, and rebirth of a king, emphasizing the central image of the circle. As the opening song, "The Circle of Life," rings out, the cast of hybrid actor-animals majestically process to the stage from the wings then through the aisles, effectively encircling the audience. The image plays out in the design as well, from the large metallic sun to the circular Pride Rock, which spirals up from the stage floor. She also brought the Zulu language and music into the piece, hiring new South African collaborators. Critics were impressed that Taymor not only masterminded the transformation from an animated film to a Broadway stage and directed it, she also designed the costumes and a portion of the masks, and she helped write new lyrics and music. *Newsweek* hailed the musical as "a landmark event in American entertainment" (Richards G01). Since opening in 1997 *The Lion King* has won a bevy of awards and played to more than 45 million people in fifteen countries, including South Africa.

Taymor's work in mime, mask, experimental, and Asian theatre all influence her work with performers. When casting, Taymor seeks actors who move well and are inventive. She comes into rehearsals with a clear vision, but she also improvises with actors and encourages their input. Because her productions are often physical, she gets actors on their feet early, adding textual interpretation as they progress. Assistant Director Michele Steckler observes, "She has a very straightforward approach to directing—she's fairly specific about what she wants from people in terms of moving from here to there. But she's also very open. . . . It's a nice combination of being open and collaborative and yet ultimately very clear about her vision" (Taymor 144).

After directing Carlo Gozzi's *The Green Bird* on Broadway in 2000, Taymor found herself ready for new challenges and turned her attention to film and opera, though she was enticed back to Broadway to direct and co-create *Spider-Man: Turn Off the Dark*, which opened in 2011 after numerous delays due in part to performers' injuries. While still in previews, producers replaced Taymor with another director and reworked the musical, deemphasizing her darker, mythological elements and focusing instead on the romance between the leading characters. Whether in film, opera, or theatre, Taymor has proved herself to be a director with a fantastical visual sense and a fertile imagination.

Susan Stroman

Unlike Taymor, Susan Stroman worked her way into directing from a career as a Broadway choreographer. Born in 1956 in Wilmington, Delaware, she grew up in a household filled with music and dancing and knew from an early age she wanted to choreograph and direct. Stroman earned a bachelor of arts in English from the University of Delaware in 1976, then headed to New York City, where she found work touring as a dancer in musicals. By 1987 her career as a choreographer began in earnest, and she quickly gained awards and critical recognition for her Broadway choreography.

It was not until her conception, direction, and choreography of the Broadway hit *Contact* that Stroman's career as a director became prominent. More dance-theatre than traditional musical theatre, *Contact* tells three distinct stories through music and dance, all linked by the theme of isolation. The production opened Off Broadway in 1999, then transferred to a Broadway theatre. Calling Stroman the alchemist of a new anti-depressant, Brantley raved, "*Contact* is a sustained endorphin rush of an evening, that rare entertainment that has you floating all the way home" ("Musical" E1). He gave Stroman credit for defining character through dance, a trait for which she is proud to be known. The same year *Contact* transferred to Broadway, Stroman opened her Broadway revival of Meredith Wilson's *The Music Man*. She was nominated for two Tony Awards for direction in 2000, a first for any woman.

Stroman's next Broadway production, *The Producers*, catapulted her further into the limelight. Originally hired as the choreographer, Stroman took over the direction of the show when the director, her husband, was stricken with leukemia. Soon after his death, she reported that her work in theatre had become her salvation, explaining, "My nighttimes and my mornings are simply unbearable. I find great solace in being in a studio with music and being with actors" (Simonson 28). An admitted workaholic, at one point Stroman found herself rehearsing the national touring company of *Contact* in the mornings, auditioning for *The Music Man* in the afternoon, and tweaking details on *The Producers* in the evenings.

Based on the 1968 film of the same title, Mel Brooks's *The Producers* revolves around a failing Broadway producer, Max, who lassos his accountant, Leo, into a scheme to make money off of a theatrical flop. Critics and audiences guffawed at Brooks's slapstick humor and Stroman got credit for keeping pace with her divinely silly staging. Brooks wrote, "What an imagination she has! I would write a song, and then she would take over. It was her imagination that made the show the monster hit it is. . . . She knows the human heart so well, she knew what Leo would be fantasizing about, and she put it right there on the stage" (n.p.). *The Producers* broke all previous Tony Award records, winning twelve, including awards for Stroman's directing and choreography. The show ran for six years and surpassed twenty-five hundred performances, and Stroman made her debut as a film director in 2005 with the musical version of *The Producers*.

In the rehearsal hall, Stroman brings joy, inventiveness, humor, and a sense of rhythm, a trademark of her work. Against the trend for big Broadway musicals, she is known for casting actors who are not big stars as her leads, helping them find success. When coaching actors who are not dancers, she says, "They have to have great rhythm. All the actors that I work with have to have rhythm. And once I have that, then I can do wonders with any of them" (CNN). The rewards of the job drive Stroman in her career. "I'm not a material person, so it's not about the money," she states. "It's about the art. But I do feel responsibility that my shows are successful so people who write the checks to produce them also consider women [to direct them]" (Brooke 24).

Since the stunning success of *The Producers*, Stroman's projects have ranged widely in subject matter: from the film-to-stage transformation of Brooks's *Young Frankenstein* in 2007 to a musical based on the historical rape trial and attempted lynching of nine black youths, *The Scottsboro Boys*, in 2010. Stroman continues to make her name as one of Broadway's busiest director/choreographers.

Mary Zimmerman

While LeCompte, Taymor, and Stroman are known primarily for their work in New York City, Mary Zimmerman operates out of Chicago, where her visual adaptations of old texts and myths are developed and premiered.

Born in Nebraska in 1960, Zimmerman had aspirations of becoming an actor as a child. She attended Northwestern University in Illinois, where she obtained three degrees: a bachelor of arts in theatre in 1982, followed by a master of arts and a doctorate in performance studies in 1985 and 1994. She balances her career as a director with that of an academic as a full professor at Northwestern.

Her connection with Northwestern led Zimmerman and other graduates to found the Lookingglass Theatre in 1988. It is there and in her classes that Zimmerman usually develops her works, which are also shown at Chicago's Goodman Theatre, where Zimmerman is an artistic associate and was the first woman director on the staff.

The 1990s were particularly fruitful for Zimmerman as a director-auteur. In 1994 she won awards for the Goodman's production of *The Notebooks of Leonardo Da Vinci*, which she directed and wrote. She continued to win accolades the following year for the Lookingglass production of *The Arabian Nights*, which she directed and adapted from the classic tales. The play, which featured stylized movement and song, also won her a New York Drama Desk Award for best director with her 1994 Off Broadway debut. The same year, the Goodman presented Zimmerman's *Journey to the West*, which she directed and adapted from the Chinese epic of the journeys of a Buddhist monk. The visually stunning production featured Eastern music and was named one of the top ten best productions of the year by *Time* magazine, winning numerous awards throughout the country. Another award-winning tale was Zimmerman's direction and adaptation of the Persian epic poem *Mirror of the Invisible World*, produced at the Goodman in 1997.

Zimmerman is perhaps best known for her 2002 Broadway success, *Metamorphoses*. Based on Ovid's myths of transformation, Zimmerman wrote and directed the action in and around a pool of water. Originally presented at Northwestern, the play won awards at the Lookingglass and in California before opening Off Broadway, shortly after the terrorist attacks of September 11, 2001. Brantley later examined the timing, writing, "[T]he show's ritualistic portrayal of love, death and transformation somehow seemed to flow directly from the collective unconscious of a stunned city. . . . Every night you could hear the sounds of men and women openly crying" ("Dreams" E1). Zimmerman added that the play's stories, "have something to say because they are so ancient that they help you take the long view. . . . We've suffered incredible disasters and transforming events, and yet the story goes on" (n.p.). The award-winning Off Broadway production transferred to Broadway the next year, where it won further awards, including a Tony Award for best director.

Zimmerman enjoys creating works from ancient texts that come from the oral tradition. When choosing a text, Zimmerman needs to visualize images to select it. She prefers working with the same performers, who understand her methods, and casts an ensemble. Since the play is developed during rehearsals, the assignment of roles may occur before or during development, and performers may play more than one part. Zimmerman takes creative license with texts that she uses to make her productions work—adding, cutting, or altering elements ranging from characters to the sequencing of events.

Zimmerman does not begin rehearsals with a script but brings in an image, such as a photograph or one from a dream (Smith 14). She lets the cast take turns reading from the text on which the piece will be based and leads a discussion. Culling from the physical improvisations of the performers, she writes the script in between rehearsals, often tailoring the text to specific performers or the venue. From her rehearsals, Zimmerman creates a production with text and rich visual images. Her unique presentations of ancient stories resonate in the present for audiences.

In New York City, where competition is most fierce for directing jobs, American women stage directors still struggle for work. Off Broadway, men direct four out of five productions. On Broadway, women have made little progress since the 2001–02 season, when only one play was directed by a woman; in the 2012–13 season only three plays were directed by women (Healy). While big successes such as those of Taymor, Stroman, and Zimmerman are rare, women directors continue to strive for excellence and recognition throughout the United States as they pave the way for future generations.

Notes

1. Taymor won best director (musical) for *The Lion King*, and Hynes best director (play) for *The Beauty Queen of Leenane*. See also a profile of Hynes in the chapter on Ireland.

2. According to the Internet Broadway Database, Evelyn Ellis preceded Carroll, directing seven performances of *Tobacco Road* on Broadway in 1950.

Sources

Brantley, Ben. "A Case for Cubism and Deals With Devils." Review of *House/Lights* by The Wooster Group. *New York Times*, February 3, 1999, E1.

———. "Dreams of 'Metamorphoses' Echo in Larger Space." Review of *Metamorphoses* by Mary Zimmerman. *New York Times*, March 5, 2002, E1.

———. "Musical Elixir Afoot." Review of *Contact*, book by John Weidman, conceived by Susan Stroman and John Weidman. *New York Times*, October 8, 1999, E1.

Brooke, Jill. "Art of the Matter." *Avenue*, December 1, 2001, 22–24.

Brooks, Mel. "Broadway Director: Susan Stroman." *Time*, July 9, 2001.

CNN. "America's Best: Artists and Entertainers." *CNN Presents*. Television transcript. July 1, 2001. Available at transcripts.cnn.com (accessed August 11, 2010).

Daniels, Rebecca. *Women Stage Directors Speak: Exploring the Influence of Gender on Their Work*. Jefferson, N.C.: McFarland, 1996.

Dolan, Christine. "Vinnette Carroll: Looking at the Whole Picture." *Journal for Stage Directors and Choreographers* 18.2 (Fall/Winter 1999): 15–19.

Fliotsos, Anne, and Wendy Vierow. *American Women Stage Directors of the Twentieth Century*. Urbana: University of Illinois Press, 2008.

George, Nelson. "Ms. Carroll Brings Black Richness to the Stage," *New York Amsterdam News*, March 5, 1977, D9.

Gussow, Mel. "The Year's Best: Stage View; Civilization and Savagery Collide in Metaphor." *New York Times*, December 24, 1989, sec. 2, 3.

Healy, Patrick. "Staging a Sisterhood." *New York Times*. January 31, 2013.

Housely, Helen. M. "The Female Director's Odyssey: The Broadway Sisterhood." From *Women & Society*, proceedings of the 2nd Annual Seminar on Women, Marist College, Poughkeepsie, N.Y., 1993.

Jonas, Susan, and Suzanne Bennett. "Report on the Status of Women: A Limited Engagement?" [Executive Summary]. New York: New York State Council on the Arts, 2002.

Kelly, Kevin. "Experimental Wooster Group Survived; The Wooster Group Performs Elizabeth LeCompte's 'L.S.D.'" *Boston Globe*, April 15, 1984, 1.

McClinton, Calvin A. *The Work of Vinnette Carroll: An African American Theatre Artist.* Studies in Theatre Arts. Vol. 8. Lampeter, Wales: Edwin Mellen, 2000.

Mee, Susie. "Chekhov's *Three Sisters* and the Wooster Group's *Brace Up!*" *Drama Review* 36.4 (Winter 1992): 143–53.

Norman, Marsha. "Not There Yet: What Will It Take for Women to Achieve Equality in the Theatre?" *American Theatre*, November 2009.

Richards, David. "The Pride of Broadway; Julie Taymor Turns *The Lion King* into Brilliant Theater." *New York Times*, December 28, 1997, G01.

Simonson, Robert. "The Idol Maker." *Playbill,* May 2000, 26, 28.

Smith, Sid. "Director, Actor, Artist, Scholar; Where Else but the Theatre Could Mary Zimmerman Play Out All the Roles She Lives?" *Chicago Tribune Magazine*, November 22, 1998, 14.

Taymor, Julie, with Alexis Greene. *The Lion King: Pride Rock on Broadway.* New York: Hyperion, 1997.

Vierow, Wendy. "The Status of Early to Mid-Career Women Stage Directors." New York State Council of the Arts in collaboration with the Women's Project. Unpublished paper presented at the Conference of the Association for Theatre in Higher Education. Denver, Colo., 2008.

———. "Women on Broadway: 1980–1995." PhD diss., New York University. Ann Arbor: UMI, 1997.

Zimmerman, Mary. Interview with Bill Moyers. "Transcript: Bill Moyers Interviews Mary Zimmerman." *NOW*, March 22, 2002. Available at www.pbs.org (accessed August 11, 2010).

Contributors

Ileana Azor, PhD, is a professor of theatre at Universidad de las Américas, Puebla (Mexico). Her books include *Origen y presencia del teatro en Nuestra América, Temas de Teatro latinoamericano, El neogrotesco argentino,* and *Teatralidades y carnival: Danzantes y color en Puebla de los Ángeles.*

Dalia Basiouny, PhD, is an assistant professor of theatre at the American University in Cairo (Egypt). She is a theatre director with fifteen plays to her credit, performed in Egypt and overseas. In addition to playwriting, she also writes reviews, translates, and performs.

Kate Bredeson, DFA, is an assistant professor of theatre at Reed College (United States), a director, and a dramaturge. She has published on French theatre in journals including *Theater, Modern and Contemporary France, Theatre Symposium,* and the book *May 68: Rethinking France's Last Revolution.*

Miřenka Čechová, PhD (Academy of Performing Arts in Prague, Czech Republic), is an active performer, director, and choreographer in both Europe and the United States. She is the founder of Spitfire Company and Tantehorse, which both focus on experimental physical theatre.

Marié-Heleen Coetzee, DTech, is head of drama at the University of Pretoria in Gauteng (South Africa) and has written on theatre and performance practice in South Africa.

May Summer Farnsworth, PhD, is an associate professor of Spanish and Hispanic studies at Hobart and William Smith Colleges in Geneva, New York (United States). She has published essays on the early stages of Latin American feminist theatre in *Latin American Theatre Review, e-misférica, MIFLC Review,* and the *South Atlantic Review.*

Anne Fliotsos, PhD, is a professor of theatre at Purdue University (United States). Books include *American Women Stage Directors of the Twentieth Century, Teaching Theatre Today: Pedagogical Views of Theatre in Higher Education,* and *Interpreting the Play Script: Contemplation and Analysis.*

Laura Ginters, PhD, is a senior lecturer in performance studies at the University of Sydney (Australia). She has written on Australian playwrights and directors, historical and contemporary rehearsal, and production histories. Her translations of German plays have been published, adapted, and produced.

Iris Hsin-chun Tuan, PhD, is a professor of humanities and social sciences at National Chiao Tung University (Taiwan). Books include *Intercultural Theatre, Alternative Theatre in Taiwan, Drama and Hakka,* and *Western Canon in Taiwan Theatre.*

Maria Ignatieva, PhD, is an associate professor of theatre, Ohio State University at Lima (United States). She has published numerous journal articles on Russian contemporary theatre and theatre history, and she wrote *Stanislavsky and Female Actors: Women in Stanislavsky's Life and Art.*

Adam J. Ledger, PhD, is a Lecturer in Drama and Theatre Arts at the University of Birmingham (England) and a director. He publishes on performance practice, including the book *Odin Teatret: Theatre in a New Century.*

Roberta Levitow is the Senior Program Associate International with the Sundance Institute Theatre Program (United States). Co-founder/director of Theatre Without Borders, she is a theatre director, dramaturge, and teacher, and a former Fulbright Specialist grantee and Fulbright Ambassador emerita. Publications include *American Theatre Magazine,* among others.

Jiangyue Li, BA and MA in theatre and film studies (China), is a PhD student in theatre history at the University of Illinois at Urbana-Champaign (United States). Her research interests include cross-cultural theatre, dramaturgy, directing, and translational studies of theatre.

Lliane Loots, MA, is a lecturer in the drama and performance studies program at the University of KwaZulu-Natal (Howard College Campus) in Durban (South Africa) and has written extensively around gender revisions of African contemporary performance histories.

Diana Manole, PhD (University of Toronto), is a Romanian-born assistant professor at Trent University (Canada), a stage and TV director, and an award-winning writer. She has published eight collections of poems and plays and several academic articles and book chapters.

Karin Maresh, PhD, is an associate professor of theatre at Washington & Jefferson College (United States). She has written for the journals *Theatre Journal* and *Theatre Survey* and has an article in the forthcoming book *Performing Motherhood.*

Gordon McCall, MFA, is the head of the Purdue University directing program (United States). Former artistic director of Montreal's Centaur Theatre, he has directed numerous productions at major theatres in Canada, the United States, Ireland, and Australia. He is also a playwright, screenwriter, and journalist.

Erin B. Mee, PhD, assistant professor of dramatic literature at New York University (United States), is the author of *Theatre of Roots: Redirecting the Modern Indian Stage* and co-editor of *Antigone on the Contemporary World Stage.* She has directed numerous productions at major U.S. theatres and directed two of Panikkar's plays in India with his company, Sopanam.

Ursula Neuerburg-Denzer, PhD, born in Cologne, Germany, teaches theatre at Montreal's Concordia University (Canada). With a strong background in performing and directing, her research centers on the performance of extreme emotion.

Claire Pamment, MPhil, is foreign faculty (HEC) at Beaconhouse University, Lahore (Pakistan). Research interests include popular South Asian performance cultures. Her work is published in *TDR, Asian Theatre Journal, Journal of South Asian Popular Culture, Comedy Studies,* and *Sohbet.*

Magda Romanska, PhD, is an associate professor of theatre and dramaturgy at Emerson College (United States) and an award-winning author and scholar. Books include *The Post-Traumatic Theatre of Grotowski and Kantor, Boguslaw Schaeffer: An Anthology, Comedy: Theory and Criticism* (forthcoming), and *The Routledge Companion to Dramaturgy* (forthcoming).

Avra Sidiropoulou, PhD, is a stage director and a lecturer of theatre arts at the Open University of Cyprus (Republic of Cyprus). She has studied and worked internationally. She wrote *Authoring Performance: The Director in Contemporary Theatre.*

Margaretta Swigert-Gacheru, PhD, is a lecturer at Kenya Methodist University and theatre critic for *The Nation Media Group* (Kenya). A former actor with the University of Nairobi's Free Traveling Theatre, she is author of *Creating Contemporary Kenyan Art: Art Networks in Urban Africa.*

Alessandra Vannucci, PhD, is a professor at the Universidade Federal de Ouro Preto (Brazil) and a visiting professor/artist at Pontifícia Universidade Católica do Rio de Janeiro. An award-winning playwright and director, she has written books about the travels of actors.

Wendy Vierow, PhD, is an educator, director, performer, and writer (United States). She is the co-author of *American Women Stage Directors of the Twentieth Century,* has written and directed performance art, and has performed in works shown internationally.

Vessela S. Warner, PhD, is an assistant professor of theatre at the University of Alabama at Birmingham (United States). She has contributed to *Theatre and Performance in Eastern Europe: The Changing Scene* and *Performing Worlds into Being: Native American Women's Theatre.*

Brenda Werth, PhD, is an associate professor of Latin American studies at American University, Washington, D.C. (United States). Her research focuses on Latin American theatre, performance, memory studies, and human rights. She is author of the book *Theater, Performance, and Memory Politics in Argentina.*

Index

The University of Illinois Press
is a founding member of the
Association of American University Presses.

———————————————————————

Based on a design by Dennis Roberts
Composed in 10/13 Adobe Garamond Pro
by Celia Shapland
at the University of Illinois Press
Manufactured by Sheridan Books, Inc.

University of Illinois Press
1325 South Oak Street
Champaign, IL 61820-6903
www.press.uillinois.edu